The Complete Guide to Adobe Premiere Pro 2025

Master video editing with expert tips, techniques, and workflows

Najihah Najlaa

The Complete Guide to Adobe Premiere Pro 2025

Publishing Product Manager: Nitin Nainani
Book Project Manager: Sonam Pandey
Senior Editor: Nathanya Dias
Technical Editor: K Bimala Singha
Copy Editor: Safis Editing
Indexer: Pratik Shirodkar
Production Designer: Aparna Bhagat
Senior DevRel Marketing Executive: Nivedita Pandey

First published: February 2025

Production reference: 1280125

Published by Packt Publishing Ltd.
Grosvenor House
11 St Paul's Square
Birmingham
B3 1RB, UK.

ISBN 978-1-83898-193-8

www.packtpub.com

To all the dreamers and doers, this is my first book, born from countless late nights and endless cups of coffee. May it inspire you to chase your own dreams with relentless passion.

To Aurora, whose questions turned dreams into pages.

– Najihah Najlaa

Contributors

About the author

Najihah Najlaa is an Adobe Certified Expert and Instructor with over seven years of experience. Since 2017, she has conducted 200+ training sessions, helping 500+ students achieve Adobe Certified Professional credentials. From 2017 to 2019, she was an Instructor at an Adobe Authorized Training Centre in Malaysia. In 2020, she became the only Malaysian Behance featured stream artist and spoke at Adobe MAX in 2021. Najihah now leads A Lifetime Project, providing top-tier training in Malaysia and internationally. She holds a BSc Hons in IT from Universiti Teknologi PETRONAS. Passionate about creativity and education, she inspires students and explores new artistic mediums.

My heartfelt thanks go to everyone who has been there for me, with special appreciation for my cats, Kedo, LJ, Nyaii, and my parents.

About the reviewers

Nathanael Rothschild is a skilled video editor and tech professional with five years of experience in the audio/visual industry. Proficient in Adobe Premiere Pro, he handles diverse projects, from corporate to personal. Nathanael excels in editing, filming, audio recording, and streaming. He's passionate about his craft and seeks to improve himself every day. Nathanael also runs a YouTube channel, *Manfred Plus Magic*, sharing his love for Magic: The Gathering. Dedicated to growth, he continually hones his skills. Outside work, Nathanael cherishes his role as a husband and father, enjoying time with his wife and two daughters.

Francisco Lepe-Salazar is currently the managing director of Ludolab, the director of the Observatorio Nacional de la Industria de los Videojuegos with DevsVJ MX, the creator and organizer of the Games4Empowerment international contest, a founding member of the Código Frida educational program, and a teacher with the University of Colima, Mexico, and the Deggendorf Institute of Technology, Germany. His research interests include entertainment computing, human-computer interaction, and user empowerment.

Prashant Bhakuni is an experienced multimedia professional with over 5 years of expertise, bringing a wealth of knowledge to his role as a technical reviewer. He has a background in video post-production and has collaborated with numerous businesses, top content creators, and video editing agencies on various multimedia projects. While he has worked with different editing software, his focus on Adobe Premiere Pro is evident in his work. Currently, he focuses on the emerging trend of short-form social media content. His keen eye for detail and dedication to quality make him a valuable asset to any team, ensuring projects meet the highest standards of professionalism and creativity.

Agbele Ololade Abel is a video editor with a passion for literature and technology. He offers a unique perspective that blends creativity with analytical thinking. In addition to his expertise in visual storytelling, he provides technical reviews for books, offering insights that bridge the gap between content and craft.

Table of Contents

5

Everything You Need to Know about Transitions   121

6

Enhancing Audio with Premiere Pro   151

7

Editing Audio Easily in the Essential Sound Panel 175

8

Adding and Adjusting Sound Effects to Improve Your Video 189

9

Creative Video Effects in Premiere Pro   231

10

Exploring Compositing Techniques   257

11

Adjusting and Correcting Colors Professionally   279

12

Mastering Titles and Graphics with the Graphics Templates Panel in Premiere Pro   321

13

Multi-Camera Editing in Premiere Pro   355

14

Creating and Editing Trendy Videos for Social Media   387

15

Optimizing Premiere Pro's Performance Settings for Smooth Workflows 415

16

Best Export Settings in Premiere Pro 455

17

Team Projects in Premiere Pro — Collaborating with Other Editors via the Cloud   499

18

AI-Powered Video Editing   529

Preface

Hello there! Video editing is a dynamic and creative process that transforms raw footage into compelling visual stories. Adobe Premiere Pro 2025 stands at the forefront of this field, offering a comprehensive suite of tools designed to meet the needs of both novice and professional editors.

This book is structured around three core pillars of video editing:

- Mastering the latest features and updates in Premiere Pro
- Developing essential editing skills and workflows
- Applying advanced techniques to enhance your projects

While many guides focus on the basics, this book aims to take you further, providing in-depth knowledge and practical tips to elevate your editing skills. Drawing on my extensive experience and insights from industry experts, this book will help you navigate the complexities of Premiere Pro and unlock its full potential.

As the demand for high-quality video content continues to rise, proficiency in Adobe Premiere Pro will set you apart in the competitive field of video editing. This book is your gateway to mastering the art and science of video editing with Premiere Pro 2025.

Who this book is for

This book is designed for anyone looking to master video editing with Adobe Premiere Pro 2025. Whether you are a beginner or an experienced editor, this book provides valuable insights and practical knowledge to enhance your editing skills.

The target audience of this book is as follows:

- Aspiring video editors: Individuals who are new to video editing and want to learn the fundamentals of Adobe Premiere Pro. This book will guide them through the basics and help them build a strong foundation in video editing.

- Intermediate editors: Those who have some experience with video editing and are looking to refine their skills and learn advanced techniques. This book will provide them with in-depth knowledge of Premiere Pro's features and tools, enabling them to create professional-quality videos.

- Professional video editors: Experienced editors who want to stay up to date with the latest features and best practices in Adobe Premiere Pro 2025. This book will help them enhance their workflow, improve their editing efficiency, and explore new creative possibilities.

No matter your background, this book will equip you with the skills and confidence to excel in video editing and produce stunning visual content.

What this book covers

Chapter 1, Exploring New Features in Adobe Premiere Pro 2025, introduces the latest features and updates in Adobe Premiere Pro 2025. This chapter will guide you through the new tools and functionalities that have been added to enhance your editing experience. You'll learn how to leverage these features to streamline your workflow and improve your editing efficiency. Whether it's new effects, improved performance, or enhanced user interface elements, this chapter ensures you are well-versed with the cutting-edge capabilities of Premiere Pro 2025.

Chapter 2, Essential Tools and Workflows in Premiere Pro, covers the fundamental tools and workflows for efficient video editing. This chapter will provide a comprehensive overview of the Premiere Pro interface, including the timeline, media browser, and essential panels. You'll learn how to organize your projects, import and manage media, and utilize key editing tools. By mastering these basics, you'll be able to set up your projects for success and work more effectively.

Chapter 3, Efficiently Cutting and Trimming Videos, explains techniques for cutting and trimming videos effectively to create seamless and engaging content. This chapter delves into the various methods of trimming clips, including ripple, roll, slip, and slide edits. You'll also learn about the importance of pacing and rhythm in video editing, and how to use these techniques to maintain viewer interest and enhance storytelling.

Chapter 4, Adding Motion and Animated Graphics in Premiere Pro, explores how to incorporate motion and animated graphics into your videos, enhancing their visual appeal. This chapter covers the basics of keyframing, motion paths, and using the Essential Graphics panel to create dynamic titles and lower thirds. You'll also learn how to integrate After Effects compositions into your Premiere Pro projects for more complex animations.

Chapter 5, Everything You Need to Know about Transitions, provides comprehensive knowledge about transitions and how to use them to maintain the flow and continuity of your edits. This chapter will explore different types of transitions, from simple cuts and dissolves to more advanced effects, such as wipes and morph cuts. You'll learn when and how to use transitions effectively to enhance your narrative and keep your audience engaged.

Chapter 6, Enhancing Audio with Premiere Pro, discusses techniques to enhance audio quality within Premiere Pro, ensuring your videos sound professional. This chapter covers audio editing basics, including adjusting levels, applying effects, and using audio transitions. You'll also learn about advanced techniques such as noise reduction, equalization, and mastering to ensure your audio tracks are clear and polished.

Chapter 7, Editing Audio Easily in the Essential Sound Panel, simplifies the process of editing audio using the Essential Sound Panel. This chapter will guide you through the various presets and controls available in the Essential Sound Panel, making it easier to achieve professional-sounding audio. You'll learn how to categorize audio clips, apply automatic adjustments, and use the panel's tools to enhance dialogue, music, and sound effects.

Chapter 8, Adding and Adjusting Sound Effects to Improve Your Video, covers how to add and adjust sound effects to elevate the overall impact of your videos. This chapter explores the creative use of sound effects to enhance storytelling and create a more immersive experience for your audience. You'll learn how to source, import, and synchronize sound effects with your video, as well as techniques for layering and mixing sounds to achieve the desired effect.

Chapter 9, Creative Video Effects in Premiere Pro, explores creative video effects that add a unique flair to your edits. This chapter covers a range of effects, from basic color correction and grading to more advanced techniques, such as chroma keying, time remapping, and creating custom effects. You'll learn how to use these tools to enhance the visual style of your videos and make them stand out.

Chapter 10, Exploring Compositing Techniques, delves into compositing techniques to combine multiple elements seamlessly. This chapter will teach you how to use masks, mattes, and blend modes to create complex compositions. You'll also learn about the principles of layering and how to integrate different media types, such as video, images, and graphics, to create visually compelling scenes.

Chapter 11, Adjusting and Correcting Colors Professionally, teaches how to adjust and correct colors to give your videos a polished look. This chapter covers the basics of color correction, including using scopes and color wheels, as well as advanced techniques such as secondary color correction and color grading. You'll learn how to achieve consistent color balance, enhance the mood of your scenes, and ensure your videos look professional.

Chapter 12, Mastering Titles and Graphics with the Graphics Templates Panel in Premiere Pro, covers the creation of titles and graphics using the Essential Graphics Panel. This chapter will guide you through designing and animating text and graphics, using templates, and customizing your creations to fit your project's style. You'll also learn how to create motion graphics templates that can be reused across different projects.

Chapter 13, Multi-Camera Editing in Premiere Pro, explains the intricacies of multi-camera editing to manage complex projects. This chapter will teach you how to set up and synchronize multiple camera angles, switch between them during editing, and refine your multi-camera sequences. You'll also learn about the benefits of multi-camera editing for live events, interviews, and other multi-angle productions.

Chapter 14, Creating and Editing Trendy Videos for Social Media, provides insights into creating and editing videos specifically designed for social media platforms. This chapter covers the unique requirements and best practices for social media content, including aspect ratios, video length, and platform-specific features. You'll learn how to optimize your videos for different social media channels and create engaging content that resonates with your audience.

Chapter 15, Optimizing Premiere Pro's Performance Settings for Smooth Workflows, discusses how to optimize performance settings for smooth and efficient workflows. This chapter will guide you through hardware and software configurations, project settings, and workflow optimizations to ensure Premiere Pro runs smoothly. You'll learn how to troubleshoot common performance issues and make the most of your editing setup.

Chapter 16, Best Export Settings in Premiere Pro, explores the best export settings to ensure your videos maintain high quality across different platforms. This chapter covers the various export options available in Premiere Pro, including formats, codecs, and presets. You'll learn how to choose the right settings for your project, whether it's for web, broadcast, or social media, and ensure your final output meets the highest standards.

Chapter 17, Team Projects in Premiere Pro — Collaborating with Other Editors via the Cloud, explains how to collaborate with other editors via the cloud using team projects. This chapter will teach you how to set up and manage team projects, share assets, and work collaboratively in real time. You'll learn about the benefits of cloud-based collaboration and how to streamline your workflow when working with a team.

Chapter 18, AI-Powered Video Editing, explores the exciting realm of AI-powered video editing to enhance your editing process with advanced technology. This chapter covers the latest AI tools and features in Premiere Pro, such as auto-reframe, scene edit detection, and speech-to-text. You'll learn how to leverage these tools to save time, improve accuracy, and add innovative elements to your projects.

To get the most out of this book

Before diving into the chapters, it's important to have a basic understanding of video editing concepts and familiarity with Adobe Premiere Pro. This book assumes that you have some prior experience with video editing, even if it's minimal. Additionally, having a creative mindset and a willingness to experiment will help you make the most of the techniques and tips provided.

Software/Hardware covered in the book	OS Requirements
Adobe Premiere Pro 2025	*Windows* A processor equivalent to Intel® i5-4590 or AMD FX 8350, at least 4 GB RAM, and a graphics card such as NVIDIA GeForce® GTX 970 or AMD Radeon™ R9 *macOS* macOS 10.15 (Catalina) or later versions are recommended

Software/Hardware covered in the book	OS Requirements
Adobe After Effects	*Windows* The minimum operating system requirement for Windows is Windows 10 (64-bit) version 22H2 or later. *macOS* The minimum operating system requirement for macOS is macOS 10.15 (Catalina) or later. The 24.x or later versions of After Effects will not install on Mac Pro 2013 or older systems.

Download the project files

You can download the Project files for this book at the following links:

Assets: `https://packt.link/gbz/9781838981938`

Lessons(Chapter 1 to 4): `https://packt.link/N8mee`

Lessons(Chapter 5 to 8): `https://packt.link/HoN1y`

Lessons(Chapter 9 to 14): `https://packt.link/chjEm`

Lessons(Chapter 15 to 19): `https://packt.link/HlsMF`

We also have other code bundles from our rich catalog of books and videos available at `https://github.com/PacktPublishing/`. Check them out!

Conventions used

There are a number of text conventions used throughout this book.

Bold: Indicates a new term, an important word, or words that you see onscreen. For example, words in menus or dialog boxes appear in the text like this. Here is an example: "Open the project you want to work on, then select **Window | Workspace** and the workspace you want to use."

> **Tips or important notes**
> Appear like this.

Get in touch

Feedback from our readers is always welcome.

General feedback: If you have questions about any aspect of this book, email us at `customercare@packtpub.com` and mention the book title in the subject of your message.

Errata: Although we have taken every care to ensure the accuracy of our content, mistakes do happen. If you have found a mistake in this book, we would be grateful if you would report this to us. Please visit `www.packtpub.com/support/errata` and fill in the form.

Piracy: If you come across any illegal copies of our works in any form on the internet, we would be grateful if you would provide us with the location address or website name. Please contact us at `copyright@packt.com` with a link to the material.

If you are interested in becoming an author: If there is a topic that you have expertise in and you are interested in either writing or contributing to a book, please visit `authors.packtpub.com`.

Share Your Thoughts

Once you've read *The Complete Guide to Adobe Premiere Pro 2025*, we'd love to hear your thoughts! Scan the QR code below to go straight to the Amazon review page for this book and share your feedback.

`https://packt.link/r/1-838-98193-4`

Your review is important to us and the tech community and will help us make sure we're delivering excellent quality content.

Download a free PDF copy of this book

Thanks for purchasing this book!

Do you like to read on the go but are unable to carry your print books everywhere?

Is your eBook purchase not compatible with the device of your choice?

Don't worry, now with every Packt book you get a DRM-free PDF version of that book at no cost.

Read anywhere, any place, on any device. Search, copy, and paste code from your favorite technical books directly into your application.

The perks don't stop there, you can get exclusive access to discounts, newsletters, and great free content in your inbox daily

Follow these simple steps to get the benefits:

1. Scan the QR code or visit the link below

https://packt.link/free-ebook/978-1-83898-193-8

2. Submit your proof of purchase
3. That's it! We'll send your free PDF and other benefits to your email directly

1

Exploring New Features in Adobe Premiere Pro 2025

Calling all aspiring editors and video wizards! Are you ready to unleash your inner Spielberg and craft videos that leave audiences speechless? Welcome to the electrifying world of Adobe Premiere Pro 2025, a treasure trove of cutting-edge tools designed to catapult your editing skills from novice to ninja. This isn't your grandpa's editing software – the 2025 update explodes with groundbreaking features that will have you streamlining workflows like a pro, injecting mind-blowing creativity into every frame, and pushing the boundaries of storytelling like never before.

But hold on, before we dive headfirst into this editing wonderland, let's first understand the difference between linear and **non-linear editing** (**NLE**). Then, we will learn what non-linear video editing means and go over its advantages before we introduce you to the new Adobe Premiere Pro 2025 updates!

The 2025 update introduces a brand new, user-friendly workspace designed to make navigating Premiere Pro a breeze, even for complete newcomers or those updating from previous versions. Worried about all those buttons and menus? Fear not! This streamlined interface will have you feeling right at home in no time.

Did someone say *vertical video*? Premiere Pro 2025 understands the ever-evolving social media landscape. With a dedicated workspace for vertical video editing, you can now effortlessly create Instagram Reels and other social media masterpieces that will have your followers clamoring for more.

Speaking of social media, collaboration is key! The 2025 update integrates seamlessly with Frame. io, making it easier than ever to share your projects and collaborate with fellow editors. Need to add captions for accessibility or that extra polish? Premiere Pro now boasts effortless caption integration, allowing you to focus on crafting your story without technical hurdles.

And let's not forget the power of masking! Masking allows for precise edits and creative effects, but it could be a bit cumbersome in the past. The 2025 update streamlines masking tools, making it a breeze to isolate elements and create stunning visuals.

This chapter is your launchpad into a universe of editing possibilities. We'll crack open the hood of Premiere Pro 2025, unveil its most powerful secrets, and equip you with the knowledge to become a video editing ninja. So, grab your mouse (or editing tablet – we don't judge!), unleash your inner creative genius, and get ready to dive into the exhilarating world of Premiere Pro 2025!

In this chapter, we are going to cover the following main topics:

- Linear and NLE in Adobe Premiere Pro
- The new Essentials workspace
- The new Vertical video workspace
- The new Project creation dialog
- The new Import interface
- The new Export interface in Adobe Premiere Pro 25.1
- Upgrading captions to graphics
- Frame.io integration with Adobe Premiere Pro
- Improved masking tools
- A look at Premiere Pro 2025's enhancements

By the end of this chapter, you will have learned about new workspace features, including a vertical video workspace and a new import and export interface window. You will also learn about upgrades to captions, including the ability to convert them to graphics. Finally, you will learn about improved masking tools for more precise editing and how to use the title and graphics tools in Premiere Pro to add a visual impact and production value to your videos.

Linear and NLE in Adobe Premiere Pro

NLE gives video makers a lot of freedom during the editing process. It is very flexible and doesn't require much planning to be executed. Users can apply a trial-and-error method. If you make a bad edit, you don't have to worry; just undo the changes and give it another try. This gives room for more creativity rather than just video editing and Premiere Pro is one of the best pieces of software to perform NLE.

In this section, we will learn about the fundamental differences between linear and NLE techniques. You will understand how linear editing was done traditionally using tape-based systems and how it has limitations in terms of flexibility and editing speed. On the other hand, you will learn how NLE revolutionized the industry by offering faster, more flexible, and more intuitive editing capabilities.

Linear editing

Linear editing is a traditional video editing technique that involves physically cutting and splicing together pieces of film or video footage in a sequential order to create a final edited video. Linear editing is called *linear* because the editing process must be done in a sequential manner, meaning that any changes made in the earlier parts of the sequence will affect the later parts of the sequence.

In the past, linear editing was done using tape-based systems. The video footage was recorded on film tapes, and the tapes were physically cut and spliced together to create the final edited video. Because of the physical nature of linear editing, it was a time-consuming and tedious process. Furthermore, any mistakes made during the editing process could not be undone easily, and changes made later in the sequence required redoing the entire editing process from that point onward.

With the advent of NLE systems, linear editing has become less common. However, some video producers still use linear editing for certain projects, such as for creating analog-based media such as VHS tapes, as linear editing allows them to edit the video in real time without having to rely on computer processing power.

NLE

NLE is a digital video editing technique that allows editors to manipulate video and audio clips independently of their original source files, and in any order or arrangement they choose, making it faster, more efficient, and more flexible than linear editing.

In NLE, the original video and audio clips are digitized and stored on a computer hard drive or other digital storage medium. The video and audio clips can be easily accessed, viewed, and edited using the NLE software on a computer. This allows editors to work with the original files non-destructively and create multiple versions of the same video without altering the original media files.

NLE systems offer various advantages over traditional linear editing systems. The software allows for more precise editing, such as frame-by-frame editing, with the ability to undo and redo changes easily. NLE also allows for the addition of special effects, audio mixing, color correction, and other post-production processes that can be done more efficiently than in linear editing.

Additionally, NLE makes it easier to collaborate on a project as multiple editors can work on different parts of the same video project simultaneously. The final edited video can be exported in various formats, such as high-definition video, web video, or broadcast-quality video, and can be distributed across various platforms such as television, the web, or cinema.

NLE is now the industry standard for video editing, and several NLE software options are available on the market, including Adobe Premiere Pro, Final Cut Pro, Avid Media Composer, and DaVinci Resolve.

Here is a table that summarizes the key differences between linear and non-linear video editing:

Feature	Linear Video Editing	Non-linear Video Editing
Media	Film or tape	Digital storage device
Editing process	Cut and splice footage	Trim, crop, and rearrange clips
Flexibility	Less flexible	More flexible
Efficiency	Less efficient	More efficient
Mistakes	Difficult to undo	Easy to undo
Cost	More expensive	Less expensive

Figure 1.1 – The table shows the differences between linear versus non-linear video editing

With a solid understanding of both linear and non-linear video editing methods, you've acquired a fundamental grasp of the contrasting approaches that shape the world of visual storytelling. Now, let's navigate the intriguing crossroads that editors often encounter when making the choice between these two paradigms. In the forthcoming section, we'll delve into the considerations that guide this decision-making process, examining the strengths and limitations of each approach in the context of different projects.

Making the choice

The choice between linear editing and NLE depends on several factors, including the type of project, available resources, and personal preference. Here are some considerations to help make the choice:

- **Type of project**: Linear editing may be suitable for simpler projects, such as home videos or basic corporate videos that require minimal editing. NLE, on the other hand, is necessary for more complex projects, such as feature films, documentaries, or high-end commercials that require precise editing and special effects.

- **Available resources**: Linear editing requires specialized equipment, such as tape decks, splicers, and monitors. NLE, however, requires a computer with sufficient processing power, storage, and software. Consider the available resources before deciding on the type of editing to use.

- **Budget**: Linear editing may be a cheaper option, as it requires less expensive equipment and can be done in real time without requiring extensive processing power. NLE, however, may require a higher budget due to the cost of hardware and software.

- **Timeframe**: Linear editing may be faster for smaller projects, as it does not require digitizing footage or processing large amounts of data. NLE, however, is more efficient for larger projects, as it allows for faster and easier access to footage, undo/redo capabilities, and the ability to work with multiple editors simultaneously.

- **Personal preference**: Some editors may prefer the tactile feel of linear editing or enjoy the creative process of splicing and physically arranging footage. Others may prefer the flexibility and precision of NLE software.

Ultimately, the choice between linear editing and NLE depends on the project's specific needs, available resources, budget, timeframe, and personal preference. It's essential to consider these factors before deciding which technique to use.

Having navigated the considerations and nuances of choosing between linear editing and NLE approaches, you've gained a profound insight into the dynamic landscape of video production. As we continue our exploration, let's cast our gaze forward and delve into the intriguing realm of the future of NLE within Adobe Premiere Pro. In the upcoming section, we'll peer at the horizon of technological advancements and evolving creative demands, anticipating how the software will evolve to empower editors in an ever-changing media landscape.

The future of NLE

The future of NLE is exciting, as technology continues to advance and new tools and features are developed to enhance the editing process. Here are some trends that may shape the future of NLE:

- **Artificial intelligence (AI)**: **AI** and **machine learning (ML)** are already being integrated into NLE software to automate certain tasks, such as color correction, audio leveling, and even editing decisions. As AI and ML technologies continue to evolve, they could become increasingly sophisticated and more integral to the editing process.

- **Real-time collaboration**: Real-time collaboration is becoming more common in NLE software, allowing multiple editors to work on the same project simultaneously. As internet speeds and cloud-based technology continue to improve, real-time collaboration could become more seamless and efficient.

- **Virtual and augmented reality**: Virtual and augmented reality technologies are already being used in some NLE software, such as Unity, Unreal, Vuforia, and ARCore, allowing editors to view and edit footage in 3D and immersive environments. As these technologies become more accessible and advanced, they could change the way editors work and create new possibilities for storytelling.

- **Cloud-based editing**: Cloud-based NLE is already being offered by some software companies, allowing editors to access their projects from anywhere with an internet connection. As internet speeds continue to increase and cloud-based technology becomes more reliable, cloud-based editing could become a more popular and efficient option.

- **Mobile editing**: NLE software is already available on mobile devices, and as smartphones and tablets continue to improve in processing power and screen size, mobile editing could become a more viable option for certain types of projects.

Overall, the future of NLE is likely to be shaped by advancements in technology, automation, collaboration, and new ways of storytelling. As these trends continue to develop, NLE software is likely to become even more powerful, efficient, and accessible.

Adobe Premiere Pro, one of the leading NLE tools, exemplifies these advancements by integrating cutting-edge features such as AI-driven editing, seamless cloud collaboration, and support for various media formats. Its continuous updates and user-friendly interface make it a preferred choice for both professionals and hobbyists, reflecting the broader trends in the NLE landscape.

Time to dive deeper! In the next section, we'll explore the new **Essentials** workspace in Premiere Pro, designed to optimize your editing experience.

The new Essentials workspace

The recently upgraded version of Premiere Pro offers improved organizational and creative tools to help you work more quickly and effectively throughout the program. Three new workspaces have been added in the latest release:

- **Essentials**
- **Vertical**
- **Review**

Premiere Pro is now optimized for single-screen devices, particularly laptops, under the new **Essentials** workspace. The most crucial panels are now consolidated in one location, with space for a longer timeline, eliminating the need to switch between workspaces. In the following figure, you can see the three new workflow screens, that is, **Import**, **Edit**, and **Export**:

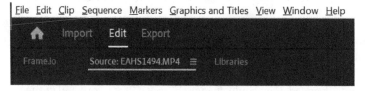

Figure 1.2 – The workflow screen tabs in the header bar

Even though **Essentials** includes much of what we use for a daily edit, all the additional workspaces that we utilize with Premiere Pro are located in the upper-right corner, beneath the workspace symbol (the blue highlighted icon):

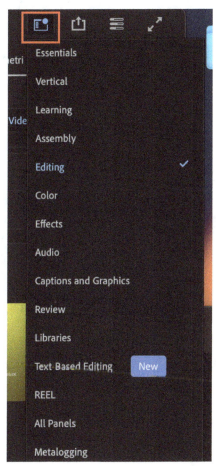

Figure 1.3 – List of workspaces in Premiere Pro

The **Essentials** workspace is designed for using Premiere Pro on a laptop or a single screen and provides editors with quick access to all basic Premiere Pro features without having to switch workspaces.

A wide timeline spans the bottom of the new **Essentials** workspace's clear and uncluttered style, which shows the panels in a logical left-to-right workflow:

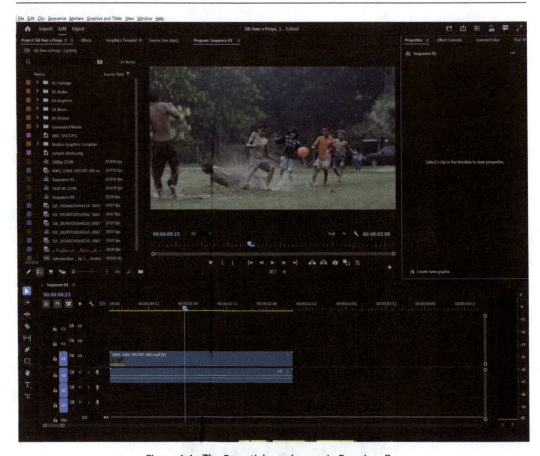

Figure 1.4 – The Essentials workspace in Premiere Pro

With a solid understanding of the **Essentials** workspace in Premiere Pro, we can now delve into the exciting realm of the new **Vertical** workspace. This innovative feature offers a fresh perspective on video editing, catering specifically to projects optimized for mobile devices and online platforms. In this section, we will explore the intricacies of the **Vertical** workspace, discovering its unique tools and functionalities that empower editors to craft captivating content perfectly tailored for vertical viewing experiences. Whether you're a seasoned editor or just starting your journey with Premiere Pro, embracing the **Vertical** workspace will undoubtedly broaden your creative horizons and enable you to stay at the forefront of modern video editing techniques.

The new Vertical video workspace

The new **Vertical** workspace has a tidy, straightforward design that is tailored for vertical content. The Program Monitor, which is configured to display vertical **9:16** video, can be found to the right of this workspace for social media creators working in this format. To activate the vertical arrangement, navigate to **Window | Workspaces | Vertical** to create the panel layout seen in the following screenshot:

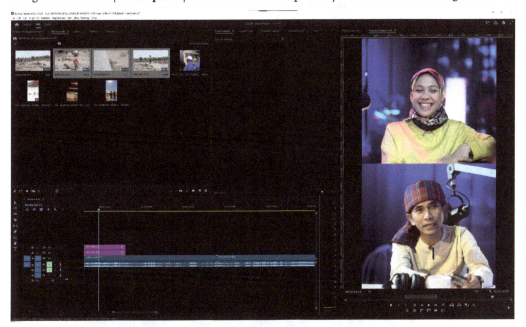

Figure 1.5 – The Vertical workspace in Premiere Pro

The panels are still laid out in the same way, but the Program Monitor now has substantially more workspace at the expense of a shorter timeframe.

Now that we've uncovered the innovative features of the **Vertical** workspace and how it optimizes content for vertical viewing, let's shift our focus to another significant enhancement: the new **Import** interface. This revamped interface streamlines the importing process, making it more intuitive and efficient than ever before. In the upcoming section, we will take an in-depth tour of the **Import** interface's revamped design, exploring its advanced organizational capabilities, metadata handling, and seamless integration with various file formats. By mastering this enhanced import process, you'll be equipped to start your editing projects on the right foot, ensuring a smoother workflow from the very beginning.

The new Project creation dialog

The New Project creation dialog is the beginning point for each video editing project in Adobe Premiere Pro. This window is where you create the foundation of your editing process, from naming your project and choosing a location to configuring critical video and audio parameters.

Let's dig in and learn how to make the most of this amazing tool. The **New Project Creation Dialog** allows you to:

- Name your project.
- Choose a location to store your project.
- Choose a template.
- Skip the Import mode (your option is sticky; if you pick it, it will remain chosen).
- Access project settings including General, Color, Scratch Disks, and Ingest Setting.

If you prefer not to utilize the Import mode, you may now import media straight from your project using the **Project** Panel.

To create a new project from the **Home** screen, first name your project; then, decide where to locate it. Click **Create** to create an empty project and allows you to follow your preferred workflow to add material:

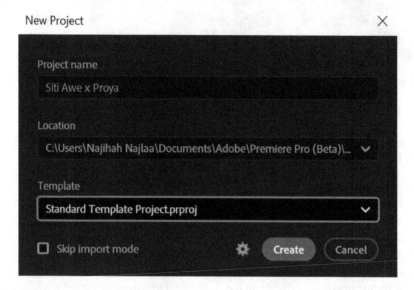

Figure 1.6 – The new project window in Premiere Pro

You can choose any of the project template options offered. Use **Standard Template Project.prproj** for normal video editing and the **Social Media Template Project.prproj** to produce social media videos to open template sizes for a variety of social networking platforms, including Facebook, TikTok, and YouTube:

Figure 1.7 – Selecting project template in Premiere Pro

Upon accessing your project panel, you will observe the pre-arranged bin folders that function as the basis for future projects for you to get started as you can see in the following screenshot:

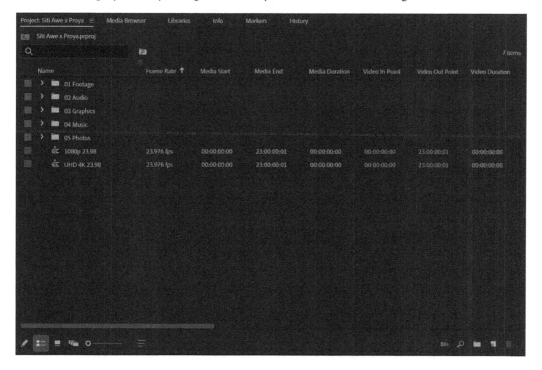

Figure 1.8 – Pre-arranged bin folders in Project panel

Project templates provide a substantial benefit by reducing the setup procedure and providing consistent results across various projects. Using a template, you may predefine project settings, sequence parameters, color profiles, and even placeholder material, saving time and work. This is especially useful for editors working on projects that have similar criteria, such as corporate films, social media material, or documentaries.

If you routinely work on a project of a similar kind, you have the option to develop your own project templates. This will save you the effort of starting from the beginning each time. Here are the methods to save your own project templates:

1. To save the templates, navigate to the **File** menu and select **Save as Template...** as seen in the following screenshot:

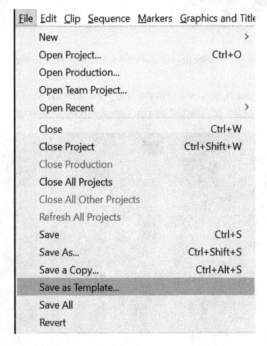

Figure 1.9 – Saving a project template from the File menu

2. Provide the name of the template and then click on the **Save** button:

Figure 1.10 – Naming the project template and hit Save

3. When initiating a new project, you will get the choice to select a template project from the dropdown **Template** menu, as seen in the following screenshot:

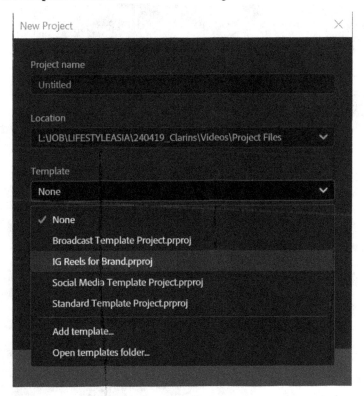

Figure 1.11 – Choosing your saved project template in the Template dropdown menu

Furthermore, templates help team members collaborate by offering a common structure for project organization. Establishing a defined process can help you improve productivity while maintaining project quality.

The new Import interface

To begin with, it is important to highlight that all the features that previously worked well during media import are still operational. Adobe has only revamped the user interface with the aim of facilitating media import.

They wanted to create it so that new users of Premiere Pro could search and import media fast and easily without having to worry about codecs, frame rates, or any of the other complicated technical aspects of video editing. Just scaled back, the technology is still there.

In this section, we will go over this new **Import** interface and look at the various options that come under this interface.

This is what the new **Import** interface looks like:

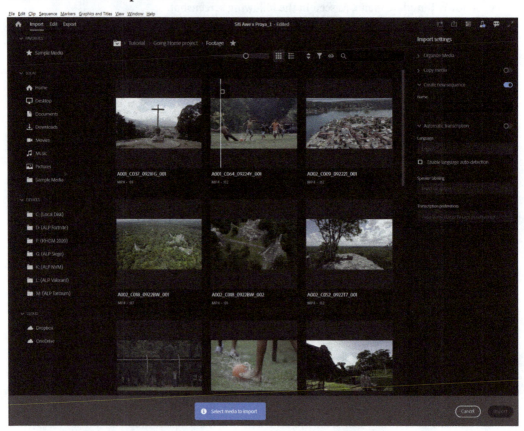

Figure 1.12 – The new Import interface in Premiere Pro

The preceding screen will display when you start a new project. On the left, you'll see common storage places, in the middle, sample media, and on the right, import settings.

For a thumbnail view of your media in the center panel, navigate to the list of the folder containing it on the left side of the panel:

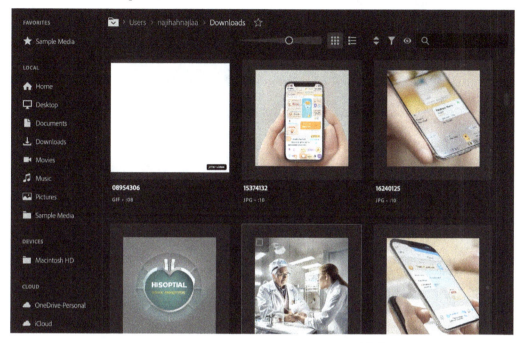

Figure 1.13 – Choosing media from the folders in the Import panel

The following figure shows all the settings across the top center of the **Import** interface:

Figure 1.14 – List of settings across the top center of the Import interface

Referring to the preceding figure, let's go over the various options:

- **1**: Changes the size of the thumbnails

- **2**: Displays thumbnails

- **3**: Displays a list view with metadata

- **4**: Changes the sort order

- **5**: Displays files by video, audio, images, or all

- **6**: Selects files by camera type

- 7: Searches for files by name

The upper left of the screen shows the current path. Click the *star* to add the current place to your **FAVORITES** list. Once more, click the star to *unfavorite* it:

Figure 1.15 – The star icon to enable Favorite location

The following screenshot shows the favorite destinations displayed in the interface's upper-left corner:

Figure 1.16 – The star icon shows the favorite folders

You can start choosing the clips as shown in the thumbnail in the following screenshot:

Figure 1.17 – Check the boxes of your selected clips

Now, let's look at the options in the **Import settings** menu, which can be found on the right-hand side of the interface:

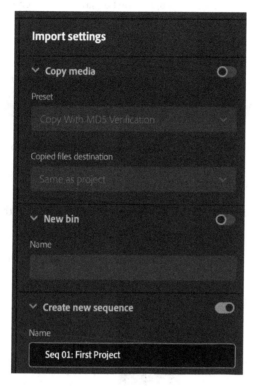

Figure 1.18 – Import settings window in Premiere Pro

The cornerstone of any editing project in Premiere Pro is the sequence. Here's how to utilize the **Create** button to get started:

- **Copy media** (off by default): This is the key to creating a copy of your media files. Adobe Media Encoder opens automatically to make copies in the background if **Copy media** is enabled.

- **New Bin** (off by default): Use this to make a new bin (folder icon) to put the media in. Media will be shown in the **Project** panel as individual files if the box is left unchecked.

- **Create new sequence** (on by default): Use this to construct and include the media in a new sequence. As a result, a reel is essentially created from the imported media that have been selected. Click on the **Create** button when you are done, as shown in the following screenshot:

Figure 1.19 – Click on the Create button to start creating a sequence

> **Important note**
>
> Once you click on the **Create** button, the project won't be saved. So, whenever the main Premiere Pro screen displays, don't forget to save the project.

When you want to add more media to a project, you should click **Import**:

Figure 1.20 – Import tab in header bar in Premiere Pro

Let's walk through these essential steps:

1. To return to the **Import** screen, click the **Import** button located on the left of the header bar.

2. The standard **Import** window is opened by selecting **File | Import**.

    The following screenshot shows the **Window** drop-down menu in Premiere Pro:

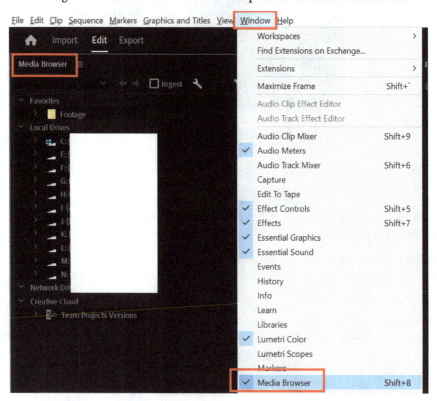

Figure 1.21 – Open the Media Browser panel

3. In the menu bar, select **Window | Media Browser** to keep all of its import, processing, and clip review features, or simply drag the required material into the project.

Having gained mastery over the new **Import** Interface, a crucial gateway to your editing endeavors, our journey now leads us to the intricacies of the **Export** interface. As every editor knows, the final stages of a project are just as crucial as its inception. In the upcoming section, we'll explore the enhanced **Export** interface of Premiere Pro, which offers an array of powerful tools and settings to fine-tune your project's output. Let's dive into the world of exporting and elevate your post-production skills to new heights.

The new Export interface in Adobe Premiere Pro 25.1

As we venture deeper into the realm of Adobe Premiere Pro, we arrive at a pivotal juncture that marks the culmination of your creative journey: exporting your meticulously crafted project to share it with the world. In this chapter, we will unravel the intricacies of the new **Export** interface, a powerful and revamped feature that empowers editors to optimize their content for various platforms, ensuring a seamless and captivating viewing experience for audiences far and wide.

Significant changes to the way we export sequences from Premiere Pro came with the introduction of the 24.5 upgrade.

Thankfully, Adobe simplified the tools without sacrificing any of their strength or adaptability. Here's how to export media in Premiere Pro:

1. Select the project you want to export either in the **Project** panel or the timeline.

2. Click the **Export** tab (or choose **File | Export Media**):

Figure 1.22 – Export tab in the header bar

3. The new **Export** interface will appear, as in the following screenshot:

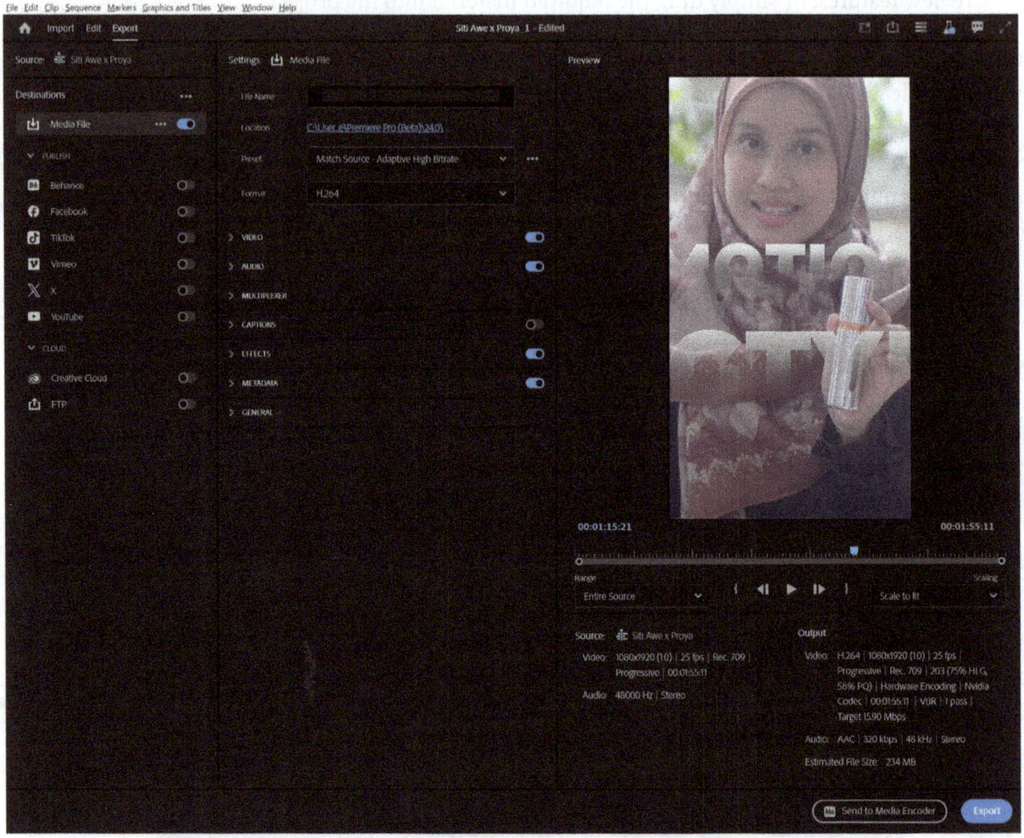

Figure 1.23 – The Export window in Premiere Pro

Let's go over this interface:

- The usual export destinations are on the left. You can enable the type of media for your export over here. Select the video destination from the options in the left-hand column, such as TikTok, YouTube, Vimeo, or your local drive (**Media File**).

- The output settings are in the center. These are the same ones that can be found in Adobe Premiere Pro normally.

A playable version of the project itself is shown on the right, along with a **Play** button and technical information presented under the **Source** and **Output** options.

The Destinations panel

It is possible to export many files from a single project using the **Destinations** panel. It will save you a ton of time. This is what the panel looks like:

Figure 1.24 – Export options in the Export window in Premiere Pro

Let's go over the options under this panel:

- **Media File**: H.264 format being the default setting, this option exports a finished file
- **YouTube** and others: These options make a compressed file that is best suited for social networking platforms
- **FTP** (**File Transfer Protocol**): Transmits a file that is often compressed to the web server of your choice

Next, let's look at the **Settings** panel.

The Settings panel

This is what the **Settings** panel looks like:

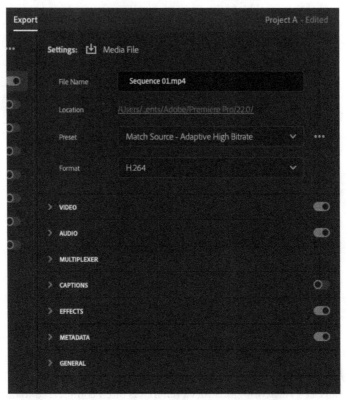

Figure 1.25 – Settings options in the Export window in Premiere Pro

Let's go over the options seen in the **Settings** panel:

- **File Name**: Here, you can give the exported file a name before selecting a storage place by clicking the blue text in the **Location** option, as highlighted in the preceding figure.

- **Location**: The file path directory of the saved file. This is where you can locate your project.

- **Preset**: You can choose a different video preset from the **Preset** menu. While individual options are available for all export parameters, **Match Source** defaults are frequently the best choice. These are adaptable presets that employ the same frame size, frame rate, and so on as your original sequence. Choose the **High Bitrate** setting to export high-quality video.

- **Format**: A media file's default export setting uses the highly compressed H.264 codec. However, switching to a higher-quality codec, such as ProRes, is simple using the dropdown.

- **VIDEO**: Toggling this on will enable video export.

    All the settings will give you access to more by clicking the chevron.

While individual settings for all export parameters are available, **Match Source** presets are frequently the best option. These are adaptive presets that employ the same frame size, frame rate, and other parameters as your source sequence. To export a high-quality video, use the **High Bitrate** preset.

> **Important note**
> We have been using Adobe Media Encoder for years with the same settings.

Now that we have looked through the **Settings** panel, let's look at the last set of panels, that is, the **Preview**, **Source**, and **Output** panels.

The Preview, Source, and Output panels

This is what the **Preview**, **Source**, and **Output** panels look like:

Figure 1.26 – The Preview, Source, and Output panels in Premiere Pro

By default, the **Preview** window exports the entire project. Marking an **In** point and an **Out** point tells Premiere Pro what part of the clip you want to use. In Adobe Premiere Pro, **In** and **Out** points refer to the designated beginning and end of a specific section of a clip or sequence you want to work with. It's essentially a way to tell Premiere Pro which part of the clip you're interested in using. The **In** specifies the beginning, and the **Out** specifies the end. To set an **In** or **Out** point in the timeline at the bottom of the **Preview** panel, however, press the *I* or *O* keys. Under the image, that is, in the **Output** panel, are the technical settings of the file. Once you are finished editing the file, you can click on **Export**.

> **Important note**
> You can also click **Edit** in the top-left corner of the **Export** interface to leave this screen if you decide not to export.

This new interface is nice! It is easy to navigate from left to right, giving users access to all the parameters they need, and feels more spacious than previous export windows did.

With export settings firmly under your command, you've gained the knowledge to ensure your projects leave a lasting impact on audiences. Now, let's explore another facet of Premiere Pro's creative toolbox: upgrading captions to graphics. In the upcoming section, we will unveil the transformative capabilities that allow you to transcend traditional captioning and transform your text into engaging visual elements.

Upgrading captions to graphics

Many options are available in Premiere Pro for styling and formatting captions. You can now turn captions into graphics for even more inventive alternatives. Once finished, you can animate the words on the screen by using effects and transitions. To have exact control over the outcomes, you can use keyframing to change the timing of impacts or transitions.

Upgraded captions can still be changed to text, either in the **Text** panel or directly in the Program Monitor. The outcome, including all of the graphics, can be exported. To upgrade captions to graphics, go to **Graphics and Titles | Upgrade Caption to Graphic**:

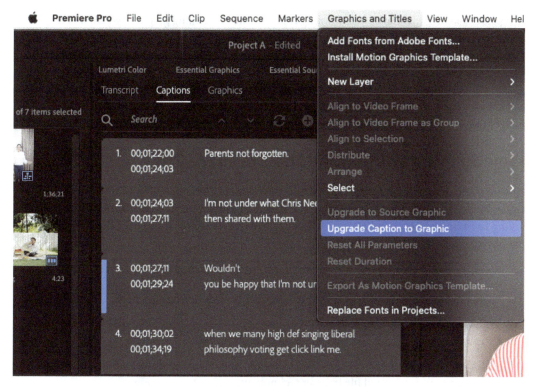

Figure 1.27 – Open Text panel to access Captions options

> **Important note**
>
> Use the standard captions instead of `sidecar` text files for images if you need to export your captions as separate files, such as `.srt` files. In Premiere Pro, a sidecar text file is a separate file that stores captions or subtitles for your video. It's called a *sidecar* because it exists alongside (but independent of) the main video file.

The following tip will come in handy.

> **Tip**
>
> Create a duplicate of the captions track and upgrade one of them to graphics if you want to export separate versions of your video. While working on the graphics track, hide the captions track. When you're ready to export, create two files—one with the original captions track as an `.srt` sidecar file and one with the visuals burned in.

Having unlocked the potential of transforming captions into compelling graphics, you're well on your way to creating content that resonates deeply with your audience. Now, let's delve into a powerful integration that amplifies collaboration and streamlines your editing process: **Frame.io** integration. In the upcoming section, we will explore how this seamless connection between Premiere Pro and Frame. io enhances real-time collaboration, feedback, and version control. By embracing this integration, you'll not only expedite your workflow but also foster a dynamic environment for sharing ideas and refining projects.

Frame.io integration in Adobe Premiere Pro

Although Adobe has included a plethora of new capabilities in Premiere Pro and After Effects, the integration of Frame.io is the standout addition. **Frame.io** provides a powerful tool for video editors working in Premiere Pro to collaborate effectively with reviewers and improve the overall video editing process.

With a Creative Cloud subscription, video producers can now do the following:

- Share ongoing projects with an unlimited number of reviewers everywhere

- Without leaving the Premiere Pro or After Effects timeline, add frame-specific comments and notes right there

- Utilize the 100 GB of dedicated Frame.io storage to upload and download material quickly with Frame.io's accelerated file transfer technology

- Together with another remote user, work on up to five projects at once

- Utilize Camera to Cloud, the quickest, simplest, and safest method for getting footage from cameras to editors, motion graphic designers, and other stakeholders

As we embrace the collaborative power of Frame.io integration, it's evident that modern video editing extends far beyond individual efforts. Now, let's shift our focus to refining the very canvas upon which your creative vision comes to life. In the following section, we'll dive into the realm of improved masking tools in Premiere Pro. These tools empower you to precisely control visual elements, allowing you to manipulate and enhance specific portions of your footage with remarkable accuracy.

Improved masking tools

You can add numerous points to a line path that you draw using the Pen tool to easily conceal items down to the tiniest of details without being hindered by rotate and scale options. With the additional 800% and 1600% zoom-level settings, you can zoom in and out in the Program Monitor for even more accuracy.

In this section, we will first learn how to apply effects to a specific part of a frame in your video using Premiere Pro's masking tools. Then, we will move on to learn how to apply a mask and then track it across the frame.

To apply effects to a specific area of a frame in your video, use Premiere Pro's masking capabilities. You can make a circular or ellipse-shaped mask with the Ellipse tool, or a four-sided polygon with the Rectangle tool.

Masking and tracking in Premiere Pro

We use masks to specify a specific area in a clip for blurring, covering, highlighting, applying effects, or color-correcting. Different-shaped masks, such as an ellipse or a rectangle, can be made and modified. Alternately, you can use the Pen tool to create free-form Bezier forms. Bezier curves are a fundamental concept used for creating smooth and natural-looking animations.

Creating a mask using shapes

The following screenshot illustrates the process of examining the choices available in Premiere Pro to make masks using shapes. This feature allows you to enhance your video edits by adding a creative touch.

To illustrate this point, let's look at the following screenshot:

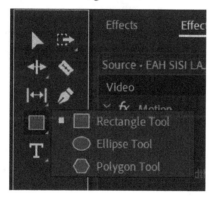

Figure 1.28 – Using Rectangle Tool, Ellipse Tool, and Polygon Tool

An elliptical or circular mask can be made using the **Ellipse Tool**, and a four-sided polygon can be made using the **Rectangle Tool**. You can find this tool in Shape button, as shown in *Figure 1.28*.

In the following screenshot, the mosaic effect is seen both before and after its application:

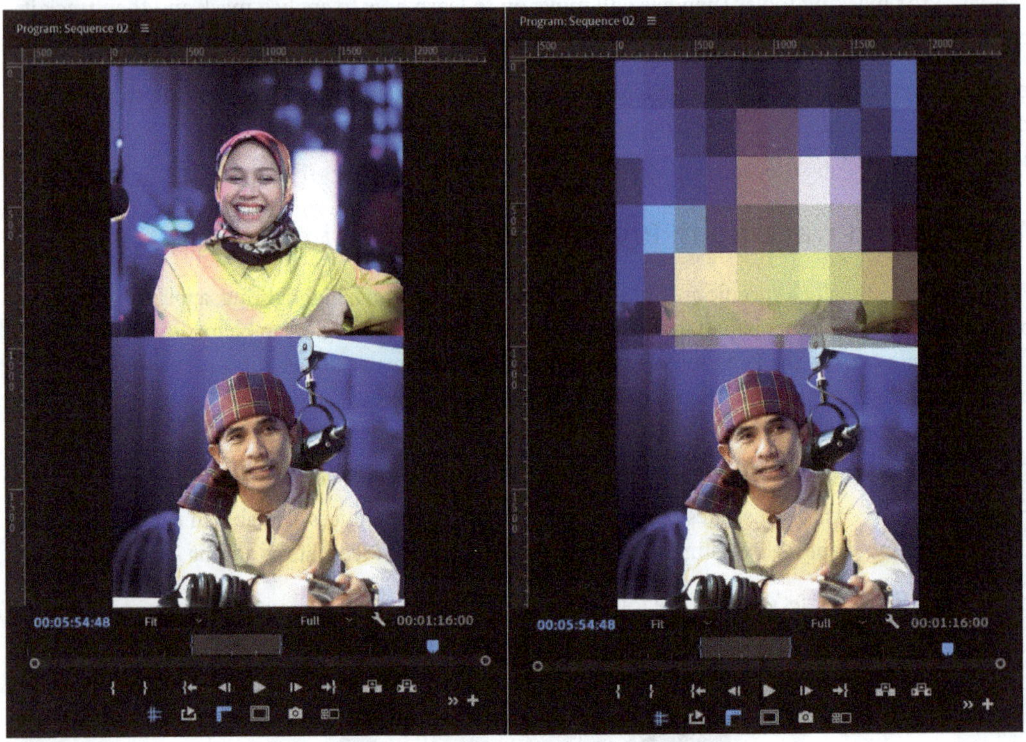

Figure 1.29 – Before and after applying the mosaic effect in the mask area

To apply effects on a masked clip, follow these steps:

1. Choose the clip you want to mask in the **Timeline** window.

2. Choose the effect you want to use on the footage from the **Effects** panel. For instance, choose **Effects | Stylize | Mosaic** to apply the mosaic effect.

Figure 1.30 – Adding the mosaic effect to a clip

3. Drag the chosen effect from the **Effects** panel to the clip in the **Timeline** panel to apply it to the clip. Alternately, you can also apply an effect by selecting the clip and double-clicking the effect in the **Effects** panel.

4. To view the effect properties, open the **Effect Controls** panel. To make the controls visible, click the drop-down arrow.

    The **Effect Controls** panel's adjustment settings can be entered manually to modify a mask. Depending on your selection, the controls vary. The following screenshot shows the controls of the **Mosaic** effect:

Figure 1.31 – Adjusting the Mosaic effect in the Effect Controls panel

5. The effect is contained within the masked region and can be seen in the clip that is shown in the Program Monitor:

Figure 1.32 – Mosaic effect in the masked area

6. Now, using the **Effect Controls** panel, you can also alter the mask's size and shape with the blue line:

Figure 1.33 – Creating a mask using the Ellipse tool and set as Inverted

> **Important note**
>
> By adjusting the settings differently each time, you can apply the same effect more than once. Masks are not stored as effect presets in Premiere Pro.

Creating a free-form shape

By using the *Pen tool*, free-form shapes can be produced. You can easily draw intricate mask forms around things using the Pen tool. From the **Effect Controls** panel, select the Pen tool. On the clip in the Program Monitor, draw immediately:

Figure 1.34 – Creating a free-form shape using the Pen tool

By drawing straight lines and curved segments, you can make various shapes. You can have more control over the mask's design by using Bezier path segments to create smooth curves.

Mask tracking in Premiere Pro

By applying a mask on an object in Premiere Pro, you may enable the mask to automatically track the item's movement as it transitions from one frame to another. For example, Premiere Pro has the capability to automatically track the motions of a face that has been masked and blurred using a form mask, from one frame to another, as the subject walks.

The **Effect Controls** panel shows controls for tracking a mask forward or backward when a mask is selected. You can decide whether to track the mask across the entire sequence or one frame at a time.

If you want to change how masks are tracked, click the wrench icon. For the best tracking, you can choose from a few options, including the following:

- **Position**: Only records the precise location of the mask from one frame to the next.
- **Position & Rotation**: Tracks the mask position while adjusting the rotation as needed per frame with **Position** and **Rotation**.

- **Position, Scale, & Rotation**: The position, scale, and rotation of the frame are adjusted automatically to match the location of the mask.

Speeding up mask tracking

Live **Preview** can slow down mask tracking in Premiere Pro (the default option). If Live **Preview** is activated for some reason, you can disable it by following these steps:

1. Choose the clip that includes the effect utilizing masks in the **Timeline** box.

2. To listen to a preview of the changes made to the music, click on the symbol that looks like a wrench for the mask and select **Preview** from the option that appears:

Figure 1.35 – Previewing Mask in Effect Controls panel

3. To deselect the **Preview** option, click on the mask wrench symbol and choose Preview from the drop-down menu:

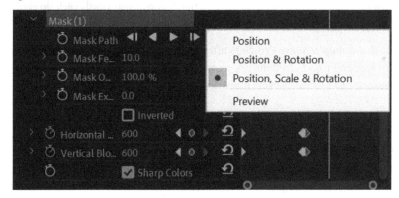

Figure 1.36 – Disable Preview mode in Effect Controls

Additionally, Premiere Pro comes with built-in tools such as **Mask Path** that improve mask tracking. Premiere Pro adjusts the frame to 1080 for clips with a height greater than 1080 before determining the track. Additionally, in order to expedite the mask tracking process, Premiere Pro employs low-quality renders.

A look at Premiere Pro 2025's enhancements

Premiere Pro 2025 brings a range of impressive upgrades aimed at enhancing your video editing workflow. The new **Properties Panel** consolidates essential editing tools, making the process more efficient. The introduction of **Generative AI** features allow for automatic video edits and effects, saving time and sparking creativity. The redesigned **Timeline** clips now feature a sleek, rounded appearance, which is easier on the eyes during long editing sessions. **Performance** has also been significantly improved, with H.264 encoding speeds up to four times faster on Apple silicon and twice as fast on Windows. These updates, along with better color management and AI-driven audio tools, make Premiere Pro 2025 a substantial upgrade for both beginners and seasoned editors.

A timeline that is five times quicker

Anyone who has extensively used Adobe Premiere Pro knows that it is prone to slowness, glitches, crashes, and everything in between. Adobe has been working hard behind the scenes to fix these unpleasant issues and position its flagship NLE as the leading choice for professional editors. Introducing a five-fold faster timeline will surely assist in reaching this aim. According to Adobe, the new high-performance timeline drawing is more engaging and responsive, allowing for buttery smooth editing and cutting.

A new recovery mode

Adobe has added a new mode called **Recovery Mode** that lets you seamlessly pick up right where you left off with automatic project recovery if something goes wrong.

When you relaunch Adobe Premiere Pro 2025 after an app crash, you will see an automated popup that allows you to reopen projects in their prior condition. Meanwhile, if you want to restore a prior version of your project, go to **File | Revert** and select the last user-saved state. Nice and simple.

Speed and efficiency in every edit

As you can see from new features such as Video Effects Manager and project templates, the latest Adobe Premiere Pro update puts speed first. With Video Effects Manager, you can easily control all third-party apps from one place. Now more than ever, you can find, troubleshoot, and disable incompatible plugins to improve system stability. This gives you more time to edit.

Meanwhile, project templates let editors store projects as templates for later usage. When you start a new project, you can use a prior template with the bins and sequences already sorted. Again, it's all about accelerating your process. A project may be saved as a template by selecting **File | Save as Template**.

New text tools for faster workflows

Regarding speed, Adobe has completely adopted AI in this Premiere Pro upgrade. The future of editing is evident, and the newest text-based editing tool is an excellent example of this. This is not a new feature, but with AI, it seems more powerful than ever. With just one click, you have the ability to eliminate all pauses and transcribe an audio file using either a specific channel or a mixture of all channels.

Here's a closer look at how it works:

Figure 1.37 – Deleting pauses and re-transcribing an audio file

These streamlined workflows for deleting pauses and re-transcribing audio in Premiere Pro empower you to edit with greater efficiency and precision. This newfound efficiency allows video editors to focus on the creative aspects of storytelling, delivering a more polished final product in less time.

Audio auto-tagging

Audio auto-tagging is now available, in addition to improved text-based editing. The program can now automatically classify audio files as conversation, music, special effects, or atmosphere using AI. When you pick a tag in the **Essential Sound** panel, all clips labeled in that category are immediately selected, making it easier and faster to create professional sound. We shall learn more in the forthcoming *Chapter 7, Editing Audio Easily in the Essential Sound Panel.*

AI-powered speech enhancement

If you were dealing with terrible audio, it may take a very long time to clear up. With Enhance Speech, AI now does the heavy lifting for you, reducing background noise and dramatically enhancing the sound of badly recorded speech in seconds. Things like these have us enthusiastic about the introduction of AI into the editing realm.

Here's a closer look at where to **Enable Enhance Speech** within the Premiere Pro interface when you right-click the audio in the timeline:

Figure 1.38 – Enable Enhance Speech in the timeline in Premiere Pro

Premiere Pro's new in-timeline Enhance Speech feature empowers editors to achieve broadcast-ready audio with minimal effort. By leveraging ML, this innovative tool tackles noise reduction and clarity issues in a single click, streamlining the editing process. This translates to more time spent crafting impactful narratives and less time wrestling with audio imperfections. The result? Crystal-clear voiceovers, interviews, and dialogue that elevate the overall production value of your videos.

Streamlined controls for effortless color grading

Color options in previous versions, were often split across many panels and preferences. In the 2025 Premiere Pro update, we see a redesign with simpler color settings, merging all of these color options into a single tab. The **Settings** tab in **Lumetri Color** combines **Preferences**, **Project** color settings, **Source Clip** color settings, **Sequence** color settings, and **Sequence Clip** color settings. Making modifications is faster and simpler than ever before. Here's where you can find the new **Settings** tab in the **Lumetri Color** panel:

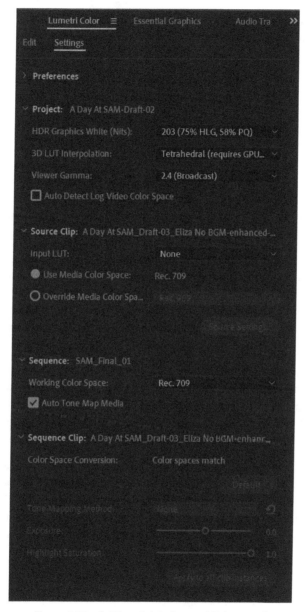

Figure 1.39 – Settings tab in Lumetri Color panel

There's lots more to be thrilled about with the latest Adobe Premiere Pro version. SRT support will allow you to stream information packets from Premiere Pro to various viewers, and H/W decoding and encoding of H264/HEVC files on *Intel Discrete Graphics* (Intel Arc) cards will improve the app's speed even more.

You may now add, edit, and save a single set of custom destinations in **Export** mode. Previously, custom destinations were kept for each sequence, and there was no simple method to distribute them between sequences andS projects.

If you're wondering how to upgrade Premiere Pro, the process is straightforward. If you're connected to Adobe Creative Cloud and have automatic updates enabled, the updated Premiere Pro 2025 will load automatically.

Summary

The topic of linear editing versus NLE explores two different methods of editing video footage. Linear editing involves physically splicing and arranging footage on tape, while NLE uses software to digitally edit and manipulate footage. The choice between the two depends on various factors, including the type of project, available resources, budget, timeframe, and personal preference.

In this chapter, we also learned about all the new features Adobe released in Premiere Pro. It introduced several new features and performance improvements, such as the new **Essentials** and **Vertical** video workspaces. Redesigned core workflows are now more intuitive and visual with new import and export interfaces, upgrading captions to graphics, Frame.io integration with Premiere Pro, and improved masking tools. This update makes Premiere Pro more efficient and allows users to easily create and share high-quality videos.

So, there are a lot of improvements and changes to digest for the 2025 edition of Adobe Premiere Pro, some major and others little. It's evident that AI is here to stay, and we're really interested to see how this technology improves and supports our video editing experience. It's not necessarily about AI taking over as editor and displacing us from a job, but more about how it can perform the heavy lifting and expedite what were previously highly monotonous, time-consuming, and frustrating tasks.

With all these useful new options, editing seems faster and easier than ever. This can only be a positive thing. As we transition to the next chapter, *Linear and Non-Linear Editing in Adobe Premiere Pro*, we'll guide you through the essential steps to set up your initial project within Adobe Premiere Pro. From creating a new project to familiarizing yourself with the interface, tools, and organizational structures, the chapter will provide you with a solid foundation to kickstart your editing journey with confidence.

2

Essential Tools and Workflows in Premiere Pro

In this chapter, you'll learn the basics of starting a new project in Premiere Pro. You'll learn how to download and install Premiere Pro, create a new project, set up project settings, and select a scratch disk. This chapter will also introduce the Premiere Pro interface, including the **Project** panel, **Source** panel, **Timeline** panel, and **Program** panel.

In this chapter, we're going to cover the following main topics:

- Introduction to Premiere Pro
- Introduction to the Premiere Pro interface
- Customizing the Premiere Pro interface
- Understanding the timeline
- Enhancing your Premiere Pro editing workflow
- Learning how the experts edit faster

By the end of this chapter, you'll have gained a better understanding of the basic functionalities of Premiere Pro, be prepared to import media, and can start to edit your project in the following chapters.

Technical requirements

The technical requirements for starting a Premiere Pro project may vary, depending on the version of Premiere Pro and the complexity of the project, but the following are the recommended system requirements for Adobe Premiere Pro CC 2025:

- **Processor**: An Intel 6th gen or newer CPU or AMD equivalent.
- **Operating system**: Windows 10 (64-bit) version 22H2 (or later), Windows 11, or macOS Monterey (version 12) or later.

- **Memory**: 8 GB or 16 GB of RAM (32 GB or more recommended).

- **Graphics card**: 2 GB or 4 GB of GPU VRAM (8 GB recommended) for GPU-accelerated performance.

- **Storage**: 8 GB of available hard disk space for installation; additional free space required during installation (can't install on removable flash storage devices).

- **Monitor resolution**: 1920 x 1080 or greater display resolution.

- **Sound card**: ASIO-compatible or Microsoft **Windows Driver Model (WDM)**.

- **Network storage connection**: 1 Gigabit Ethernet or 10 Gigabit Ethernet for a 4K shared network workflow.

Note that these are the recommended requirements; the actual system requirements may vary, depending on the project's size and complexity. Additionally, the system requirements may change with the future versions of Premiere Pro. So, it's always a good idea to check the latest system requirements before starting a new project. For more details, please visit `https://helpx.adobe.com/premiere-pro/system-requirements.html`.

Introduction to Premiere Pro

Premiere Pro is a powerful video editing software developed by Adobe Inc. It has become a leading tool for professional video editors and content creators around the world. With its advanced features, intuitive interface, and seamless integration with other Adobe applications, Premiere Pro has become the go-to choice for creating high-quality video content for a variety of platforms, including television, film, social media, and the web.

Premiere Pro allows users to import and edit videos, audio, and graphics in a wide range of formats. Its editing tools are designed to help users create visually stunning videos with precision and speed. From basic editing tasks, such as trimming and splitting footage, to advanced effects, such as color grading and compositing, Premiere Pro has all the tools necessary to bring your creative vision to life.

In the following sections, we'll learn how to install Premiere Pro, create a new project, and stay organized.

Installing Premiere Pro

To install Premiere Pro, follow these steps:

1. Visit the Adobe website (`https://www.adobe.com/my_en/products/premiere.html`) and select **Download** under **Adobe Premiere Pro**:

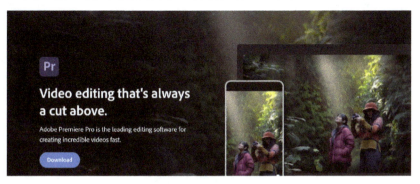

Figure 2.1 – Downloading Adobe Premiere Pro from the Adobe website

2.   Choose a plan and enter your Adobe ID and password or create a new account:

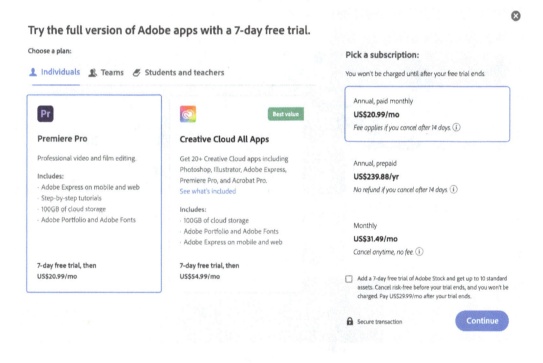

Figure 2.2 – Subscription plans available on the Adobe website

3.   Once you've purchased a plan, click the **Download** button to download the installer.

4.   Run the installer and follow the prompts to complete the installation process.

5.   When prompted, enter your Adobe ID and password to activate the software.

6.   Once the installation is complete, launch Premiere Pro to start a new project.

> **Important note**
>
> The exact steps may vary, depending on your operating system and the version of Premiere Pro you're installing. Additionally, make sure that your computer meets the minimum system requirements before installing Premiere Pro. Visit the Adobe website for more details: `https://helpx.adobe.com/premiere-pro/system-requirements.html`.

Creating a new project

To create a new project in Premiere Pro, follow these steps:

1. Launch Adobe Premiere Pro from your computer. You should see the splash screen, along with a list of recent projects.

2. To create a new project, click on the **New Project** button in the lower-left corner of the screen. Alternatively, you can go to **File | New | Project...** from the menu bar:

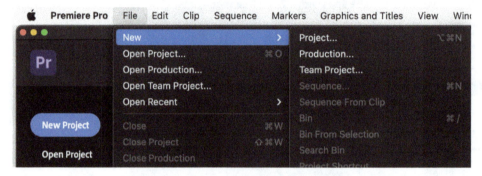

Figure 2.3 – Creating a new project file in Premiere Pro from the menu bar

You can create a new project by clicking on the dedicated **New Project** button on the home screen. This is a quicker way to initiate a new project without having to navigate menus:

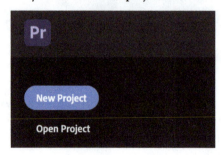

Figure 2.4 – Clicking the New Project button to create a new project on the home screen

3. In the **New Project** dialog box, you'll be prompted to choose a name and location for your project. You can also set the video and audio settings for your project, such as resolution, frame rate, and audio sample rate. Click **Create** to create the new project:

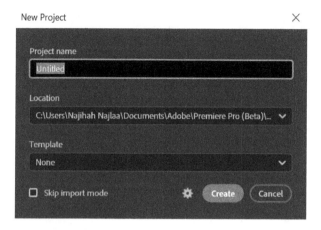

Figure 2.5 – The New Project window in Premiere Pro

4. Name your project, choose where you wish to save it, and pick a project template. You can also upload a **Template** from your own files:

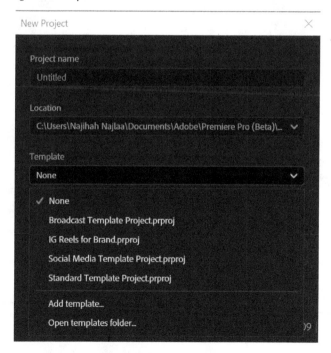

Figure 2.6 – Picking a project template in Premiere Pro

5. If you prefer to skip **Import** mode and add media directly from the **Project** panel, check the **Skip import mode** option. This will stay selected for future projects unless you change it:

Figure 2.7 – Skip import mode in the New Project window

6. Click on the **Settings** icon to open **Project Settings**, where you can adjust **General**, **Color**, **Scratch Disks**, and **Ingest Settings**.

7. Select the video clips and other media you want to include in your project.

8. As you select your media, the items will appear in the **Selection Tray** area at the bottom of the window. You can right-click on any item in the tray to remove it or clear all items if needed. The following screenshot demonstrates what your **Import** window will look like:

Figure 2.8 – Selecting media in the Import window

9. In the **Import settings** section of the **Import** desktop, choose the following options to manage your files:

    • **Organize media**: Use this option to arrange your project media before you start editing. You can create a new bin and name it, after which the media will be displayed without being copied to the new location.

    • **Copy media**: Toggle this option to copy media files from a temporary source, such as a camera card or removable drive. You can start editing while Premiere Pro copies the files in the background, using MD5 checksum verification to ensure the files aren't corrupted during the process.

    • **Create new sequence**: Toggle this option to simplify the process. Premiere Pro will automatically set the sequence settings, such as resolution and frame rate, based on the first asset you select.

    If this option is on, the new media will be added as a new sequence in your project. If it's off, the new media will go into the **Project** panel. Please refer to the following screenshot:

Figure 2.9 – Import settings in the Import window

10. Click **Create** to import your media as a sequence in Premiere Pro. After creating the new project, you'll be taken to the main workspace of Premiere Pro, where you can start importing and editing your media files.

That's it! You've successfully created a new project in Premiere Pro. From here, you can import your media files, organize your project using bins, and start editing your video footage.

Staying organized

Staying organized is essential when working with any video editing software, including Premiere Pro. This section will provide some tips to help you stay organized in Premiere Pro:

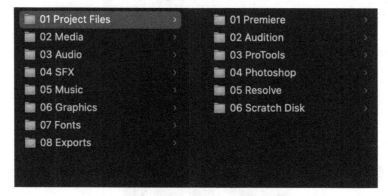

Figure 2.10 – Organizing media

It's important to note that organizing a Premiere Pro project depends on bins. Simplify the organization process by using general categories, such as *Footage* and *Audio*, provide clear labeling for all items, and employ color coding as visual indicators. Before diving into project creation, let's establish a solid foundation by exploring how to structure folders and media files for a smooth and streamlined workflow by using the methods listed here:

- **Use bins**: Bins are like folders that allow you to group and organize your media files, sequences, and other assets. Create bins for different types of footage, such as interviews, B-roll, or sound effects, and keep them organized so that you can quickly find the clips you need. In Premiere Pro, bins aren't technically folders you *add* to the project, but rather containers you create to organize your media files. Here's how to create bins:

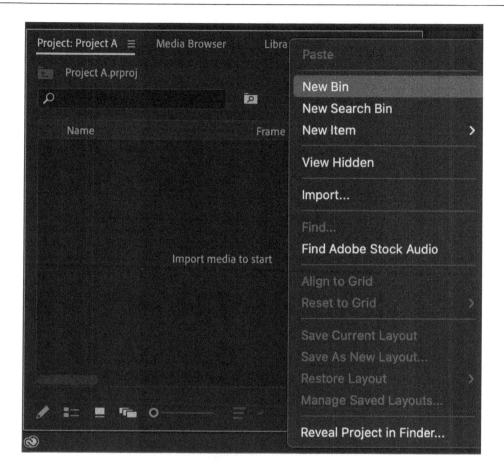

Figure 2.11 – Creating a new bin in the Project panel

Within Adobe Premiere Pro, bins function like file directories within your project, facilitating the effective organization and management of your media assets. They're essential for maintaining a neat and easily accessible workstation, particularly while working on extensive or intricate tasks. The following screenshot shows an example folder structure for managing your editing process effortlessly:

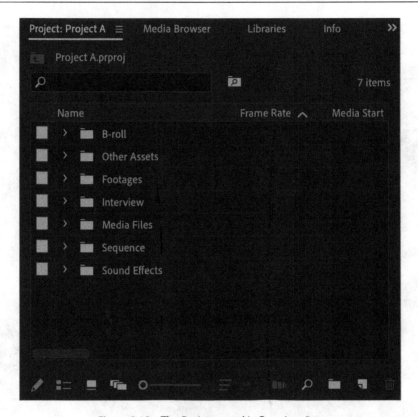

Figure 2.12 – The Project panel in Premiere Pro

- **Label your clips**: Assign labels to your clips to help identify them easily. For instance, you could label all the interview clips as *Interviews*, B-roll clips as *B-Roll*, and so on. You can also create custom labels so that they suit your project, as shown in the following screenshot:

Figure 2.13 – Adding labels from the Preferences menu

Labels in Premiere Pro save you time and annoyance while maintaining a seamless and effective workflow. The following screenshot shows how to leverage labels in Premiere Pro:

Figure 2.14 – Creating label options in the Preferences window

- **Use markers**: Markers are notes that you can place on the timeline to help you remember key points in your project. Use markers to mark important scenes or add notes for yourself or other collaborators. Don't just mark a spot – add comments to your markers! Explain what needs to be done at that point, highlight potential issues, or leave reminders for yourself or collaborators. This fosters clear communication and keeps everyone on the same page. See the following screenshot for an example:

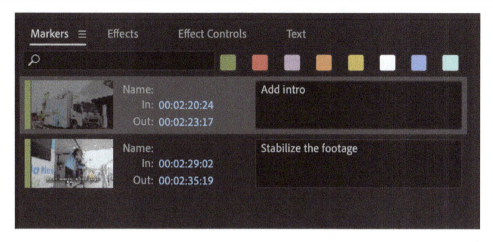

Figure 2.15 – Adding comments to your markers in the Markers panel

Markers in Premiere Pro serve as little indicators during the editing process. Visual checkpoints serve as markers that allow you to quickly navigate back to certain places, organize parts, and ensure seamless transitions. For precise editing, markers allow you to pinpoint the exact frame for surgical precision in your editing. You can see the comments on the clips, as shown in the following screenshot:

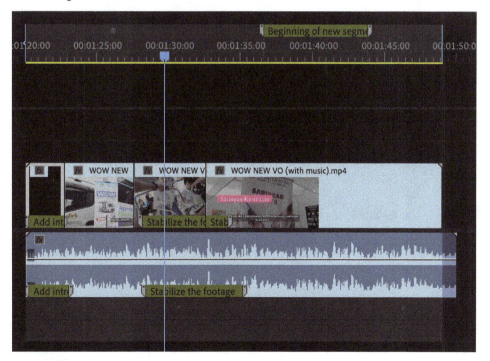

Figure 2.16 – Comments on the clips in the timeline

- **Create a naming convention**: Develop a consistent naming convention for all your project files. This will help you stay organized and quickly find the files you need. For instance, you could name your clips with a prefix that identifies the type of clip, followed by a sequence number, and a brief description of the content.

There are numerous categories from which to choose for this particular shoot, including the following:

- Shoot date

- Project ID

- Subject name

- Camera number

- Shot composition

- Audio

- Clip number

Start with a broad category for your project type. Examples include Shoot, Date-project, ID-subject, name-camera, number-clip, and number. See the following example:

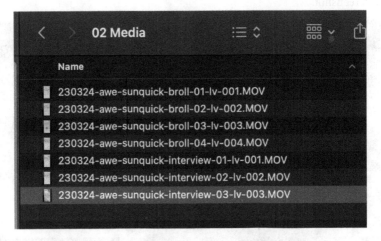

Figure 2.17 – Renaming clips to stay organized with the numbering system

File naming in Premiere Pro is your time-saving partner! Using descriptive titles that include keywords, dates, and version numbers will help you avoid the confusion of searching for certain clips, thus saving you valuable time throughout the editing process. It's like a searchable map, enabling you to discover what you need fast, keeping your project structured, and assuring easy cooperation with others. Therefore, abandon the enigmatic V3_Final_Final.mov and choose unambiguous, descriptive titles to enhance the efficiency of your editing process and promote more contented working.

- **Use workspaces**: Workspaces are customizable arrangements of panels that you can save and recall later. Use them to create different layouts for different tasks, such as editing, color grading, or audio mixing.

- **Keep your project folder tidy**: Keep your project folder organized by keeping all your files, including media files, project files, and any other assets, in their respective folders. This will help you avoid confusion and make it easier for you to back up your files:

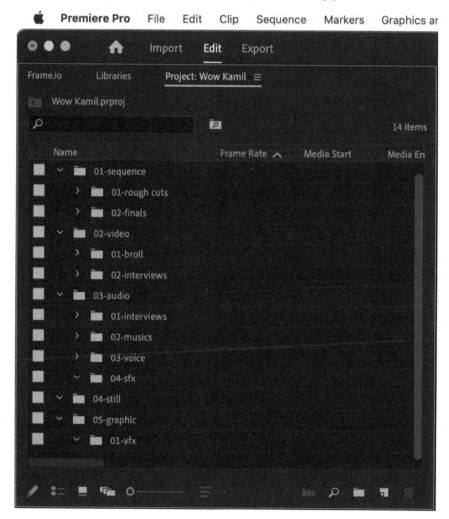

Figure 2.18 – Folder naming in the Project panel

By following these tips, you can stay organized and keep your Premiere Pro projects running smoothly.

Introduction to the Premiere Pro interface

In the following subsections, we'll assist you in understanding the workspace, transforming daunting panels into comfortable companions. It functions as a user-friendly guide, revealing the editing tools and saving you a significant amount of time that would otherwise be spent exploring. This enables you to begin creating your desired outcome immediately, without the frustration of figuring out where to click. Consider it as your intensive training program for editing, providing you with the assurance and expertise to navigate the tools and unlock your narrative capabilities effortlessly.

Workspaces

As a video editor, having a workspace and workflow that suit your needs is essential to work efficiently and effectively in Premiere Pro. In this section, you'll learn how to customize your workspace, create workspaces for different tasks, and establish a workflow that fits your editing style.

Standard workplaces

The panels that make up the Premiere Pro **user interface** (**UI**) are arranged into a layout and saved as a workspace. There are 15 standard workspaces included with Premiere Pro. Although the majority of the workspaces are designed for certain post-production activities (such as color, audio, or graphics), here are some pointers for using some of the generic workspaces:

- **Essentials**: Everything that you require is arranged for simple access. This is recommended, particularly if you just have one display.

- **Vertical**: This is perfect if you're editing vertical video. It's designed for editing Instagram Reels, TikTok videos, and YouTube Shorts. Traditional horizontal workspace limits are addressed.

- **Learning**: This workspace is ideal if you want to learn content while editing and use the in-app tutorials.

- **Assembly**: This workspace is useful for rapid review and rough-cut editing. Speed and efficiency are prioritized while building your video framework.

- **Captions and Graphics**: This workspace is excellent if you need to work with captions or graphics (`https://helpx.adobe.com/my_en/premiere-pro/using/working-with-captions.html` and `https://helpx.adobe.com/my_en/premiere-pro/using/essential-graphics-panel.html`).

- **Review**: Use this workspace if you want to use **Frame.io** for reviews.

- **Production**: Use this workspace if you're collaborating with a team on a production.

The following screenshot shows these workspaces:

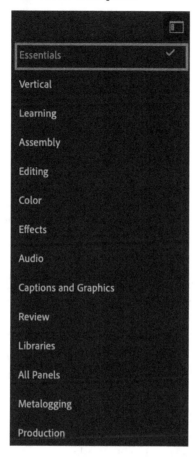

Figure 2.19 – Essential workspaces in Premiere Pro

When you first dive into the Adobe Premiere Pro interface, you may find yourself feeling a bit overwhelmed by the multitude of functions and panels it presents. However, don't be afraid! By carefully selecting the ideal workspace for your editing requirements, you can unleash a highly efficient and seamlessly flowing workflow. We've just delved into a few of the most well-known workspaces, such as **Assembly**, **Editing**, and **Color**. Each of these workspaces has been carefully designed to cater to different tasks and individual preferences.

Now that we have a perfectly arranged workspace, let's delve into changing workspaces according to your project's needs.

Changing workspaces

To access a workspace, click on the name of the respective workspace in the drop-down menu. You can also use keyboard shortcuts or the **Window** menu to open a workspace:

1. Open the project you want to work on, then select **Window | Workspace** and the workspace you want to use.

2. Individual workspaces can be accessed by pressing *Alt + Shift + 1* (up to *9*).

Customizing the workspace

Premiere Pro offers a vast range of tools and features that can be overwhelming for new users. However, by customizing the workspace, you can create a layout that suits your needs and preferences. You can rearrange panels, resize windows, and group related panels together. By creating a workspace that works for you, you can focus on your editing and increase your productivity.

Creating custom workspaces

One of the unique features of Premiere Pro is the ability to create custom workspaces. **Workspaces** are preset arrangements of panels that allow you to switch between different editing tasks quickly. For example, you can create a workspace for editing video footage, another for color grading, and another for audio mixing. By creating custom workspaces, you can improve your workflow and save time.

In Premiere Pro, **panels** refer to the various windows and interfaces that make up the software's UI. These panels allow users to access and manipulate different parts of their video editing project, such as the timeline, media browser, effects controls, and more.

The panels in Premiere Pro are fully customizable, which means users can arrange and resize them according to their needs and preferences. Users can also group related panels, creating custom workspaces that are tailored to their specific editing tasks.

Here are some of the main panels in Premiere Pro:

*   **The Project panel**: This displays all the media files and sequences in the current project
*   **The Source panel**: This allows users to preview and select clips for editing in the timeline
*   **The Timeline panel**: This displays the sequence of clips and allows users to edit and arrange them
*   **The Program panel**: This shows the final video output and allows users to preview and make adjustments
*   **The Effects panel**: This lets users add and adjust video and audio effects to their clips
*   **The Audio meters panel**: This displays audio levels for individual audio tracks
*   **The Media browser panel**: This allows users to browse and import media files from their computer or external devices

By utilizing these panels and customizing their layout, Premiere Pro users can work more efficiently and effectively in their video editing projects. Having a tidy workstation may greatly increase your Premiere Pro editing productivity. You may expedite your procedure and save a lot of time by arranging the panels to fit your workflow. To make your personalized workstation easily accessible, follow the steps outlined in the following sections.

Organizing your panels

Spend some time organizing the panels (**Project**, **Effects**, **Timeline**, and so on) so that they're both familiar and easy to use:

1. To reposition panels in Premiere Pro, drag and drop them:

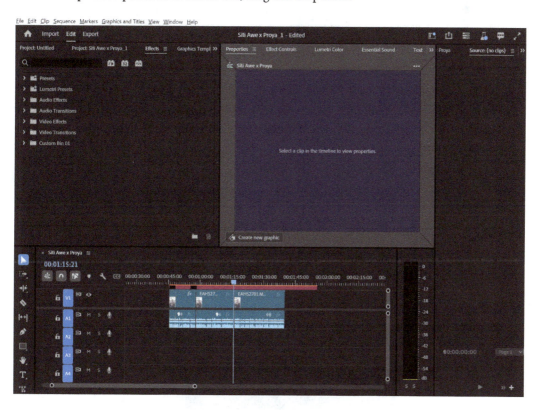

Figure 2.20 – Dragging and dropping the Panels workspace in Premiere Pro

2. Put panels together that you use regularly. To stack the panels into a group, right-click on a panel's tab and choose **Panel Group Settings**:

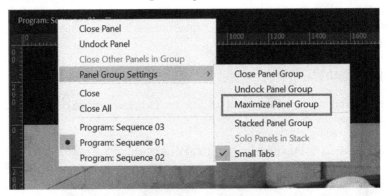

Figure 2.21 – Stacking panels in Premiere Pro

3. Drag panel groups to the window's boundaries to dock them together. As a result, the interface will be neat and well-organized.

4. To save your workspace, scroll to the **Window** menu at the top of the screen after finalizing the arrangement.

5. Select **Workspace**, then **Save as New Workspace...**:

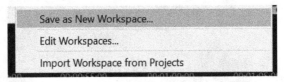

Figure 2.22 – Saving the new workspace in Premiere Pro

6. A pop-up window will emerge. Enter a descriptive name for your workspace (for example, **Editing Workspace** or **Color Grading Workspace**). This will allow you to recognize it quickly later:

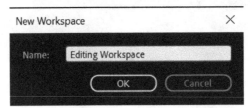

Figure 2.23 – Naming the new workspace in Premiere Pro

7. Click **OK** to save your new workspace. You may easily switch between stored workspaces at any moment. Locate the **Workspace** drop-down menu in the top-right corner of the Premiere Pro window (near the minimize and maximize buttons):

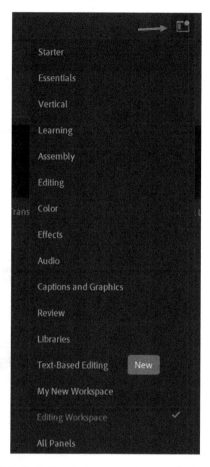

Figure 2.24 – Switching between workspaces in Premiere Pro

This menu will show all your stored workspaces. Simply choose the one you wish to use, and Premiere Pro will rearrange the panels based on the stored arrangement.

Consider creating several workspaces for various editing jobs. For example, you may wish to create a separate workspace for editing, another for color grading, and a third for audio mixing.

To improve your productivity even further, you may create keyboard shortcuts for commonly performed activities. Premiere Pro provides several customization choices to tailor your editing experience.

Customizing the Premiere Pro interface

The ability to customize the UI in Premiere Pro is of paramount importance as it grants you the flexibility to tailor the editing environment to your specific project requirements. This customization empowers you to arrange tools, panels, and functions in a manner that aligns with your workflow, ultimately boosting your efficiency and productivity. By organizing the interface to display the most relevant tools for your current task, you can eliminate clutter and streamline your editing process. This adaptability ensures that whether you're working on a fast-paced video montage or a meticulous color grading session, you have the tools you need at your fingertips, enhancing your overall editing experience and enabling you to focus on the creative aspects of your project.

Changing appearance with the new spectrum UI in Premiere Pro

Let's discover the enhanced spectrum UI in Adobe Premiere Pro and its impact on improving the accessibility of the application. The new version of Premiere Pro features a redesigned UI that incorporates Adobe's Spectrum design, resulting in a contemporary and cohesive appearance throughout the whole application.

To access the three newly added themes and the high and low contrast options, follow these steps:

1. Choose **Edit | Preferences | Appearance…**:

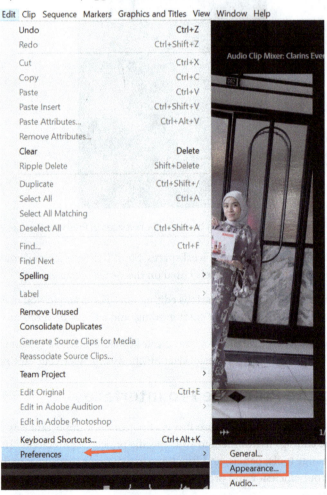

Figure 2.25 – Changing the appearance in Premiere Pro

2.   Select from **Darkest**, **Dark**, and **Light**:

Preferences

Figure 2.26 – Choosing appearance options in the Preferences panel

Additionally, there is a new toggle that allows you to choose between a high-contrast mode, which enhances visibility and accessibility, and a low-contrast option, which prioritizes your information.

3.   Opt for the settings that are most suitable for your needs and confirm by selecting **OK**.

By implementing this design approach, you will see enhanced visual coherence throughout Adobe programs, improved readability, and simplified UI interactions. The Spectrum design approach consolidates Adobe's application design based on principles that ensure inclusivity, scalability, and focus.

Importing and organizing media in Premiere Pro

In this section, you'll learn how to organize your media files in advance and then add them to your current project by dragging them into Adobe Premiere Pro or using the **File | Import** menu option.

You can import media files directly from your computer filesystem as follows:

1.   Use **File | Import** to select and import media files.

2.   Choose **File | Import** to import files using a file browsing window. To help you find the media you wish to import, a **Browse** window will open.

3.   Drag media files from a folder into the **Project** panel.

4.   Drag your media files from a **Finder** window (macOS) or an **Explorer** window (Windows) into the **Project** panel of Premiere Pro.

5.   Directly drag media files onto the **Timeline** panel. The fresh clips will be imported into the **Project** panel and added to any open sequences. A new sequence will be started with settings that match the first media file that was added if none are open at the moment.

6.   Automatically match project bin names with folder names. Bins will be created with the same names as folders if you drag them into the **Project** panel.

> **Important note**
>
> Premiere Pro will now accurately replicate the folder structure when importing folders. The import operation in Premiere Pro didn't include vacant folders and folders containing only one file in previous versions. Instead, the files were imported, but the folder wasn't. Currently, all folders will be included when importing assets using **File | Import**, **Drag and Drop**, and **Media Browser** in the most recent beta build.

Creating a sequence while importing

Before you begin intensive editing in Premiere Pro, you should understand two key concepts: content organization and sequence creation. Both of these will be crucial when creating you begin working on your video in Premiere Pro.

This is where you'll make your modifications and create your video. That being said, we'll discuss sequences in this section. Here are a few things you should know about sequences:

- A project can contain numerous sequences.

- A sequence can be inserted into another sequence. This is known as a **nested sequence**.

- You can copy and paste sequences.

- Sequences, like content, can be deleted, renamed, and searched.

You can't edit a sequence's preset once it's been generated. As a result, you want to set it up correctly creating the first time. Otherwise, you'll have to copy and paste altered snippets into the proper sequence. Although this isn't difficult to do, it requires time that could be spent on other editing duties. Before you learn how to create a sequence in Premiere Pro, let's understand what a sequence is.

What is a sequence?

A **sequence** is a compilation of video segments. The requirement is that there must be a minimum of one video track and one audio track. Sequences that include audio tracks must also include a master audio track, which serves as the destination for the combined output of the other audio tracks. Audio can be combined by utilizing multiple audio tracks.

In Premiere Pro, you can trim video segments, merge them into sequences, and customize the settings for each sequence.

A Premiere Pro project can have one or more sequences, with each sequence having its own distinct set of settings. The graphical representation of clips, transitions, and effects in sequences can be found in one or more **Timeline** panels, allowing you to combine and rearrange these elements. A sequence is formed when many video and audio tracks are played simultaneously in a **Timeline** panel.

How do you make a sequence?

Creating a sequence is simple – drag an asset from the **Project** panel to the new item icon at the bottom of the panel:

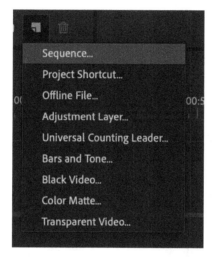

Figure 2.27 – Creating a new sequence from the new item icon in the Project panel

A sequence can also be created by choosing a preset from the **File | New | Sequence** menu option. The proper settings for typical sorts of assets are included in the Premiere Pro sequence presets. For instance, you can use a DV sequence preset if the majority of your material is in DV format. **Sequence Presets** and **Settings** are where you can find more details:

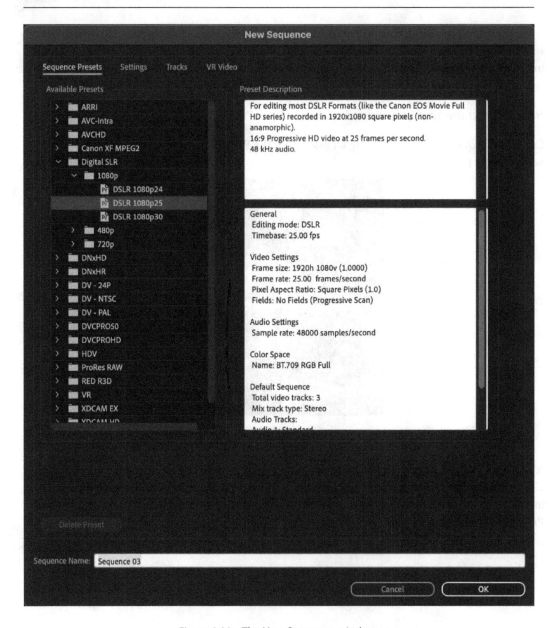

Figure 2.28 – The New Sequence window

If you want to specify lesser output quality settings, don't alter your sequence settings (such as streaming web video); alter your export options afterward instead.

In the following sections, we'll learn about the timeline in Adobe Premiere Pro.

Understanding the timeline

The **timeline** is where you organize your video clips and plan out all of the changes you want to make. As you work, you'll notice that all of your video and audio clips, effects, and transitions are organized chronologically from start to finish. All of the fundamentals of video editing are available, including reordering, trimming, and enhancing your footage. You can also play your project at any point in the timeline to see how your changes will look.

In Premiere Pro, there's no restriction to the number of audio and graphic tracks. You can employ them to include layers of simultaneous audio, image, and video files in your project.

You can layer graphics, photographs, or films that play on top of one another or arrange sound effects that play throughout music and dialog in this fashion.

The playhead and playback window

In Premiere Pro, the playhead and playback controls are essential tools for navigating and modifying your video project. The following sub-sections provide a breakdown of their roles.

The playhead

The playhead in Premiere Pro is a vertical line marker that moves along the timeline. It fulfills two primary functions:

- **Indicates current editing position**: The playhead displays the precise frame that's currently visible in the program monitor, indicating the current editing position. The corresponding video frame is displayed as the playhead is moved along the timeline.

- **Playback control**: The playhead also functions as the playback control. The playback will commence from the position of the playhead when the play button is clicked or keyboard shortcuts are used. The frame that's displayed at the playhead's location will be frozen if playback is paused or stopped.

The following are some supplementary details regarding the playhead that may be beneficial for you:

- **Playhead position counter**: This counter is situated in the top-left quadrant of the timeline and indicates the timecode (*hours:minutes:seconds:frames*) that corresponds to the playhead's position. This enables precise navigation within your sequence:

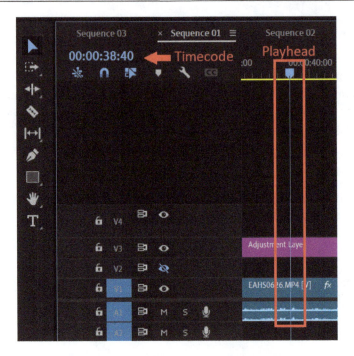

Figure 2.29 – The Playhead's position in the timeline

Premiere Pro enables the creation of multiple playheads for a variety of purposes. This can be advantageous for concurrently evaluating various segments of your video.

By comprehending the playhead's functionality, you'll be able to make precise adjustments, control replay, and navigate your projects within Premiere Pro effectively.

- **Navigation tool**:

  - Clicking at different points on the timeline moves the playhead to that corresponding location

  - Keyboard shortcuts, such as the left arrow and right arrow keys, nudge the playhead frame by frame

  - You can also drag the playhead itself to scrub through your sequence

- **Editing reference point**:

  - Many editing tools and actions in Premiere Pro are based on the playhead's position. For example, inserting clips and adding markers all happen at the playhead's location.

The playback controls

Premiere Pro has several playback options to help you browse your project and fine-tune your editing process. Here's where you can find the playback controls in Screen Monitor and Program Monitor:

Figure 2.30 – Playback controls in Premiere Pro

These controls allow you to control the play behavior of your sequence:

- **Play button (spacebar)**: This starts and pauses playback from the current playhead position.
- **Stop playback (K)**: With this, you can stop playback at any point.
- **Rewind (J)**: This rewinds the clip at a configurable rate based on how many times you hit the key. Each push increases the rewind speed. If you want to slow things down, press the *J* key twice or three times to get the desired speed.
- **Fast-forward (L)**: This plays and fast-forwards the clip at a variable speed based on the number of presses. Simply press the *L* key twice to double the speed, or three times to triple the thrill.
- **Step forward or backward (right or left arrow)**: This navigates forward and backward through your sequence, typically frame by frame.
- **Next or previous edit (up or down arrow)**: This moves the playhead to the next or previous edit point in the sequence.
- **Play from the beginning (Enter)**: With this, you can begin playback from the beginning of your sequence, regardless of the playhead's position.
- **Mark In and Mark Out (I and O)**: These buttons allow you to set the *in* and *out* points of a clip based on the playhead's position. This is a handy way to mark selected footage at the beginning or end of a clip.

  With the playhead and playback controls working together seamlessly, you'll have full command over how you view and manipulate your video project. With a deep understanding of these tools, you'll be able to navigate your timeline, execute precise edits, and seamlessly preview your work effortlessly, resulting in a highly efficient and effective editing workflow in Premiere Pro. Look at the following example:

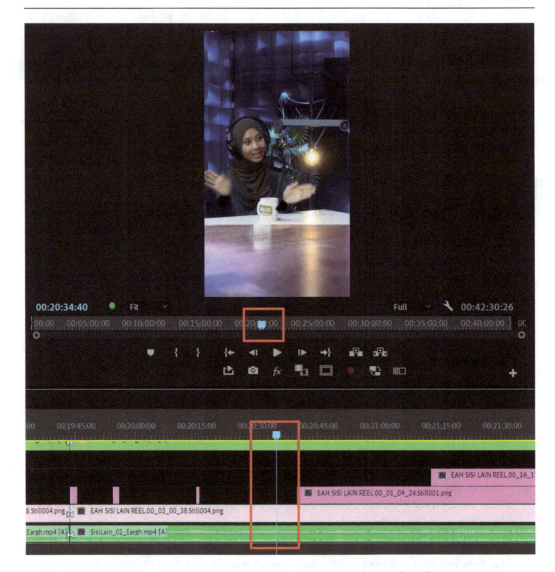

Figure 2.31 – Playhead position in the Program window and timeline

Your timeline is framed by a blue line that has a clickable marker at the top. This is the *playhead* you're using. To move it between frames in your project, click and drag it. Look up at the *playback window* above your timeline and press the play button to view a preview of your project. In the playback box, you may also make adjustments to your clips. To alter how clips or videos look in your film, change their proportions and drag them to different locations in the window.

The eight primary timeline tools

Eight tools are displayed to the left of your timeline as icons. You can employ them to carry out the following fundamental tasks:

- **Selection tool (V)**: To edit clips, you can either choose them from your timeline or the playback window. To cut, copy, or remove clips, you can use the right or control clicks. To change the length of clips, simply hover your cursor over their edges:

Figure 2.32 – The Selection tool allows you to perform basic selections and edits

- **Track Select Forward tool (A)**: You can use this tool to choose every clip after the one you click on your timeline:

Figure 2.33 – The Track Select Forward tool lets you select all clips in a forward sequence

Instead, you may click and hold the tool to make it the **Track Select Backwards** (*Shift + A*) tool, which picks out all previous clips:

Figure 2.34 – The Track Select Backwards tool lets you select all clips in a backward sequence

- **Ripple Edit tool (B)**: With this tool, you can fill in any gaps left by your adjustments by clicking on either side of an empty area:

Figure 2.35 – The Ripple Edit tool will fill in the blanks between the two editing points

- **Razor tool (C)**: Wherever you click, this tool splits video clips into smaller chunks:

Figure 2.36 – The Razor tool helps to carefully cut or split clips into multiple parts

- **Slip tool (Y):** You can cut the beginning and end of the following clip so that the overall length of the two clips is the same:

Figure 2.37 – The Slip tool "slips" in and out with the slip tool, but it doesn't move on the timeline

- **Pen tool (P):** In the replay area of your project, you can use this tool to draw free-form forms. You may also click and hold the Pen tool to show the Ellipse and Rectangle tools. After that, you can insert unique modifications or artwork inside your new shape:

Figure 2.38 – The Pen tool allows you to click on any point on your clip

- **Hand tool (H):** With the help of this tool, you can browse your chronological sequence without making any selections:

Figure 2.39 – The Hand tool helps you navigate and pan around your timeline and project

- **Type tool (T):** Use the **Type** tool to add text directly onto your video clips. It allows you to create text elements, customize their appearance, and integrate them seamlessly into your project:

Figure 2.40 – The Type tool is primarily used to edit text within your video projects

We can see these tools in the following screenshot:

Figure 2.41 – List of tools available in Premiere Pro

Premiere Pro is filled with an array of robust tools that will elevate your edits to new heights. There's so much more to discover in Premiere Pro, with a wide range of tools and features at your disposal. Keep exploring the software to unlock its full potential.

Workflow tips for timeline editing

As you edit your video content, follow a procedure to prevent lost footage and streamline your production. Back up all of your videos before you begin on an external hard drive. After that, upload or ingest your video into a new Premiere Pro project. Your clips will be pulled onto the editing timeline from this bucket. From your project library, go through and remove any clips you don't want.

After, drop a few clips onto the timeline, then start making your first cuts. Bring in the soundtrack or any sound effects that you plan to use to assist you in conceiving your sequence. It helps to color-code your sound clips. For example, you could use one color for dialog and another for music or sound effects.

Enhancing your Premiere Pro editing workflow

Here are some advanced tricks you can implement to supercharge your editing workflow in Premiere Pro:

- **Master keyboard shortcuts**: Forget menus! Learn basic keyboard shortcuts for operations such as clip trimming and timeline navigation. This will dramatically increase your editing speed.

- **Organize with nested sequences**: Organize big projects into smaller, nested series. This makes them easier to maintain and edit without disrupting the overall project.

- **Smooth proxy workflows**: Using high-resolution film might slow things down. Create lower-resolution proxy files for editing before switching back to high-quality files for export.

- **Simplify with adjustment layers**: Use adjustment layers to apply effects to numerous clips simultaneously, simplifying the process. Edit the layer once, and the changes will ripple down to all clips underneath it, saving you a lot of time.

- **Fine-tune speed with Rate Stretch**: The **Rate Stretch** tool allows you to alter clip speed without changing pitch. This is ideal for slow motion or accelerating sluggish areas.

- **Customize your workspace**: Premiere Pro provides customizable workspaces for editing, color, audio, and more. You may also customize your arrangement to put your most often-used tools within easy reach.

- **Explore third-party plugins**: Extend Premiere Pro's capabilities using plugins and extensions. These tools include specialized effects, complex editing options, and automated workflows.

- **Editing style**: Develop your editing style by experimenting with ways that work best for you. Experiment with your editing approach to achieve the ideal blend of speed and creativity.

Mastering these strategies can significantly increase your editing speed and efficiency in Premiere Pro, enabling you to focus on bringing your creative vision to life.

Learning how the experts edit faster

Learning how to edit quicker isn't about magic tricks; it's about mastering the tools and procedures that help you get things done faster.

Here are some important tactics that are utilized by professionals to accelerate their Premiere Pro editing:

- **Pancake timelines**: You can open numerous timelines in Premiere Pro or switch back and forth between them. You can view and access a lot of videos at once by using this feature to edit between timelines. A fantastic blog post about using pancake timelines has been written by the Hollywood editor Vashi Nedomansky: `https://vashivisuals.com/the-pancake-timeline-maximum-limit-is-24-hours/`.

- **Source track patching**: You can work more quickly when editing with the keyboard by creating your own keyboard shortcuts for patching and assigning keyboard presets when routing tracks for three-point editing. Scott Simmons has written a fantastic post about this: `https://www.providecoalition.com/day-3-28daysofquicktips-2018-track-patching-keyboard-premiere-pro/`.

- **Assembly edits in the Project panel**: You can preview, mark, arrange, and edit clips directly into sequences from the **Project** panel.

- **Grade in the application**: To complete your project without leaving Premiere Pro, you can use the advanced colorimetry of the **Lumetri Color** tools for color grading and creative color correction.

- **Essential sound panel**: Loudness settings are automatically determined, and music is muted behind vocals. With this, long manual audio editing can be completed in a few clicks.

- **Motion Graphics templates (MOGRT)**: A MOGRT in Premiere Pro is a pre-animated graphic or element that can be imported and customized in your project effortlessly. With these templates at your disposal, you'll be able to enhance your videos with stunning animations, captivating titles, seamless transitions, and a variety of other visually striking elements. These templates offer a time-saving and efficient way to add professional-looking animations, titles, lower thirds, transitions, and other visual elements to your videos.

- **Copy and paste between Premiere Pro and After Effects**: Because Premiere Pro and After Effects are compatible with one another, editors can drag or copy and paste clips to share their original work.

Summary

In this chapter, we learned about the world of Premium Pro. We began by learning about the platform's main features and functions. We also thoroughly investigated the Premium Pro interface, learning how to navigate it properly.

To personalize the workplace, we learned how to tailor the Premium Pro interface to specific tastes and workflows. Then, we learned how to manage projects efficiently by understanding the timeline function. With this information, we looked into sophisticated strategies to improve our Premiere Pro editing process. Finally, we discovered time-saving techniques by looking at how editing professionals streamline their operations.

Building on this basis, the next chapter will delve into the art of video editing, including effective cutting and trimming procedures in Premiere Pro.

3

Efficiently Cutting and Trimming Videos

In this chapter, you will learn how to efficiently cut and trim videos using Adobe Premiere Pro, one of the leading video editing software in the industry. You will start by exploring the different tools and techniques available for cutting and trimming videos in Premiere Pro, including the razor, selection, and ripple edit tools.

You will also learn how to use keyboard shortcuts and how to customize hotkeys to speed up your workflow and increase your productivity when cutting and trimming videos. You will see how to trim your clips using the Trim Edit tool, as well as how to use the Mark Selection and In and Out points to define the start and end of your clips. The Trim Edit feature allows you to see the frames that were incoming or outgoing of the trim you are editing, which is useful for fine-tuning edits. Adobe Premiere Pro's Mark Selection enables you to easily mark the start and end of a selected region of clips in an open sequence. The ability to export a portion of the sequence, chapter markers, or notes for your project can be useful in many ways.

In this chapter, we're going to cover the following main topics:

- Editing – type of cuts
- The 5 Shots, 10 Seconds rule
- Getting the perfect shot perfect every time

Editing – type of cuts

Video editing involves merging video footage and audio recordings into a final product. A complex and imaginative technique conveys narratives, induces feelings, or communicates messages.

The use of cuts is a crucial aspect of video editing. The transitions between scenes or shots are known as **cuts**. Their function can either advance the plot, modify the surroundings, or produce a specific effect.

Various types of cuts in video editing can be used to transition from one shot to another or to create a specific visual effect. Some common types of cuts include the following:

- **Hard cut or rough cut**: A quick and immediate cut from one shot to the next, without any visual effects or transitions

- **Jump cut**: A cut between two shots that are very similar or nearly identical, creating a jarring effect

- **Cross cut**: A cut between two or more shots that are happening simultaneously, often used to create tension or suspense

- **Match cut**: A cut that links two shots together based on visual or audio similarity, creating a smooth and seamless transition

- **L-cut and J-cut**: These are audio-based cuts, where the audio from the previous shot continues over the following shot (L-cut), or the audio from the following shot starts before the previous shot ends (J-cut)

- **Cutaway**: A cut to a shot unrelated to the previous shot, often used to provide context or show a reaction

- **Contrast cut**: A contrast cut juxtaposes two frames with dramatically distinct views, sounds, or emotions

The choice of cut used depends on the desired effect and the overall tone of the video. Each type of cut can be used to create a different mood or convey a specific message, and a skilled editor will choose the appropriate cut to enhance the visual storytelling of the video.

Hard cut or rough cut

In video editing, a **hard cut** is a straightforward technique used to transition from one shot to another without any visual effects or transitions. It involves cutting abruptly from the end of one clip to the beginning of the next clip, resulting in a quick and immediate change in the scene.

Hard cuts are often used in fast-paced or action-packed videos, where a smooth transition or fancy effect may not be necessary or appropriate. They are also commonly used in news broadcasts or documentaries to quickly switch between interviews or locations.

While hard cuts may seem simple and easy to achieve, they still require careful planning and execution to ensure that they don't disrupt the flow of the video or cause any visual jarring. It's important to consider the timing and pacing of the cuts, as well as the content and context of the shots being cut together. Your rough cut will look something like this in the timeline:

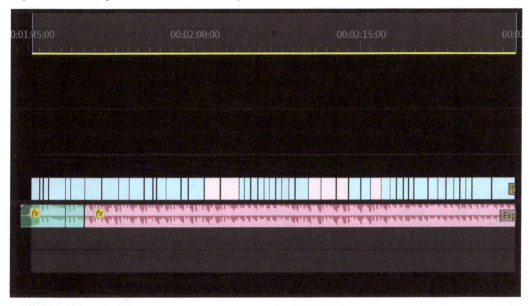

Figure 3.1 – Rough cut example in the timeline

Overall, hard cuts can be a useful and effective technique in video editing, but they should be used thoughtfully and in appropriate situations.

Jump cut

A **jump cut** is a type of cut in video editing where the editor cuts between two shots that are very similar or nearly identical, creating a jarring effect that can be used for stylistic or narrative purposes. Jump cuts are often used to compress time or show a character's thought process, as they can create a sense of discontinuity or interruption in the flow of the scene.

Jump cuts can be achieved by cutting out a portion of a shot or by using a different camera angle, creating a noticeable change in the image. They can also be used intentionally to convey a sense of confusion, disorientation, or anxiety, depending on the context of the scene. See the jump-cut edit used in *Catch Me If You Can*.

While jump cuts can be an effective technique for creating a specific visual effect, they can also be distracting or disorienting if used excessively or inappropriately. As with any editing technique, it's important to consider the desired effect and the context of the scene before using a jump cut in video editing.

Cross cut

A **cross cut** in video editing involves cutting between two or more shots that are happening simultaneously, often used to create tension or suspense. Cross-cutting is commonly used in action sequences, or to show the parallel events happening in different locations, as it provides a sense of continuity between the shots.

Cross cuts are achieved by alternating between different shots in quick succession, creating a sense of urgency and immediacy in the scene. This technique can also be used to convey contrast or comparison between two different events or situations. One of the famous examples of the cross cut technique used you can see in Christopher Nolan's *Inception*.

While cross-cutting can be an effective way to create a specific mood or effect in a scene, it's important to use it appropriately and with care, as overuse can lead to a sense of disorientation or confusion for the viewer. A skilled editor will use cross-cutting judiciously to enhance the visual storytelling of the video.

Match cut

A **match cut** links two shots together based on visual or audio similarity, creating a smooth and seamless transition. Match cuts are often used to create a sense of continuity or to show a character's progression, as they can provide a sense of visual cohesion between different shots.

Match cuts can be achieved in various ways, such as matching the movement of an object in one shot to the movement of another object in the following shot, or matching the color or texture of two different shots to create a visual link. They can also be achieved through audio cues, such as matching the sound or music of one shot to another shot.

Match cuts can be an effective way to create a sense of narrative coherence and enhance the visual storytelling of the video. However, it's important to use them appropriately and with care, as overuse can lead to a sense of monotony or predictability for the viewer.

Here are the steps for implementing a match cut in Premiere Pro video editing:

1. Open Premiere Pro and import your footage:

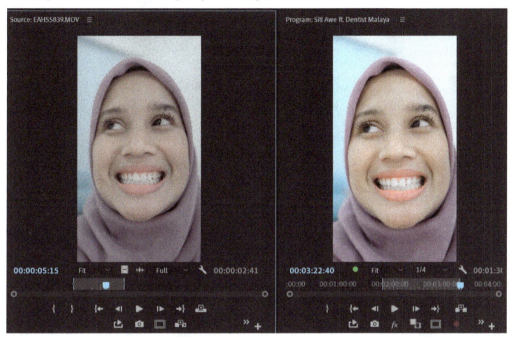

Figure 3.2 – Two clips for match cut

2. Make two clips, one for each shot you want to include in the match cut:

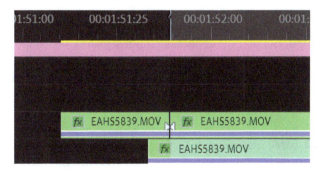

Figure 3.3 – Clip that we are working on at the beginning of the timeline

3.   Drag the first clip to the beginning of the sequence in the **Timeline** panel:

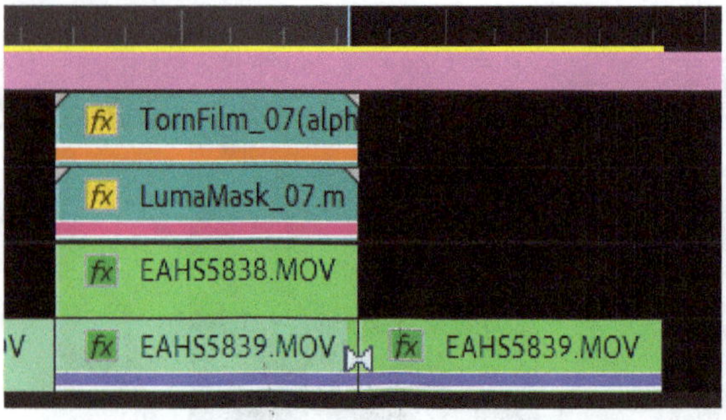

Figure 3.4 – Positioning the same clip that we are working on at the end of the timeline

4.   Place the two clips you want to match cut on the timeline, one after the other. You can overlap them slightly to identify the exact frames for the cut.

5.   Drag the second clip to the sequence's end.

6.   Make sure the two clips are aligned so that the common object or element appears in both shots.

7.   Make the two clips the same length by adjusting their durations.

8.   Check the match cut to ensure it looks smooth and seamless.

For many years, this technique has been used. It's most effective when you need to move the story forward while also finding a way to connect the dots seamlessly. Two films in particular do this exceptionally well, and they are among the most acclaimed films in history.

Explore this captivating film to delve into the intricacies of the match cut technique employed in *2001: A Space Odyssey*. Witness how Stanley Kubrick masterfully orchestrates a seamless transition from the primal *Dawn of Man* sequence to the awe-inspiring *Space Station* sequence in a mere blink of an eye. He illustrated this by depicting a scene where a primitive man tosses a bone into the air, only to be replaced by a spaceship gracefully drifting through the vastness of space. The seamless transitions between scenes captivated the audience, making for an incredibly effective experience.

Dynamic cut

A **dynamic cut** is a fast-paced and energetic technique used in video editing to create a sense of excitement, action, or urgency. It involves using quick cuts, fast transitions, and special effects to create a visually dynamic sequence.

Dynamic cuts are commonly used in action movies, music videos, and sports highlights. The purpose of this technique is to keep the audience engaged and energized, while also conveying a sense of movement and progression.

In a dynamic cut, the editing style is often characterized by rapid cuts, quick camera movements, and abrupt changes in shot size and angle. This creates a sense of motion and energy, as well as emphasizes the pace of the action or the music.

Special effects and visual treatments, such as speed ramps, color grading, and motion blur, are also commonly used in dynamic cuts to enhance the impact of the visuals and to create a unique visual style.

Overall, dynamic cuts are a powerful technique in video editing that allows filmmakers to create a sense of excitement, action, and urgency in their sequences. When used effectively, dynamic cuts can create a memorable and impactful visual experience for the audience.

L-cuts and J-cuts

L-cuts and **J-cuts** are audio-based cuts used in video editing to create a smooth transition between two shots while maintaining the continuity of the audio.

An L-cut is when the audio from the previous shot continues to play over the footage of the following shot, creating a sense of continuity and linking the two shots together. This technique is often used in dialogue-heavy scenes, where the audio can help to establish the tone and mood of the scene. Here is how the L-cut and J-cut clip sequences appear in the timeline:

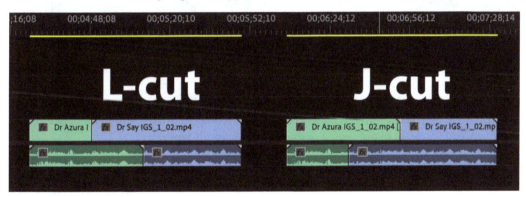

Figure 3.5 – Trim clips in L-cut and J-cut

On the other hand, a J-cut is when the audio from the following shot starts before the previous shot ends, creating anticipation or tension for the viewer. This technique is often used in action sequences or montages, where the audio can provide a sense of momentum or urgency.

Both L-cuts and J-cuts are useful in enhancing the overall flow and pacing of the video and can be used to create a sense of cohesion between different shots. However, it's important to use them appropriately and in moderation, as overuse can lead to a sense of monotony or predictability for the viewer.

Cutaway

Cutaways are used in video editing to show a different angle or detail related to the main action or subject in the scene. Cutaways are often used to provide context, establish a setting or mood, or create visual interest in a scene.

Cutaways can be achieved by cutting to a shot of a different subject or object, often related thematically to the main action or subject of the scene. For example, in a scene of a character cooking, a cutaway shot may show a close-up of the ingredients being prepared or the stove being turned on. Here's how the cutaway clips look in a timeline:

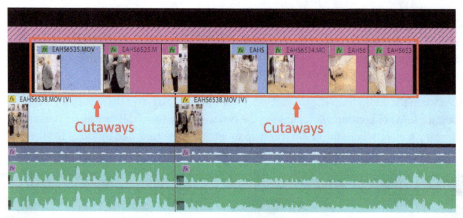

Figure 3.6 – Cutaway clips in the timeline

Cutaways are useful in enhancing the visual storytelling of the video, providing a sense of depth and complexity to the scene. However, it's important to use them appropriately and in moderation, as overuse can lead to a sense of distraction or disorientation for the viewer.

Contrast cut

A **contrast cut** is a technique in film editing that emphasizes differences or contrasts between two consecutive shots. It is the opposite of a match cut, which emphasizes similarities between shots.

A contrast cut can be achieved in several ways, such as through differences in lighting, color, or composition. For example, a filmmaker might cut from a bright and sunny outdoor scene to a dark and gloomy interior shot, creating a stark contrast between the two scenes. Another example could be cutting from a wide shot of a crowded city street to a close-up of a character's face, emphasizing the contrast between the chaotic external world and the character's inner emotions.

The purpose of a contrast cut is to create an impact on the audience, to highlight a change in mood or atmosphere, or to draw attention to a specific element in the film. By highlighting differences between shots, the contrast cut can help create a sense of tension or drama, as well as provide a visual storytelling element that can add depth and complexity to the film's narrative.

Overall, a contrast cut is a powerful tool in the filmmaker's arsenal, allowing them to create contrast and tension between different shots and to convey different emotions and messages to the audience.

Morph cut

This unique transition is ideal for eliminating the usage of filler words such as *ums* and *uhhs*, as well as reducing lengthy pauses during interviews. If the A and B frames of an edit are substantially identical, using **morph cut** will seamlessly blend the cut, making it appear as if it doesn't exist.

Now, you can efficiently cleanse interview dialog by eliminating undesired segments of a tape and subsequently using the morph cut video transition to seamlessly eliminate jarring jump cuts. Morph cut may be utilized to seamlessly reorganize clips in your interview material, guaranteeing a coherent visual flow without any abrupt transitions.

Morph cut employs a sophisticated blend of facial tracking and optical flow interpolation to provide a smooth and uninterrupted transition between video segments. When used skillfully, the morph cut transition may achieve such a high level of seamlessness that it appears as though the video was shot without any disruptive pauses or words that could disrupt the narrative continuity.

Applying morph cut

The following screenshots demonstrate how to apply the morph cut effect onto clips:

1. Set In and Out points on the timeline to the specific area of the clip that you wish to eliminate.

2. Perform this action for each segment of the video that you wish to eliminate.

3. In the **Effects** panel, select **Video Transitions | Dissolve | Morph Cut**. Then, move the effect to the specific location where the clips in the timeline meet:

Figure 3.7 – The Morph Cut effect in the Effect panel

4. To prevent lip sync issues, utilize the **Morph Cut** feature at the points where the speech's last or first words reach their highest intensity. Additionally, audio waveforms may be utilized to detect sections with pauses, facilitating precise editing at certain points.

5. While applying the **Morph Cut** effect, the clips will be analyzed in the background. An **Analyzing in background** status appears in the Program Monitor to indicate that the analyzing process is taking place. While the clips are analyzed, you can continue working on the film or any other aspect of the project.

Figure 3.8 – Analyzing the Morph Cut effect on a clip in Program Monitor

Once the analysis is finished, a symmetrical transition is generated, with the edit point in its center. The transition time corresponds to the default value of 30 frames set for **Video Transition Default** time. To modify the default duration, use the **Preferences** dialog.

> **Important note**
>
> To achieve optimal outcomes, utilize the **Morph Cut** feature on stable photos that feature a solitary individual speaking and a motionless backdrop.

The 5 Shots, 10 Seconds rule

The *5 Shots, 10 Seconds* rule is a guideline used in video editing to help create dynamic and engaging visual sequences. The rule states that for every 10 seconds of video, you should aim to include 5 different shots, each with a different angle, framing, or focus.

The idea behind this rule is that by varying the shots in a sequence, you can create a sense of movement and visual interest that keeps the viewer engaged. It also allows you to convey information more effectively and efficiently by showing different perspectives or details of a subject or scene.

It's worth mentioning that the *5 Shots, 10 Seconds* guideline isn't set in stone and should be tailored to each project and scene. Depending on the needs of the scene, fewer or more shots may be necessary, and the length of each shot can vary depending on the scene's pace and tone. The main objective of adhering to this rule or other editing guidelines is to produce a visually captivating video that effectively delivers the intended message to the viewers.

Here's an example of how the *5 Shots, 10 Seconds* rule can be applied in a video:

Figure 3.9 – Series of images on how to apply the 5 Shots, 10 Seconds rule

You are not required to edit it in this order, but it should provide you with enough material to work with.

You'll need the following shots:

- Hands
- Face
- Hands and face
- Over-the-shoulder or point-of-view shot
- A creative shot

A creative shot could be an important detail, an unusual angle, or a shot with a shallow focus.

By following the *5 Shots, 10 Seconds* rule, we've created a sequence that is visually dynamic, engaging, and effectively conveys the musician's performance. We've used a variety of shots to show different aspects of the scene, such as the musician's technique, the audience's reaction, and the energy of the performance.

Getting the perfect shot every time

Perfect shots in videography have different characteristics depending on the desired effect and the context of the shot. However, the following are some general characteristics of perfect shots:

- The subject of the photograph should be in sharp focus, while the background should be blurred. This can be accomplished by employing a shallow depth of field.
- **Proper exposure**: The shot should be properly exposed so that the subject is not overly dark or overly bright. This is accomplished by adjusting camera settings, such as aperture and shutter speed.
- **Good composition**: The shot should be well composed so that the subject is nicely arranged. This can be accomplished through the use of the rule of thirds or other compositional techniques.
- **Smooth camera movement**: To avoid distracting the viewer, the camera movement should be smooth and steady. A tripod or other stabilizing equipment can be used to accomplish this.
- **Framing**: The shot should be properly framed so that the subject is not cut off or obstructed. This can be accomplished by paying close attention to the frame's edges.
- **Proper lighting**: The shot should be well lit so that the subject is visible and the mood is conveyed. This can be accomplished through natural light, artificial light, or a combination of the two.
- **Angles of interest**: The shot should be captured from an interesting angle to keep the viewer interested. This can be accomplished by utilizing low, high, or other creative angles.

Aside from these general characteristics, numerous other factors can contribute to a flawless shot. The important characteristics will vary depending on the desired effect and the context of the shot. Following these general guidelines, however, will allow you to create shots that are both technically and creatively sound.

Getting the perfect shot in video involves several factors, such as planning, execution, and post-production. Here are some tips to help you get the perfect shot:

- **Plan your shots**: Before you start filming, take the time to plan your shots. This includes choosing the right camera angle, composition, lighting, and sound. Create a storyboard or shot list to help you visualize the shots you need.

- **Use a tripod or stabilizer**: A steady shot is essential for a professional-looking video. Use a tripod or stabilizer to keep your camera steady and minimize shakiness.

- **Focus on the subject**: Make sure your subject is in focus and well lit. Use manual focus to ensure that the camera is focused on the subject and not the background. Use lighting to highlight the subject and create depth and texture.

- **Shoot in the right frame rate and resolution**: Choose the right frame rate and resolution for your project. A higher frame rate is better for capturing motion, while a higher resolution produces a sharper image.

- **Record good audio**: Good audio is just as important as good video. Use a high-quality microphone to record clear audio. Make sure to position the microphone close to the subject and avoid background noise.

- **Edit your footage**: Finally, edit your footage to create a cohesive and polished final product. Use editing software to trim the footage, adjust the color and exposure, and add music and sound effects.

Remember, getting the perfect shot takes practice and patience. Keep experimenting with different techniques and tools until you find what works best for you and your project.

Summary

This chapter discusses the different types of cuts used in video editing, including jump cuts, cross cuts, match cuts, L-cuts, J-cuts, and morph cuts. Each type serves a different purpose and can be used to convey different emotions and ideas in a video.

The chapter also introduces the *5 Shots, 10 Seconds* rule, which is a technique used to create visually dynamic and engaging video sequences. The rule involves breaking a video clip down into three 10-second sequences, each containing five shots. By following this rule, filmmakers can create a sequence that effectively conveys their message and keeps the audience engaged.

Lastly, the chapter provides tips on how to get the perfect shot in video, which includes planning your shots, using a tripod or stabilizer, focusing on the subject, shooting in the right frame rate and resolution, recording good audio, and editing the footage. By following these tips, filmmakers can produce high-quality videos that effectively convey their message and captivate their audience.

The next chapter will build upon the foundational concepts of video editing introduced in this chapter. It will provide filmmakers with a more comprehensive toolkit for creating engaging and impactful videos by incorporating advanced editing techniques, adding motion, and animating graphics in Premiere Pro. These additional skills and knowledge will enable filmmakers to take their video production to the next level, delivering content that effectively communicates messages and captivates their audience.

4

Adding Motion and Animated Graphics in Premiere Pro

In this chapter, we will explore the process of adding motion and animating graphics in Adobe Premiere Pro. We will cover the basics of animation and explore the different tools available in Premiere Pro to create animations and add motion to your video projects.

The chapter will introduce the concept of keyframe animation and the basics of animation. We will then explore the types of motion that can be added to graphics, including position, rotation, scale, and opacity. We will also look at using motion paths to create more complex animations.

Next, we will dive into the various tools available in Premiere Pro to create animations and add motion to graphics. This will include the Transform effect, which allows you to add motion and keyframes to graphics, and the *Motion* effect, which offers more advanced animation options including zoom effects and split screen as we will discuss further in the chapter.

We will also cover using masks and the **Track Matte Key** effect to create complex animations and effects, such as text animations that follow a specific path or objects that appear to move behind other objects.

Throughout the chapter, we will provide step-by-step tutorials and examples to help you master adding motion and animating graphics in Premiere Pro. By the end of the chapter, you will have a solid understanding of creating professional-looking animations and adding motion to your video projects in Premiere Pro.

In this chapter, we're going to cover the following main topics:

- Understanding keyframes
- Effects with keyframes
- Picture-in-Picture video
- Create a split-screen effect

- The Ken Burns effect – position and scale

- The difference between aspect ratio and resolution in video

Understanding keyframes

Keyframes are markers you place on a timeline or effect controls panel that define the starting and ending points of a change in a property (such as *position*, *scale*, or *opacity*). Imagine them like snapshots of your clip's state at specific moments. Premiere Pro automatically interpolates (calculates) the values in between the keyframes, creating the animation or movement. Here's a collection of keyframes available in Premiere Pro:

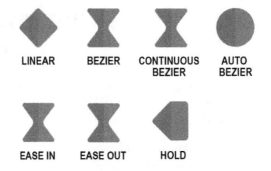

Figure 4.1 – Various types of keyframes in Premiere Pro

Here's a breakdown of the keyframe types in Premiere Pro:

1. **Temporal Interpolation (time-based)**: These control how the property changes over time:

    - *Linear*: Creates a straight line between keyframes, resulting in a constant speed change. (Think of a car moving at a steady pace.)

    - *Auto Bezier*: Creates a smooth, curved path between keyframes, often used for natural-looking motion with acceleration and deceleration. (Imagine a car starting slow, gaining speed, and then slowing down to stop.)

    - *Bezier*: Offers the most control, allowing you to independently adjust the handles of each keyframe to create custom speed changes. For example, consider a car with precise control over speed and braking.

2. **Spatial Interpolation (position-based)**: These control how the property changes across the screen (mainly for motion paths):

    - *Hold*: The property stays at the same value until the next keyframe. (Think of a picture frame staying still.)

    - *Continuous Bezier*: Creates a smooth, curved path between keyframes. (Imagine a picture frame moving smoothly across the screen.)

Here are some resources that might help you visualize:

- *Video tutorial*: https://www.youtube.com/watch?v=pjcW8JYUHJc

- *Keyframe tips and tricks*: https://m.youtube.com/watch?v=Y3NhNgLVpOo

Remember, keyframes are a powerful tool for creating animations and motion graphics. As you get more comfortable with them, you can combine them to achieve complex and creative effects in your Premiere Pro projects.

Effects with keyframes

You can use keyframes to animate the values of these properties over time. For example, you could create a slow zoom-in on a clip by setting an opacity keyframe at the start and then another keyframe at the end, with the opacity value increasing between the two keyframes.

Here are some other things to remember about keyframes in Premiere Pro:

- The **Effect Controls** panel stores keyframes

- Keyframes can be added, deleted, and moved as needed

- Keyframes can also be copied and pasted between clips or effects

- Different interpolation methods, such as Linear, Ease In, Ease Out, and Bezier, can be used to animate keyframes

One of the most common techniques used in video editing is the zoom-in and zoom-out effect. This effect can be used to emphasize a particular part of a scene or give a sense of movement to an otherwise static shot. This chapter will explore how to create the zoom-in and zoom-out effect using keyframes in Adobe Premiere Pro.

Setting up the project and footage

Before adding keyframes, it's important to ensure our project is set up correctly. We will cover how to import footage into Premiere Pro and how to create a sequence with the correct settings. We will also talk about selecting the footage that we want to animate an object and how to trim it as necessary.

Adding keyframes to move an object

Here's a step-by-step guide on adding keyframes to move an object in Premiere Pro:

1. Select your object: In your **Timeline** panel, locate the clip containing the object you want to animate. Click on the clip to select it.

2. Open the **Effect Controls** panel: Go to the **Windows** menu at the top and select **Effects Controls**. Alternatively, use the keyboard shortcut *Shift + 3*.

3. Locate the **Position** property: Scroll down in the **Effects Controls** panel until you find the **Position** property. This controls the object's location on the screen.

4. Set the starting keyframe: Move the playhead (the vertical line in the timeline) to the point where you want the animation to begin. Click the stopwatch icon next to the **Position** property. This sets the starting keyframe, marking the object's initial position.

5. Move the object to its final position: Drag the playhead to the point where you want the animation to end. In the **Position** property, adjust the **X** and **Y** values to move the object to its desired final location.

6. Set the ending keyframe: Click the stopwatch icon next to the **Position** property again. This creates the ending keyframe, defining the object's final position.

7. Preview your animation: Press the spacebar on your keyboard to play back the video and see your object move.

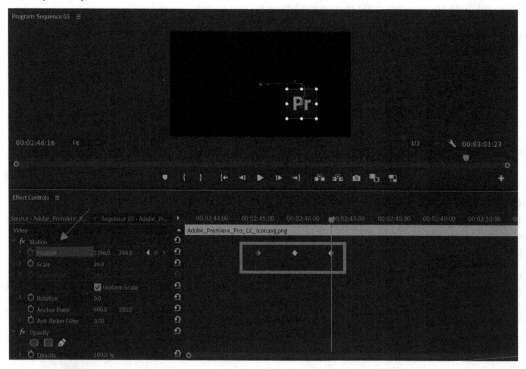

Figure 4.2 – Adding keyframes to the Position property in the Effect Controls panel

8. When the video is played, the movement appears quite abrupt due to its angled positioning. To enhance the logo movement, simply right-click on the middle of the keyframe and choose **Spatial Interpolation**. By enhancing the interaction between keyframes, a significant improvement can be achieved. Next, we will adjust the keyframes to create a smoother movement for the logo.

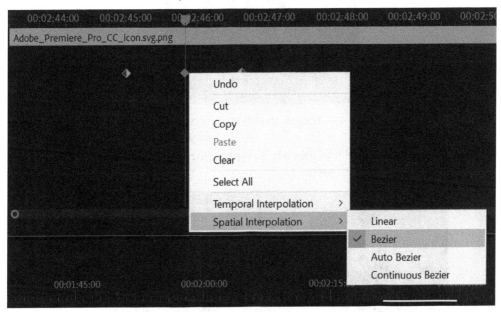

Figure 4.3 – Converting Linear keyframes to a Bezier curve

In Adobe Premiere Pro, *Spatial Interpolation* refers to the process of producing interim frames between two frames to simulate motion or change. It is an essential component in video editing and animation, allowing for seamless transitions and motions between frames. This approach is used to estimate an object's values at unseen places using values from known locations.

Spatial Interpolation can be either **Linear** or **Bezier**. Premiere Pro uses *Linear Spatial Interpolation* to generate a straight route between keyframes, whereas *Bezier Interpolation* produces a curved path. The sort of spatial interpolation used in a video may have a significant impact on its aesthetics since it controls how the object travels from one keyframe to the next.

Linear generates a consistent rate of change between keyframes, whereas **Bezier** allows you to vary the rate of change on either side of the keyframe, and **Auto Bezier** modifies the rate of change based on the surrounding keyframes. The option is determined by your project's particular requirements.

9. Look at the motion path; it is now curved and no longer an angled line.

Figure 4.4 – The motion path is now a curved line

10. Now let's look at Temporal Interpolation. Navigate to the **Effect Controls** panel and click the drop-down arrow on the property.

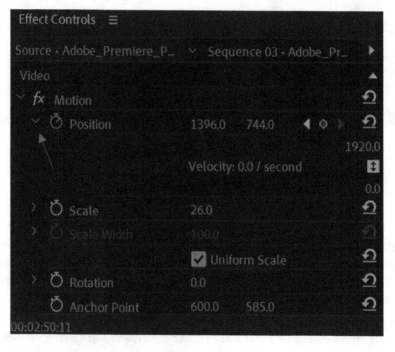

Figure 4.5 – Drop-down property in the Effect Controls panel

In the first place you will see a straight-line motion path, which is a horizontal line. The motion path is defined by specifying keyframes, which are specific points in time when the object's position changes. The path can be straight or curved, and the item can move at either a constant or variable pace. Other attributes, such as scale, rotation, and opacity, may also vary throughout the motion path seen in the following screenshot:

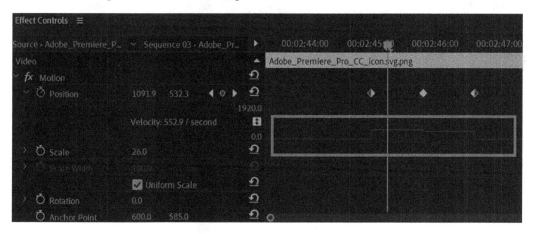

Figure 4.6 – Linear curve in Effect Controls panel

11. Now, we want to smoothen the animation by creating **Ease In** and **Ease Out** effects on those keyframes. Right-click on the first keyframe and choose **Temporal Interpolation** | **Ease Out**.

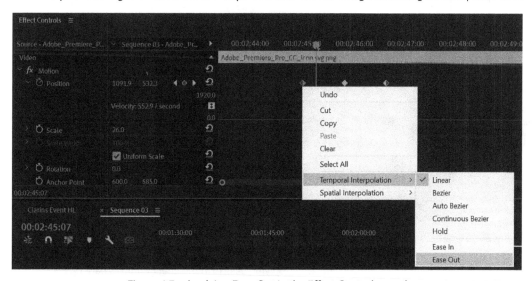

Figure 4.7 – Applying Ease Out in the Effect Controls panel

12. The first keyframe needs to ease out because that's where the animation starts. The last keyframe needs to ease in because that's where the animation ends, so apply **Ease In** to the final keyframe, as shown in the following screenshot:

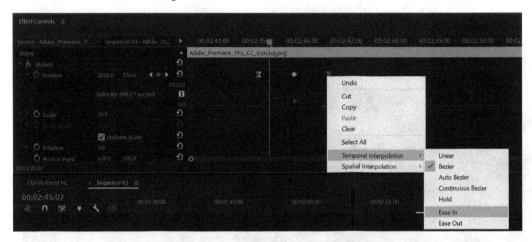

Figure 4.8 – Applying Ease In in the Effect Controls panel

13. When we look at our **Effect Controls** panel, we can see that we have created a curve. When you move the levers, you can change the speed of the animation. You can choose which parts of the animation to slow and which to speed up. You can play around with this and explore many possibilities.

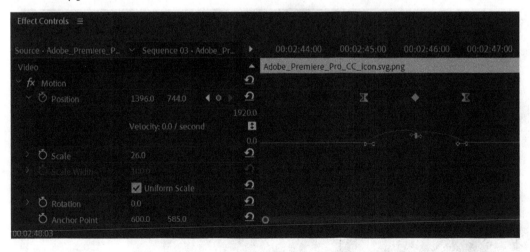

Figure 4.9 – Curved motion path after applying Ease In in the Effect Controls panel

14. Next, you can ensure all your keyframes become a smooth curve by applying **Auto Bezier**. **Auto Bezier** in Premiere Pro serves the function of automatically creating smooth transitions between keyframes, particularly when animating object movement. Here's how to apply it:

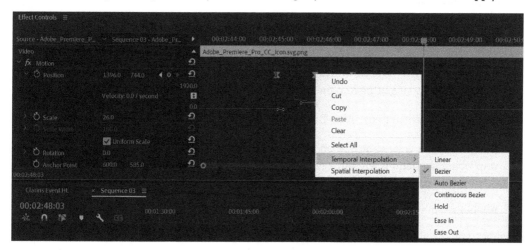

Figure 4.10 – Applying Auto Bezier in the Effect Controls panel

15. Auto Bezier automatically calculates and generates a curved path between keyframes, resulting in a natural and visually pleasing animation with acceleration and deceleration. This is ideal for simulating realistic movement, avoiding the jarring effect of a constant speed change (linear interpolation). And this is how it appears once applied:

Figure 4.11 – Auto Bezier graph in the Effect Controls panel

In essence, as you can see in *Figure 4.11*, **Auto Bezier** takes the workload off you by automatically creating those smooth curves, letting you focus on the bigger picture of your animation.

Here's the benefits of applying Auto Bezier:

- *Natural movement*: Auto Bezier eliminates the need for manually adjusting Bezier handles in most cases, saving time and effort while still achieving realistic animation

- *Intuitive and beginner-friendly*: It's a great option for beginners who want to create smooth animations without getting into the complexities of manual Bezier curves

Next, let's understand when to use Auto Bezier:

- Auto Bezier is a great choice when you want to achieve smooth, natural-looking motion for your object animations without having to delve into the intricacies of manual Bezier curves.

- It's particularly useful for basic movements such as panning, zooming, or object transitions where precise control over the path might not be necessary.

Remember, you can always switch between different interpolation types within the same animation if needed, allowing you to combine the strengths of each approach for a more nuanced effect.

Creating multiple zoom levels with keyframes

We can add multiple zoom levels using additional keyframes to create a more dynamic zoom effect. This will make more gradual transitions between each zoom level and give us more control over the final effect.

We will cover how to add additional keyframes and how to adjust the scale and position of our footage to create a multi-level zoom effect. We will also cover adjusting the timing and ease in and out of our keyframes to create a smooth and polished effect.

By using keyframes in Premiere Pro, we can easily create a zoom-in and zoom-out effect that will add emphasis and movement to our footage. With the tips and techniques covered in this chapter, you will be able to create professional-looking zoom effects in no time.

Step 1 – setting the zoom's starting point

One technique to consider is zooming in or out on specific elements within your video. Premiere Pro offers precise control over this effect. Here's how to set the starting point for your zoom:

1. Choose a clip from your personal project, then drag the playhead to the desired beginning of the movement.

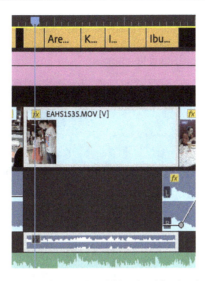

Figure 4.12 – Dragging the playhead (the thin blue line) in the Timeline

2.   Locate the **Scale** and **Position** properties by opening the **Effect Controls** panel.

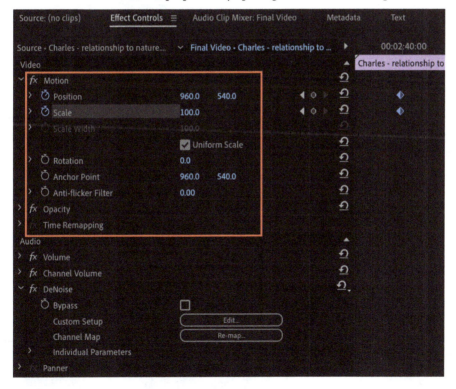

Figure 4.13 – The Effect Controls panel

3. Click the stopwatch to enable keyframing and establish a keyframe for both **Scale** and **Position**. When keyframing is active, the stopwatch will become blue, and any further changes to those parameters will also be recorded via keyframes.

Figure 4.14 – Enable keyframes in the Effect Controls panel

With the starting point set for your zoom, you've laid the groundwork for this dynamic effect. Remember, to animate the zoom smoothly, you'll need to enable keyframes in the **Effect Controls** panel. This lets you define the zoom's starting position (which we just set) and then create another keyframe later to define the ending zoom level, essentially telling Premiere Pro how to transition between the two points over time. We'll explore creating the zoom animation in the next step.

Step 2 – animating the zoom effect

In this step, we'll explore how to animate the zoom itself. We'll leverage the power of keyframes to define the ending zoom level and create a smooth transition, resulting in a polished and engaging zoom animation for your video. Follow these steps:

1. You can zoom in and frame your subject by moving the playhead to the location where you want the movement to stop and adjusting the **Scale** and **Position** parameters. If keyframing is enabled, new keyframes will be captured.

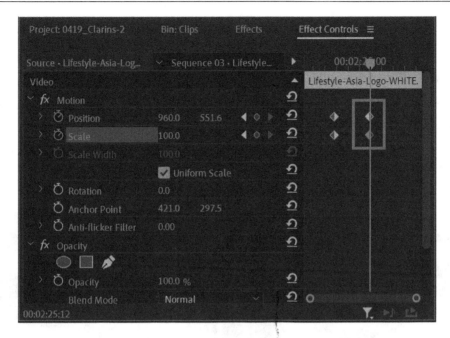

Figure 4.15 – Adjusting the Scale and Position parameters with keyframes

2. Replay it in real time and make any necessary modifications. Move the keyframes closer together to speed up the movement. Increase the distance between them to slow it down.

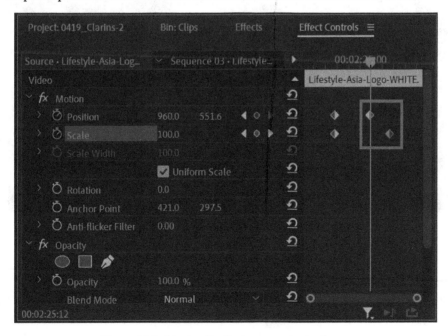

Figure 4.16 – Moving the Scale parameter keyframe

With the keyframes set for your zoom animation, you've established the start and endpoint. Now, let's refine the effect to create a polished and impactful zoom.

Step 3 – polishing and completing your zoom

Here's how to use the **Scale** and **Position** parameters within the keyframes to fine-tune your zoom for an exceptional final result:

1. You may have noticed that the movement suddenly starts and ends. Select your first keyframe, and right-click it for a few alternatives for a more non-linear motion.

2. Try using **Ease Out** at the start of the movement and **Ease In** at the conclusion.

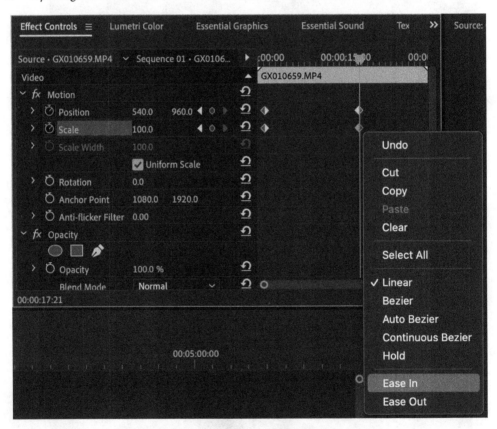

Figure 4.17 – Enable Ease In in the Effect Controls panel

You have learned how to apply Ease In and Ease Out onto keyframes to adjust object position and scale which is a useful technique for adding depth and engagement to your video projects.

Next, **Picture-in-Picture (PiP)** will take your video editing skills to the next level. It enables you to overlay multiple video clips or images within your main video, giving you a plethora of creative options.

PiP is a great way to add context or commentary to your videos and a powerful storytelling tool that can add layers of information. This section delves deep into the Adobe Premiere Pro techniques and tools that allow you to seamlessly integrate PiP elements into your projects.

So, now that you've mastered the art of zooming with keyframes, you're ready to take your video editing skills to the next level by learning how to effectively incorporate PiP videos.

Picture-in-Picture video

Creating a video card to play a clip while some other footage is playing underneath is one of the most common strategies for enhancing the engagement of YouTube channel videos. This is also known as the PiP effect:

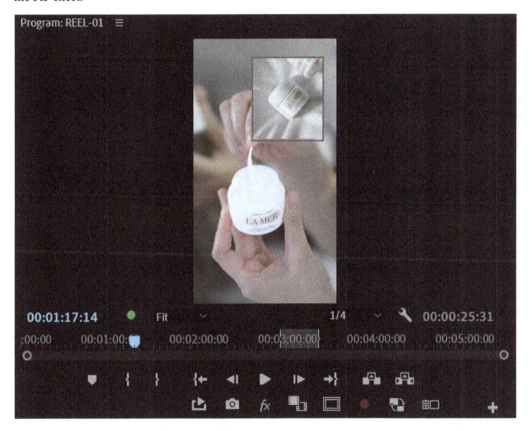

Figure 4.18 – Adding Picture-in-Picture video

Here's how you can create your own PiP-styled video in your project. Let's go over a more stylized version of this effect, which is quite simple to create!

Step 1 – creating a footage card

Assume you have a video of someone doing some activities. The purpose of PiP here is to incorporate a small framed image or video into the footage, akin to a news broadcast. To make this footage card, follow these steps:

1. If the individual is in the center of the screen in the shot, move them to the left side of the screen. You can do this by utilizing **Scale** and **Position** in the **Effect Controls** panel.

Figure 4.19 – Moving an individual to the left of the screen

2. Then, import the shot with which you want to create the footage card. In the Timeline, place it above your original clip.

3. Then, in the **Effect Controls** panel, resize the image to make it small enough to fit in the right-hand corner. It is recommended that the size be reduced by 35-40%. This will give you some buffer space around the footage card.

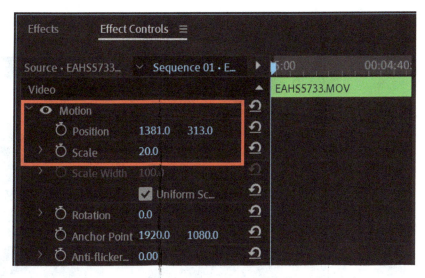

Figure 4.20 – Adjusting options in the Effect Controls panel

4. You can move the footage around by using the **Position** sliders. You can now edit the clip to ensure that only the appropriate portion of the video is used.

Step 2 – adding a colored border

You've now created the PiP effect, but you can do a few more things to make it look more professional. Because you want the footage card to stand out from the underlying video, you could place a solid rectangular box behind it. Here's how you do it:

1. Use the rectangle shape tool and draw a rectangle box on top of the video to add a shape.

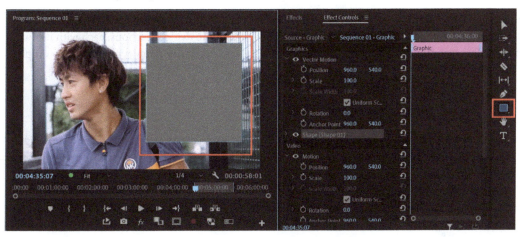

Figure 4.21 – Add a rectangle shape using the shape tool

2. Adjust the **Shape (Shape01)** options in the **Effect Controls** panel. Enable **Stroke** and adjust the thickness value to **20.0**:

Figure 4.22 – Adjust the shape options in the Effect Controls panel

3. If you wish to modify the color of the box, you can do this in the **Essential Graphics** tab.

You've explored the exciting world of PiP video editing in Premiere Pro and used the power of overlaying multiple videos to enhance your storytelling. Let's move on to our next creative endeavor, creating a split-screen effect with borders.

While PiP is a great way to contrast different visual elements, the split-screen effect takes it a step further. This section will teach you how to divide your screen into distinct sections, each with its own content. This technique can be used to compare two scenes, emphasize parallel narratives, or simply create visually stunning compositions.

Creating a split-screen effect

As the name implies, a split screen divides your video frame into multiple sections, each displaying a distinct visual element. This technique is visually appealing and serves a variety of creative and practical functions. Split screens enable you to present multiple perspectives at the same time, compare scenes, highlight parallel storylines, or convey a wealth of information in a single frame. They are a versatile storytelling tool that can improve the quality of your video projects, whether you're making tutorials, vlogs, documentaries, or dramatic narratives.

How to create a split screen

A split screen simply divides the screen space so that different clips can be viewed at the same time. Most split screens will require cropping, which you can learn everything about here:

1. Add all the clips you want to see on screen and stack them in the sequence.

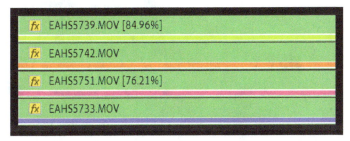

Figure 4.23 – Add clips for trimming in the Timeline

2. Trim the clips to ensure that they are all the same length.

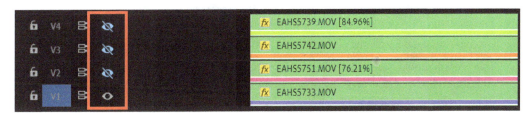

Figure 4.24 – Hide the top three tracks

3. Turn off the top three tracks, leaving only the lowest one visible.

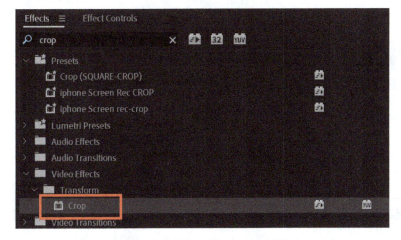

Figure 4.25 – Add the Crop effect from the Effects panel

4.   Open **Effect Controls** from the **Window** menu. Add the **Crop** effect to the **Effect Controls** panel.

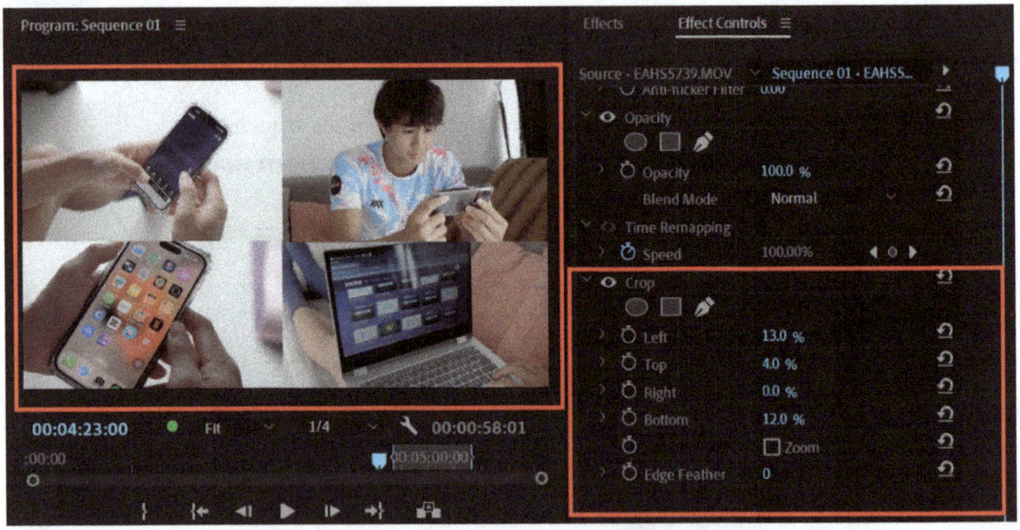

Figure 4.26 – Adjust Crop effects accordingly

5.   Crop, position, and scale the clip until you're satisfied with how it looks.

6.   This process should be repeated for each clip in the series. You may need to go back and modify additional clips so that everything fits properly. To make things easier, enable snapping in the Program Monitor, as follows:

Figure 4.27 – Enabling snapping in the Program Monitor

7. Once you enable the snapping feature, go to the **Effect Controls** panel and click on the **Motion** property to enable the bounding box (blue color) while repositioning your media in a video. Red-dashed snap lines will appear as you can see in the following screenshot:

Figure 4.28 – Snap lines in the Program Monitor

8. The snap lines are used to help you to move any object for example here, we added on a logo to the right position but if you want to move more freely, all you need to do is deselect the snapping icon and freely move your logo.

These are the fundamentals of manipulating your clips and arranging them in a split-screen manner. You can use this technique to be creative with your composition, although it isn't extremely precise.

The Ken Burns effect – position and scale

Do you want to add motion to your still photos in a video? The Ken Burns effect is a popular method in video editing. This popular effect in video editing allows you to create a progressive zoom or pan across a still image. It is named after a well-known documentary filmmaker, Ken Burns, who used this technique frequently in his work. The Ken Burns effect can be used to draw attention to specific elements in an image or to add variety to a series of static photographs.

You can create the Ken Burns effect in Premiere Pro. Although this effect doesn't come as a preset function, it can still be created in a few comparatively easy steps with keyframes and the **Effect Controls** panel. You can save your Ken Burns effect results as a preset to use again later once you are satisfied with the results.

How to create the Ken Burns effect in Premiere Pro

In just a few quick steps, you can add a Ken Burns effect to an image in Premiere Pro:

1. Launch Premiere Pro and initiate a fresh project.

2. Within the editing window, bring in the image you desire to utilize for the Ken Burns effect.

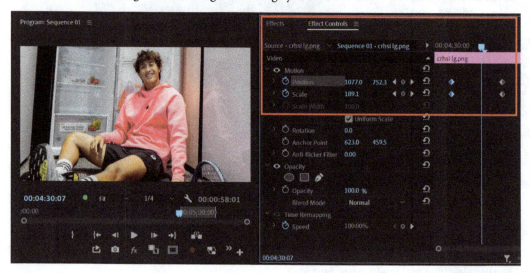

Figure 4.29 – Add keyframes in Effect Controls

3. Select the specific frame from which you would like the Ken Burns effect to commence. Position the playhead at the desired starting point to achieve the desired effect. Activate the **Scale** animation button, resembling a stopwatch.

4. The first keyframe will then be added. Increase the **Scale** value by clicking later in the clip where you want the effect to terminate. You'll get your second keyframe as a result. If you want all effects to take effect at once, repeat this procedure for the **Position** and **Rotation** attributes.

5. Until you get the outcome you want, keep modifying **Position**, **Scale**, **Rotation**, and keyframes as necessary. Once you're pleased, you can either choose **File** | **Export** | **Media** or press *Ctrl + M* to export the video. The video format, resolution, and quality can all be changed in the Export window.

With its smooth and dynamic motion, the Ken Burns effect brings images to life by panning and zooming within the frame. It gives your video projects depth and storytelling finesse, allowing you to create visually engaging content. To truly master the art of video editing, however, you must first understand the foundation upon which every frame is built – aspect ratios.

Aspect ratios determine the shape and dimensions of your video frames, influencing how your content appears on different-sized screens. Understanding aspect ratios is not only important, but is also an artistic decision that can have a significant impact on the visual appeal of your videos.

Deeper understanding of aspect ratios

You might not always detect the variation in aspect ratios as a spectator. However, to create high-quality video content, it is essential for content creators to understand aspect ratios. Aspect ratios, in short, are more than just technical details; they are tools for maintaining consistency, engaging audiences, and unleashing creativity. In today's multimedia landscape, mastering them is essential for content creators. You will discover more about video aspect ratios in this article. We'll talk about some of the most widely utilized aspect ratios nowadays and how to use them in your projects.

What is the aspect ratio in a video?

The proportionate relationship between a video frame's width and height is referred to as the aspect ratio in videos. Using a colon to divide two numbers, it is expressed in the form of 4:3 or 16:9.

The frame's width is indicated by the first number, and its height by the second. A video with a 16:9 aspect ratio, for example, has a width that is 16 units long and 9 units tall.

The difference between aspect ratio and resolution in video

Although you might mix up aspect ratio and resolution, these are two distinct ideas. Resolution is the number of pixels that make up the video frame, whereas aspect ratio is the proportion between width and height. The number of pixels in a video frame, such as 1920 x 1080 or 3840 x 2160, is commonly used to describe resolution.

Popular aspect ratios used in video

Aspect ratios are important in video editing because they determine the dimensions of your video frame. There are several popular aspect ratios in Premiere Pro, each serving a specific purpose:

Aspect Ratio	Purpose
16:9 (1.78:1)	Commonly known as widescreen, this is the industry standard for HD and many online platforms. Ideal for a wide range of content, from vlogs to feature films.
4:3 (1.33:1)	This is the aspect ratio used in classic television and early film. Some presentations or retro-style projects still use it.
(Square): 1:1	Instagram and TikTok, popular social media platforms, use this aspect ratio. It has a distinct, intimate feel and is ideal for vertical content.
3:2	This is used to create a video that has a more cinematic look. It can also be used to create a more balanced composition, as the width and height are more evenly distributed.

Aspect Ratio	Purpose
2.39:1 (Cinemascope)	Used in film productions to achieve a cinematic, widescreen look. Makes for an impressive and immersive viewing experience.
9:16 (vertical)	Designed specifically for mobile devices and vertical video formats. Ideal for smartphone-optimized stories and content.

Table 4.1 – Aspect ratios for video production

The aspect ratio you use is critical for visual consistency, storytelling impact, and platform compatibility. The versatility of Premiere Pro allows you to work with these popular aspect ratios while also allowing you to customize them as needed to realize your creative vision.

4:3 aspect ratio

While widescreen formats such as 16:9 dominate today's screens, the 4:3 aspect ratio has a rich history and distinct qualities. This format, resembling a square but slightly wider, was once the standard for televisions and computer monitors. Let's delve into the characteristics, applications, and continued relevance of the 4:3 aspect ratio in the digital age.

Figure 4.30 – 4:3 aspect ratio

Early television broadcasts and video production frequently used the almost-square aspect ratio known as 4:3. It has a boxy frame with a width to height ratio of 4:3, which is somewhat broader than it is tall. Up until the introduction of **high-definition television (HDTV)** and widescreen aspect ratios, the 4:3 aspect ratio was the norm for television transmissions for a long time.

The ability to give a video a classic, nostalgic, or retro vibe is one benefit of the 4:3 aspect ratio. This can be helpful for content intended to conjure up memories of the past or that is regarded in a sentimental light. The 4:3 aspect ratio can also be an effective tool for filmmakers to develop a certain aesthetic or visual style. Because many films are shot in the 4:3 aspect ratio, it can also be used to create a more cinematic look.

4:5 aspect ratio

The 4:5 aspect ratio stands out for its unique proportions. Taller than the standard widescreen format (16:9) but narrower than a square (1:1), 4:5 offers a distinct visual aesthetic. Often associated with social media platforms such as Instagram and popular for mobile viewing, this ratio presents an interesting choice for creative video content. Let's explore the advantages, applications, and potential considerations for using the 4:5 aspect ratio in your video projects.

Figure 4.31 – 4:5 aspect ratio

The most recent addition to the list of typical aspect ratios for videos is 4:5. The 4:5 ratio, made popular by Instagram's vertical video mode, is perfect for social media since it fills more screen space and commands more attention.

4:5 is a vertical aspect ratio, which means that the width is 4 units and the height is 5 units. This is a common aspect ratio for mobile phones and social media videos because it allows the video to fill the screen without cropping the top or bottom.

The 4:5 aspect ratio can be used in video editing to create a more vertical composition, which is useful for videos that focus on people or objects that are taller than they are wide.

1:1 aspect ratio

Among the aspect ratios discussed here, the 1:1 aspect ratio stands out for its perfectly square dimensions. Often associated with social media platforms such as Instagram and photography, this ratio offers a balanced and visually striking canvas for creative expression. Whether you're showcasing static images or crafting captivating square videos, the 1:1 aspect ratio presents a unique opportunity to tell your story in a visually engaging way. Let's delve into the benefits, applications, and considerations for incorporating the 1:1 aspect ratio into your video projects.

Figure 4.32 – 1:1 aspect ratio

For both photographs and videos, the 1:1 aspect ratio square format is frequently used on social media sites such as Instagram and Facebook. This aspect ratio offers a square frame that is balanced and might be helpful for producing aesthetically appealing and compelling content.

The 1:1 aspect ratio is frequently used in marketing and advertising because it enables companies to present their goods or services in a way that stands out in a crowded social media feed and is visually appealing. In addition, the 1:1 aspect ratio can contribute to the sense of balance and symmetry in the frame, which can be especially helpful for close-up portraits or product pictures.

16:9 aspect ratio

This 16:9 format, characterized by a width that stretches nearly twice its height, has become the standard for widescreen televisions, computer monitors, and a significant portion of online video content. From action-packed movies to captivating documentaries, the 16:9 aspect ratio offers a natural and immersive viewing experience that perfectly complements modern high-definition displays. Let's explore the reasons behind its dominance, the advantages it presents for creators and viewers alike, and how to leverage this format to its full potential in your video projects.

Figure 4.33 – 16:9 aspect ratio

This aspect ratio offers a large frame suited for a variety of content, including online videos and social media content you view on YouTube and Vimeo as well as movies and TV series. This suggests that videos created in the 16:9 aspect ratio is more likely to be watched in its original aspect ratio without letterboxing or cropping, which might impair the video's visual quality.

Additionally, the 16:9 aspect ratio is a flexible format that may be utilized for a variety of content, including documentaries, corporate videos, fiction, and more. It also permits a wider field of vision, which is advantageous for capturing expansive landscapes, group photographs, and action scenarios.

9:16 aspect ratio

As mobile devices and social media platforms have grown in popularity, so has the 9:16 aspect ratio, a vertical video format. When using mobile devices held vertically, this aspect ratio creates a tall and thin frame that is perfect for viewing.

Figure 4.34 – 9:16 aspect ratio

One of the main benefits of the 9:16 aspect ratio is that it makes mobile viewing more immersive and interesting. This is because it makes use of the typical way that users hold their phones, which is with one hand holding the phone vertically. This format is especially popular on social media sites such as Instagram and TikTok, which focus on brief, visually appealing material made for mobile-first viewing.

Portraits, close-ups, and other vertically oriented images work well with the 9:16 aspect ratio for content capture. As a bigger frame that highlights the subject's features and expressions is possible, it can be very helpful for taking pictures of people's faces.

3:2 aspect ratio

The 3:2 aspect ratio is suitable for certain types of video production, such as documentaries and creative films. Compared to other more frequently used aspect ratios, this can create a cinematic feel like the 35mm film format.

Figure 4.35 – 3:2 aspect ratio

3:2 is an almost-square aspect ratio, with a width of 3 units and height of 2 units. This aspect ratio is common for DSLR cameras because it allows the sensor to capture more of the scene. Many popular photo formats, such as 4x6 and 5x7, use this aspect ratio.

Because many movies are shot in this aspect ratio, the 3:2 aspect ratio can be used in video editing to create a more cinematic look. Because the width and height are more evenly distributed, it can also be used to create a more balanced composition.

It's important to note that most video-sharing services do not often support the 3:2 aspect ratio, therefore some platforms or devices may require that videos in this aspect ratio be letterboxed or pillarboxed in order to display them appropriately.

21:9 aspect ratio

The ideal aspect ratio for cinematic videos is 21:9. On larger monitors, it produces an immersive viewing experience by creating an ultra-widescreen effect that gives depth to an image.

Figure 4.36 – 21:9 aspect ratio

Despite being more frequently utilized for filming movies, the 21:9 aspect ratio is becoming more and more common for smartphone media consumption. This is because turning a smartphone to landscape mode makes it simple to watch Netflix and YouTube films because it properly fits this aspect ratio.

Here are some examples of films and television shows that use various aspect ratios:

- *Movies*:

  - *The Grand Budapest Hotel* (2014) by Wes Anderson uses three different aspect ratios: 1.37:1, 1.85:1, and 2.35:1. This reflects the different time periods and moods of the film.

  - *The Lord of the Rings trilogy* (2001-2003) by Peter Jackson uses a 2.35:1 aspect ratio, which is the standard widescreen aspect ratio. This helps to create a sense of epic scale and scope.

  - *The Witch* (2015) by Robert Eggers uses a 1.66:1 aspect ratio, which is a narrower aspect ratio than 2.35:1. This helps to create a more claustrophobic and intimate feel.

- *TV series*:

  - *House of Cards* (2013-2018) by David Fincher uses a 2:1 aspect ratio, which is wider than the standard 16:9 aspect ratio. This helps to create a more cinematic feel for the series.

  - *The Crown* (2016-present) by Peter Morgan uses a variety of aspect ratios, depending on the time period being depicted. This helps to create a sense of historical accuracy.

  - *WandaVision* (2021) by Matt Shakman uses a variety of aspect ratios, including 4:3, 1.33:1, and 16:9. This reflects the different decades that the series is set in.

Summary

In this chapter, we delved into the intricacies of incorporating motion and animated graphics within Adobe Premiere Pro. We talked about the fundamentals of animation, starting by discussing keyframe animation and then proceeding to examine various types of motion, such as position, rotation, and scale. The Transform and Motion effects in Premiere Pro were thoroughly explained to help you create stunning animations.

In this chapter, you walked through detailed tutorials on the process of creating zoom in/out effects using keyframes, PiP videos, and split-screen effects with borders. Each step was carefully explained to ensure you could easily follow along and achieve the desired results. Next, we explored the concept of the Ken Burns effect, which allows for adding motion to still photos. We also highlighted the importance of aspect ratios in the realm of video editing. In the last section of the chapter, various aspect ratios that are frequently employed in video production were discussed.

Next, we will cover everything you need to know about transitions. The next chapter will give you a detailed guide on transitions in Adobe Premiere Pro, covering all the essential information you need to seamlessly connect and enhance your video sequences.

5

Everything You Need to Know about Transitions

Transitions play a crucial role in video editing, allowing smooth and seamless visual and auditory changes between shots. In Adobe Premiere Pro, a powerful and versatile video editing software, transitions provide an array of creative options to enhance the flow and impact of your video projects. Transitions are a powerful tool to improve the flow and impact of a video. They can be used to indicate a change in scene, mood, or tone, or to simply enhance the visual appeal of the video. Transitions, when used correctly, can help to keep viewers engaged in and hooked on the content. In this chapter, we will explore everything you need to know about transitions in Premiere Pro, from the basics to advanced techniques.

In this chapter, we're going to cover the following main topics:

- Adding video transitions in Premiere Pro
- Customizing video transitions in Premiere Pro
- Adding audio transitions and creating custom audio fades
- Creating custom transitions with adjustment layers
- Creating directional blur and motion blur transitions

Adding video transitions in Premiere Pro

Adding transitions to your video clips in Adobe Premiere Pro is a straightforward process that can be accomplished through the **Effects** panel. This section will provide a step-by-step guide on accessing the **Effects** panel and browsing through the available transitions. Additionally, we will explore the convenient drag and drop technique to add transitions to the timeline effortlessly.

Step 1 – accessing the Effects panel

To begin, launch Adobe Premiere Pro and open your video project. Make sure you have your clips imported and arranged on the timeline.

In the workspace, locate the **Effects** panel. If you can't find it, go to the top menu and select **Window | Effects**.

Figure 5.1 – Accessing the Effects panel from the Window menu

The **Effects** panel will appear, typically on the left side of the screen. It consists of different tabs that categorize various effects and presets.

Step 2 – browsing and selecting transitions

The **Effects** panel offers a wide range of transitions to choose from, and you can explore and choose different video or audio transitions to enhance the flow and visual appeal of your video project. Transitions are used to smoothly move from one video clip or audio track to another, creating a seamless and engaging viewing experience for your viewer.

Click on the **Video Transitions** tab within the **Effects** panel to access the available video transitions.

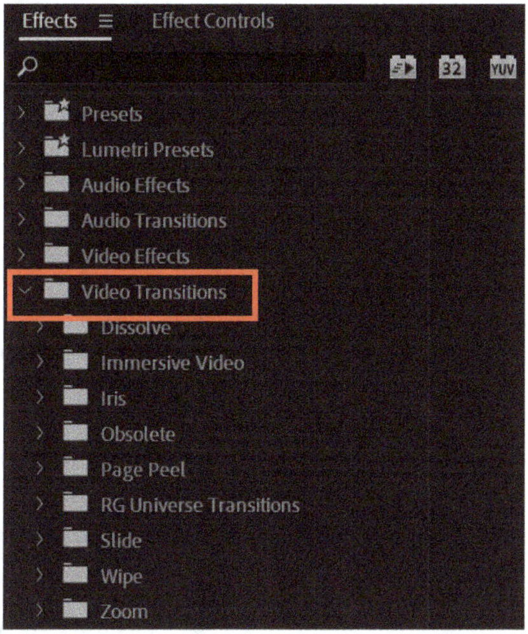

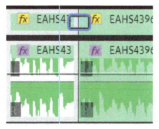

Figure 5.2 – Opening the Video Transitions panel

Next, we will continue with *step 3*. We will focus on the technique of applying transitions using drag and drop to enhance the overall visual narrative in your projects.

Step 3 – applying transitions using drag and drop

Premiere Pro offers a convenient drag and drop method to apply transitions directly to your clips on the timeline. Follow these steps to use this technique:

1. Select the transition you want to apply from the **Effects** panel.

2. Click and hold the transition, and then drag it to the desired edit point on the timeline. The edit point is the exact location where you want the transition to occur between two adjacent clips.

Figure 5.3 – Applying the transition between two clips

3. As you drag the transition, a small icon representing the transition will appear, indicating the position of the transition on the timeline.

4. Release the mouse button to drop the transition onto the edit point. The transition will be automatically applied to the selected area, creating a smooth visual transition between clips.

5. To further explore a transition, drag it onto a clip. Click on the transition applied to the clip, and then open the **Effect Controls** panel, where you can modify specific properties of the transition, such as duration or direction.

Important note

You can also adjust the duration of a transition by dragging its edges on the timeline. Lengthening the transition duration will create a more gradual effect, while shortening it will result in a quicker transition.

This is the visual representation of your footage after applying a transition at the beginning. This will ensure a seamless and professional transition between scenes.

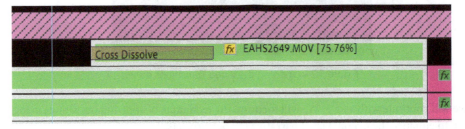

Figure 5.4 – Applying a transition to the beginning of the clip

We learned about the different types of video transitions available in Adobe Premiere Pro and how to apply them to clips in a sequence. In the next section, we will learn how to customize the properties of video transitions to create unique and interesting effects.

Customizing video transitions in Premiere Pro

Transitions are not just limited to their default settings. In the following subsections, we will explore transition alignment, working with transition handles, and various transition properties such as opacity adjustments, speed modifications, and motion effects.

Transition alignment and handles

Premiere Pro provides meticulous control over transition alignment and handles to accomplish your editing objectives.

Transition alignment

Transitions are the bridges between your edits. They help guide the viewer's eye and maintain a natural flow throughout your video. But to ensure these bridges are sturdy and seamless, here's the transition alignment that you should know.

- **Center at Cut (Default)**: This is the most prevalent approach. Take the transition effect from the Effects panel and place it on the dividing line between two clips. This positioning of the transition ensures that it is precisely centered, resulting in a seamless integration of the clips.

- **Single-Sided Transitions**: Premiere Pro provides enhanced creative autonomy with its support for single-sided transitions. While dragging the transition, hold down the *Ctrl* key on Windows or the *Cmd* key on Mac. You have the option to select either the **Start at Cut** or **End at Cut** icons:

  - *Start at Cut*: Places the beginning of the transition at the start of the second clip. The first clip plays in full, then the transition effect begins.

  - *End at Cut*: Places the end of the transition at the end of the first clip. The transition effect starts, then the second clip cuts in abruptly.

Handle manipulation

After positioning your transition, grasp the little grips located on both sides of it. By pulling them in an outward direction, the transition is extended, enabling the impact to gradually occur over a greater period of time. On the other hand, pulling them towards the center reduces the duration of the change.

To make more precise modifications, use the **Effect Controls** panel by selecting the transition in the timeline and clicking on it. Within this interface, you will see sliders labeled **Start** and **End** that allow you to precisely adjust the transition % applied to each individual clip.

Premiere Pro does not include distinct ease in/out handles inside the **Effect Controls** panel, unlike some other products. Nevertheless, you may attain comparable outcomes by utilizing the **Work Area Bar** and implementing velocity modifications inside that specific segment.

The visual impact of your transitions is greatly influenced by this fundamental aspect, giving you the freedom to select between smooth blends and more noticeable shift effects.

Understanding transition alignment

Transition alignment refers to how a transition is applied in relation to the cut or edit point between two clips. Adobe Premiere Pro offers two alignment options:

- **Applied to a cut point**: When a transition is applied to a cut point, it starts exactly at the edit point where the two clips meet. This alignment creates a more abrupt transition effect.

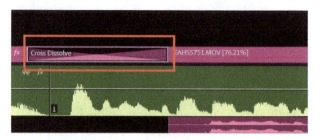

Figure 5.5 – Adding a transition to a cut point

- **Centered between clips**: When a transition is centered between clips, it extends equally into each adjacent clip, creating a smoother and more gradual transition.

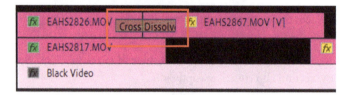

Figure 5.6 – Adding a transitional center between clips

To adjust a transition alignment, follow these steps:

1. Select the transition on the timeline.
2. In the **Effect Controls** panel, navigate to the **Alignment** drop-down menu.
3. Choose either **Center at Cut** or **Center at In/Out Points** to change the transition alignment.

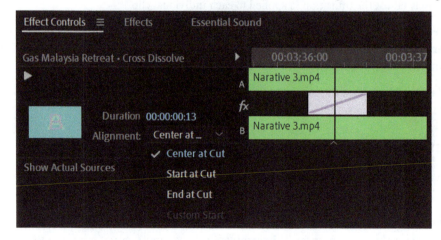

Figure 5.7 – Adjust the transition in the Effect Controls panel

The effect controls provide a great foundation for customizing transitions, but there's another tool in your editing arsenal: transition handles. These offer even finer control over the start and end points of your transitions, allowing for a more precise and professional edit.

Working with transition handles

Transition handles are the editable areas at the beginning and end of a transition on the timeline. These handles allow you to precisely control the timing and duration of the transition effect. By adjusting the handles, you can make the transition shorter, longer, or change the speed of the transition.

To work with transition handles, follow these steps:

1. Select a transition on the timeline.

2. Locate the handles at the beginning and end of the transition.

3. Click and drag the handles inward or outward to adjust the duration of the transition.

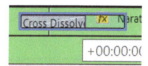

Figure 5.8 – Working with transition handles

4. Dragging the handles inward makes the transition shorter, while dragging them outward increases the duration.

Important note

Be careful not to extend the transition handles beyond the adjacent clips, as this can result in unwanted gaps or overlaps in your timeline.

---

5. You can also click twice on the transition in the timeline. A dialog box will appear to set the transition duration. Adjust the duration value by dragging it or entering a new value. Then, click **OK**.

Figure 5.9 – Setting the transition duration

> **Important note**
>
> Double-clicking on a transition will open up a window, **Set Transition Duration**.

Smooth opacity transition using the Effect Controls panel

There are various settings and attributes that you can change to control how transitions between video clips are applied and appear in your video project, such as **Opacity** in the **Effect Controls** panel. Adjusting **Opacity** allows you to control the transparency of a transition, creating gradual fade-ins and fade-outs within the transition effect. This technique can add elegance and polish to your video transitions.

To adjust opacity within a transition, follow these steps:

1. Select the clip you want to adjust in the timeline.

2. In the **Effect Controls** panel, locate the **Opacity** property.

3. Create keyframes at the desired points in the timeline where you want the opacity to change.

4. Adjust the opacity value of each keyframe to control the fade-in and fade-out effect.

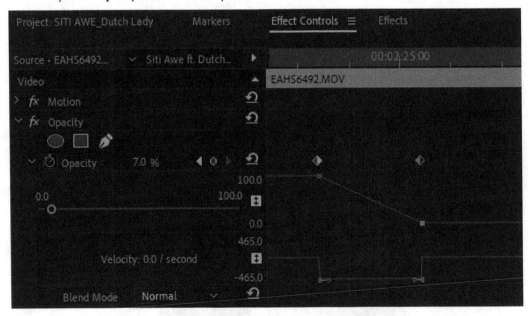

Figure 5.10 – Working with opacity in the Effect Controls panel

Opacity control in video editing lets you create layered effects by making elements partially transparent. This is useful for blending clips, creating subtle reveals or ghosting effects, and introducing smooth transitions such as fades. You can use it for anything from picture-in-picture effects to stylized intros and outros. Next, we will learn how to use speed ramping as a transition.

Making smooth speed ramping transition

Changing the speed of a transition can significantly impact its visual impact. Slowing down a transition can create a more dramatic and deliberate effect, while increasing its speed can make it quicker and snappier. In this section, we will use the speed ramping technique.

Speed ramping, also known as time remapping, is a powerful technique in Premiere Pro that allows you to manipulate the playback speed of a clip over time. This means you can go beyond simple slow or fast motion, creating more dynamic effects by gradually changing the speed throughout the clip. We'll also explore how to smooth out the transitions between different speeds for a polished and natural look in your edits.

Here's a breakdown of how speed ramping works:

1. Select the transition on the timeline.

2. In the **Effect Controls** panel, locate the **Time Remapping | Speed** property.

3. Adjust the speed value to increase or decrease the transition's speed. A higher value will speed up the transition, while a lower value will slow it down.

4. To add a speed ramp to the desired clip, simply right-click on it and select **Show Clip Keyframes | Time Remapping | Speed**. Now, you'll be able to see the speed shifts in your clips.

Figure 5.11 – Enabling the Time Remapping view on a clip

5. To create a keyframe, you can either press the **P** key or select the **Pen** tool from the toolbar. Next, select the desired starting and ending points on the white line of your video track. This will generate keyframes that allow you to fine-tune the velocity between the two points.

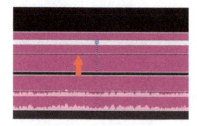

Figure 5.12 – Adding the start and end points to the white line

6. To modify the speed, simply click on the white line between the two keyframes, and move it upward to increase the video's pace or downward to create a slow-motion effect. The more you extend it, the more significant the alteration in time.

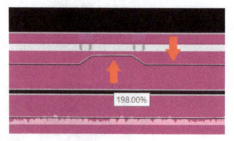

Figure 5.13 – Increasing and decreasing the video speed using the white line

7. Refine the transition by using the **Selection** tool and effortlessly adjusting the keyframe marker on your clip to create a seamless transition in slow or fast motion. (If you fail to complete this step, the transition will happen instantly.) This enhances the flow of the transition. Once more, when you extend the distance between the keyframes, the transition becomes more gradual.

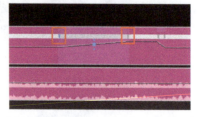

Figure 5.14 – Smoothing the speed transition by refining the keyframe marker

Speed ramping is a versatile tool that adds another layer of creative control to your video editing in Premiere Pro. By mastering keyframes and the use of handles, you can manipulate time within your clips, enhancing the flow, impact, and overall storytelling power of your edits. Next, let's look into how to add audio transitions in Premiere Pro.

Adding audio transitions and creating custom audio fades

Audio transitions and fades play a crucial role in ensuring a smooth and professional audio experience in video projects. Adobe Premiere Pro's powerful tools allow you to control the volume levels and seamlessly blend audio clips. The following subsections will explore the techniques of adding audio transitions, adjusting their properties, and creating custom audio fades to enhance the overall audio quality of your videos.

Understanding audio transitions and fades

Audio transitions are techniques used to create smooth and seamless connections between different audio clips. They eliminate jarring audio jumps, create a natural flow, and enhance the listening experience for viewers. Understanding the importance of audio transitions helps you appreciate their role in maintaining audio continuity and overall video quality.

Types of audio transitions

Premiere Pro offers several types of audio transitions to choose from. Understanding the different types and their effects will allow you to select the most suitable transition for your project. Common audio transitions include the following:

- **Exponential Fade**: A transition where the audio gradually fades out to silence (dip to black) or fades in from silence (dip to white), often used for transitions between scenes or to emphasize certain moments.

- **Constant Power**: A smooth transition where the audio levels are maintained consistently during the transition, providing a natural flow between clips.

- **Constant Gain**: An audio is increased or decreased at a consistent rate as you transition between clips. It changes the volume at a constant rate (linearly).

Applying default audio transitions

In the `Audio Transitions` effect folder, look for the transition with a blue outline or highlight. This indicates that it's the current default transition:

Figure 5.15 – Applying a default transition

To add audio transitions to your project, follow these steps:

1. Ensure that your audio clips are placed on the timeline in the desired order.

2. Locate the **Effects** panel by going to the **Window** menu and selecting **Effects**.

3. In the **Effects** panel, navigate to the **Audio Transitions** folder.

4. Browse through the available transitions and preview them by hovering over each one.

5. Once you find a suitable transition, simply drag and drop it between the two audio clips on the timeline.

Figure 5.16 – Applying audio transition onto clips

6. Adjust the duration of the transition by dragging its edges on the timeline, allowing you to achieve the desired blend between the audio clips.

Adjusting an audio transition duration

Premiere Pro allows you to customize the duration of audio transitions to achieve the desired blend between clips. To adjust the duration of an audio transition, follow these steps:

1. Select the audio transition on the timeline by clicking on it.

2. Look for the transition handles, represented by small squares or circles at the beginning and end of the transition.

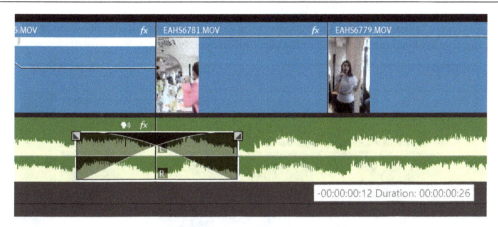

Figure 5.17 – Adjusting audio duration in clips

3. Drag the transition handles inward or outward to decrease or increase the duration of the transition, respectively.

4. Preview the transition to ensure that it creates a seamless blend between the audio clips.

Creating custom audio fades

Using Adobe Premiere Pro to create custom audio fades, you can have precise control over how audio levels transition between two clips or within a single clip. Custom audio fades are especially useful when you want to tailor an audio transition to your project's specific needs.

Creating fade-in and fade-out effects

Fade-in and fade-out effects are essential for creating professional audio transitions. To create a fade-in or fade-out effect, follow these steps:

1. Select the audio clip on the timeline by clicking on it.

2. Locate the **Effect Controls** panel by going to the Window menu and selecting **Effect Controls**.

3. In the **Effect Controls** panel, look for the **Opacity** parameter.

4. To create a fade-in effect, set a keyframe at the beginning of the clip with an opacity value of 0%, and another keyframe at the desired point with an opacity value of 100%.

5. To create a fade-out effect, set a keyframe at the desired point with an opacity value of 100%, and another keyframe at the end of the clip with an opacity value of 0%.

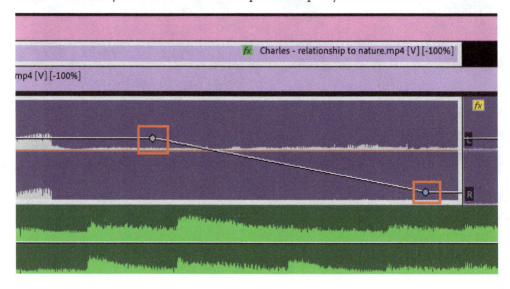

Figure 5.18 – Adjusting the timing and duration using keyframes on the audio file

6. Adjust the timing and duration of the fade-in and fade-out effects by dragging the keyframes onto the timeline.

Customizing audio transition curves

Premiere Pro provides control over the shape of audio transition curves, allowing you to create custom transitions with specific volume adjustments. To customize the audio transition curves, follow these steps:

1. Select an audio transition on the timeline by clicking on it.

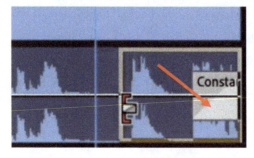

Figure 5.19 – An audio transition on the timeline

2.   Look for the transition in the **Effect Controls** panel.

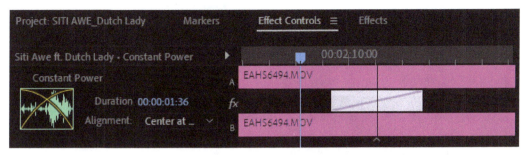

Figure 5.20 – The transition in the Effect Controls panel

3.   Click on transition to reveal the handles that control the shape of the transition curve.

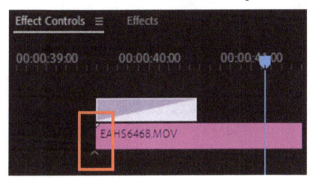

Figure 5.21 – The handle in audio transitions

4.   Drag the handle to adjust the curve shape, controlling the volume levels during the transition.

5.   Preview the transition to ensure that it produces the desired audio effect.

Fine-tuning and refining audio transitions and fades

To fine-tune the timing and placement of audio transitions, ensure that the transitions are precisely aligned with the desired audio cues or moments. Drag the transitions onto the timeline to adjust their timing, ensuring they align seamlessly with the visual and auditory elements of your video.

See the following example on how to refine the audio:

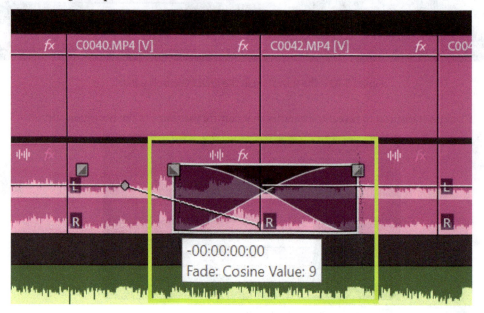

Figure 5.22 – Fine-tuning a transition in timeline

You can also use real-time previewing of audio transitions and fades, enabling you to evaluate the effectiveness of your transitions. Use the Program Monitor to preview your transitions and make necessary adjustments, based on real-time feedback.

Here's a sample of a real-time preview in Premiere Pro:

Figure 5.23 – Real-time previewing of audio transitions and fades

As we delve into the complexities of audio transitions and fades in Adobe Premiere Pro, let's uncover some valuable troubleshooting insights and essential tips to guarantee a seamless and polished auditory experience in your video projects.

Troubleshooting and tips for audio transitions and fades

Audio transitions and fades are essential for creating smooth transitions in your Premiere Pro edits. Here's a breakdown of troubleshooting common issues and some tips for achieving those professional-sounding results:

Troubleshooting common issues

The following are some common issues while troubleshooting audio in Premiere Pro:

- **Audio popping or clipping**: Adjust the volume levels and transition curves to prevent abrupt changes in audio levels, which can cause popping or clipping sounds.

- **Unwanted audio artifacts**: Ensure that the audio transitions are smooth and seamless, without any unintended artifacts such as clicks or gaps.
- **Disruptive audio changes**: Make sure the audio transitions blend well with the overall video flow, avoiding abrupt changes that may distract or confuse viewers.

Tips to create effective audio transitions and fades

Here are some tips to create effective audio transitions and fades in Premiere Pro:

- **Smooth transitions**: Experiment with different types of audio transitions to find the most suitable ones for your project. Aim for seamless and natural-sounding transitions that enhance the storytelling.
- **Gradual volume adjustments**: Utilize fade-ins and fade-outs to gradually increase or decrease volume levels, providing a smooth and pleasing listening experience.
- **Audio layering**: Consider layering multiple audio tracks to create complex and engaging audio transitions, combining dialogue, music, and sound effects to enrich the viewer's experience.

Creating custom transitions with adjustment layers

Adjustment layers are a powerful tool that allows you to apply effects and modifications to multiple clips simultaneously, giving you the ability to create unique and seamless transitions. By leveraging adjustment layers, you can enhance the visual storytelling in your videos and add a professional touch to your editing.

Understanding adjustment layers

Adjustment layers are transparent layers that can be added to the timeline above multiple clips. They act as a container for effects, allowing you to apply modifications to all the clips below the adjustment layer. The purpose of adjustment layers is to provide a non-destructive way to apply effects, color corrections, and transitions to multiple clips at once.

The benefits of using adjustment layers for transitions

Now, let's explore the significant benefits of using adjustment layers for transitions in Adobe Premiere Pro. This feature offers a versatile and efficient tool to enhance the visual consistency and creative flexibility of your video editing projects:

- **Flexibility and efficiency**: Adjustment layers offer flexibility in terms of modifying and fine-tuning transitions, making it easy to experiment and iterate. They also provide an efficient workflow by allowing you to apply transitions to multiple clips with a single adjustment layer.

- **Consistency and coherence**: By applying transitions through adjustment layers, you ensure a consistent and coherent look across all the clips involved in the transition. This helps maintain visual continuity and enhances the overall quality of your video.

Creating custom transitions with adjustment layers

With an adjustment layer, you can create unique and stylized visual effects between clips or throughout your entire video. Adjustment layers are a powerful video editing tool that can affect multiple clips at the same time.

Adding adjustment layers to the timeline

To add an adjustment layer to the timeline, follow these steps:

1. Go to the **Project** panel and click on the **New Item** button.

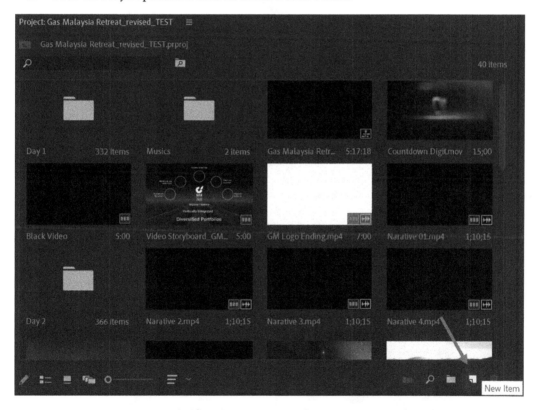

Figure 5.24 – The Project panel in Premiere Pro

2.   Select **Adjustment Layer…** from the drop-down menu.

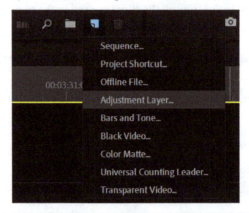

Figure 5.25 – Adjustment Layer… in the Project panel

3.   Specify the video settings for the adjustment layer – **Width**, **Height**, **Timebase**, and **Pixel Aspect Ratio**.

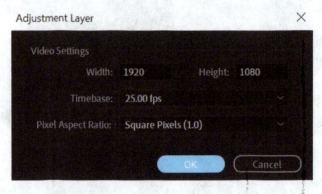

Figure 5.26 – Creating an adjustment layer

4.   Click **OK** to create the adjustment layer.

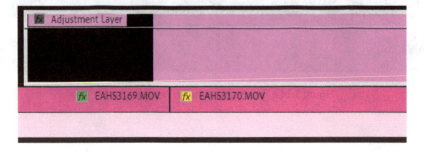

Figure 5.27 – Adding an adjustment layer to the timeline

5. Drag the adjustment layer to the desired track in the timeline, above the clips where you want to apply the custom transition.

Applying effects and modifications to adjustment layers

Once you have added the adjustment layer to the timeline, you can apply effects and modifications to it using the **Effect Controls** panel. Here's how:

1. Select the adjustment layer on the timeline.

2. Open the **Effect Controls** panel by clicking on the Window menu and selecting **Effect Controls**.

3. In the **Effect Controls** panel, you can add various effects and modifications to the adjustment layer. For example, you can add a transform effect to create scale or position changes, or apply a color correction effect to adjust the overall color balance.

Creating transition effects using keyframes

Keyframes are essential for creating custom transition effects. They allow you to control the timing and behavior of effects over time. Here's how to create custom transitions using keyframes:

1. Select the adjustment layer on the timeline.

2. Open the **Effect Controls** panel.

3. Go to the effect applied to the clip you want to animate and enable keyframing for the desired property.

4. Move the playhead to the beginning of the transition.

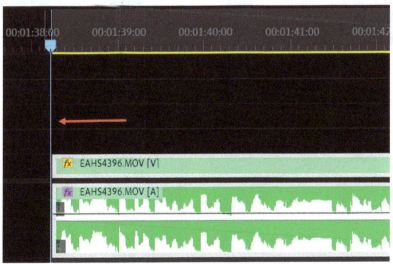

Figure 5.28 – Moving the playhead to the beginning of the transition

5.   Set the initial value for the keyframe.

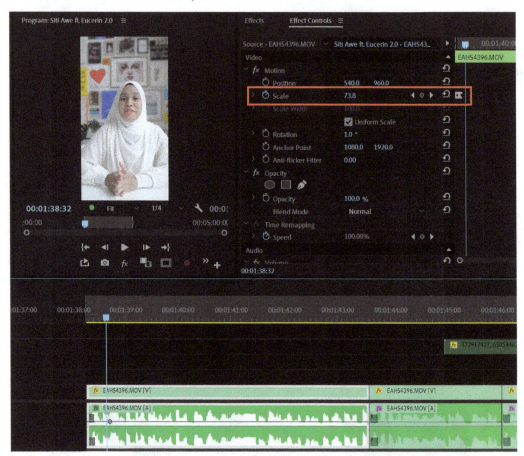

Figure 5.29 – Adding the value to the first keyframes

6.   Move the playhead to the end of the transition.

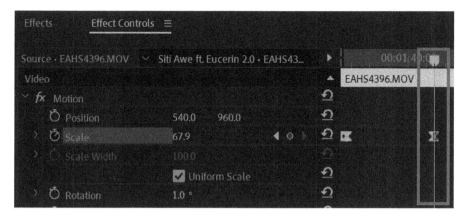

Figure 5.30 – Moving the playhead to the end keyframe and adding the value

7. Adjust the value of the keyframe to create the desired effect.

8. Premiere Pro will automatically create a smooth transition between the two keyframes.

Fine-tuning and refining custom transitions

Mastering the art of custom transitions requires finesse and precision, akin to a skilled artist wielding a brush. Listed are the various tools and techniques that allow you to masterfully manipulate every pixel and frame, creating transitions that will leave your viewers in awe:

- **Transition timing and duration**: To fine-tune the timing and duration of custom transitions using adjustment layers, you can adjust the properties of the adjustment layer in the **Effect Controls** panel. This includes modifying the duration of the adjustment layer on the timeline and making precise adjustments to keyframe positions and values.

- **Previewing and adjusting transitions in real time**: Premiere Pro provides real-time preview capabilities that allow you to evaluate and refine your custom transitions as you work. Use the Program Monitor to preview your transitions, making adjustments as needed based on visual feedback. This iterative process ensures that your custom transitions are seamless and visually appealing.

Troubleshooting and tips for custom transitions with adjustment layers

You can effectively create and troubleshoot custom transitions with adjustment layers in Adobe Premiere Pro by following these troubleshooting tips and adhering to best practices. This method gives you a lot of creative freedom and can boost the visual appeal and storytelling impact of your video projects.

Troubleshooting common issues

Overcoming technical challenges is not an insurmountable task. You can unravel the mysteries of common issues with adjustment layers and confidently discover solutions to them, as follows:

- **Rendering errors**: If you encounter rendering errors with adjustment layers, ensure that your project settings and sequence settings are configured correctly

- **Performance issues**: Adjusting the playback resolution or rendering previews can help alleviate performance issues when working with complex adjustment layers

- **Misaligned clips**: Double-check the placement and timing of the adjustment layer on the timeline to ensure proper alignment with the clips involved in the transition

Tips to create effective custom transitions

Envisage transitions that go beyond mere technical connections and, instead, serve as powerful conduits for emotions. Through a deep understanding of custom creation, you can imbue your edits with purpose and intrigue, leading your viewer on a captivating journey through time and space using compelling visual cues:

- **Experiment with effects**: Try different effects and modifications on adjustment layers to create unique and visually appealing transitions

- **Timing and duration**: Pay attention to the timing and duration of your transitions to ensure that they flow naturally within the context of your video

- **Sound design**: Consider incorporating sound effects or music to complement your custom transitions and enhance the overall viewer experience

Creating directional blur and motion blur transitions

Directional blur and motion blur provide dynamic and eye-catching effects that add a sense of motion and energy to your videos. By understanding the techniques and tools involved in creating directional blur and motion blur transitions, you can elevate the visual storytelling of your projects and captivate your viewer.

Understanding directional blur transitions

Directional blur transitions are effects that simulate a directional motion while blurring the footage. They are commonly used to transition between two clips or introduce a new scene. The purpose of directional blur transitions is to create a visually appealing and engaging transition that captures the viewer's attention.

The benefits and applications of directional blur transitions

Directional blurs can add a lot of dynamism and style to your videos in Premiere Pro. Here's a breakdown of their benefits and applications:

- **Visual impact**: Directional blur transitions add a dynamic and energetic element to your videos, enhancing the overall visual impact

- **Scene transitions**: They are effective for transitioning between different scenes or locations, creating a seamless connection

- **Style and creativity**: Directional blur transitions allow you to showcase your creative flair and unique style in video editing

Applying directional blur transitions

To apply a directional blur transition in Premiere Pro, follow these steps:

1. Import the footage clips you want to transition between into your project.

2. Place the two clips on the timeline, with the outgoing clip preceding the incoming clip.

3. Locate the **Effects** panel by going to the **Window** menu and selecting **Effects**.

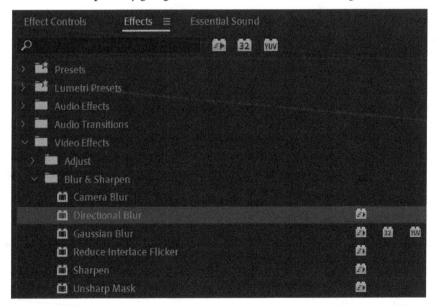

Figure 5.31 – The Effects panel in Premiere Pro

4. In the **Effects** panel, search for the **Directional Blur** effect.

5. Drag and drop the **Directional Blur** effect onto the outgoing clip on the timeline.

6. In the **Effect Controls** panel, adjust the parameters of the **Directional Blur** effect to control the amount of blur and the direction of the directional blur.

7. Preview the transition to ensure that it achieves the desired effect.

Customizing directional blur transitions

Premiere Pro provides various options to customize directional blur transitions, allowing you to achieve the desired look and feel. Here are some customization options:

- **Blur amount**: Adjust the intensity of the blur effect by modifying the blur amount parameter.

- **Blur length**: Control the center point of the directional blur effect to determine the focal point of the transition.

- **Direction**: Experiment with different directions and rotation angles to create unique motion blur transitions.

- **Keyframes**: Utilize keyframes to animate the directional blur effect over time, adding more complexity and visual interest to the transition.

Understanding motion blur transitions

Motion blur transitions involve a motioning effect combined with blurring to create a sense of motion and depth. These transitions simulate the camera moving in or out, adding a cinematic touch to your videos. The purpose of motion blur transitions is to smoothly transition between clips while adding a dynamic and visually captivating element.

The benefits and applications of motion blur transitions

But what is the reason for motion blur? Why not stick with the established fades and dissolves? Well, motion blur provides a wide range of advantages, enhancing the smoothness of your edits and adding emotional impact and visual appeal. Here are what you need to focus on when applying motion blur transitions:

- **Depth and dimension**: Motion blur transitions create a sense of depth and dimension, making your videos visually engaging

- **Emphasis and focus**: They can draw attention to specific elements within a scene or highlight key moments in your storytelling

- **Cinematic touch**: Motion blur transitions add a cinematic quality to your videos, giving them a professional and polished look

Applying motion blur transitions

To apply a motion blur transition in Premiere Pro, follow these steps:

1. Arrange two clips on the timeline, with the outgoing clip preceding the incoming clip.

2. Locate the **Effects** panel in Premiere Pro.

3. Search for the **Transform** effect in the **Effects** panel.

Figure 5.32 – Transform in the Effects panel in Premiere Pro

4. Drag and drop the **Transform** effect onto the outgoing clip on the timeline.

5. In the **Effect Controls** panel, adjust the parameters of the **Transform** effect to control the motion and blur settings.

6. Preview the transition to ensure that it achieves the desired effect.

Customizing motion blur transitions

Premiere Pro offers customization options to tailor motion blur transitions to your specific needs. Here are some customization options:

- **Motion amount**: Adjust the intensity of the motion effect by modifying the motion amount parameter.

- **Blur amount**: Control the level of blur applied during the transition by adjusting the blur amount parameter.

- **Center point**: Set the center point of the motion effect to determine the focal point of the transition.

- **Keyframes**: Utilize keyframes to animate the motion and blur effects over time, creating dynamic and intricate motion blur transitions.

Tips and best practices for directional blur and motion blur transitions

No more abrupt transitions and stagnant edits! The following techniques will elevate your scenes, seamlessly connecting them with a captivating cinematic allure. Imagine seamless scene transitions reminiscent of action-packed films, ethereal dissolves found in romantic comedies, and a wide range of other captivating visual effects.

However, before we dive into the incredible capabilities of blur, let's first acknowledge some important aspects of the technique that you can explore:

- **Experimenting with speed and timing**: Try different speeds and timing for your directional blur and motion blur transitions to find the most visually appealing effect. Varying the speed can create different moods and impact the overall pacing of your video.

- **Combining blur with other transitions and effects**: Don't be afraid to combine directional blur and motion blur transitions with other transitions and effects in Premiere Pro. Experiment with crossfades, dissolves, and other visual effects to create unique and captivating transitions.

- **Previewing and refining**: Always preview your directional blur and motion blur transitions to evaluate their effectiveness. Make necessary adjustments, such as modifying parameters or timing, to refine the transitions and achieve the desired visual impact.

Next, picture this – a single edit effortlessly transitioning between screens of different orientations, from TikTok's vertical scroll to Twitter's landscape feed. Say goodbye to the tedious process of manually cropping and the frustration of zoomed-in shots. Auto Reframe assumes control, employing advanced analysis of your footage to effortlessly optimize it for seamless viewing across all platforms.

Summary

In this chapter, we covered a wide range of topics related to transitions in Adobe Premiere Pro. We started by explaining how to add video transitions using the **Effects** panel, including the drag and drop method. Then, we explored modifying transitions by discussing alignment options and working with transition handles for precise timing and duration control. Additionally, we delved into transition properties such as opacity adjustments, speed modifications, and motion effects, enabling users to create unique and visually appealing transitions.

We then moved on to audio transitions, explaining how to add them and creating custom audio fades for seamless audio blending. We also discussed the creation of custom transitions using adjustment layers and explored the concepts of directional blur and motion blur transitions, providing step-by-step instructions on their application and customization. By mastering these topics, users can elevate their video editing skills and create captivating content with smooth and engaging transitions.

Having a strong audio foundation is equally important to captivate your viewer. In the next chapter, we'll delve into techniques to get better audio with Premiere Pro. This will ensure your videos not only look great but also sound professional.

6
Enhancing Audio with Premiere Pro

In the world of video production, high-quality audio is just as crucial as stunning visuals. Whether you're working on a short film, documentary, or marketing video, audio can make or break the overall experience for your audience. Adobe Premiere Pro, leading video editing software, offers a comprehensive set of tools and features to help you achieve professional-grade audio in your projects. In this chapter, we'll delve into the techniques and best practices for achieving better audio with Premiere Pro.

In this chapter, we're going to cover the following main topics:

- Understanding audio in Premiere Pro
- Adjusting audio levels – how to make it louder and quieter
- Removing background noise in Premiere Pro
- Using audio presets to adjust audio

Understanding audio in Premiere Pro

Before we dive into the practical aspects, let's take a moment to understand the key concepts related to audio in Premiere Pro:

- *Audio formats and settings*: Premiere Pro supports various audio formats, including WAV, AIFF, MP3, and more. It's essential to select the appropriate format based on your project's requirements. Additionally, pay attention to sample rates and bit depths to ensure the best audio quality.

- *Audio channels*: Understanding audio channels is crucial to proper audio management. Premiere Pro allows you to work with mono, stereo, and even multi-channel audio. Knowing how to handle different channel configurations will improve your audio editing efficiency.

- *Audio meters and monitoring*: Premiere Pro provides audio meters to help you monitor audio levels. Learn how to interpret these meters to maintain consistent audio levels and avoid distortion or clipping.

- *Audio effects and transitions*: Premiere Pro offers a wide array of audio effects and transitions. These tools can enhance your audio, fix issues, and add creative touches. We'll explore some essential audio effects and how to use them effectively.

Adjusting audio levels – how to make it louder and quieter

Some of the most common effects to adjust in audio editing are the **equalization** (**EQ**), reverb, compression, and delay of audio level to help properly control the volume of your audio clips and ensure a balanced and pleasant listening experience for your audience. Throughout this chapter, we will delve into different techniques for adjusting the audio levels within Premiere Pro. These methods will enable you to enhance your video projects by mastering the skill of audio volume control.

Understanding audio levels

Before we begin, let's briefly cover some essential concepts related to audio levels in Premiere Pro:

- **Decibels (dB)**: Audio levels are measured in dB, representing the volume or amplitude of sound. Positive values represent louder audio, while negative values indicate quieter audio.

- Peak versus **root mean square** (**RMS**): Premiere Pro displays both peak and RMS audio levels. Peak levels show the highest amplitude of the audio waveform, while RMS levels indicate the average loudness over time.

- Normalization: Normalizing audio adjusts the overall level of a clip so that the loudest peak reaches a specified dB value. This process can be helpful to bring all your audio clips to a consistent volume.

Making audio louder

There are several ways to make audio louder in Premiere Pro. The simplest method is to use the clip volume slider in the **Essential Sound** panel. However, if you need to significantly increase the volume of audio, you may need to use the **Audio Gain** dialog box.

Everything you need to know about the Essential Sound panel

The Essential Sound panel is a powerful tool designed to streamline audio editing and mixing within Premiere Pro. It offers a simplified interface, making it accessible even for users without extensive audio production experience. Let's explore more about the Essential Sound panel.

Here are the key features of the Essential Sound panel:

- *Audio type categorization*: It categorizes audio into four main types: dialog, music, **sound effects** (**SFX**), and ambience. This categorization helps tailor adjustments and effects specifically to each audio type.

- *Presets and controls*: Each audio type has dedicated presets and controls that optimize the sound for its intended purpose. For example, dialog presets might focus on noise reduction and speech clarity, while music presets could adjust EQ and stereo width.

Accessing the panel

The Essential Sound panel in Premiere Pro is a powerful tool designed to simplify audio mixing and editing, especially for users who might not have extensive audio experience. Here's the walkthrough on how to access the panel:

1. Go to the **Window** menu in Premiere Pro. Select **Essential Sound**.

    Figure 6.1 shows the features you can find in the **Essential Sound** panel:

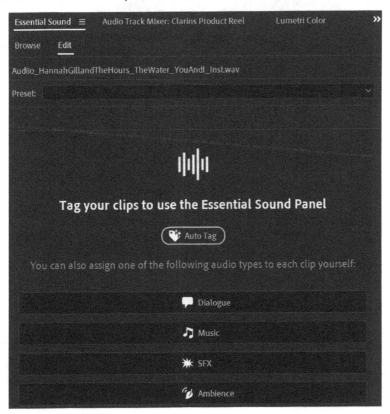

Figure 6.1 – The Essential Sound panel in Premiere Pro

2. The panel categorizes audio into four main types:

    - **Dialogue**: Focuses on speech clarity and reducing background noise
    - **Music**: Emphasizes volume consistency and stereo enhancement
    - **SFX**: Provides options for adding punch and shaping the sound
    - **Ambience**: Offers tools for adjusting the background atmosphere and reducing unwanted noise

3. Once you choose the audio category, you will see more options like the following:

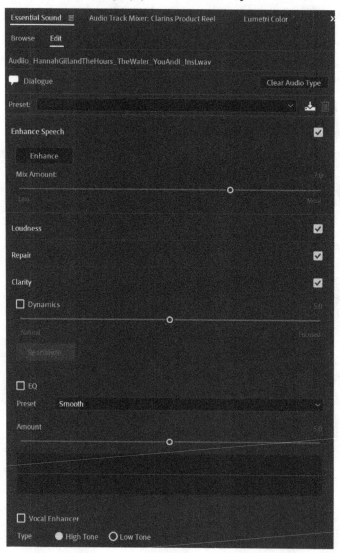

Figure 6.2 – Audio options in the Essential Sound panel in Premiere Pro

Here are the essential audio editing tools that you should pay attention to:

- *Level meters*: Monitor audio levels and adjust gain for optimal levels
- *Faders*: Control the volume of individual audio tracks for precise mixing
- *Panning*: Adjust the stereo positioning of audio tracks to create a wider or narrower soundstage
- *Loudness*: Ensure consistent audio levels across different clips for a balanced mix
- *Repair*: Reduce noise, hum, clicks, and other unwanted sounds for cleaner audio
- *Effects*: Apply basic audio effects such as EQ, reverb, compression, and more for creative sound design
- *Fade handles*: Easily create fade-in and fade-out transitions for smooth transitions between audio clips

There are more settings accessible inside each feature, such as the following:

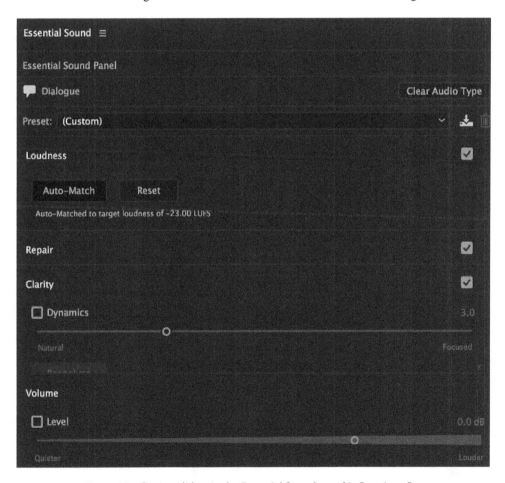

Figure 6.3 – Setting sliders in the Essential Sound panel in Premiere Pro

Here are some additional features of the Essential Sound panel:

- *Auto-match*: Automatically adjust the volume of background ambience to match the level of dialog, ensuring a consistent soundscape

- *Duration*: Modify the length of audio clips directly within the panel for precise timing

- *Custom presets*: Create and save your own custom presets for frequently used adjustments

Remember, the Essential Sound panel is a powerful tool for basic audio editing. For more advanced audio work, you can access additional tools within Premiere Pro or switch to dedicated audio editing software such as Adobe Audition.

Using the clip volume control

Learn how to adjust the audio gain by using either the selection tool or the timeline method. Follow these steps to get started:

1. Open your Premiere Pro project and select the audio clip you want to make louder on the timeline:

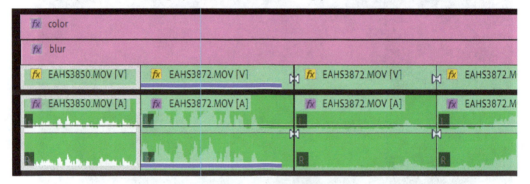

Figure 6.4 – Audio clip on the timeline

2. In the **Effect Controls** panel, locate the **Volume** section. Increase the slider to raise the clip's volume. Be cautious not to increase it too much, as this may result in distortion or clipping. Here's how to adjust the clip volume in the **Effect Controls** panel:

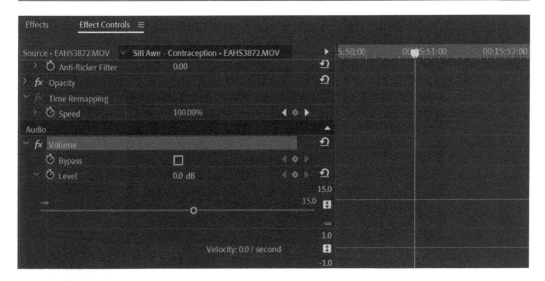

Figure 6.5 – Adjusting clip volume in the Effect Controls panel

3. For alternative volume adjustment, use the shortcut keys: press [to decrease and] to increase. Simply select the audio clip in your timeline and use the keys for on-the-fly volume control.

Adjusting audio gain

Learn how to adjust the audio gain by using either the selection tool or the timeline method. Follow these steps to get started:

1. To modify the volume of your selected audio, simply right-click on it and choose **Áudio Gain...**:

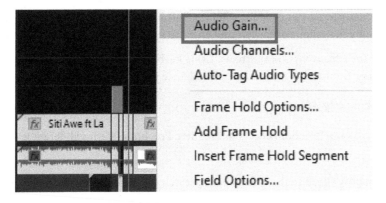

Figure 6.6 – Adjusting Audio Gain for a clip on the timeline

2. Enter a value in the field that appears in the dialog box for adjusting the gain. If you wish to amplify the volume, input a positive value. To decrease the volume, simply input a negative value:

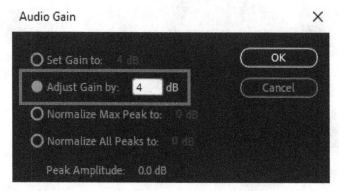

Figure 6.7 – Enter an Adjust Gain value in the field

3. The **Adjust Gain by:** feature allows you to conveniently raise or lower the volume by a specified number of dB without having to set it to a specific dB level.

4. For example, to raise the volume by 4 dB, just enter *4* and click **OK**.

5. Additionally, the **Audio Gain** panel can be accessed by using the *G* shortcut key.

As you further develop your video editing skills in Premiere Pro, keep these important points in mind:

*   Remember to pay attention to the balance of your audio. The volume of your content can greatly impact your audience's engagement. Strive for a harmonious blend that enhances your video content without overshadowing it.

*   Utilize keyframes to achieve dynamic volume adjustments. This is particularly helpful when you want to modify the volume of background music to suit voiceovers or other audio components.

*   Remember the effectiveness of shortcuts. Using keyboard shortcuts such as *[* and *]* for volume adjustment or *G* for audio gain can greatly enhance your workflow efficiency.

Applying the Amplify effect

There are two ways to amplify audio effects in Premiere Pro, both offering different levels of control and precision:

1. Add the Amplify effect: In the **Effects** panel, search for the **Amplify** effect and apply it to the audio clip:

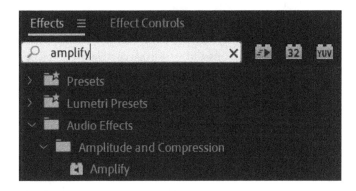

Figure 6.8 – Finding the Amplify effect in the Effects panel

2. Adjust amplitude: In the **Effect Controls** panel, you can adjust the amplitude using the **Amplification** parameter. Increase it to make the audio louder. Use the audio meters to monitor the levels and avoid over-amplification:

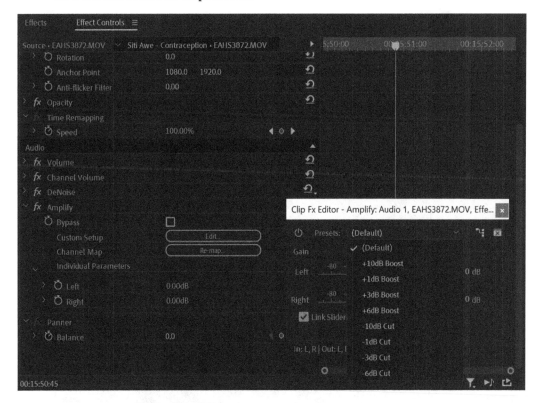

Figure 6.9 – Adjusting the Amplitude effect

Sound is a crucial element in the creation of videos. It is crucial in crafting a captivating experience for the viewer. The audio component plays a crucial role in establishing the atmosphere and ambience of a video. It has the power to evoke emotions and establish a captivating ambience. Additionally, it has the ability to direct the viewer's focus and elevate the overall enjoyment of the viewing process. Having high-quality audio is crucial for a video to captivate and engage the viewer, ensuring their undivided attention. When it comes to enhancing the audio of a video project, there are various methods to achieve this in Adobe Premiere Pro – all detailed previously.

Making audio quieter

The volume of your video is a crucial element that should not be overlooked. Playing music at excessively high volumes can not only irritate your audience but also potentially provoke their anger. Conversely, having the volume set too low can lead to a frustrating experience. Luckily, for those utilizing Adobe Premiere Pro, there are multiple methods available to manage the volume.

Using the clip volume control (again)

Adjusting clip volume within the **Effect Controls** panel in Premiere Pro offers a precise way to modify audio levels. Here's how:

1. Select the audio clip: Similar to making audio louder, select the audio clip you want to make quieter on the timeline.

2. Adjust clip volume: In the **Effect Controls** panel, locate the **Volume** section. Decrease the slider to lower the clip's volume:

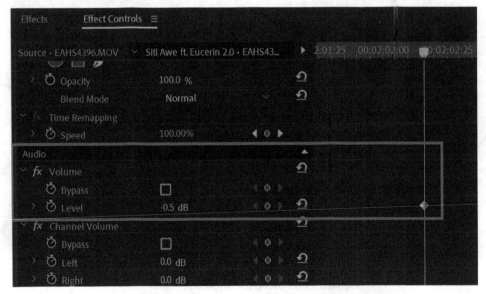

Figure 6.10 – Adjusting clip volume in the Effects panel

Using the clip volume control effectively shapes the sonic landscape of your video. But what about those annoying silences or distracting background noises that persist within your clips? Have no fear, audio enthusiasts, because Premiere Pro has a powerful tool at your disposal: the Auto Gate effect. It's here to help you eliminate unwanted silence and enhance the clarity of your audio tracks.

Applying the Auto Gate effect

An auto gate is essentially a noise gate, acting like a volume control that automatically opens and closes based on a set threshold. The Auto Gate effect is a powerful tool that expertly eliminates any pesky moments of silence or distracting background noise that may be hiding in your audio tracks. It functions as a digital gatekeeper, filtering out the noise during moments of silence and allowing only the most captivating sounds to reach your audience's ears.

Follow these steps to get started:

1. Add the Auto Gate effect: In the **Effects** panel, search for the **Dynamics** effect and apply it to the audio clip:

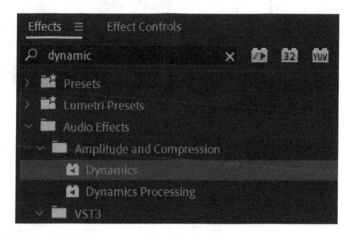

Figure 6.11 – Adding the Dynamics effect

2. Configure threshold and reduction: In the **Effect Controls** panel, pay attention to these four controls: threshold, attack, release, and hold. Adjust the **Threshold** parameter to set the level at which the gate starts to reduce the volume. Use the **Reduction** parameter to determine how much quieter the audio becomes when it falls below the threshold. So, think of a noise gate as an on/off switch that automatically turns that channel on or off when the volume reaches a certain threshold. We'll showcase a screenshot next to visually demonstrate how you can adjust the threshold in Premiere Pro.

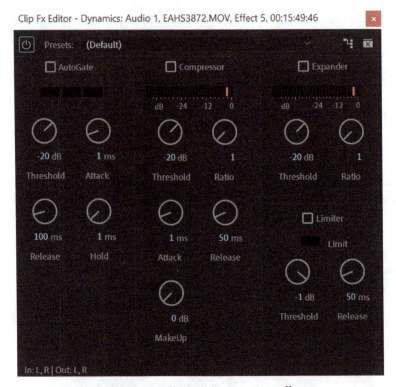

Figure 6.12 – Adjusting the Auto Gate effect

3. We established a threshold that triggers the channel to turn on and allow you to hear it when the voice breaks it. Conversely, if the voice drops below the threshold due to no talking, the channel is automatically turned off.

Let's look at the following figure to understand further:

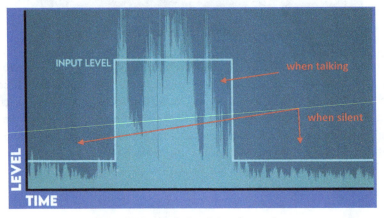

Figure 6.13 – Audio level signal over time

For example, the input audio level may be the signal received from a microphone. When you don't say anything, the audio signal will be low. When you start talking, the audio signal will increase to a specific level. When you're done talking, the audio signal will return to a low level. Even if you are not talking, the low-level audio stream will cause some noise on the channel, as indicated in the red area in *Figure 6.14*:

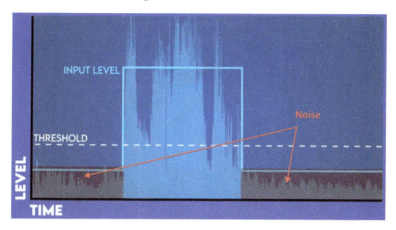

Figure 6.14 – Audio noise when silent

The aim of the Auto Gate effect is to establish the **Threshold**, which will silence the microphone when the audio volume drops below that **Threshold**. When the input level is below the **Threshold**, the final output is muted; when the audio level is above the **Threshold**, it opens up the gate or unmutes the channel.To truly understand how threshold and reduction perimeter work, let's take a look at the following screenshot. It will visually represent the auto gate effect *cutting through* the audio level below the threshold you set.

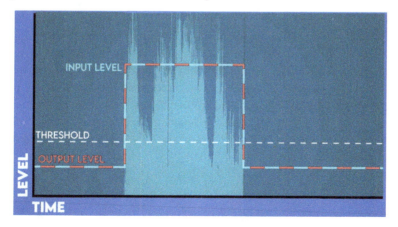

Figure 6.15 – Cutting through the audio level below the Threshold

When you set the **Threshold** to a certain audio level, be aware. The higher the **Threshold**, the more amplitude and volume you require in your input signal to pass through the **AutoGate**. The lower you set the **Threshold**, the simpler it is for background noise to pass through the gate since you are lowering the bar. Now, let's look at the following screenshot. It will show you exactly where to adjust the threshold within the Auto Gate effect controls panel in Premiere Pro.

Figure 6.16 – Adjusting the Threshold

By adjusting different parameters, you can hear how they impact the sound of the voice. It's essential to be cautious while setting these parameters. If the threshold is too high, the voice may stutter as it switches on and off too quickly. Alternatively, if the threshold is set too low, even minor disturbances could activate the auto gate due to its heightened sensitivity. Thus, it is essential to strike a harmonious equilibrium between embracing the speaker's unique voice and filtering out any distracting background noise. Beyond the threshold, the auto gate effect offers even more control with **Attack** and **Release** knobs. The next screenshot will take you inside the **AutoGate** panel and visually demonstrate how to adjust these knobs to fine-tune the gating behavior.

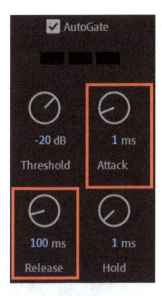

Figure 6.17 – Adjusting the Attack and Release knobs

The **Threshold** is the volume at which the noise gate begins to operate. Next, the **Attack** and **Release** knobs allow you to control how quickly the channels are turned back on after the threshold is broken. Think of it as a *fade in* effect where it allows the audio to linearly increase to avoid a *pop* sound in transitioning volumes between two clips. **Hold** specifies the duration of time the option will remain active after the threshold is surpassed, while **Release** specifies the rate at which it will terminate when the volume falls below the threshold. As the following screenshot shows, pay attention to the colored indicator, which helps visualize the audio currently being reduced by the effect.

Figure 6.18 – Auto Gate color indicator

The three-color audio meter at the top lets you see what Auto Gate is doing as well. This is what it implies:

- *Red*: The gate is muting the track
- *Yellow*: The audio level is nearing the threshold line
- *Green*: The gate is unmuting the rails and all signals are passing through

If you are using Auto Gate for the first time, set the threshold to extremely high and progressively reduce it. Once it reaches where most of your signal wants to come through, begin to dial in the other settings, Attack, Release, and Hold.

Finally, it is up to you to experiment with the settings and discover the finest sound. Mastering this skill requires patience and careful observation. By attentively studying the mechanics of the gate and striving to replicate its organic sound, you can achieve the desired result.

Keyframing audio levels

For more precise control over audio levels, you can use keyframes to create volume changes over time as follows:

1. Access the audio clip: Select the audio clip and open the **Effect Controls** panel:

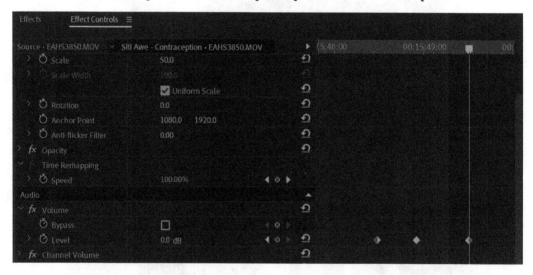

Figure 6.19 – Add keyframes to the Volume effect

2. Set keyframes: Click the **Volume** stopwatch icon to enable keyframing. Then, add keyframes at specific points on the audio track.

3. Adjust keyframes: Drag the keyframes up or down to increase or decrease the volume at those specific points. Smoothly adjust the curve between keyframes for natural-sounding audio transitions. The next screenshot will show you the timeline and how to use keyframes to create precise volume changes over time within your audio clip.

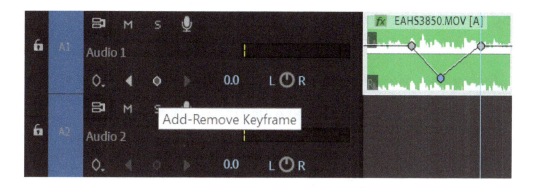

Figure 6.20 – Adjusting audio keyframes on the timeline

Now, after carefully adjusting your audio using keyframes, you might be wondering about those bothersome background noises such as the air conditioner's hum or the distant traffic rumble. Have no worries, as a fresh solution is about to unfold, revealing the techniques to eliminate bothersome noise and guarantee your audio sparkles with crystal-clear perfection!

Removing background noise in Premiere Pro

Background noise can be a common nuisance in audio recordings, diminishing the overall quality and professionalism of your video projects. Fortunately, Adobe Premiere Pro offers powerful tools and techniques to help you effectively remove background noise and improve the clarity of your audio. In the next sub-sections, let's explore step-by-step instructions on how to tackle background noise using Premiere Pro's built-in features.

Understanding background noise

Before diving into the removal process, it's essential to recognize the different types of background noise that can occur in audio recordings:

- *Constant background noise*: Steady background sounds, such as air conditioning hums, traffic noise, or electrical buzzing, remain consistent throughout the recording

- *Random background noise*: Occasional or sporadic noises, such as footsteps, door slams, or sudden external sounds, can disrupt an otherwise clean audio track

- *Background hum or hiss*: Often encountered in older recordings or recordings made with poor equipment, this noise presents itself as a low hum or hissing sound

The Noise Reduction effect in Premiere Pro is a powerful tool for improving the audio quality of your videos. It is a straightforward effect with numerous applications. Whether you're making a personal video or a professional video for work, using the Noise Reduction effect is a great way to improve the sound quality of your video.

Using the Noise Reduction effect

The Noise Reduction effect in Premiere Pro is useful for several reasons:

- *To improve your video's overall sound quality*: Background noise can be distracting and make it difficult to hear dialog or other important sounds. The Noise Reduction effect can assist in removing this noise, resulting in a clearer and more professional-sounding video.

- *To make your video more appealing to viewers*: A video with good sound quality is more likely to be watched and enjoyed by viewers. Background noise can be annoying and distracting, making it difficult to focus on the video's content. Using the Noise Reduction effect can help to make your viewers viewing experience more enjoyable.

- *To meet technical standards*: When submitting your video to certain platforms, such as YouTube or Netflix, you may be required to meet technical requirements. Some platforms, for example, require that the audio level of your video be within a certain range. The Noise Reduction effect can assist you in meeting these technical requirements.

Let's proceed with applying the Noise Reduction effect to the entire audio track:

1. Select the audio clip: Choose the audio clip you want to clean up and ensure it's selected on the timeline.

2. Access the **Effects** panel: Go to the **Effects** tab, then navigate to **Audio Effects | Noise Reduction/ Restoration** and find the **DeNoise** effect:

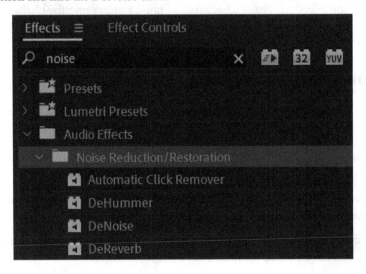

Figure 6.21 – Apply the Noise Reduction/Restoration effect in the Effects panel

3. Apply the effect: Drag and drop the **Noise Reduction (process)** effect onto the audio clip on the timeline.

4. Adjust the Noise Reduction settings: In the **Effect Controls** panel, adjust the **Noise Reduction** slider to determine the strength of the noise reduction. Be cautious not to overdo it, as excessive noise reduction can negatively impact the audio quality. The next screenshot will take you inside the **Effects Controls** panel and demonstrate how to adjust the Noise Reduction effect for broader noise reduction across your audio clip.

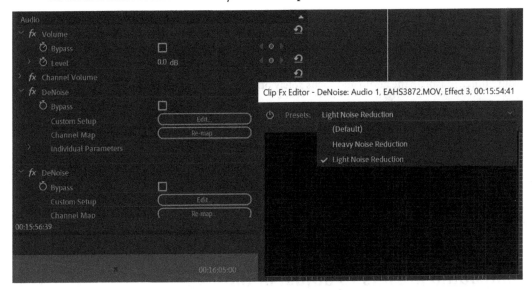

Figure 6.22 – Adjusting the Noise Reduction effect

The Noise Reduction effect serves as your primary tool for combating unwanted noise. Simply drag it onto your noisy clip and witness how Premiere Pro skillfully analyzes and eliminates undesirable background sounds. Fine-tune the reduction amount by adjusting the sliders for a more natural audio balance. Keep in mind that a moderate amount of noise removal can greatly enhance your audio quality. However, excessive noise removal can result in a thin and lifeless sound.

Now, with your audio track expertly crafted, we'll embark on a new journey in the next topic. Here, we'll explore the techniques of enhancing and enriching your sound, adding layers of depth and richness to elevate your audio masterpieces to new heights.

Fine-tuning with additional settings

Premiere Pro offers additional settings to further refine the noise reduction process:

- **DeHummer** and **DeEsser**: Use this setting to target and reduce background hum or hiss if present in your audio.

- **DeNoise**: These settings allow you to adjust the frequency range targeted for noise reduction. For instance, if the background noise is mostly low-frequency hum, reduce the **Noise Reduction Low** setting.

- **Sensitivity:** This setting controls how sensitive the noise reduction process is to background noise. A higher sensitivity value may remove more noise but can potentially affect the desired audio.

- **Frequency smoothing:** Use this setting to smooth out the frequency response after noise reduction, preserving the natural tonal balance of the audio.

Preview and adjust

Once you've applied the Noise Reduction effect and adjusted the settings, it's important to listen closely to the audio track. Make sure the unwanted noise is reduced without affecting the important sounds in your audio. To isolate the audio and focus solely on noise reduction, use the Solo Track feature.

Now that you've become an expert in perfecting your audio, it's time to enhance it with some captivating SFX! But before you delve into the intricacies of EQ and compression, let's discover a powerful tool that can enhance your workflow and take your audio skills to new heights: presets. Premiere Pro provides a wide range of pre-configured audio settings that effortlessly enhance your tracks with a touch of professionalism and creative finesse.

Premiere Pro audio presets are a great way to save time when adjusting audio. With a single click, you can apply a set of audio effects to a clip. This is especially useful if you need to apply the same effects to multiple clips or are unfamiliar with audio effects.

Using audio presets to adjust audio

In the fast-paced world of video production, efficiency is paramount. Adobe Premiere Pro offers a valuable feature known as audio presets, which can save you time and effort when adjusting audio settings. These presets are pre-configured settings that can be applied to your audio clips, eliminating the need to manually adjust each parameter. In this sub-section, we'll explore how to use audio presets effectively to expedite the audio adjustment process and enhance your workflow in Premiere Pro.

Understanding audio presets

Audio presets in Premiere Pro are pre-defined combinations of effects and settings that can be saved and re-used across different projects. These presets enable you to achieve specific audio treatments quickly without having to recreate them from scratch. Premiere Pro comes with a selection of built-in audio presets, and you can also create and save your own custom presets.

Accessing audio presets in Premiere Pro

Remember, these presets can also be a starting point for further customization to achieve your desired sound. Let's proceed with applying the audio effect to the entire audio track:

1. Open the **Effects** panel: Launch Premiere Pro and navigate to the **Effects** tab, typically located in the bottom-left corner of the interface:

Figure 6.23 – Open the Effects panel

2. Locate the audio presets: Expand the **Audio Effects** folder and look for the various sub-folders that contain audio presets. These sub-folders might include **Modulation**, **Reverb**, **Special**, and more:

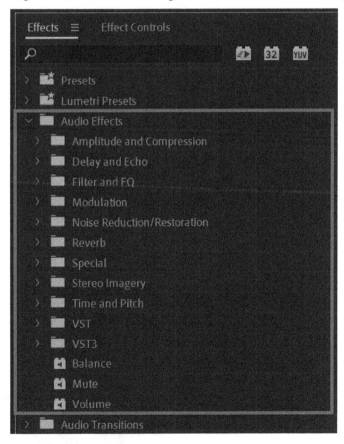

Figure 6.24 – The Audio Effects folder in the Effects panel

3. Apply the audio preset: Select the audio clip on the timeline that you want to apply the preset to. Then, simply drag and drop the desired preset onto the clip. Premiere Pro will automatically apply the preset's settings to the audio clip. The next screenshot takes you to the timeline, demonstrating how to easily apply these presets to your audio clips.

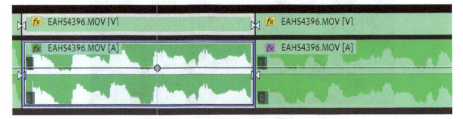

Figure 6.25 – Apply the preset on the timeline

However, it's important to keep in mind that applying effects is only the initial stage. After establishing your presets, it's crucial to adjust the settings to cater to your unique requirements. Feel free to explore, adjust the settings, and pay close attention to the way the sound develops. Becoming skilled at these adjustments is like crafting your audio, taking it from *good* to *breathtaking*.

Armed with presets and the ability to make precise manual adjustments, you now have the tools to turn your audio tracks into extraordinary sonic creations. Always remember, achieving the ideal harmony between the pre-configured magic and your own unique creative flair is the key to true artistry. So go forth, brave editor, and confidently wield these audio tools!

Now, get ready to explore more about customizing the audio presets.

Customizing audio presets

While using the built-in audio presets can be time-saving, creating your own custom presets allows for personalized and consistent audio treatments across projects:

1. Customize the audio effects: Apply the audio effects and adjust the settings on an audio clip until you achieve the desired sound treatment.

2. Save the custom preset: Once you've created your custom audio treatment, right-click on the audio clip and select **Save Preset...**. Give your preset a descriptive name and choose an appropriate folder to save it in. AS the below screenshot will show you how to save your customized audio preset directly within the **Effects** panel. This will allow you to quickly apply the same settings to future projects, saving you valuable time and effort.

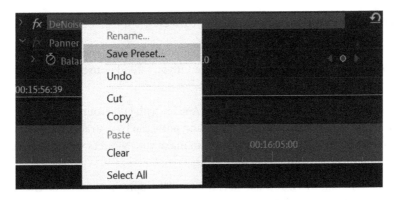

Figure 6.26 – Saving the preset in the Effects panel

3. Reusing custom presets: Your custom audio preset will now be available in the appropriate folder in the **Effects** panel. To apply it to other audio clips, simply drag and drop the preset onto the desired clips.

Organizing audio presets

As your library of audio presets grows, organizing them becomes essential for efficient usage:

- *Create custom folders*: Premiere Pro allows you to create custom folders within the Effects panel to categorize and store your audio presets based on different criteria, such as effect type or project requirements.

- *Rename and group presets*: Give descriptive names to your custom presets to make them easily identifiable. Additionally, you can group similar presets together within the same folder.

- *Delete unnecessary presets*: Regularly review your audio presets and remove any redundant or obsolete ones to keep your library clutter-free and organized.

In this section, we learned about three essential audio editing features in Premiere Pro:

- *Adjusting audio levels*: This allows you to make audio louder or quieter, which is important for ensuring that your audio is consistent and easy to hear

- *Removing background noise*: Removing background noise can help to improve the overall sound quality of your videos and make them more engaging for viewers

- *Using audio presets*: When adjusting audio, this can save you a lot of time and effort, especially if you need to apply the same effects to multiple clips

You can gain a number of benefits by mastering these features:

- *Your videos will sound more professional*: When your audio is good, your videos will appear more professional. This is especially important if you intend to use your videos for business or marketing purposes.

- *Your videos will be more interesting to viewers*: A video with good sound quality is more likely to be watched and enjoyed by viewers. Background noise can be distracting and make it difficult to concentrate on the video's content. You can make your viewers viewing experience more enjoyable by using the Noise Reduction effect.

- *You will save time and effort*: You can quickly and easily apply the same audio effects to multiple clips by using audio presets. This can save you a significant amount of time and effort, particularly if you're working on a large or complex video project.

Overall, mastering Premiere Pro's audio editing features can help you create better-sounding and more engaging videos. If you are serious about video editing, it is worth your time to learn how to use these features properly.

Summary

By combining the knowledge gained from each chapter, you can now confidently approach audio editing in Adobe Premiere Pro, making significant improvements to the audio quality of your video projects. From adjusting audio levels to removing background noise and applying custom presets, you have a comprehensive set of tools and techniques at your disposal.

Remember that audio is a crucial component of storytelling, and thoughtful audio editing can enhance emotions, engagement, and overall impact. Continue to experiment, learn, and refine your audio skills in Premiere Pro to create captivating and immersive video experiences for your audience.

As you progress in your journey as a video editor and audio enthusiast, stay up-to-date with the latest features and advancements in Premiere Pro to leverage the full potential of this powerful software. Keep exploring new possibilities, and don't hesitate to push the boundaries of your creativity to produce audio that captivates and resonates with your viewers. This chapter equips you with a solid foundation in audio editing.

The next chapter ushers in the Essential Sound panel, empowering you to make precise adjustments and enhance your audio with ease by learning techniques like ducking music for seamless dialogue and crafting dynamic remixes to elevate your project's audio impact.

7

Editing Audio Easily in the Essential Sound Panel

The **Essential Sound** panel is a feature within Adobe Premiere Pro designed to simplify the audio editing process. It provides a visually intuitive interface that enables both beginners and seasoned professionals to make precise adjustments without the need for complex audio engineering knowledge. The panel offers a range of options, including basic audio mixing, noise reduction, and background music adjustment.

In this chapter, we're going to cover the following main topics:

- Ducking music with the Essential Sound panel
- Remixing music

By the end, you'll have the skills to enhance your audio tracks with ease using the ducking music exercise. You'll also be able to turn your video creations into captivating sonic experiences by remixing music.

Ducking music with the Essential Sound panel

Ducking music is a crucial technique in audio and video production to create a seamless balance between background music and dialogue or narration. It involves reducing the volume of the music track automatically when someone is speaking, allowing the spoken words to be heard clearly without overpowering the background music. The Essential Sound panel offers an efficient and user-friendly way to achieve this effect. In the following subsections, we will explore how to duck music using the Essential Sound panel.

Preparing your project

Before you start ducking music, ensure you have your audio tracks and video clips properly imported into your Premiere Pro project. Organize your timeline by placing the music track on a separate audio track above the dialogue or narration track. This setup is crucial for implementing the ducking effect effectively.

To help you visualize the key steps involved in preparing your project, take a look at the following screenshot:

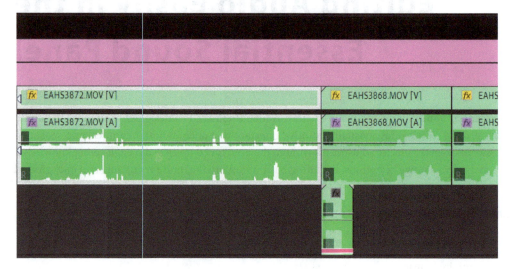

Figure 7.1 – Importing video and audio tracks into the timeline

Now that you've primed your project for seamless music ducking with the Essential Sound panel, let's tackle identifying the all-important dialogue track. Pinpointing the dialogue amongst your various audio clips is crucial for applying the ducking effect precisely. In the next section, we'll explore several methods to confidently distinguish your dialogue track, ensuring that your audio sounds polished and your audience hears every word clearly.

Identifying the track types using Audio Tag

To begin ducking the music, you need to identify the track types. In the **Essential Sound** panel, click on the audio clip that contains the dialogue or narration or use *Shift + click* to choose all the clips in that track. Once you've made your selection, navigate to the **Essential Sound** panel and click on **Audio Tag** to assign the **Dialogue** audio type.

Here's where you can find **Audio Tag** in the **Essential Sound** panel:

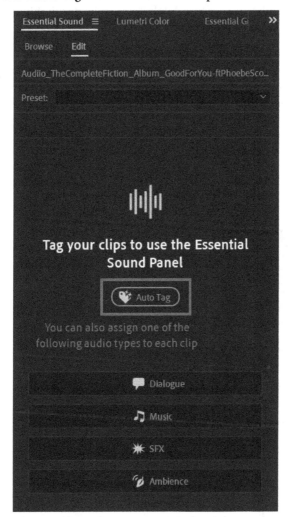

Figure 7.2 – Audio Tag in the Essential Sound panel

The **Essential Sound** panel in Premiere Pro streamlines audio editing by categorizing your audio clips into four distinct types: **Dialogue**, **Music**, **Sound Effects** (**SFX**), and **Ambience**. Each category offers tools and presets designed to enhance that type of audio, as listed here:

- **Dialogue**: This category focuses on spoken voices within your project. Tools here help with clarity, reducing background noise, and evening out volume levels for consistent intelligibility.

- **Music**: This category caters to background music or scores. You'll find tools for adjusting the overall feel of the music, such as adding EQ or spatial effects, to better complement your visuals.

- **SFX**: This category handles all the sound effects you add to your project, such as explosions, foley (everyday sounds), or UI beeps. Tools here can help with things such as emphasizing specific aspects of the sound effect or adding a sense of distance.

- **Ambience**: This category deals with background sounds that set the scene and atmosphere. It could be nature sounds for a forest scene or city noise for a street scene. Tools here can help with things such as balancing the ambience level or adding subtle effects for a more realistic soundscape.

In conclusion, **Dialogue** has clarity boosters, **Music** has mood adjusters, **SFX** has detail editors, and **Ambience** has atmosphere enhancers. This categorization helps you fine-tune each audio element for a clear and polished final mix.

Next, if you choose to tag the audio type manually, you can assign it by right-clicking on the audio clip and selecting **Audio-Tag AudioTypes**, as shown in the following screenshot:

Figure 7.3 – Manually assigning audio types

The new power of AI with audio category tagging enables you to effortlessly explore audio controls and produce professional-grade sound quality videos in Adobe Premiere Pro. With the incredible power of AI, your clips are effortlessly categorized into **Dialogue**, **Music**, **SFX**, or **Ambience**, complete with a brand-new interactive badge. Choose to instantly access the most relevant tools for that specific audio type in the **Essential Sound** panel, as shown in the following screenshot. After the auto-tagging process is finished, you will be able to see interactive Essential Sound badges displayed on every audio clip. By simply selecting the badge, you will be granted automatic access to the **Essential Sound** panel, where you can find a plethora of tools tailored specifically to the type of audio you are working with.

Here's what the timeline looks like with the **Essential Sound** badges applied:

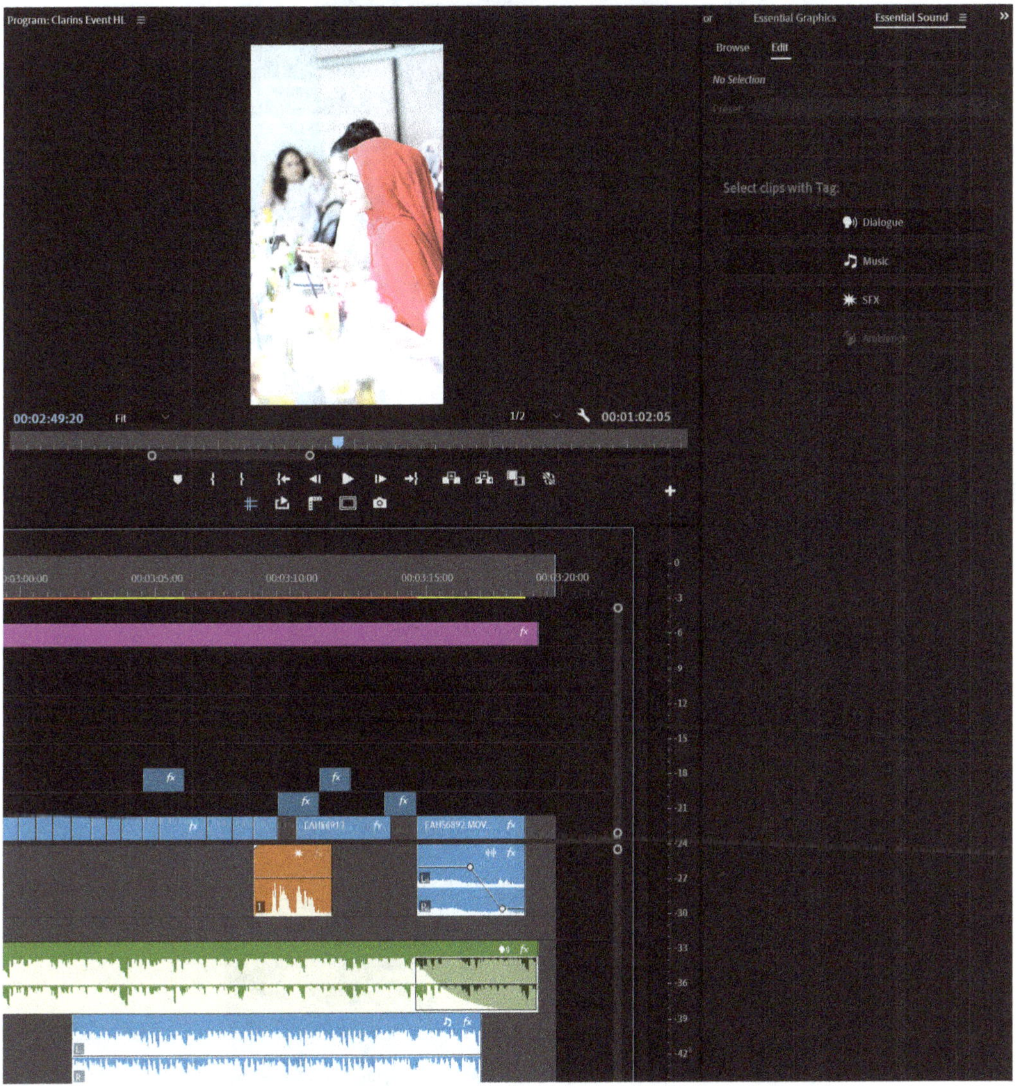

Figure 7.4 – Essential Sound badges applied to audio clips in the timeline

AI automatically detects if your clips are Dialogue, Music, SFX, or Ambience and assigns a new interactive badge. Select an audio type to have fast access to the most relevant tools in the Essential Sound panel.

Interactive audio badges

It's like having a team of expert sound designers at your fingertips. When the badge is selected, it opens up the Essential Sound panel, granting you easy access to a range of useful audio tools. See the following screenshot for reference:

Figure 7.5 – The power of AI automatically adds Essential Sound badges

The audio files will be automatically assigned to different categories, and you can untag them by selecting **Clear Audio Type**.

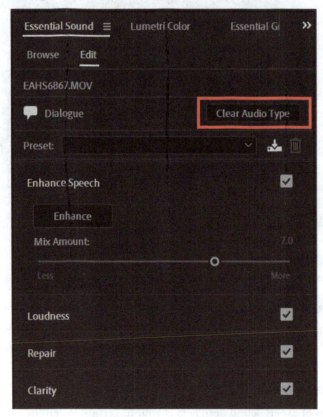

Figure 7.6 – Clearing the audio type in the Essential Sound panel

With the right processes at your disposal, you'll easily identify your audio hero and bring it into the limelight. Keep in mind that effectively communicating with your audio recordist or production team can be a game-changer, helping you save precious time and avoid unnecessary stress down the line. With the knowledge you've gained and a proactive mindset, you can confidently begin your editing journey, assured that any audio mysteries you come across will be easily resolved. Next, let's see how we can apply the ducking effect in audio.

Applying the Ducking effect

With the dialogue track identified, you can now apply the **Ducking** effect to the music track. Click on the audio clip containing the music in your timeline, and the Essential Sound panel will recognize it as **Music**. Next, click on the **Ducking** checkbox in the **Essential Sound** panel for the music track.

The following screenshot provides a snapshot of the key steps involved in applying the **Ducking** effect in your Premiere Pro project:

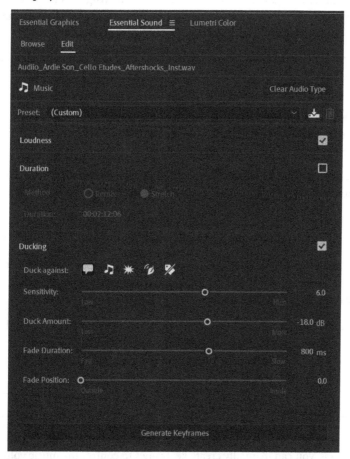

Figure 7.7 – Adjusting the Ducking option in the Essential Sound panel

With the **Ducking** feature of the **Essential Sound** panel, you can effortlessly create smooth and balanced audio conversations. This allows your dialogue to shine while still maintaining the richness and liveliness of your background music and sound effects. Keep in mind that creating an engaging audio mix requires a careful balance and seamless coordination. Through meticulous adjustments to the **Ducking** settings and a keen ear for your mix, you can craft captivating soundscapes that effortlessly transport your audience deep into the core of your narrative.

Next, we'll delve into further details on adjusting the **Ducking** parameters.

Adjusting Ducking parameters

After enabling the **Ducking** effect, you'll notice a set of parameters that you can adjust within the **Essential Sound** panel. These parameters control how the music volume responds when dialogue is present:

- **Sensitivity**: This slider adjusts how responsive the **Ducking** effect is to dialogue volume. Increasing **Sensitivity** triggers the effect of quieter dialogue while decreasing it lessens the effect of soft-spoken words.

- **Duck Amount**: This slider determines the amount of volume reduction applied to the music when there is dialogue. Higher values result in more aggressive ducking, while lower values offer a subtler effect.

- **Fade Duration**: This setting controls how quickly the music volume fades in and out when the **Ducking** effect is applied. Longer fade times create a smoother transition between the music and dialogue, preventing abrupt changes in volume.

- **Fade Position**: This slider allows you to decide on the placement of the background audio fade in relation to the dialogue: either outside, inside, or in the middle.

The Essential Sound panel in Premiere Pro includes a variety of audio presets and tools for fine-tuning. These tools allow you to change the volume, equalizer, and other audio properties of your clips.

In contrast, audio keyframes enable you to make precise and dynamic changes to audio properties over time. You could, for example, use audio keyframes to fade a clip's volume in and out or to boost the bass frequency of a clip at a specific point.

The main difference between using Essential Sound to fine-tune audio and using audio keyframes is that the latter gives you more precise control over your audio. Essential Sound restricts you to using the presets and tools provided. With audio keyframes, you can create any type of audio change that you want.

Applying keyframes

In some cases, the Essential Sound panel's automatic ducking may not provide the precise control you need. In such situations, you can manually create keyframes to control the music volume. To do this, expand the audio track containing the music in your timeline and locate the audio keyframe (a small diamond-shaped icon). Add keyframes at the points where dialogue begins and ends and adjust the music volume between these keyframes to achieve the desired ducking effect.

Here are the necessary steps to apply keyframes in the timeline:

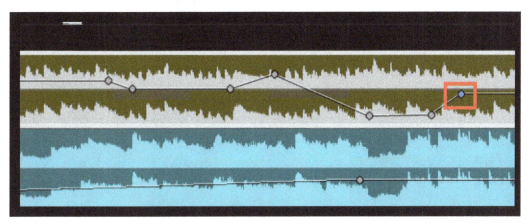

Figure 7.8 – Adjusting audio keyframes in audio clip in the timeline

After you add the keyframes to the audio clip in the timeline, you can see the same **Volume** keyframes added in the **Effect Controls** panel. Here's what it looks like:

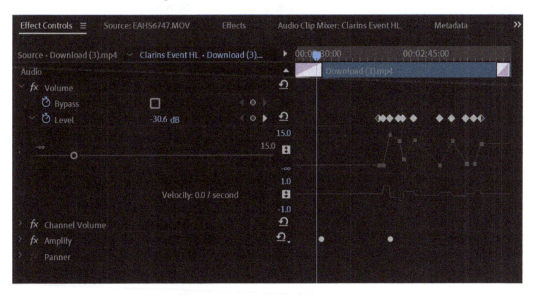

Figure 7.9 – Adding audio keyframes in the Effect Controls panel

With that audio keyframe adjustment, you know how to create engaging audio excursions that ebb and flow with precision and emotion, like a conductor. You must balance technical control and artistic expression to master keyframes. Now, with your audio clips expertly crafted, let's explore the world of musical transformation! In the upcoming section, we'll delve into the world of remixing music, revealing techniques to creatively transform existing songs into custom soundscapes that beautifully enhance the visual narrative of your video.

Remixing music

The Remix feature in Premiere Pro allows you to automatically shorten or lengthen an audio clip without losing any of the content. This is a great way to adjust the length of a song to fit your video project or to create a custom version of a song with a different tempo or feel.

Remix in Premiere Pro, powered by Adobe Sensei, saves hours of cutting, rippling, adding fades, and previewing results while attempting to fit a piece of music to the length of a scene.

> **Important note**
>
> Adobe Sensei is a platform for AI and machine learning developed by Adobe. It powers a variety of features in Adobe Creative Cloud applications such as Photoshop, Illustrator, InDesign, and Premiere Pro.

Whether your music clips are from a favorite stock audio service such as Adobe Stock, your personal or commercial libraries, or even your neighbor's garage band, Remix can find the best cut points or loops for retiming and rearranging your songs almost instantly.

Remixing in Premiere Pro offers various ways to manipulate and reimagine existing music tracks to fit your video's needs. Next, we'll delve into how to do remixing music in Adobe Premiere Pro.

How does Remix work?

When you use Remix, Premiere Pro analyzes each beat in a song by measuring several qualities and comparing them to every other beat. Based on those qualities, Remix then finds the path of greatest confidence to create a musically coherent and seamless song remix, including cuts and crossfades. The Premiere Pro Remix feature analyzes audio patterns and dynamics in a song using Adobe Sensei to create new arrangements of the song that match the duration you require. This can be used to make shorter or longer versions of songs for your videos, as well as custom remixes.

How to remix audio in Premiere Pro

Simply select the song clip in your timeline and right-click to activate the **Remix** feature. Then, from the context menu, choose **Remix**. The song will then be analyzed by Premiere Pro, and a new arrangement will be created to match the duration you specify.

To remix audio in Premiere Pro, follow these steps:

1. Import your audio clip into Premiere Pro:

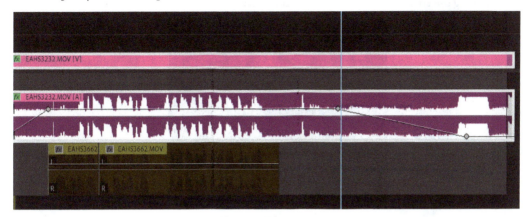

Figure 7.10 – Importing an audio clip into the timeline

2. In the **Essential Sound** panel, select the **Music** track and enable the **Remix** option:

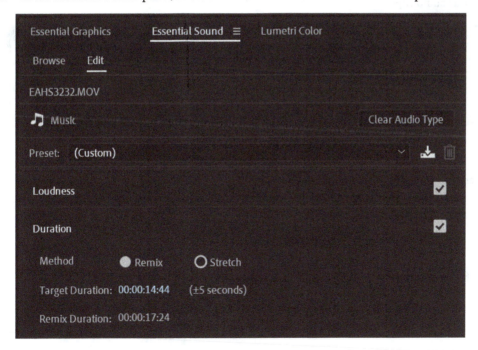

Figure 7.11 – Adjusting the music track by using the Essential Sound panel

3. In the **Remix** section of the panel, specify the desired target duration for your audio clip.

4. You can also use **Remix Tool** to manually shorten or lengthen the audio clip. To do this, click and drag the end of the audio clip in the timeline:

Figure 7.12 – Using Remix Tool to remix

5. Once you have specified the desired target duration, Premiere Pro will automatically remix your audio clip:

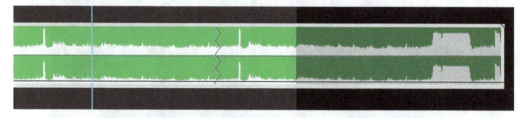

Figure 7.13 – Audio clip in the timeline stretched out after Remix

Premiere Pro remixing requires imagination and experimenting. Find the best video approach by trying several ones. These capabilities let you turn music into captivating soundscapes that boost your video production.

I hope this clarifies Premiere Pro remixing!

Tips for remixing audio in Premiere Pro

The **Remix** feature can also be used to create variations of the remixed song. Simply click the **Variations** button in the **Essential Sound** panel to do so. This will bring up a dialogue box.

Here are some more tools for using the **Remix** feature in Premiere Pro:

- **Segments**: This slider controls the number of cuts that Premiere Pro makes when remixing your audio clip. A higher segment value will result in a smoother remix, but it will also take longer to process. A lower segment value will result in a rougher remix, but it will process faster.

- **Variations**: This slider controls the amount of variation in the remixed audio. A higher variation value will result in a more varied remix, but it may also introduce some artifacts. A lower variation value will result in a less varied remix, but it will be less likely to introduce artifacts.

The following screenshot unveils the powerful tools of Premiere Pro's remixing arsenal. These help you bend music to your will, from beat detection to pitch shifting, and create sonic journeys that captivate your audience.

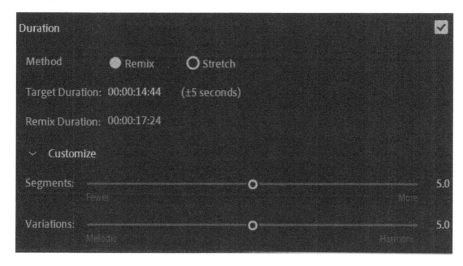

Figure 7.14 – Applying Remix in the Essential Sound panel

Here are some tips for getting the best results when using the **Remix** feature in Premiere Pro:

- Use a high **Segments** value for smooth remixes

- Use a low **Variations** value for less varied remixes

- Experiment with different target durations to see what works best for your project

- Listen to the remixed audio carefully to make sure that it sounds good

The Remix feature is a powerful tool that can help you quickly and easily adjust the length of your audio clips. With a little practice, you can use this feature to create custom versions of your favorite songs or to create original music for your video projects.

Summary

In this chapter, we explored two powerful techniques that elevate your video productions to new heights: ducking and remixing. We learned how ducking ensures clarity and prominence, lowering background music volume when dialogue, narration, or key moments demand our full attention. This simple yet effective tool adds polish and professionalism, ensuring your story takes center stage.

Ducking and remixing let you craft your video's sounds with precision and finesse. Crisp, compelling language, seamlessly blended music, and dramatic soundscapes may boost your video's emotional impact and create a lasting impression.

But our audio adjustment continues! In the next chapter, we'll cover noise removal, sweetening, and advanced effects to improve your video in professional audio editing. Prepare to perfect your audio and turn your videos into audio masterpieces!

8

Adding and Adjusting Sound Effects to Improve Your Video

Adding sound effects to your videos can be a great way to improve the overall production value and make your videos more engaging. In this chapter, we will show you how to add and adjust sound effects such as utilizing built-in audio presets, **equalization (EQ)**, and noise reduction in Premiere Pro. In addition to these specific benefits, you will also gain a general understanding of how sound effects work and how they can be used to improve videos with a wide range of sounds. From eerie silence to comedic slapstick, sound effects enhance the overall experience of your video. They bring a sense of immersion, evoke emotions, improve clarity, and add a touch of finesse, creating a truly captivating sensory feast.

This knowledge will allow you to be more creative and effective when using sound effects in your own videos.

In this chapter, we delve into the enthralling world of audio enhancement, investigating the powerful tools and techniques available in Adobe Premiere Pro to help you take your video projects to the next level. A well-crafted video isn't complete without great audio, and this chapter will teach you how to turn your footage into an immersive audiovisual experience.

In this chapter, we're going to cover the following main topics:

- The significance of sound—understanding its importance
- Creating audio presets in Essential Sound
- Using the Audio Track Mixer to adjust and add effects to entire tracks
- Adjusting audio gain in Premiere Pro
- Learning sound design
- Syncing audio and video with one click
- Syncing multiple audio clips in Premiere Pro

The significance of sound – understanding its importance

Indeed, while your film may possess visually striking elements, the absence of sound effects might result in a lack of depth and vitality. Sound effects serve as a covert tool, amplifying certain elements of your video:

- **Storytelling**: The appropriate sound effect has the ability to enhance the emotional intensity of a scene. The eerie sound of a creaking door in a horror film evokes a chilling sensation, yet a humorous whoosh sound may transform a basic jump cut into a comedic moment.

- **Clarity**: Sound effects have the ability to elucidate events that are happening on the screen. Consider the gratifying auditory experience of a basketball effortlessly passing through the net, producing a resonant *thunk* sound, or the enticing sound of food making contact with a heated pan in a culinary movie.

- **Engagement**: Sound effects enhance viewer engagement by providing an additional level of sensory input. They enhance the viewing experience by making it more immersive and energetic.

Sound effect arsenal – what's in your toolkit?

The world of sound effects is extensive, but here are a few fundamental classifications to begin your exploration:

- **Foley**: Foley sounds refer to the replication of daily noises in a controlled studio environment in order to enhance the authenticity and realism of audiovisual productions. Consider the sounds of footfall, door creaks, garment rustles, and interactions with objects.

- **Whooshes and impacts**: These striking auditory elements generate a perception of motion, velocity, or collision. They are ideal for action scenes, smooth transitions, and emphasizing pivotal moments.

- **Ambiance**: The use of background noises such as recordings of nature, cityscapes, or workplace sounds may create a certain atmosphere and help to establish the setting of your scenario.

- **Music and soundtracks**: Although not only sound effects, music plays a key part in establishing the overall atmosphere and sentiment of your video.

Sound effects play a crucial role in crafting a captivating narrative and captivating the audience. By implementing the strategies and methods outlined in this chapter, you can tap into their full potential and take your videos to new heights. Embrace the thrill of experimentation, indulge in the joy of creativity, and witness your videos transform into vibrant masterpieces through the enchanting realm of sound!

Creating audio presets in Essential Sound

Audio presets are a great way to save time and effort when mixing audio in Premiere Pro. They allow you to store a set of audio settings, such as EQ, compression, and noise reduction, so that you can easily apply them to other audio clips. With audio presets in **Essential Sound**, you can save and apply various audio tweaks to various clips, maintaining consistency across the project. When working on extensive projects or wishing to maintain a consistent audio aesthetic over several scenes, this is quite helpful, and to those who are seeking seamless sonic transitions, the audio presets in Premiere Pro can be a hidden gem. Picture the incredible efficiency achieved through optimizing your workflow, eliminating redundant adjustments, and seamlessly integrating each scene into the next, all while maintaining your distinctive sonic style. This incredible tool is not limited to experienced filmmakers alone. Even up-and-coming podcasters and YouTubers can take advantage of presets to establish their brand and enhance their productions.

Next, let's delve into a step-by-step guide to creating audio presets, enabling you to streamline your workflow and achieve consistent, professional-quality sound.

Step-by-step guide to creating audio presets

Creating audio presets can save you time and effort. Learn how in this step-by-step guide:

1. Open your project in Premiere Pro and select the clip or clips you want to adjust.

2. **Access Essential Sound**: Navigate to the **Essential Sound** panel by going to the **Window** menu and selecting **Essential Sound**:

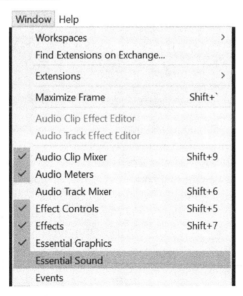

Figure 8.1 – Opening Essential Sound using the Window menu

3. **Choose audio type**: In the **Essential Sound** panel, choose the audio type that best suits your clip—options include **Dialogue**, **Music**, **SFX**, and **Ambience**:

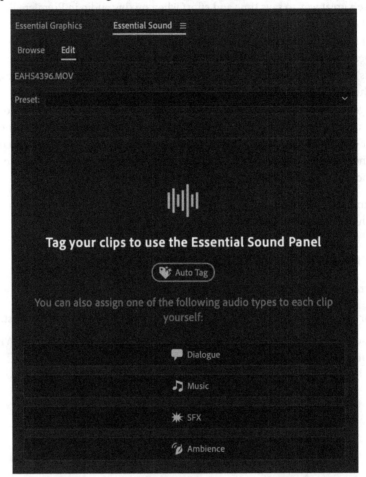

Figure 8.2 – Choosing audio type in the Essential Sound panel

4. **Adjust parameters**: Utilize the various controls within the **Essential Sound** panel to fine-tune your audio. This may include adjusting **Loudness**, **Clarity**, **Dynamics**, and more. You can create a harmonious auditory environment by utilizing **Loudness** controls to achieve a balanced soundscape, reduce undesirable noise using **Clarity**, and regulate variations in volume with **Dynamics**. Do not feel overwhelmed by complex terminology—straightforward explanations and visual aids will assist you throughout the entire process. Unleash your imagination and uncover the latent possibilities within your audio. The **Essential Sound** panel allows for limitless creative possibilities:

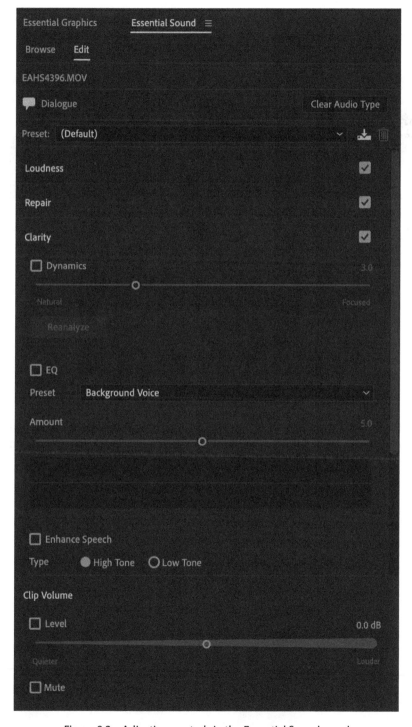

Figure 8.3 – Adjusting controls in the Essential Sound panel

5. **Save the preset**: Once you've dialed in your desired audio settings, click on the **Save Preset** icon next to the **Preset** dropdown to trigger the save procedure in the **Essential Sound** panel and select **Save Preset**:

Figure 8.4 – Saving preset in the Essential Sound panel

6. Now, give your preset a descriptive name in the **Save Preset** window and click **OK**:

Figure 8.5 – Naming preset in the Save Preset window

7. **Apply the preset**: To apply your newly created preset to other clips, select the target clips, navigate to the **Essential Sound** panel, and choose your preset from the drop-down menu:

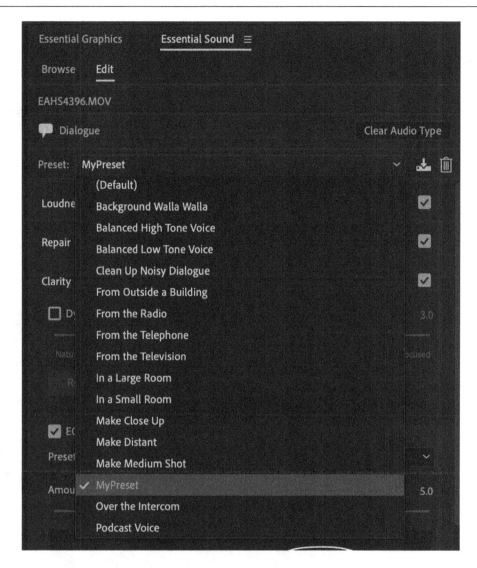

Figure 8.6 – Choosing the saved preset from the drop-down menu and applying it to the dedicated audio

If your audio clips have varying sounds, relying on audio presets might not provide a solution. However, it seems that we find ourselves repeatedly making the same adjustments to our audio, time and time again. With the help of audio presets, applying these adjustments becomes incredibly swift.

Next, for even more control and nuanced edits, let's delve into the world of track adjustments and effects. In the next section, we'll explore the powerful Track Mixer, for fine-tuning individual tracks and adding creative effects to take your audio to the next level.

Using the Track Mixer to adjust and add effects to entire tracks

By carefully arranging individual sound effects, you may enhance the complexity of your film. However, the Premiere Pro **Track Mixer** allows you to improve the overall auditory experience of your complete audio track. This section explores how to effectively utilize this potent tool to create a unified and influential auditory encounter.

Understanding the Track Mixer

A complete audio control panel that provides a visual representation of your audio tracks is Adobe Premiere Pro's Track Mixer. It offers a single location where you can fine-tune the audio components of your project by tweaking levels, adding effects, and so on. You may use the Track Mixer by going to the **Window** drop-down menu and choosing **Audio Track Mixer**. This opens a window with all your audio tracks displayed vertically and a horizontal area for each track, including a volume fader, mute button, and effects rack:

Figure 8.7 – Audio Track Mixer panel

Within Premiere Pro's **Audio Track Mixer**, every Audio track tab functions as a compact control hub for its respective track. By clicking on one, you'll be able to adjust its volume, panning, effects, and many other options. In addition, users can view all their tracks simultaneously, allowing for efficient management of track order and visibility. This feature ensures that audio files remain organized and easily manageable, even within intricate projects.

The volume fader

The volume fader is a vertical slider that directly adjusts the overall loudness of the audio track. Here's how to use it for optimum balance:

Figure 8.8 – Volume fader in the Audio Track Mixer panel

To achieve audio-level balance, import your talk, music, and sound effects into distinct audio tracks. Utilize the volume faders in the Track Mixer to modify the levels of each track until they attain a harmonious equilibrium. For example, you may choose to somewhat decrease the volume of the music track in relation to the dialogue in order to guarantee the distinct comprehensibility of spoken words. Next, you see a list of music tracks available in this project:

Figure 8.9 – Audio track tab in the Audio Track Mixer panel

As you can see in *Figure 8.9*, there are a certain number of track mixers (**Audio 1**, **Audio 2**, **Audio 3**, **Audio 4**, **Audio 5**), and that number corresponds to the total number of audio tracks that are included in this timeline (**A1**, **A2**, **A3**, **A4**, **A5**), as you can see in *Figure 8.10*. Each of the audio tracks manages a distinct track.

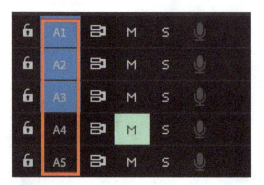

Figure 8.10 – Audio Track in timeline

Next, let's look at adding effects with the effects rack.

Adding effects with the effects rack

The magic truly unfolds within the effects rack of each audio track. Here's how to utilize it to enhance your audio:

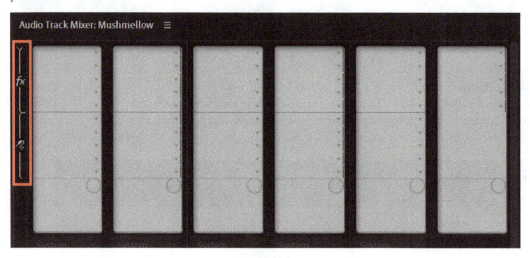

Figure 8.11 – Effects rack in the Audio Track Mixer

To add basic effects, simply click the downward arrow located next to the effects rack on the selected audio track. Upon activation, a menu will be displayed, offering a selection of pre-installed effects such as EQ, dynamics (compression), and reverb:

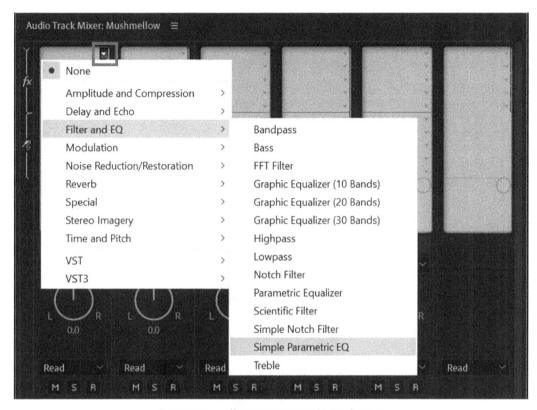

Figure 8.12 – Effects menu in Audio Track Mixer

Conduct experiments with these effects to enhance the sound quality of the entire recording. Applying EQ may effectively diminish undesired ambient noise in a speech recording, while incorporating modest reverberation into a music track can provide a more expansive and captivating auditory encounter.

Premiere Pro has an extensive collection of supplementary effects accessible through the **Effects** window in your workspace. You may easily move and place these effects into the effects rack of your audio track to enhance your creative control. Envision using a chorus effect on a conversation track to produce a surreal sequence or employing a distortion effect on a music track to attain a more intense, rock concert ambiance.

Keep in mind that subtlety is key! Although you are encouraged to explore, excessive use of effects can distort the audio and create an artificial sound. Commence by making little modifications and attentively observe the effect on your entire auditory environment.

Expanding upon our knowledge of the Track Mixer, we will now shift our attention to perfecting the volumes of each individual track to create a harmonious and powerful soundscape.

Adjusting audio levels with precision

Mastering the art of audio editing requires finesse and precision. Premiere Pro provides a wide range of powerful tools, although at times, the editing process focused on video frames may not be as precise for making subtle adjustments to the sound. Do not be afraid, masters of sound! In this section, you will explore the intricacies of precise level adjustments in Premiere Pro.

Track volume

The Track Mixer enables precise control over a **track's volume**. Adjust the slider for a gradual increase or decrease in volume. Right-clicking on the slider reveals additional options such as creating keyframes for dynamic changes:

Figure 8.13 – Volume slider in the Audio Track Mixer panel

Let's go to work on changing the volume now. If the music track is, for example, excessively loud, we can simply turn it down in the Track Mixer.

There are two ways we can go about that. To adjust the volume, we may either enter a value here where it reads 0 (see *Figure 8.9*). A number between -infinity **decibels (dB)** and +15 dB will cause the volume to increase. Any negative number entered will result in a lower track volume.

However, we can also use this slider to move it up or down and accomplish the same thing. Let's pull it down to turn down the volume:

Figure 8.14 – Adjusting volume in the Audio Track Mixer panel

Additionally, the music is considerably quieter now, as can be heard. If you need to change the general settings of a really long video, anything longer than 10 minutes, for example, it is a quick and straightforward approach to save time. But those are the fundamentals of using the **Audio Track Mixer** to change the volume of the music. Come back up here, and let's look at a few more features:

Figure 8.15 – Mix track in the Audio Track Mixer panel

As you can see, there is a track named **Mix** to the right of every track we have here. The fact that this track manages the loudness of everything at once makes it unique. Not only will it save all the modifications you have made to the individual tracks, but it will also go above and beyond to provide you with simultaneous control over everything. The overall volume will change in accordance with any adjustments you make to a clip's volume before adjusting the **Mix** slider while maintaining the original proportions.

Adding effects to the Mix track

To add the effects to the **Mix** track, locate the effects rack in the **Mix** track and direct your attention to the horizontal section. Click the down-arrow icon next to the effects rack:

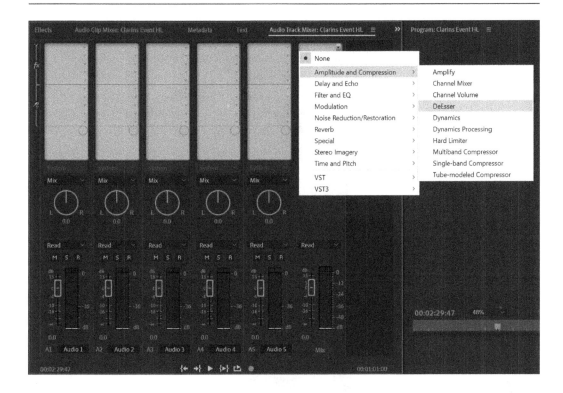

Figure 8.16 – Adding effects to Mix track in the Audio Track Mixer panel

This reveals a menu showcasing various built-in effects offered by Premiere Pro. These effects provide powerful tools to enhance the overall sound of your entire audio track. Some common options include the following:

- **EQ**: This is a process used to adjust the frequency balance of audio. It may be used to remove undesirable background noise or enhance certain ranges to improve the clarity of conversation or music.

- **Dynamics (compression)**: Manage the variation in volume levels, minimizing the disparity between loud and soft sections in order to create a more uniform and harmonious audio environment.

- **Reverb**: Help to enhance the spatial and ambient qualities of audio, creating the illusion that it was recorded in a particular setting such as a concert hall or a cathedral. This is especially beneficial for music songs.

To choose and apply an effect, just choose the appropriate effect from the menu in the effects rack. By clicking on the effect, it will be added to the vacant space in the effects rack for the corresponding audio track.

Mute (M), Solo (S), Record (R)

The next thing you'll notice is that we have the letters **M**, **S**, and **R** above our fader:

Figure 8.17 – M, S, R buttons in the Audio Track Mixer panel

Here, **M** represents **Mute**. It will become *green* when you click it, and playing that audio will be stopped completely. Now for the **S** phase, which represents **Solo**; to hear just that layer, hit this button. It will, therefore, mute everything else. Lastly, there is the **R** button, which represents **Record**. It allows you to record audio straight onto the timeline track in question.

Automation modes

Under this section, the automation modes are the next in line. **Automation modes** should be configured to read by default, but if you click on any of them, you should see **Write**, **Off**, **Read**, **Latch**, and **Touch** options:

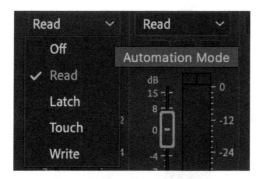

Figure 8.18 – Automation modes in the Audio Track Mixer panel

Let me briefly describe each of them as they won't all immediately make sense to you:

- **Off**: During playback, track settings and current keyframes are ignored. In this mode, changes are not recorded.

- **Read**: Represents the default state and hence reflects any adjustments made to the track volume. You won't first notice a change because, by default, you shouldn't have any.

- **Latch**: It functions similarly to **Touch** but doesn't go back to its initial position unless you pause playback and then restart it.

- **Touch**: In order to maintain the position of your audio slider, you need to continuously interact with it, as it will record your adjustments over time. When you hold it in that position, it will dutifully record for future playbacks. However, the moment you release your grip, it gracefully fades back to its original position. Depending on the type of audio editing you're doing, this tool can be quite enjoyable and beneficial.

- **Write**: You may think of **Write** mode as a continuous keyframe recording for your slider. As the device remains in write mode, it diligently captures our movements over time and securely preserves them. This becomes particularly evident when we play our clip and manipulate the slider in real time.

However, it will continue to write over anything we play over as long as we have this set to **Write (W)**. Thus, when you've completed making your edits, remember to return it to **Read (R)**. After that, you may see what you just completed.

Adjusting the track volume on the timeline

There is a simpler approach to visualize it if you want to know what your track keyframes are doing without having to go back and watch the entire thing again. Keyframe settings can be added by navigating to the relevant track and double-clicking on the left side. By default, these are the options for your clip keyframes:

Figure 8.19 – Expanding audio track in timeline to enable Clip Keyframes option

The rubber band function in the **Timeline** panel allows for effortless adjustment of the volume level of a track or the creation of a dynamic volume shift over time in an audio track. These options have the following uses:

- **Clip Keyframes**: It is possible to animate audio effects for a clip, such as adjusting the volume level. These keyframes exclusively pertain to the clip that has been selected.

- **Track Keyframes**: Keyframes can be used to animate audio track effects, such as adjusting the volume or muting the audio. These keyframes are applicable throughout the entire track.

- **Track Panner**: You have the ability to modify the volume level of a track. To obtain additional details, please refer to the topics of panning and balancing.

   However, if you click the *diamond* on the left and choose **Track Keyframes | Volume**, you will see that all of the keyframes that we recently recorded onto the track are readily visible here. Refer to the following screenshot to understand more:

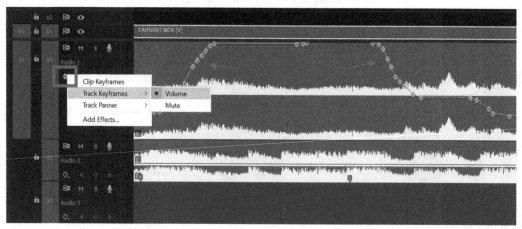

Figure 8.20 – Enabling Track Keyframes to see written keyframes

To generate keyframes, utilize the *Ctrl* + click function on Windows or the *CMD* + click function on macOS. The **Pen** tool (**P**) can also be used to generate keyframes.

To adjust the volume, use either the Selection tool (**V**) or the Pen tool to manipulate the volume-level rubber band by moving it upward to increase the volume or downward to decrease the volume.

Important note

To modify the volume effect over time, position the current-time indicator at the desired spot for each change, select the **Add/Remove Keyframe** button in the audio track header, then adjust the keyframe by moving it upward (increasing volume) or downward (decreasing volume).

- **Track Panner** is the next item on this list. This is where we adjust the balance between the left and right sides of the audio source for each track. We can only hear the audio for that track coming from the right side of our speakers or headphones if we slide this all the way to the right:

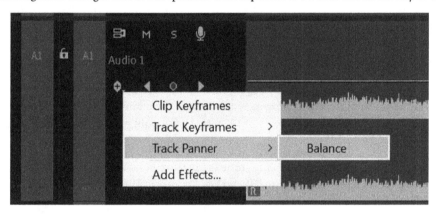

Figure 8.21 – Enabling Track Panner to balance the right and left sides of the audio

- If needed, one can achieve a balanced clip by utilizing the **Balance** audio effect. Only proceed with this step once you have determined that track balancing is not enough.

Next, let's look into how we can balance the audio using automation mode for **Track Panner**.

The automation modes we just looked at also affect this area of the Track Mixer. For example, by setting it to **Touch**, we may move our panner while capturing real-time footage of it moving, and then release it to enable it to return to its initial position:

Figure 8.22 – Track Panner in the Audio Track Mixer panel

The **Audio Track Mixer** offers a range of controls to adjust the panning and balance of your audio. When a mono or stereo track outputs to a stereo track, a round knob will appear. With a simple twist of the knob, you have the power to effortlessly adjust the audio, seamlessly shifting the balance between the left and right output track channels. Next, let's see panning and balancing in the **Audio Track Mixer**.

Panning (Track Panner) and balancing in the Audio Track Mixer

In the **Audio Track Mixer** of Premiere Pro, you'll find the pan/balance control. This nifty feature is usually displayed as a knob or slider, allowing you to adjust the panning of your audio. The values range from -100% (for a full left placement) to 100% (for a full right placement), while 0% signifies a center placement.

With this control, you have the power to fine-tune the balance of an audio track's signal, ensuring that it is perfectly distributed between the left and right speakers of your stereo output. Adjusting the knob/slider to the left or right directs the audio to the corresponding speaker, while keeping it centered evenly distributes the sound between both speakers.

Allow me to share with you some important insights regarding panning in the **Audio Track Mixer**:

- The impact extends to entire tracks, rather than just individual clips within a track. To achieve individual clip panning, **Audio Clip Mixer** is the tool you need.
- When the audio track and output track have the same channel configuration, panning and balancing options are not accessible. The channels of both tracks align perfectly.
- Adjusting the panning of a track doesn't alter its overall volume but rather positions it within the stereo soundscape.
- Take advantage of the panning controls to position audio within the stereo field. This is invaluable for creating a sense of space and depth in your audio mix:

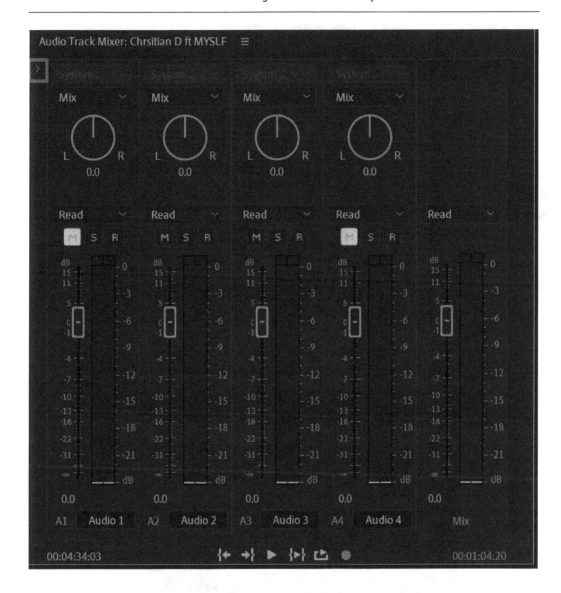

Figure 8.23 – Track Panner in the Audio Track Mixer panel

The icon is located at the upper-left corner of your panel. This drop-down arrow should reveal a series of slots where you may insert various effects and send assignments. You may view every effect that can be applied to the entire track by clicking on one of the open slots for the master track or any specific track:

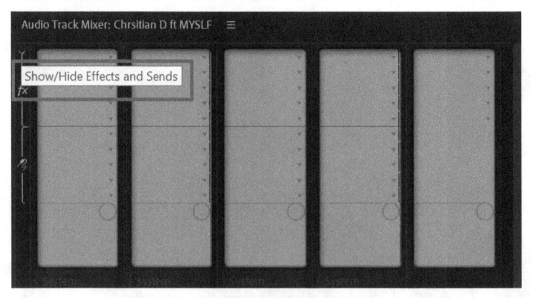

Figure 8.24 – Track effects in the Audio Track Mixer panel

Now, let's move on to an effect that you may not utilize as often but for which it is really simple to distinguish between the two: **Pitch Shifter**. When you click on it, a drop-down box will appear as follows:

Figure 8.25 – Pitch Shifter effect in the Audio Track Mixer panel

When you click on it, the settings of this effect may be adjusted in the box down below. Thus, we can plainly hear that the audio's pitch is changing when we click and drag this effect up or down. Additionally, you can click the small **fx** button in the corner to maintain the effect while only muting it. Additionally, we may add more effects to happen simultaneously:

Figure 8.26 – Muting effect in the Audio Track Mixer panel

You can bypass the effects rack by opening the **Audio Track Mixer** panel and locating the specific track. Located in the top-right corner of the track, within the mixer panel, there is a little **fx** button. Press the **fx** button. This activates or deactivates the bypass capability for all effects on the specified track.

When the button is highlighted, it signifies that the effects are being bypassed and not being implemented. When the button is not highlighted, the effects are in operation.

Keep in mind that disabling the effect or bypassing the effects rack will fully eradicate the influence, as opposed to merely muting it. This means that you will lose the specific changes you have made to the sound.

To temporarily quieten and reactivate effects without totally disabling them, use the **Solo** button on the chosen track. When the **Solo** function is engaged, just the selected track is audible, effectively silencing all other tracks and their associated effects. However, this is only a temporary solution while the mixer panel remains accessible.

To eliminate an effect, just click on it and choose **None** to replace it:

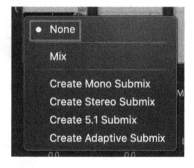

Figure 8.27 – Deleting effect in the Audio Track Mixer panel

We haven't yet discussed one particular kind of audio track, though, and I believe it may be quite helpful to you. It is known as a submix. We'll learn more about this in the next section.

Adding a submix

A submix is a track where audio signals from multiple tracks are blended together into a unified whole. Imagine the possibilities of making modifications to the submix, allowing you to effortlessly apply different adjustments to various tracks without the need for repetitive changes. It appears to resemble an adjustment layer applied to audio.

Additionally, you may add one by right-clicking on the left side of your timeline, choosing **Add Audio Submix Track**, and then adding one. You may now adjust the audio slider here, which is a little bit darker. Additionally, it has a submix label.

Here's how you can add a submix track to your timeline:

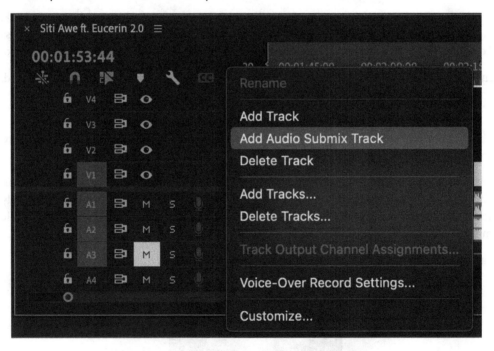

Figure 8.28 – Adding audio submix track on timeline

To add a submix track, go to the audio track in the sequence timeline, right-click, and select **Add Audio Submix Track**. A slightly darker track is added to the **Audio Track Mixer** that is labeled as **Submix 1**:

Figure 8.29 – Submix track in the Audio Track Mixer

Upon adding the **Pitch Shifter** effect once more to the submix and playing our footage, no discernible alterations occur. However, now that we've gone up here and changed the track output assignment on each of our channels from **Master** to **Submix 1**, we can hear the impact happening. With this slider right here, we can adjust every track that we've attached to **Submix 1**:

Figure 8.30 – Assigning audio track to Submix 1 track in the Audio Track Mixer

Finally, you may wonder how to go about erasing keyframes that have already been set on a track in the event that you discover a mistake. It's easy; just navigate to the disputed track in the timeline and confirm that keyframe tracking is enabled:

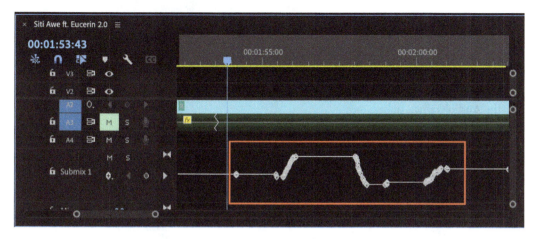

Figure 8.31 – Removing submix track's keyframes in timeline

Next, select every keyframe you wish to remove with your **Pen** tool, then press the *Delete* key. That's it—you're back at the beginning.

And there, folks, is the essence of the **Audio Track Mixer**. I hope this makes it easier for you to use and that it helps you grasp another feature of Premiere Pro that you may utilize down the road.

With Adobe Premiere Pro, editors have dynamic control over the audio design of their projects, thanks to the Track Mixer. You may do more with your audio editing if you are aware of its subtleties and powers. With the Track Mixer, you can create an engaging audio experience for your listeners by modifying effects, panning, and level adjustments. Accept its power, try out various methods, and let the quality of your audio tracks come through in the edited version.

Adjusting audio gain in Premiere Pro

Gain in clips refers to the input level or loudness. The **Audio Gain** command is utilized to modify the gain level of one or many chosen clips. The **Audio Gain** command operates autonomously from the output level configurations in the **Audio Track Mixer** and **Timeline** panels. The value is integrated with the track level to create the final mix. The **Normalize Master Track** command allows you to modify the gain for an entire sequence.

For optimal sound levels and to avoid conflicts between tracks, it is important that your video goods comply with particular audio standards. The primary audio, which usually includes narration, interviews, or dialogue, should always have a volume level ranging from -12 to -6 dB. The recommended range for secondary audio, such as natural sound, is -30 to -18 dB. It is crucial to bear in mind that audio levels and loudness are distinct entities. The audio level refers to the fundamental level of your audio, while the volume pertains to the audio that may be adjusted by the observer.

To modify audio gain, utilize either the **Selection** tool or the timeline approach, according to the instructions provided next:

1. Select **Audio Clips | Audio Options | Audio Gain…** or the *G* keyboard shortcut.

2. You can perform a right-click action on one of the audio clips that have been selected to access the **Audio Gain…** option too:

Figure 8.32 – Right-clicking an audio clip to select Audio Gain… option in timeline

3.   Select the **Audio Gain...** option from the pop-up menu:

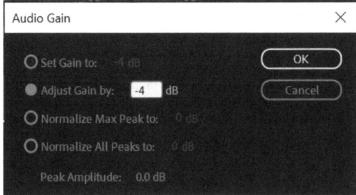

Figure 8.33 – Adjusting dB value in the Audio Gain window

4.   In the **Audio Gain** box, adjust the dB value to the desired level. Use a positive number to increase it and a negative number to decrease it.

5.   Click **OK**.

The dialog box for adjusting audio gain is shown. Premiere Pro automatically computes the maximum amplitude of the chosen clips. The value is shown in the **Peak Amplitude** field. After being computed, this value is then kept for the purpose of selection. This value can be utilized as a reference to fine-tune the gain.

Choose one option from the following list and assign a value to it:

- **Set Gain to**: Adjust the gain to the desired level. The initial value is 0.0 dB. This feature enables the user to manually adjust the gain to a predetermined amount. The value is consistently updated to reflect the current gain, even if the option is not chosen, and the value is displayed as muted.

- **Adjust Gain by**: Modify the amplification level. The initial value is 0.0 dB. This feature enables the user to modify the gain by increasing or decreasing it by a certain number of dB. Inputting a nonzero value in this field automatically adjusts the **Set Gain** to dB value to accurately represent the gain applied to the clip.

- **Normalize Max Peak to**: The initial value is 0.0 dB. Users have the ability to adjust this value to any number that is lower than 0.0 dB. The option allows the user to modify the maximum peak amplitude in the chosen clips to a value defined by the user.

- **Normalize All Peaks to**: Standardize all peaks to a common level. The initial value is 0.0 dB. Users have the ability to adjust this value to any number that is lower than 0.0 dB. The normalization option modifies the peak amplitude in the chosen clips to the value given by the user.
- **Peak Amplitude**: The **Peak Amplitude** display field shows the current peak amplitude of the chosen clip(s), which represents the highest volume level.

When adjusting the gain to the desired level, please input the required gain value in dB in this section. A positive value (for example, +3 dB) amplifies the gain, resulting in an increase in audio volume. In contrast, a negative number (for example, -6 dB) reduces the gain, resulting in a drop in audio volume.

It is recommended to refrain from beyond a gain of +6 dB since doing so may result in the introduction of undesirable noise or distortion. When decreasing the gain, strive to make modifications in smaller increments to prevent the music from becoming excessively quiet.

Conduct experiments and attentively observe the effects of your modifications to attain the appropriate audio level.

Learning sound design

Sound design is a potent catalyst in the field of video editing that helps shape the emotional environment and narrative effect of your visual works. With the extensive toolkit for sound design offered by Adobe Premiere Pro, editors may create a symphony of captivating audio components for their viewers. This section takes us on an exploration of the craft and methods of sound design in the context of Adobe Premiere Pro.

In order to improve storytelling, arouse feelings, and draw viewers into the visual narrative, sound designers create and manipulate sounds. Video editing is more than just technical; it's a creative process that turns a series of images into a multi-sensory experience.

Tips to optimize your sound design in Adobe Premiere Pro

The following tips will show you how can you improve your sound design:

- **Gathering sound**: Attempt to capture as many sounds as you can while filming. You may either use this as the real sound or make your own foley later. **Foley sound** refers to the art of recreating and adding everyday sound effects specifically in post-production (for example, footsteps, clothing, objects, foods, drinks, and many more). You can find everyday objects that can be manipulated to create a vast array of sound effects. These are sounds that are either not captured well during filming or need enhancing to create a more impactful and realistic experience for the audience. You can even mimic particular sounds with your mouth or with equipment. Try searching for and downloading noises from internet libraries such as www.freesound.org and www.pond5.com if you're still unable to record them.

- **Creating ambient sound**: Make your own room tone. While filming in a particular setting, such as a factory, for instance, make every effort to ensure that the factory ambient noise is as precise as feasible. That implies pushing buttons and levers, machinery, people, and so on. While all of these sounds work together to form an ambient, they must be carefully blended in terms of volume.

- **Reverb and EQ**: Reverb and EQ should be added to your sound design during mixing. The **cutoff method** is a clever way to achieve a good reverb. After adding reverb, use keyframes to progressively lower the volume at the conclusion. The echo effect fades smoothly when the clip ends, improving audio quality and eliminating abruptness. Try different fade speeds and reverb settings to get the right mix! In the last moments of your video, add more keyframes. The reverb will be audible even if the sound of the clip will no longer play.

- **Audio panning**: One effective technique to provide your viewers or listeners with a novel experience is through audio panning in videos. You may animate the panner by selecting your clip and using the **Effect Settings** panel. You may make an interesting animation where the audio moves from the left to the right or vice versa by utilizing keyframes.

- **Pitch shifting**: There are two methods to go about this: one is to employ Premiere's **Pitch Shifter** effect. Alternatively, you may change the timing of your sound by using the **Rate Stretch (R)** tool. A slower speed will produce a deeper sound, whereas a quicker speed will provide a higher tone. This method adjusts audio playing speed. Slowing the playback rate lowers the pitch, like a slow-motion speaker. Increasing playback speed raises the pitch, like a chipmunk. To adjust the speed or duration without altering the pitch, simply select the **Maintain Audio Pitch** option in the **Clip Speed/Duration** dialog.

Every audio component of your project adds to its overall emotional resonance, making sound design an exploratory and creative process. With its wide range of tools and capabilities, Adobe Premiere Pro enables editors to become sound designers, creating aural landscapes that push the boundaries of narrative. In order to create really immersive audio experiences in the field of video editing, embrace experimentation, sharpen your listening skills, and follow your creative impulses when you set out on your sound design endeavors.

Syncing audio and video with one click

The *secret sauce* that elevates a final video effort to a new level is outstanding sound. Make sure that the audience doesn't miss a word, whether recording a feature film or a business interview. Having access to industry-standard microphones and recording equipment that can capture clear, concise dialogue is perfect for achieving excellent audio quality.

When you enter the editing studio, you are met with distinct audio and video files that you must carefully synchronize to avoid having your dramatic conversation sequence appear to be a foreign-language dub.

Fortunately, there are a few simple ways to sync your audio and video media files perfectly if you're using Adobe Premiere Pro, so you can spend more time creating content rather than reading lips. But beforehand, let's take a look at what is causing audio and video to be out of sync.

What's causing audio and video to be out of sync?

There are several possible reasons why your audio and video might not be in sync. One possible explanation is that the audio was recorded using a different device than the one used for the video, and it is almost impossible to synchronize files flawlessly on-site when using *off-camera* audio.

This explains why a scene slate has a *clap* feature; during the era of film-based filming, this particular function played a crucial role in synchronizing sound and video. Its purpose was to ensure that a crystal-clear, distinct sound was captured alongside a visual signal, simultaneously on all devices.

Thanks to technology, you can now smoothly sync your audio and video tracks even if you didn't *slate* your shots correctly. These technologies are sophisticated.

It's also possible that your audio track *slipped*, a problem more prevalent in the digital era, meaning that there was a lag in the filming process that caused the audio track to get out of sync with the video. Editing allows for the correction of this as well.

How to sync audio and video in Premiere Pro

Adobe has *baked* some very time-saving technologies into the most recent versions of Premiere Pro in response to the difficulties faced by video editors with the sometimes laborious process of sound synchronization.

See the next three methods for synchronizing audio and visuals in Adobe Premiere Pro.

Method #1 – Merging clips to sync audio and video

The **Merge Clips** option in Premiere Pro is the best option if you're searching for a quick and easy approach to sync audio and video.

The **Merge Clips** option synchronizes audio and video and then creates a new combined clip without overwriting your original audio and video files. You may relocate all of the merged clips to this bin in your **Project** panel and prevent combining merged clips with the original files if you have many video and audio clips that need audio synchronization. Just call the bin *merged clips*.

To fast synchronize audio and video in a single procedure, follow these steps to combine clips:

1. Import all your audio and video clips.

    I.   I advise you to rename your audio files before importing them into Premiere Pro, as you may have a few video files that require synchronization. You may localize which audio tracks go with which video clip in this way.

    II. Choose **Import** from the **File** menu, then go to the folder holding your video and audio clips. To import, you may choose which audio and video tracks to use. All of them will show up on your **Project** panel.

2. Merge clips from the **Project** panel.

    I.   Choose the audio track and the video that you wish to synchronize with first. For non-continuous clips, use *Ctrl* + click; otherwise, use *Shift* + click to choose neighboring audio and video. To choose individual audio and video clips on a Mac, press *CMD* + click.

    II. Select a clip by right-clicking on it, then select **Merge Clips...** from the drop-down menu.

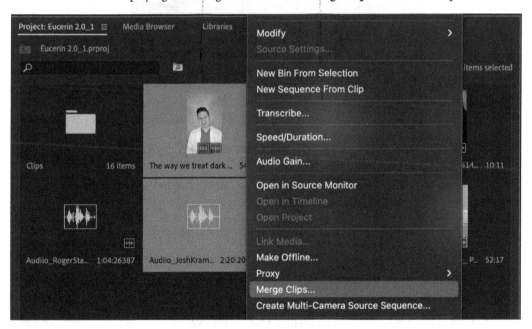

Figure 8.34 – Merge Clips in Project panel

III.   In the **Merge Clips** dialog box, you may give the newly combined clip a new name. It will, by default, finish with - **Merged** and the original name:

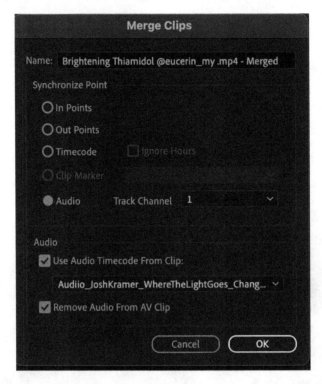

Figure 8.35 – Selecting a synchronization point in Merge Clips window

IV.   Once your combined clip has been renamed, you may select a synchronization point. With Premiere Pro, you have the following choices:

- **In Points** is a sync point based on an in point that will be used.

- **Out Points** is for audio synchronizing depending on the out point.

- **Timecode**, to use a different audio timecode between each clip to timecode audio and visual synchronization.

- **Clip Marker** will sync both audio files. Only in the event that every component clip has a clip marker will this option be accessible.

- **Audio** will be combined and synchronized using a reference audio track such as **Track 1**, **Track 2**, and **Mix Down**.

V. Choose a camera audio track in **Track Channel** as the reference track after selecting the **Audio** option.

VI. Select the **Remove Audio From AV Clip** checkbox located in the **Audio** section. Your reference audio track will be immediately removed as a result, leaving only the synchronized audio track and video.

VII. To exit the **Merge Clips** window, click **OK**.

VIII. Your selected name for your combined clip will appear on the **Project** panel.

IX. You may arrange the clips and prepare them for a new sequence by doing this from the **Project** panel. This way, you won't have to worry about audio clip synchronization when editing.

3. Add your merged clip to your sequence.

Now that your video track and audio are synchronized, you may edit the audio track like any other clip.

Method #2 – Synchronizing audio and video with Premiere Pro's Synchronize feature

Another simple way that you can only utilize from the timeline is **Synchronize**, a function of Adobe Premiere Pro. Here, the distinction is that **Synchronize** simply affects the active sequence; it won't produce a new merged clip in your **Project** panel.

You need to synchronize the clips on each timeline or, if you like, build a combined clip after synchronizing if you wish to utilize the same clip in many sequences.

Let's take a look at how to synchronize audio and video with Premiere Pro's **Synchronize** feature:

1. Arrange audio and video clips in your sequence.

2. Arrange your audio and video clips on the timeline by either creating a new sequence or choosing an existing one. The audio files must be placed on separate tracks rather than being near each other on the same track or stacked on top of each other.

   By using the **Synchronize** feature, you have the ability to meticulously synchronize individual audio and video tracks by utilizing a range of reference points such as waveforms or markers:

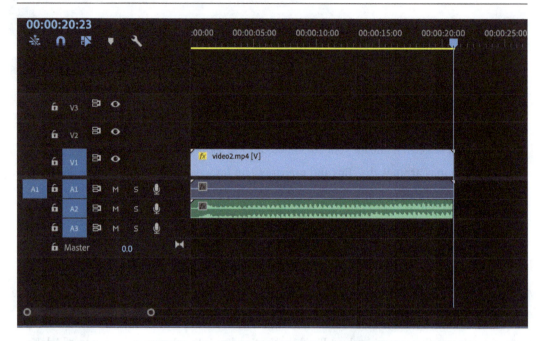

Figure 8.36 – Selecting both clips to synchronize in timeline

3.   Choose any of the ordered clips in the timeline, then use the right-click menu to select **Synchronize**.

You must select a synchronizing point based on the start and finish of the clip, a timecode, a marker, or an audio track reference when the **Synchronize** dialog box appears:

Figure 8.37 – Synchronizing clip and audio

4. In the **Synchronize Clips** pop-up window, choose the **Audio** option for the synchronize point. Then, select the track of the reference audio, which in this case is track **1**. Then, select the **OK** option:

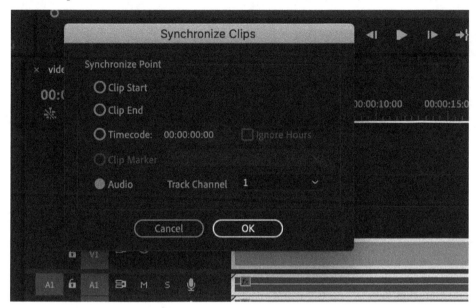

Figure 8.38 – Choosing Audio as your synchronization point and a track to sync

The clips will automatically align, as you will observe. The synchronization of the audio waves may be determined by observing them.

5. Select the reference audio clip and hit *Delete* or *Backspace* to remove it from the video track.

6. Link audio and video.

In order to prevent your synchronized tracks from becoming out of sync, you may now additionally choose to *link* them together. It is highly advised to take this action to prevent unintentional audio slips.

If you move the clips throughout the timeline, they will remain linked and not break apart. Here's how to do it:

7. Choose videos from the timeline:

Figure 8.39 – Linking your synced tracks together

8. Select **Link** from the drop-down menu by performing a right-click on them.

9. Your video and audio clip can be rearranged in the timeline because they are connected together.

If you prefer manual adjustments, **Synchronize** allows finer control. Visually align waveforms and adjust audio channels using a reference point (in point, timecode, and so on). While more laborious, this method provides accurate synchronizing for your needs. It is important to consider that the duration of your clips directly affects the time required for synchronization. Syncing videos that are over an hour long can be quite a challenge. Sometimes, it seems like they just refuse to sync unless you give them at least an hour to do their thing. Utilizing concise snippets and gradually expanding upon them can facilitate a clearer understanding if that concept resonates. Next, let's see how to sync audio and video using the manual synchronization method.

Method #3 – Syncing your audio and video using manual synchronization

Adobe Premiere Pro has automatic functionalities to interpret and evaluate the audio waveform, enabling optimal adjustments. But even Premiere Pro may make mistakes from time to time, so the final output can still be out of sync, and you'll need to manually synchronize the clips in the timeline.

If a clapboard, clap, or other sound is not utilized during recording and you have to locate another reference or visual cue to manually sync clips, this approach will still assist you.

Here is how to sync audio and video manually with a reference track:

1. Place both the audio and video tracks on your timeline:

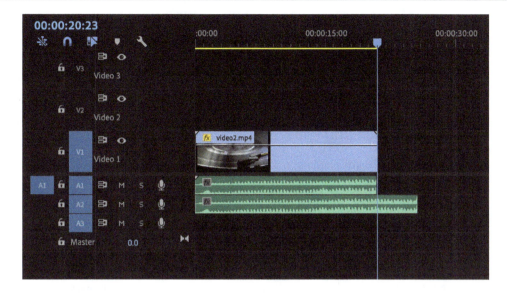

Figure 8.40 – Placing both audio and video tracks in the timeline for synchronization

2. Look for a reference mark:

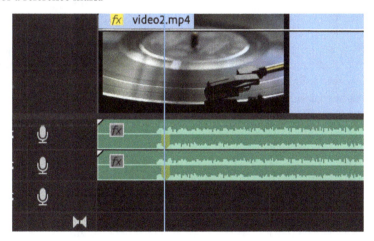

Figure 8.41 – Putting marker on the reference audio

In both audio recordings, look for a spike in the audio waveform. Verify that the audio sounds the same by listening to it.

Once you've found a solid reference point, make a marker by selecting the clip and pressing the *M* key. Repeat with the remaining clips.

3. Align audio clips:

    I.   Slide the clips around until the marks you made in the previous step are in line with them.

    II.   To make sure the two audio snippets and the video are in sync, play the clips and listen. It could take some time to locate the ideal location.

    III.   If you see distinct spikes that coincide during the footage, you may add more markers and try to align them all for better synchronization.

4. Link the clips and delete the reference track (if needed).

    Whatever your circumstances, Adobe Premiere Pro makes audio and video synchronizing comparatively easy.

    Next, let's see the process of synchronizing audio and video without relying on a reference track. This approach is slightly more intricate than syncing with a reference track, and it works most effectively when your shot is properly *slated*.

5. Find your video track slate first. Watch each frame until the clapper stick reaches the slate board. Mark that frame when you see it. Next, expand the audio clip and look for a big sound spike at the start.

6. Verify, by listening to it, that the sound is the *clap* the slate emits when the clapper stick descends. After you've marked the peak of the clap sound in the waveform and compared it to the previously created video marker, play the clips together while the sound is playing.

Properly aligning your audio and video would have been advisable had you accurately labeled both of these elements. There was a slight discrepancy in their synchronization. Adjust the audio by making small increments either forward or backward until perfect synchronization is achieved with the utilization of the **Slip Edit** tool (**Y**). When you zoom in to the maximum level, you gain the ability to meticulously analyze each individual frame of a clip and proceed to merge the clips.

Syncing multiple audio clips in Premiere Pro

Premiere Pro lets you combine up to 16 soundtracks in any mix of mono, stereo, and 5.1 audio as it supports numerous audio files for a single video clip. One track is equivalent to one mono clip, two tracks are included in stereo audio, and six tracks are included in surround 5.1.

To combine many clips, arrange them in the timeline by selecting each clip that is a part of the video clip you wish to sync sounds with. Recall that you can only combine numerous audio tracks into a single video clip. You will need to synchronize each video separately if you need to sync several video files.

The steps are the same: select every track, pick **Audio** as a synchronization point, pick a reference track, and choose **Merge Clips** or **Synchronize** from the **Clip** menu or by right-clicking.

When choosing a reference track, exercise caution. As soon as you place the recordings in the timeline, start listening to each one and choose which one is your reference track.

Adobe Premiere Pro's automatic functions let you synchronize clips fast and effectively. Always remember to have loud, clear audio recordings and a visual signal to utilize as a sync point when synchronizing audio from the camera and microphone for future recordings.

Summary

This chapter provided you with the necessary tools to build a polished and influential soundscape for your videos in Premiere Pro. We started by examining the features of the **Essential Sound** panel, with a specific emphasis on the development of personalized audio presets. These presets optimize your productivity by enabling you to preconfigure commonly used sound effects, ensuring consistent implementation across your project.

Subsequently, we explored the capabilities of the Track Mixer. This panel provides you with centralized management of all audio tracks in your project. You will get the knowledge of how to employ the Track Mixer in order to enhance the overall sound qualities of your audio by utilizing built-in effects such as EQ and dynamics. In addition, we will discuss how to use creative effects such as reverb to improve the ambiance of your film.

Moreover, this chapter focused on the pivotal element of audio gain control in Premiere Pro. There are two main techniques we examined to do this: the **Audio Gain** dialog box and the **Clip Gain** feature within the timeline. Acquiring proficiency in these methods enables you to guarantee the best audio levels throughout your project, resolving problems such as clear conversation or excessive ambient noise.

The chapter established the foundation for further examination of sound design concepts in later parts where editors could gain expertise in basic to advanced spatial approaches and creative effects by understanding the *Learning sound design* topic. We learned automated syncing features to highlight time-saving with the notion of single-click audio and video synchronization. This feature is really important as it helps to streamline your editing routine. By acquiring expertise in the techniques delineated in this chapter, you will make significant progress in creating videos that possess a professional tone and effectively captivate your viewers.

In the next chapter, we will explore the enchanting world of visual effects in Premiere Pro. Get ready to delve into a world of invaluable resources and strategies that go beyond the mundane. Prepare to explore the depths of video speed and frame rates, video stabilization, smoothing slow motion video, nesting sequences, and removing green screen background seamlessly. With the ability to delicately adjust colors and create captivating transitions, you'll be able to push the boundaries of creativity and captivate your audience with visually stunning masterpieces.

9
Creative Video Effects in Premiere Pro

This chapter will cover the essentials of video editing with Adobe Premiere Pro, emphasizing important abilities and methods. You will learn how to apply and adjust effects with accuracy to make your movie more dramatic. You will learn about the advantages of nesting and the tactical considerations that guide its use in video editing procedures. You will also learn how to remove green screen backdrops so that you can quickly incorporate topics into different settings.

Understanding frame rates gives you influence over the smoothness and style of your video. High frame rates offer a hyperrealistic sensation for fast-paced action, whereas lower rates produce a more theatrical picture. Nesting organizes your project by grouping clips and effects, making complex edits more approachable. Removing the green screen background from your talent enables you to position them in any virtual scene, expanding your creative choices. Finally, using effects such as color grading, transitions, and text overlays adds polish to your video and allows you to visually express your message. By mastering these techniques, you can transform your edits from simple cuts to professional-looking productions that capture your audience's attention.

This chapter offers a strong foundation to utilize Adobe Premiere Pro's features in your video editing endeavors through helpful advice and professional techniques.

In this chapter, you will learn how to create a variety of creative video effects in Premiere Pro, using both built-in effects and third-party plugins.

In this chapter, we will cover the following main topics:

- An introduction to video speed and frame rates
- Stabilize shaky video footage
- Smooth slow motion in Premiere Pro
- Nesting – how and why we use the nesting feature

- Removing the green screen background
- The creative cloud workflow
- On the big screen – Premiere Pro in film and television

An introduction to video speed and frame rates

The speed at which a video plays back is known as its **video speed**. It is measured in **frames per second (fps)**. The video will look smoother and more realistic the higher the frame rate. The number of distinct pictures, or frames, that are shown in a video each second is known as the **frame rate**. Videos are usually made at a higher frame rate, like 24 or 30 frames per second. It's at this higher rate that the human eye can start to notice motion. This is so that slow-motion effects can be rendered more smoothly and motion blur can be minimized at higher frame rates.

Frame rate and video speed are tools used in filmmaking to achieve various effects and moods. For instance, fast-motion can be used to convey humor or excitement, while slow-motion is frequently employed to evoke drama or tension.

Understanding the history of frame rates

In the early days of film (1890–1915), frame rates ranged from 8 to 30 frames per second (fps), which made uniformity in cranking more important than design skills. As movies became more famous, 18 frames per second became the standard to keep things running smoothly and save money.

The transition to talkies in 1927 necessitated a frame rate change for better audio quality, leading to the industry-wide adoption of 24 fps. The introduction of television in the 1930s synchronized with AC power pulsing at 60 cycles per second, resulting in the widely used 30 fps video.

Post-World War II, a global shift to 50 Hz cycles led to 25 fps video in many regions. By the HD era in the 1990s, the industry, although previously fragmented, converged on a standardized frame size and rate, culminating in the current standard.

Frame rate and video speed in the film industry

Here are some instances of how frame rate and video speed are applied in the film industry:

- *24fps*: The usual frame rate for feature films and television broadcasts is 24 fps. It strikes a decent balance between realism and fluidity.
- *30fps*: For quick action, sports, and TV compatibility, this is smoother than 24fps. It can generate a *soap opera*-like hyperrealism that may not fit all projects.

- *60fps*: This frame rate is frequently utilized in video games and slow-motion film. It gives slow motion a highly lifelike feel and reveals subtleties unnoticed at regular speeds.

- *120fps and above*: High-speed slow-motion videos of objects such as balloons exploding or bullets in flight are frequently captured at these frame rates.

Methods used to adjust the frame rate and video speed

Filmmakers can also adjust the frame rate and pace of their videos using several methods, including the following:

- **Overcranking**: Shooting at a greater frame rate than the video will be played back at is known as overcranking. This takes additional fps, smoothing the slow motion. Imagine slowing time with excellent resolution. The *bullet time* effect in *The Matrix* (1999) and Peter Jackson's *Hobbit* trilogy (2012–2014) are examples.

- **Undercranking**: Shooting at a lower frame rate than the video would be played back at is known as undercranking. This produces the illusion of quick speed. Music videos can utilize undercranking for artistic effects. Undercranking and frame mixing allowed Radiohead's *No Surprises* (1997) music video to slow down and become dreamy.

- **Ramp**: In this technique, the video speed is progressively changed from one speed to another. Many effects may be produced with this, such as a seamless change from slow motion to normal speed. Ramping may warp time and generate bizarre images. In *2001: A Space Odyssey* (1968), ramping creates the mind-bending *star gate* scenario.

- **Time-remapping**: With this technique, you can now manipulate the playback speed of specific sections, giving you the power to create stunning slow-motion and fast-motion effects with utmost precision. The climactic chase scene in *Mad Max: Fury Road* (2015) employs extensive time remapping to generate spectacular slow-motion scenes with shifting speeds.

- **Frame blending and interpolation**: To make those transitions between frames look smooth, even slow-motion videos shot at lower frame rates can be turned into a beautiful visual experience. Interpolation preserves quality and smoothness in 24fps slow-motion video, in sports films such as *Free Solo* (2018).

- **Shutter speed manipulation**: By adjusting the shutter speed, you can control the amount of motion blur, ultimately impacting the perceived speed of the action on screen. The slow shutter speed in the initial vehicle pursuit in *Drive* (2011) creates motion blur, indicating speed and recklessness.

- **Zooming**: Accelerating zoom shots infuses them with a sense of energy and excitement, while decelerating zooms can heighten tension or draw attention to specific elements. The *Jaws* (1975) zoom shot increases tension by progressively revealing the shark, increasing danger.

- **Warping and distortion**: This technique results in mesmerizing temporal effects that can transport viewers into a dreamlike state. These tools can also play with the perceived speed of specific elements, adding an extra layer of intrigue to the visual experience. The *star gate* section in *2001: A Space Odyssey* (1968) exploits temporal distortion to produce a psychedelic visual experience.

- **Sound design and music**: Thoughtfully selected sound effects and music have the power to enhance pace and tension, creating a truly immersive experience for the audience. The powerful soundtrack and sound effects in *The Raid 2* (2014) emphasize the fast-paced action and intensity.

- **Editing pacing**: The pacing of a film is heavily influenced by various editing techniques, such as cutting, shot lengths, and transitions. These elements play a crucial role in shaping the overall rhythm and flow of a film, regardless of the frame rate used. The rapid edits and montage in *Baby Driver* (2017) complement the hectic vehicle chases and soundtrack, making the action feel quicker.

Filmmakers can produce more aesthetically pleasing and emotionally impactful movies by understanding the relationship between video speed and frame rate. It affects how viewers perceive motion on screen, making it an important part of filmmaking.

The importance of frame rates in filmmaking

Let's understand the importance of frame rates in filmmaking:

- **Smoothness of motion**: Smoother motion produced by higher frame rates might be visually more appealing and give the impression that a movie is more realistic.

- **Motion blur**: Motion blur is the optical phenomenon that causes moving objects to seem out of focus. Frame rate has an impact on motion blur. Motion blur is lessened at higher frame rates such as 60 fps or above is considered a high-speed frame rate and increased at lower frame rates. Motion blur can be employed to provide movement or a sensation of speed, as well as enhance the cinematic aspect of a movie.

- **Mood and atmosphere**: Altering the frame rate can also provide a variety of moods and settings. Slow motion, for instance, can be employed to convey drama or suspense, whereas quick motion can convey humor or excitement.

Essential concepts for slow motion

It is crucial to grasp the basic principles of slow motion before delving into the specifics of making slow-motion videos in Premiere Pro.

So, let's examine the concepts:

- **Frame rate**: The smoothness of a video is defined by its frame rate, which is the number of images shown per second. The typical frame rate for **high-definition** (**HD**) video is 30 fps, whereas the standard frame rate is 24.

- **Temporal interpolation**: Premiere Pro must create extra frames to keep smoothness when slowing down footage shot at a standard frame rate. It examines the current frames and makes new ones that blend in with the original footage, a process that is called temporal interpolation.

- **Frame blending**: Frame blending is another technique that can be used to make slow motion. To achieve a more seamless transition, this method makes a copy of an existing frame and then fades them together, rather than producing new frames from scratch.

Learning the fundaments of frame rates

The fundamentals of frame rates are constant regardless of the editing program you use – Adobe, Apple, Avid, or another – on different devices:

- For best performance, try to shoot, edit, and export at the same frame rate.

- Video shot at its original frame rate appears more professional than converted video.

- Frame rates for streaming and downloaded media on the web are adjustable.

- Frames cannot be split, stretched, or compressed; they are indivisible.

- The frame rate of your project supersedes the frame rate of the original material.

- In a 25 fps project, each frame in the movie has a defined length of 1/25th of a second.

- Clips are automatically adjusted by video editing software to fit the frame rate of a project.

- Even if a project includes clips with varying frame rates, it can only have one frame rate.

- Converting from a faster frame rate – such as 50 fps – to a slower one – such as 25 fps – is typically more seamless than the opposite.

Imagine video like a comic book coming to life. Each picture in the comic is like a single frame in the video. The faster you flip through the pages (or show the frames), the smoother the action looks. This speed of flipping is called the frame rate.

Movies use different frame rates to create different moods. For example, a fast, smooth rate like 30 fps makes action scenes feel exciting. A slower rate, such as 12 fps, can make things seem dreamlike or suspenseful. By choosing the right frame rate, you can control the feeling of your video, just like a filmmaker!

Next, we'll learn how to change frame rates and what your options are.

Conversion options

To make sure that action appears at a constant speed when a clip is played at the appropriate frame rate, you can utilize **frame rate conversion**, which entails copying or deleting frames.

Although most video editing software takes care of this automatically, it can still be helpful to know the following basic options:

- **Easy conversion:**

  - For 50 fps to 25 fps or 60 fps to 30 fps, simply delete every other frame, maintaining smooth playback

  - For 29.97 fps to 59.94 fps or 25 fps to 50 fps, duplicate every frame, preserving the original motion

- **Mostly easy conversion:**

  - To convert 24 fps to 25 fps, increase speed by 4%, maintaining overall visual quality with a slightly faster pace.

- **Hard conversion:**

  - Filmmakers can change the frame rate of their video footage, but it's a bit like trying to change gears on a bike while you're already riding. There are two main ways to do it:

    - **Hard conversion:** This is like slamming on the brakes and then speeding up again. It can be tricky and sometimes cause problems such as stuttering or jerky movements.

    - **Soft conversion:** This is like gently changing gears while riding. It's smoother and generally better for your video, but it doesn't actually change the number of frames.

  - Here's an example. Imagine you filmed a video at 60 fps (fps), like a super-smooth flip book. However, you want it to look more like a movie, which is usually filmed at 24 fps (a slightly slower flip book):

    - **Hard conversion:** You could try to remove frames to get down to 24 fps, but this can make the video jumpy and look choppy. It's like ripping pages out of your flip book!

    - **Soft conversion:** You could slow down the playback speed of your 60 fps video to match the 24 fps feel. This keeps all the frames intact, but it might not look quite as smooth as native 24 fps footage.

The best advice? Whenever possible, film, edit, and play your video at the same frame rate throughout. It's like riding your bike at a steady pace – smoother and more enjoyable for everyone! But if conversion is necessary, try soft conversion methods whenever possible for a better viewing experience.

Put simply, maintaining native frame rates is essential for the best quality, since conversions might cause **visual artifacts**. The frame rate isn't the only factor in creating a cinematic image, and while methods such as optical flow try to create additional frames, they frequently don't provide the intended results.

Filmmakers manipulate frame rates utilizing optical flow. It's a method to estimate motion between frames, especially for transcoding film between speeds. *Camera-native frame rates always look better than converted frame rates* (Larry Jordan, 2016, *Frame Rates are Tricky Beasts*: `https://larryjordan.com/articles/frame-rates-are-tricky-beasts/`) is still the guiding philosophy.

Picking the right video frame rate

The slower the speed (frame rate), the blurrier moving objects appear. Back in the olden days of film, cameras were cranked by hand, which meant the speed wasn't always consistent. Once sound was added to movies, they needed a standard speed to keep the picture and sound in sync. That's why most movies are filmed at 24 fps – it was a good balance between cost and quality.

Today, filmmakers sometimes use even faster speeds, such as 48 fps, to get extra sharp images with less blur, especially for action scenes, as seen in films such as *The Hobbit*. It's like having a super-zoom that can still capture everything clearly! This also allows for brighter movie theater experiences without any flickering on the screen.

> **Important note**
> It's important to note that higher frame rates often mean faster shutter speeds, resulting in sharper but potentially less smooth motion.

Here are some practical considerations on frame rate priorities:

- Web content is flexible with frame rates.
- Cable or broadcast television often uses 60 fps in North America and 50 fps elsewhere. In most of Europe and other nations, 25 or 50 fps (PAL) is utilized.
- Theatrical releases stick to the traditional 24 fps, while digital projection offers more options.

The key takeaway is to always confirm your project's requirements before shooting, as it's easier to shoot at the right frame rate than to convert it after filming.

Stabilizing shaky video footage

Using a handheld camera to record video has the advantage of allowing for instantaneous shot movement. The unfortunate part about shaky film is that it might cause motion sickness in viewers.

In filmmaking, **stabilization** is the process of minimizing unwanted camera movements that can cause shakiness, jitter, or blur in the final footage. Picture a scene captured with an unsteady hand or during a turbulent car journey – the purpose of stabilization is to eliminate these flaws and produce a visually steady and appealing image.

Here are some common types of stabilization used in filmmaking:

- **In-camera stabilization**: Some cameras have built-in magic (in-camera stabilization) that helps smooth out bumps and wobbles when you're filming handheld. It uses tiny sensors to detect shakes and adjusts the image ever-so-slightly to keep things steady. This is great for situations where you can't use a tripod, such as filming a concert or playing catch in the park.

- **Post-production stabilization**: This method goes through your video frame by frame, like a super-careful checker, and fixes any wobbles it finds. It gives you more control than in-camera stabilization, but it takes a lot of computer power and might slightly cut off the edges of your video.

- **Gimbal stabilizers**: These are gadgets you can attach to your camera that use motors and sensors to magically smooth out shaky footage. They're perfect for handheld filming, whether you're walking around or zooming in for a close-up. They let you focus on capturing great shots without worrying about wobbles.

- **The Steadicam**: The Steadicam is a fancy stabilizer that uses a vest and arm system to keep the camera super steady, even when the operator is moving around. This lets filmmakers capture smooth, professional-looking footage, perfect for elaborate action scenes or following actors on the move. (Think of how smooth a chicken's head stays when it walks – kind of like a Steadicam! While the *Chicken Head Stabilizer* isn't a real feature, it's a fun analogy to illustrate the Steadicam's remarkable stability.)

Here are the advantages of stabilization:

- **Crafting a polished and professional look**: The importance of smooth and stable footage cannot be overstated. It elevates the overall viewing experience, leaving a lasting impression on the audience.

- **Using your own creativity**: With creative freedom, filmmakers can effortlessly wield handheld cameras or employ dynamic movements, all while maintaining impeccable image quality.

- **Emphasizing the content**: With stable footage, viewers can fully immerse themselves in the story and connect with the characters, free from any distractions caused by camera shake.

However, there are some important factors to keep in mind about stabilization:

- **Stabilization**: Excessive stabilization can result in an unnatural, almost soap opera-like effect

- **Image cropping**: It's worth noting that certain stabilization techniques might result in the image being slightly cropped

- **Resolution**: Achieving greater effectiveness in stabilization is often associated with the use of higher-resolution footage

Ultimately, the decision to stabilize or not, and how to do it, will be influenced by the unique requirements of your project, the camera you're working with, and the artistic look you want to achieve. By gaining a comprehensive understanding of the various forms of stabilization and carefully weighing their advantages and disadvantages, you can make a well-informed choice to elevate the visual excellence of your film.

How it works in Adobe Premiere Pro

Thankfully, Adobe Premiere Pro has a strong effect that helps stabilize unsteady footage. In Premiere Pro, clip stabilization uses a powerful tool called **Warp Stabilizer** to smooth out shaky footage.

> **Reminder**
> Stabilization only affects entire clips, not segments. Ensure to make a cut before stabilizing any part of the footage.

Here's how Warp Stabilizer works in Premiere Pro:

- **While analyzing shaky footage**:

  - When the **Warp Stabilizer** effect is applied, Premiere Pro meticulously examines every frame of your clip, tracking distinct points of reference within eachimage

  - Through this analysis, the software gains a deeper understanding of the camera movements that result in unwanted shakiness

- **While compensating for the movement**:

  - After identifying the movement, **Warp Stabilizer** swiftly calculates the precise counteractive motion required

  - Each frame is meticulously manipulated, **Warp Stabilizer** digitally shifting, rotating, and scaling them with precision

  - Envision each frame as a miniature puzzle piece. The position of each piece is adjusted by **Warp Stabilizer** to create a cohesive and stable image

- **While balancing stabilization and quality**:

  - As the footage is smoothed, the **Warp Stabilizer** algorithm places great emphasis on preserving the overall quality of the clip

  - With a variety of modes such as **Position**, **Scale**, and **Rotate**, users can meticulously adjust the stabilization to their liking

  - Additionally, you have the option to select either **Smooth Only** or **Smooth Stabilize** to prioritize either achieving a seamless result or preserving the initial framing

Although formidable, **Warp Stabilizer** falls short of perfection. Finding the perfect balance in stabilization settings is of utmost importance, as an overdone stabilization can lead to unsightly artifacts or a wobbly *jello* effect. Mastering intricate camera movements or dealing with excessive shakiness can still present some obstacles. Stabilization can sometimes be a time-consuming process, depending on the length and resolution of the footage.

A step-by-step guide to stabilizing video files in Premiere Pro

The **Warp Stabilizer** effect can be used to stabilize unsteady footage. It eliminates the jitter brought on by camera movement, enabling the conversion of handheld, shaky video into stable, fluid images.

Use the **Warp Stabilizer** effect to stabilize motion by doing the following:

1. Choose the clip that needs stabilizing.

2. It is only possible to apply stabilization to timeline clips. Apply **Effects** | **Video Effects** | **Distortion** | **Warp Stabilizer** after selecting the clip.

Figure 9.1 – Applying the Warp Stabilizer effect on a clip

3. Premiere instantly analyzes your footage. Later, the shakiness will subside. You can pre-render your footage for optimum results, but it's not required. **Pre-rendering** enables smooth editing previews. You can be creative because it saves minutes during export. You can also edit offline, collaborate, and export quickly. Premiere Pro pre-rendering lets your computer preview your creation. Specific timeline parts receive temporary preview files. Previews encode effects, transitions, and complex components for smoother playback. Pre-rendering ensures a smooth editing experience and lets you spot flaws before export, saving time and stress. While Warp Stabilizer is a powerful tool, it's worth noting that it doesn't always work well with other effects, particularly ones that change a clip's scale or speed. For example, if you've previously performed temporal remapping or scaling to your video, Warp Stabilizer may fail to evaluate it properly. In certain circumstances, you may see mistakes or undesired artifacts in the stabilized footage.

However, you have a number of alternatives to enhance the outcome of using the **Warp Stabilizer** effect (see *Figure 9.2*):

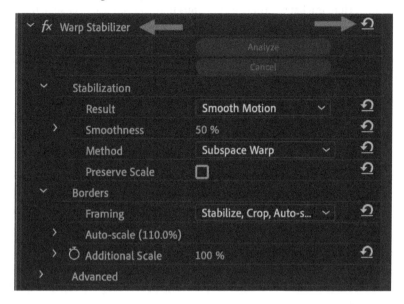

Figure 9.2 – The Warp Stabilizer effect in the Effect Control panel

As shown in *Figure 9.2*, click the *curved arrow* to the right of the setting you wish to reset (indicated by the *right red arrow*) to reset the effect as a whole or just a particular setting.

4. To get a smoother transition, it is also possible to modify the stabilization procedure using the **Stabilization** settings, as shown here:

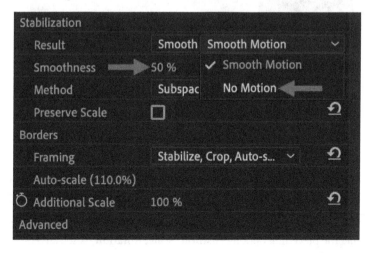

Figure 9.3 – Adjust the smoothness of the Stabilization settings

To change the amount of shaking eliminated, modify the **Smoothness** level; lower settings remove less wobble. For example, you can adjust the image by 10 pixels to eliminate a 20-pixel tremor from the frame. Here is a list of drop-down menus that you can use to change the adjustment:

- **Outcome**: This determines whether smooth or no motion is the desired outcome for the video.

- **Smooth Motion** (default): This is a setting that controls how smoothly the camera moves when it is chosen.

- **No Motion**: This tries to eliminate any camera movement from the picture. In the **Advanced** section, the **Crop Less Smooth More** function is disabled when it is chosen. This option is utilized for films when the primary subject is in the frame for the entirety of the range being analyzed.

- **Smoothness**: This determines the degree of original motion stabilization applied to the camera. Higher numbers are smoother, and lower values are closer to the actual motion of the camera. More picture cropping is necessary for values greater than 100. When the result is set to **Smooth Motion**, it becomes enabled.

The level of smoothness available in Premiere Pro's **Warp Stabilizer** tool allows for precise adjustments to reduce jitter and shakes in your footage. It complements the stabilization method you select (such as **Position**, **Subspace Warp**, or **Perspective**) to help you achieve your desired look.

The **Method** option offers the most intricate process the Warp Stabilizer does to stabilize video (see *Figure 9.4*):

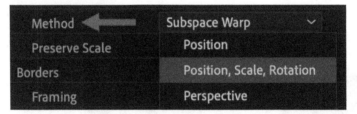

Figure 9.4 – The Warp Stabilizer options in the Effect Controls panel

You might want to adjust the method in **Warp Stabilizer** for a few reasons, depending on your specific needs and the characteristics of your footage. Here's a breakdown:

- **Position**: The simplest method of stabilizing film is position-based stabilization, which just uses position data.

- **Position, Scale, Rotation**: This information is the foundation for stabilization. If there aren't enough areas to track, Warp Stabilizer chooses the choice before this one (Position).

- **Perspective**: This employs a kind of stabilization where the frame is essentially corner-pinned throughout. The preceding option (**Position, Scale, Rotation**) is selected by Warp Stabilizer if there are insufficient regions to track.

- **Subspace Warp**: This is the default option. It tries to stabilize an entire frame by warping different areas of it in different ways. If the Warp Stabilizer cannot detect enough regions, it will select the preceding option (**Perspective**). Depending on the tracking precision, the technique used on any particular frame may change during the clip.

- **Preserve Scale**: The clip's scale remains unchanged if this item is checked.

Whether you are filming an exciting action scene, a touching moment, or the beauty of nature, I hope your footage is not only stable but also a demonstration of your skill in stabilizing shaky moments and creating a visually compelling story that resonates with your viewers.

Smooth slow motion in Premiere Pro

For a considerable time, **slow motion** has been an enthralling cinematic method, enhancing the dramatic impact, emotional depth, and visual style of films, television shows, and even social media videos. Although capturing slow-motion footage directly with specialized equipment and expertise is necessary, Adobe Premiere Pro provides a flexible and easily accessible solution to produce slow-motion effects during the editing process.

When the *shooting frame rate* is greater than the *playback frame rate* (i.e., more than 30fps!), slow motion can be achieved. For example, if you shoot video at 60 fps, it can be played back at a slow-motion rate.

Shooting at a high frame rate is ideal, and luckily, the majority of cameras offer the option to shoot at a rate between 60 and 240 fps. To capture footage with such a stunningly slow-motion effect, a dedicated camera is required that offers high frame rates (up to 240 fps) and large sensor sizes for excellent image quality, such as Sony a7S III, Canon EOS R5, or Nikon Z9.

In Premiere Pro, use high frame rate footage and choose the **Optical Flow** option for smooth slow motion.

Remember to adjust the **Smoothness** setting to fine-tune the shake removal from 0 to 100%. Begin with a low setting and slowly increase it, while monitoring for any potential artifacts. When your footage is a bit shaky, the **Warp Stabilizer** tool can help smooth it out; just be cautious of any distortion it may cause.

Keep in mind that achieving a balance is crucial; while clear visuals are important, focus on maintaining natural camera movements to prevent artifacts from appearing.

How Premiere Pro simulates a high frame rate camera

Adobe Premiere Pro needs to produce additional frames sometimes to increase the *shooting* frame rate, which is an issue with artificial slow motion. To achieve this, it can either analyze your footage and automatically generate new frames or repeat existing ones.

The outcome is somewhat jagged when the program recycles previous frames (which is also useful in its own right!). Imperfections in the interpretation can lead to artifacts and warping errors when it generates new frames. However, fear not – the finest outcomes are within your reach if you take the time to learn how to use the resources at your disposal.

When incorporating slow-motion effects in Premiere Pro, the software must generate extra frames to achieve the intended result. It may either replicate current frames (creating a choppy appearance) or produce completely new ones (potentially causing artifacts). Understanding these methods can lead to achieving outstanding slow-motion results, despite their limitations.

Changing speed and duration

Making slow-motion video is a breeze with Adobe Premiere Pro's **Speed/Duration** module. Pick **Speed/Duration** from the context menu when you right-click a clip. A percentage less than 100% will slow down your clip. To double the length of a clip, for instance, you can set the speed to 50% and play it back at half the original speed.

Conversely, you can tell Premiere how long you want your clip to be by entering the desired duration in the **Duration** section. Press G on the keyboard until this window appears (see *Figure 9.5*). This will allow you to independently adjust the duration or speed without affecting the other parameter.

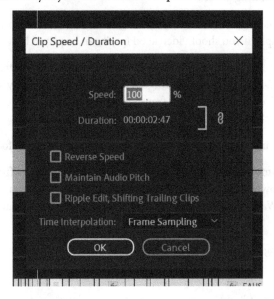

Figure 9.5 – The speed and duration options in the timeline

Quick and dirty jobs, such as giving a clip a stylized look, adjusting a clip that only needs a little tweak, or making slow motion footage even slower, are perfect for Adobe Premiere Pro's **Speed** and **Duration** adjustments.

Speed ramps, achieved by using time remapping in Premiere Pro, provide detailed control over video speed. This method enables you to control how viewers perceive time, enabling you to highlight important moments, create tension, or fine-tune pacing to suit your video's content.

Creating a speed ramp with time remapping

Through the manipulation of video speed via time remapping, you can craft compelling slow-motion sequences, highlight pivotal instances, or quicken the tempo for an exhilarating impact. With this technique, you have complete control over the flow of time in your video, enabling you to create a captivating experience for your audience:

1. Before you start applying a speed ramp, make sure you can see what you're doing by clicking and dragging the video track to make it taller. **Speed** can be accessed by right-clicking a clip and then choosing **Show Clip Keyframes | Time Remapping**, as shown in *Figure 9.6*:

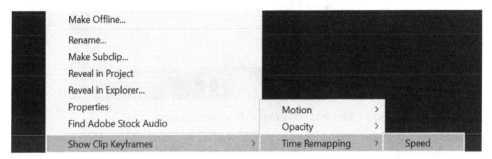

Figure 9.6 – Right-click a clip to enable Time Remapping in the timeline

2. In *Figure 9.7*, we can see a horizontal band that lets us adjust a clip's speed. To change the clip's speed and, by extension, its length, simply drag the band vertically.

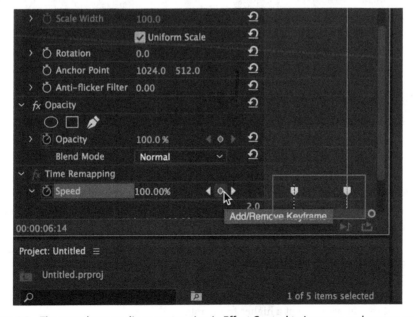

Figure 9.7 – The speed ramp adjustment option in Effect Control to increase or decrease speed

3. The use of keyframes is required in order to generate a progressive speed change. Two keyframes, effectively dividing a clip into three parts, are required to achieve an effect where the speed ramps up or down to emphasize a motion before returning to normal speed.

    To make keyframes, press *Command* + click (Mac) or *CTRL* + click (PC) on the band. To change the speed of the video, click and drag the middle section up or down.

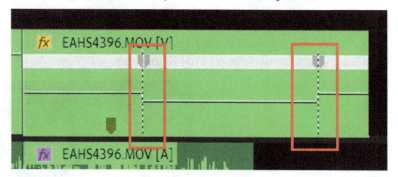

Figure 9.8 – Add keyframes to time remapping in a clip

4. Here, the change in speed is sudden. Use the mouse to split your keyframe and smooth out the ramp. When you want an even smoother result, use the Bezier handles. Get the look you want by experimenting with the ramp.

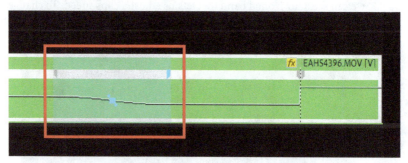

Figure 9.9 – Smoothing the speed with curve

With Bezier handles in Premiere Pro, you have precise control over the smoothness of your speed transitions. Adjust the acceleration and deceleration curves within the ramp by manipulating the handles. With this feature, you can craft authentic or artistic speed effects to enhance your video edits with a dynamic and polished touch.

Using the Optical Flow feature

To make your slow-motion effect look more natural, you can use the **Optical Flow** feature. This will make it appear as though you shot at a higher frame rate.

When you turn this feature on, Premiere Pro will intelligently create new frames to insert between your current ones by analyzing your current frames. Instead of choppy motion, the outcome is smooth motion.

Premiere Pro's **Frame Sampling** feature also allows users to achieve the slow-motion effect, by duplicating existing frames. It gets the job done, but it's not very smooth.

To activate **Optical Flow**, set the **Time Interpolation** setting to **Optical Flow** before adjusting the **Speed** or **Duration** setting.

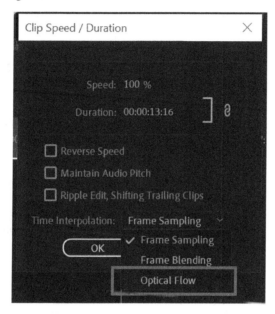

Figure 9.10 – Applying Optical Flow to a clip

To apply Optical Flow to a speed ramp, select **Optical Flow** from the **Time Interpolation** menu by right-clicking (see *Figure 9.10*). Then, make a rendering.

You will need to render the footage after making this change before you can play it back. Click on **Sequence** and then on **Render In to Out**.

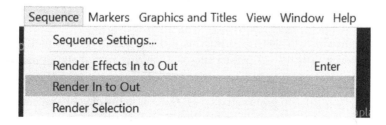

Figure 9.11 – Render In and Out on the Sequence menu

The **Render In to Out** feature in the **Sequence** menu is a great tool to streamline your editing workflow. This focused rendering method enables you to focus on particular regions with effects or lagging playback, increasing efficiency and assuring a smooth editing experience. Remember, planned rendering paired with good preview management will result in shorter project turnaround times and a more pleasurable editing experience.

Time and velocity of an Optical Flow clip

Premiere Pro can invent new images in between the real ones you filmed. This is called **Optical Flow**. It helps get rid of choppiness and makes the slow motion look smoother.

However, there's a catch! Sometimes, inventing new images can lead to weird distortions or blurry spots in your video. This is less likely if you filmed in front of a simple background, such as a wall.

The bottom line? **Optical flow**, analyzes the video and predicts where the image will go to produce the missing frames in the gaps. The outcomes from optical flow will be smoother and more natural. However, low-quality film may distort the image. This option can efficiently produce a slow-motion effect. Next, let's learn how to use nesting in Premiere Pro!

Nesting – how and why we use the nesting feature

You can simplify your timeline, organize your project, and make more complex edits in Adobe Premiere Pro using the nesting sequences technique. **Nesting sequences** allow you to combine numerous clips, which can subsequently be used independently in your project. As your project expands in scope and complexity, this can become an invaluable tool for project management.

Why is Premiere Pro's nesting necessary?

Using nesting in Premiere Pro might be useful for a number of reasons. Here are a few advantages:

- **Organization**: Nesting is a great tool for project organization because it allows you to group clips that are related together. You can keep track of your project and easily locate the clips you need with this.

- **Simplification**: Eliminating unnecessary clips from your timeline is one way that nesting can make your life easier. As a result, you may find it less of a hassle to make changes to your project and maintain tabs on them.

- **Flexibility**: More leeway to alter your project as you see fit is one benefit of nesting. To make elaborate edits such as picture-in-picture effects or multi-camera shots, for instance, you can nest sequences.

- **Reusability**: By using nesting, you can increase the reusability of your sequences. A series of lower thirds, for instance, can be *nested* and reused across various projects.

How to nest sequences in Premiere Pro

Now, let's learn how to nest sequences in Premiere Pro:

1. Choose the video clips. To nest clips in the timeline, select them.

2. To select multiple clips at once, right-click on them, and then select **Nest…** from the menu.

Figure 9.12 – Nesting clips in the timeline

3. Give your sequence a descriptive name in the **Nest Sequence Name** dialog box.

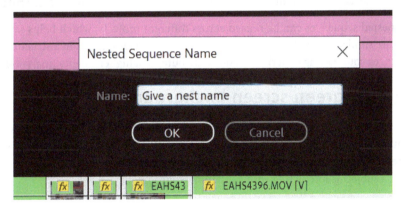

Figure 9.13 – Naming the nested sequence

4. To make a new sequence, right-click the clip, and then click on the **Nest** menu.

5. When you nest a sequence, it will appear in your timeline as a single clip. When you double-click on a nested sequence, a new timeline will open up. From there, you can edit the clips that are part of the sequence.

Figure 9.14 – A nested sequence as one clip

You can streamline your workflow, add more complexity to your edits, and improve project organization with the help of nesting sequences. It helps you keep your timeline organized by grouping related clips and effects in a single *clip*, which ultimately reduces visual clutter. Enhancing workflow efficiency is crucial by allowing you to make edits or apply effects to the entire nested sequence simultaneously, ultimately saving time and effort. Nesting essentially creates a new sub-composition of your clip, allowing stacking effects on the original footage without any pre-existing effects interfering.

Furthermore, nested sequences can be reused across different projects, which helps save time on projects that share similar elements. Utilizing nesting effectively helps maintain a structured project hierarchy, enhances your editing experience, and contributes to a higher-quality final product.

Removing the green screen background

Video editors frequently use Adobe Premiere Pro to **remove green screen backgrounds**. One way to combine multiple layers of video or images is using a green screen, which is also called **chroma keying**. A different background image or video can be used to replace the green screen, giving the impression that a subject is interacting with a different environment.

Preparing your footage

Get the lighting and camera angles just right before you start cutting out the green screen. To be well-prepared, consider the following:

- **Even green screen lighting**: To keep the green screen backdrop from casting shadows or showing color variations, it is important to use uniform lighting. Premiere Pro may struggle to properly differentiate between the subject and the green screen in environments with uneven lighting.

- **A solid green screen color**: To make a striking contrast with the subject, go for a solid, vibrant green screen color such as apple green or chroma green. Premiere Pro may have trouble isolating the subject if you use dark or dull green shades.

- **Subject separation**: Place the subject far in front of the green screen so that there is little background overlap and the subject has clean edges. By doing so, Premiere Pro will be able to distinguish between the subject and the green screen with more precision.

Removing the green screen in Premiere Pro

The **Ultra Key effect** is a flexible tool available in Adobe Premiere Pro that can be used to eliminate green screen backgrounds. To successfully remove the green screen, follow these steps:

1. **Import footage**: To import footage into Premiere Pro, simply drag and drop your green screen footage onto the timeline.

2. **Apply the Ultra Key effect**: Find the **Effects** panel and click on the green screen clip in the timeline to apply the **Ultra Key** effect. Find the **Ultra Key** effect in your search results and drop it onto the video.

Figure 9.15 – Applying the Ultra Key effect to a clip

3. **Adjust the key color**: To change the key color, go to the **Key Color** section of the **Effect Controls** panel. Use the *eyedropper* tool to extract a small sample of the clip's green screen color.

Figure 9.16 – Changing the key color using the eyedropper

4. **Fine-tune the settings**: Adjust the **Ultra Key**'s settings to fine-tune the process of removing green screens. Use this effect to make any color in an image transparent, with extra parameters to fine-tune the outcome. For control over the edges, use the **Matte Cleanup** slider, and for spill suppression, use the **Spill Suppression** slider.

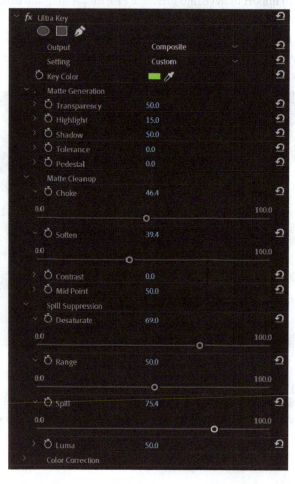

Figure 9.17 – Adjusting the settings in Effect Controls

5. **Preview and adjust**: Try it out in the program or source monitor to see how it will look before making any changes. Once you've successfully isolated the subject and eliminated the green screen, tweak the **Ultra Key** settings one more time.

Never forget that precise lighting and color settings, as well as high-quality footage, determine how well you can remove green screens. If you know what you're doing and use Premiere Pro's **Ultra Key** effect correctly, you can make stunning visual effects that look professional. However, it should be noted that Ultra Key is a unique form of color key effect. Premiere Pro has a bigger category called **Color Key** effects, which includes capabilities such as Ultra Key but targets a wider spectrum of hues.

The creative cloud workflow

Premiere Pro acts as the central hub for your video editing project. Here, you can assemble your video clips, arrange them in a timeline, and perform basic edits such as trimming, cutting, and color correction.

When you need mind-blowing **visual effects** (**VFX**) or complex motion graphics, After Effects comes to the rescue. Here's a breakdown of how Premiere Pro works with After Effects to create advanced video effects:

- **Green screen magic**: Premiere Pro can remove a green or blue background from your footage. You can then send that clip to After Effects to composite your subject onto a new background or create fantastical environments.

- **Animations and motion graphics**: Want animated titles, intros, or dynamic graphics? After Effects is your playground. You can create stunning animations and import them directly into your Premiere Pro timeline.

- **Advanced compositing**: For complex layering and compositing of multiple elements (such as explosions, smoke, or creatures), After Effects offers powerful tools to bring your vision to life.

The power of integration

The beauty of the Adobe Creative Cloud lies in its tight integration. Here's how it streamlines your workflow:

- **Dynamic link**: This feature allows you to make changes to your graphics (in Photoshop or Illustrator) or animations (in After Effects) and see those changes reflected instantly within your Premiere Pro project, eliminating the need for constant exporting and re-importing.

- **Shared assets**: Create a library of graphics, logos, or illustrations in Photoshop or Illustrator, and easily access them for use within Premiere Pro. This ensures consistency and saves time.

Premiere Pro and After Effects comprise a formidable creative suite for video editing. By combining the characteristics of each app and employing seamless collaboration features, you can create professional-looking video projects with beautiful visual effects, animations, and graphics, all inside a single workflow.

Adobe Premiere Pro is the industry standard for film and television editing. However, how exactly do editors use this powerful tool to bring our favorite shows and movies to life? Let's look at the procedure with a specific sample in the next section.

On the big screen – Premiere Pro in film and television

As the movie industry evolves and well-known editors and filmmakers migrate to Adobe Premiere Pro for video creation, independent films and even large-budget Hollywood films are making the switch to software that anybody can download and use.

Here are my top three movies and TV series that employed Premiere Pro in the editing process, along with some background information on each.

Deadpool (2016)

Miller, the editor of *Deadpool*, wasn't initially familiar with Premiere Pro. However, after learning that David Fincher used it for *Gone Girl* and hearing positive feedback about its stability and focus on filmmaker needs, Miller decided to give it a try.

Premiere Pro's seamless integration with After Effects, crucial for handling Deadpool's action and effects, combined with its efficiency in basic editing tasks and stability, made it a perfect fit for the project. The software allowed Miller to quickly bring his vision to life.

Gone Girl (2014)

Despite being the first feature film shot on 6K RED Dragon and edited in Premiere Pro CC, *Gone Girl* achieved smooth editing thanks to a powerful combination of different technologies. The footage was initially edited at a lower resolution for efficiency, and then converted to 6K using Premiere Pro and After Effects. This process relied heavily on Adobe's Mercury Playback Engine utilizing NVIDIA GPUs for real-time processing, along with optimized storage configurations by OpenDrives to handle the massive data demands.

Monsters (2010)

Gareth Edwards, the director and filmmaker credited Premiere Pro's tapeless workflow for streamlining footage import and its connection with After Effects for seamless pre-visualization. He highlighted the software's ability to handle full HD footage smoothly and the efficiency of Dynamic Link for real-time collaboration, allowing him and his collaborator to quickly create previsualization effects that seamlessly integrated into the final film.

Summary

This chapter took you on a comprehensive journey through the essential aspects of video production, covering topics such as understanding video speed and frame rates, stabilizing shaky footage, creating smooth slow-motion sequences in Adobe Premiere Pro, utilizing nesting for efficient editing workflows, and removing green screen backgrounds.

Premiere Pro shines as the central hub for your video editing project, allowing you to assemble clips, make basic edits, and manage the overall structure. But the true magic happens when you tap into the power of other Creative Cloud applications. After Effects swoops in for mind-blowing visual effects, crafting anything from green screen composites to dynamic motion graphics. Need high-quality titles or retouched video frames? Photoshop steps up to the plate for graphic design and precise image editing. Finally, Illustrator lends its expertise to create scalable vector graphics such as logos, icons, or infographics that seamlessly integrate into your project. This dream team doesn't work in isolation – Premiere Pro's Dynamic Link ensures changes made in any app are reflected instantly, and shared libraries keep your project consistent. The result? A powerful and collaborative workflow that unlocks a world of advanced video effects, animations, and graphics, allowing you to bring your creative vision to life with stunning results.

To clarify the concept of creative processes in Premiere Pro, we looked at how it simplifies the editing process, such as how editors strategize their timelines and use technologies to maximize productivity. To emphasize this point, we examined instances of well-known films and television series that used Premiere Pro for editing, demonstrating the software's strength and adaptability in the industry.

After delving into various creative video effects in Premiere Pro, in the next chapter, we will explore the realm of compositing techniques. Compositing involves skillfully merging various video elements to create a unified image. Exploring a new dimension of visual storytelling involves seamlessly blending footage, incorporating special effects, and crafting illusions that challenge the limits of reality. Prepare yourself to delve into the world of layers, masks, and blending modes in Premiere Pro!

10
Exploring Compositing Techniques

Compositing involves more than just the act of stacking items together. It is a creative discipline that involves careful contemplation of several elements, such as the arrangement of the shot. Comprehending and implementing the essential principles of shot composition will enable you to direct the viewer's gaze, establish visual equilibrium, and elicit particular emotions in your composites.

This chapter looks into the fundamentals of composition and compositing in film production. We will look at the historical history of cinema composition, the significance of knowing aspect ratios, and practical methods for enhancing shot composition and framing. We will also look at the many sorts of photographs and their compositional qualities, as well as the important components that make up a successful composition.

Furthermore, we will look at the notion of compositing, which includes integrating many visual components from various sources. We'll break down compositing techniques and look at sophisticated compositing technologies utilized in current film production. Mastering these approaches will allow you to make visually appealing and compelling films that engage your viewers.

We will examine several methodologies for integrating components from diverse origins, encompassing the following:

- The evolution of film composition
- The canvas and the frame – understanding aspect ratio
- Improving your shot composition and framing
- Understanding different types of shots and composition aspect
- Delving into the key elements of a strong composition
- What is compositing?
- Compositing technique – a breakdown
- Advanced compositing in film – Modern compositing techniques

The goal of this chapter is to provide you with the information and abilities required to make visually appealing and powerful films by delving into the principles of composition and compositing.

The evolution of film composition

Movie-making relies heavily on its visual elements, with **composition** playing a crucial role in conveying its narrative impact. Crafting the composition of visual elements in a frame is a delicate process that directs the viewer's gaze, stirs feelings, and weaves a captivating narrative. Exploring the historical roots, key elements, and practical applications of film composition is the focus of this chapter.

Exploring the world of film composition reveals a captivating evolution that parallels the dynamic nature of cinematic storytelling. Early silent films were greatly dependent on theatrical staging techniques, using static compositions with subjects placed in the center.

As the medium evolved, filmmakers such as D.W. Griffith started to explore camera movement and framing, bringing dynamism and visual storytelling elements into play. The significance of composition in directing the viewer's attention and defining the spatial relationships between characters and their environment was further highlighted with the introduction of sound.

In the 20th and 21st centuries, various **film movements** emerged, each demonstrating unique approaches to composition to convey artistic visions and evoke specific moods. For example, German Expressionism utilized distorted perspectives, while the French New Wave embraced minimalist framing.

Delving into the historical context enables one to truly grasp the intricate techniques that have influenced the art form, setting the stage for delving into the essential elements of effective compositions.

The canvas and the frame – understanding aspect ratio

The **aspect ratio**, which is the width-to-height ratio of the image, sets the foundation for your composition to take shape. Various aspect ratios can evoke different emotions and influence how the viewer perceives the content. The traditional 1.33:1 *Academy ratio*, widely employed in the early days of cinema, provides a more intimate and concentrated viewing experience.

In modern cinema, the widescreen 2.35:1 format offers a more expansive and captivating visual experience, frequently used to highlight vast landscapes or grand action scenes. By grasping the strengths and weaknesses of various aspect ratios, you can make informed decisions that align with your storytelling objectives and elevate the visual impact of your film. The following sub-sections show some common aspect ratios.

Common aspect ratios

When working with video, it's important to understand the different aspect ratios. Here are some of the most common ones:

- *Standard Definition (SD)*: 4:3 (width:height)
- *High Definition (HD)*: 16:9
- *Ultra High Definition (UHD or 4K)*: 16:9
- *Vertical*: 9:16
- *Horizontal*: 1:2.35 (also known as CinemaScope or widescreen)
- *Square*: 1:1

Each aspect ratio has distinct properties that may be employed to achieve various **visual effects** (**VFX**) and moods. Understanding aspect ratios is critical for you to properly compose your work.

Types of aspect ratios

The aspect ratio is the proportionate connection between the width and height of an image or video. It is usually written as two integers separated by a colon (e.g., 16:9). Here are some common types of aspect ratios:

- *2K resolution*: Typically, 2,048 x 1,080 pixels. It's widely utilized in digital cinema.
- *4K resolution*: 3,840 x 2,160 pixels (4K UHD) or 4,096 x 2,160 pixels (4K DCI). It has four times the pixel count of 2K, resulting in more detail and clarity.

Orientation refers to the direction in which a video or image is displayed. There are three main orientations:

- *Horizontal (Landscape)*: Wider than it is tall (16:9). Commonly used in film, television, and web video.
- *Vertical (Portrait)*: Taller than it is broad (for example, 9:16). Commonly used for mobile content, social networking platforms, and some advertising formats.
- *Square (1:1)*: Has equal width and height. Frequently used on sites such as Instagram for postings to provide a consistent image.

The aspect ratio is determined by several criteria, including the content, target audience, and the production's technological limits. Understanding the various aspect ratios and their ramifications allows you to make more educated judgments about how to frame your pictures and create the intended visual impact.

How to use the aspect ratio

Your composition's mood, tone, and visual impact can all be strongly influenced by the aspect ratio you choose. The aspect ratio is determined by a number of elements:

- *Horizontal (landscape)*: Ideal for movies, television shows, YouTube videos, and gaming as it mimics human peripheral vision, resulting in a more immersive experience.

- *Vertical (portrait)*: Best for mobile videos, Instagram or Snapchat stories, and some advertisements. Ideal for single-handed viewing on mobile devices, as consumers hold their phones vertically.

- *Square (1 to 1)*: Best for social media posts, especially on Instagram. It provides a balanced appearance and is ideal for viewing on several devices without cropping.

If you need to change the aspect ratio of your content, you may do it using the **Auto Reframe** effect in Premiere Pro. It automatically changes the video frame to retain the aspect ratio while adjusting to various screen sizes and orientations. This is especially handy when creating films for several platforms, such as social media or mobile devices, where aspect ratios vary.

Choosing the right aspect ratio

Consider where the media will be screened (e.g., cinema, television, or social media). Selecting an aspect ratio that maximizes the viewing experience based on how viewers interact with the content. Higher resolutions (such as 4K) should be used when detail is critical, such as in film productions or on large displays.

In conclusion, knowing aspect ratios and their respective contexts is critical for efficient visual communication and content production.

Improving your shot composition and framing

A masterful composition rests upon a foundation of carefully considered elements that work in concert to guide the viewer's eye and tell the story visually. Let's learn more about the key elements of a composition in the subsequent sections.

The Rule of Thirds

By dividing the frame into a grid of nine squares and strategically placing your subject at the intersections or along the lines, you can achieve a more visually appealing composition.

Figure 10.1 – Applying the Rule of Thirds technique

Visualizing the frame as a 3x3 grid is a fundamental aspect of cinematic composition known as the **Rule of Thirds**. Strategically positioning characters, horizons, and objects along the grid lines or at the intersections of *power points* enhances the visual appeal of compositions. This observation aligns with our innate inclination to be drawn towards these focal points.

Although highly beneficial, the Rule of Thirds should not be seen as a strict guideline. Experts in the field often use it with finesse, understanding when to bend the rules. Placing the horizon in the center can evoke sterility, while central symmetry can create a sense of unease or power. In some cases, the Rule of Thirds may not be as important, such as in extreme close-ups or fast-paced action sequences where the main focus is on something else.

In addition to creating engaging compositions, the Rule of Thirds is a useful tool for filmmakers to deconstruct films and comprehend the intentional decisions made in their visual storytelling. Applying the Rule of Thirds during filming or using it as an analytical lens can empower filmmakers to enrich their storytelling through the power of composition.

Balance and symmetry

Creating a sense of stability and harmony in the shot can be achieved through techniques such as **balance** and **symmetry**. Creating a composition involves ensuring that elements on either side of the frame mirror each other while arranging the elements in the shot to achieve visual balance.

Figure 10.2 – Applying the balance and symmetry technique

The next composition rule, in addition to using thirds, is to produce symmetry. Balance and symmetry are essential elements in film composition, providing filmmakers with a valuable toolkit for creating visually compelling stories. Creating symmetrical compositions by mirroring elements across the frame can evoke feelings of order, stability, and formality. Picture the precise, balanced composition of buildings and characters in Wes Anderson's films, evoking a feeling of controlled harmony. Introducing a dynamic counterpoint, asymmetry creates tension, disequilibrium, and even unease.

Deliberately arranging elements of different sizes, weights, or positions creates a sense of movement, conflict, or disruption of the expected visual order. Similar to the meticulously planned yet unbalanced fight scenes in *Crouching Tiger, Hidden Dragon*, the unconventional framing and moving camera work together to create suspense and highlight the characters nimbleness.

In certain situations, using symmetry is an excellent approach to convey your message:

- To express a scene's attractiveness
- To assist your audience in focusing on your subject

In fact, symmetry is an exception to the rule of thirds. Put your subject dead center in the picture if you want it to stand out. When a character is having a powerful moment, symmetry is frequently used. It attracts the viewer's attention in an unusual way.

Filmmakers use different types of balance to shape the mood of their stories. When compositions are *symmetrical*, they can create a sense of calm and tranquility, such as in peaceful monastery scenes. On the other hand, *asymmetrical* arrangements can evoke suspense or emphasize the disorder in a war-torn setting. Even when not perfectly centered, compositions can still convey balance and add a hint of movement and possible conflict.

Intentionally creating an unbalanced composition can highlight certain emotions or create a feeling of unease or disorientation, as demonstrated by the unsettling tilted shots used in *The Shining* to show the protagonist's descent into madness.

Let's look at a few examples from well-known films:

- *Wes Anderson's films*: These films are known for their meticulous attention to symmetry, with nearly every frame in movies like *The Grand Budapest Hotel* meticulously balanced. This signature style extends to his use of nature and architecture in *Moonrise Kingdom*, and even the quirky family tableaus in *The Royal Tenenbaums*.

- *Ang Lee's Crouching Tiger, Hidden Dragon*: Seek out the fight sequences, especially those in the bamboo forest, for masterful use of asymmetrical balance and dynamic movement.

- *Stanley Kubrick's The Shining*: Watch for the off-kilter camera angles and unbalanced hallway shots that create a constant sense of unease. Clips and analyses are readily available on YouTube. Here's an example: `https://www.youtube.com/watch?v=fI1v4_8SAU8`.

However, symmetry is a powerful tool, but use it wisely. It's best used in moderation. If you overdo it, you risk sending inconsistent messages to your audience.

Leading lines

Within the expanse of film composition, **leading lines** serve as pathways, directing the viewer's gaze on a visual expedition across the frame. Roads, architectural features, the natural environment, or the characters gaze are just a few examples of the various factors that can shape these lines. Their strength is found in their capacity to subtly guide the viewer's gaze and shape their understanding of the scene.

Figure 10.3 – Applying the leading lines technique

Filmmakers can utilize leading lines to achieve different storytelling objectives. Utilizing converging lines such as converging hallways or railway tracks can evoke a feeling of claustrophobia or imminent action. On the other hand, lines that branch out, like roads spreading from a central point, can inspire a sense of liberation and potential. *Diagonal lines*, commonly seen in staircases or the path of a falling object, bring a dynamic and lively feel to the composition.

Implied lines can also create leading lines, not just physical elements. You can be guided to observe a character's emotions and focus by paying attention to where they are looking, just as how objects are positioned within the frame can evoke feelings of tension, anticipation, or resolution depending on their alignment with or against the dominant lines.

It's important to look for situations where you may use leading lines in your photos, like in the preceding example. You'll be astonished at how simply you can locate them once you start looking!

Depth

Developing a sense of **depth** in the shot enhances visual appeal and contributes to a more engaging viewing experience. One way to accomplish this is by utilizing different techniques, such as incorporating foreground, middle ground, and background elements, along with shallow or deep focus.

Crafting depth in filmmaking composition is akin to a magician's sleight of hand, conjuring the illusion of three-dimensionality on a two-dimensional screen. This mesmerizing illusion, crafted through a skillful blend of elements, immerses the viewer in the unfolding world.

Figure 10.4 – Applying the depth technique

Each shot consists of a distinct foreground, midground, and background. The selection of elements to include or exclude in your photo reveals significant information about its content.

Occasionally, you may desire to have only your character present in the frame, without any other elements. However, it is crucial to primarily build your character within the setting you have constructed. It is important to demonstrate the connection between your subject and the world, encompassing elements that are not the main focus.

Camera placement and movement also play a significant role in establishing depth. Filming a scene from a **low angle** can make characters or objects appear more imposing and add a sense of depth, whereas a **high-angle** shot can create a feeling of looking down on the scene, offering a wider perspective. Additionally, camera movement, such as **panning** or **tracking** shots, can add dynamism and simulate how we explore the world in real life, further enhancing the perception of depth.

The spatial dimensionality of your scene is influenced by the following:

* *Location*: The place where the shooting occurs
* *Lens*: Specify the type of lens you use and its ability to create a sense of depth

The selection of your lens is crucial as it directly influences the depth of field. A wide-angle lens has a greater depth of field, so rendering it more challenging to achieve target focus while intentionally blurring the backdrop. The perceived distance between the subject and the background will likewise be magnified.

Using a lens with a greater focal length will facilitate the attainment of a shallow depth of focus, even while employing the same F-stop. Fundamentally, it will let your subject be more distinguishable from the background. Additionally, it causes background objects to appear closer than when you use a wide-angle lens.

The choices you make in this context will enable your viewers to discern their focal points, identify the crucial elements in the scene, and comprehend the character's relationship with the surrounding world.

By skillfully combining these techniques, filmmakers breathe life into their compositions, creating a sense of depth that draws viewers into the film's universe. Whether it's the layered beauty of a natural landscape or the deliberate isolation of a character within a room, mastering depth in composition allows filmmakers to transport their audience to the heart of their stories.

Understanding different types of shots and composition

Filmmakers use a variety of shot types and compositions to visually shape their narratives. The decisions we make influence our interpretation of characters, settings, and the narrative's progression.

Picture the contrast between an extreme close-up, capturing every detail of a character's trembling hand, and a wide shot showcasing a vast landscape, making the figures within it seem small. Each one evokes a distinct emotional response.

Typical shot types consist of **close-ups** to convey intimacy, **medium shots** for dialogue and interaction, and **wide shots** to establish scope and context. Moreover, different variations, such as the medium close-up or the extreme wide shot, help to refine the visual language even more.

Particular compositions, such as the stark *over-the-shoulder* shot employed to intensify tension in a negotiation, add extra depth to the way characters are positioned within the frame.

Mastering shot types and composition allows filmmakers to convey their stories beyond just dialogue and action, but through the very essence of the images. Understanding various shot compositions can enhance a filmmaker's ability to convey emotions and establish the mood of a scene, ultimately leading to a more compelling story.

Within this section, we will delve into various types of shot composition:

- **Extreme close-ups**: Intimate and intense. Extreme close-ups can evoke psychological discomfort, suggesting scrutiny or overwhelming emotion. Consider how it fragments the body, turning details into abstract images.

Figure 10.5 – Extreme close-up shot

This kind of shot zooms in on a specific detail or feature of the subject, such as the eyes, mouth, or hands. This shot has the ability to convey strong emotions or highlight a specific detail.

- **Close-ups**: Revealing the soul. Close-ups make us hyper-aware of micro-expressions, letting a flicker of fear or a hint of a smile dominate the scene.

Figure 10.6 – Close-up shot

The photograph captures the subject from the shoulders up, offering a close-up view of their face. In dialogue scenes, close-ups are frequently utilized to capture facial expressions and communicate emotions.

- **Medium shots**: Conversations and context. Medium shots balance intimacy and broader action. They are good for dialogue, where character gestures are important.

Figure 10.7 – Medium shot

By framing the subject from the waist up, a more detailed view of the subject's body language and gestures is captured. Medium shots are frequently utilized in dialogue scenes to establish the connection between characters.

- **Wide shots**: Scope and significance. Wide shots can dwarf characters in landscapes to convey isolation or insignificance, but also reveal complex spatial relationships.

Figure 10.8 – Wide shot

The photograph captures the subject from head to toe, offering a glimpse of their surroundings and providing context. Long shots are frequently employed to set the scene, convey distance, and show the scale of the surroundings.

Exploring various shot compositions can assist filmmakers in effectively communicating their vision and crafting a more engaging narrative. Next, let's see what makes a good composition.

Delving into the key elements of a strong composition

Creating a powerful composition in filmmaking involves carefully arranging visual elements to do more than just capture the scene – they should also narrate a story. Crafting a visual composition involves a delicate balance of intentionality and visual guidance. Every element, from subject placement to color palette, serves a purpose, while techniques such as the Rule of Thirds and leading lines subtly direct the viewer's eye.

Going beyond appearances, a well-crafted piece stirs feelings by skillfully manipulating light, color, and composition. The visual elements enhance the story's message, such as portraying a character's isolation through a doorway frame or creating tension with converging lines. Emphasizing technical expertise in focus, exposure, and understanding of the chosen aspect ratio is essential, but true brilliance stands out through uniqueness. A well-crafted piece can be quite surprising, incorporating unique perspectives, framing, or even a purposeful departure from traditional norms, ultimately making a lasting impact on the audience.

Crafting the ideal composition doesn't adhere to a strict formula, but certain crucial elements consistently distinguish exceptional compositions from average ones:

- *Intentionality*: Deliberate choices are reflected in a well-crafted composition by the filmmaker. Every aspect, from the placement of subjects to the choice of colors, must enhance the narrative and evoke the intended emotional response.

- *Visual guidance*: Effective compositions lead the viewer's eye, subtly highlighting key elements while preserving visual balance. One way to accomplish this is by utilizing techniques such as the Rule of Thirds, leading lines, and incorporating negative space.

- *Emotional resonance*: A well-crafted piece goes beyond mere visual appeal, connecting with the audience on an emotional level. One way to express this is by contrasting light and shadow, selecting colors, or achieving balance or intentional imbalance in the composition.

- *Narrative support*: Composition should always enhance the story without drawing attention away from it. Capturing a single figure in a doorway can effectively portray isolation without the need for words, and converging lines can create a feeling of imminent conflict.

- *Technical expertise*: Having a solid concept is crucial, but it's equally important to have the technical skills to bring it to life. Mastering focus, exposure, and the selected aspect ratio are essential for creating a beautifully composed image.

- *Uniqueness*: Uniqueness is key in a well-crafted piece, often achieved through surprising angles, framing, or purposeful deviations from traditional norms.

It is worth considering that the quality of composition can be subjective; it can vary depending on the specific requirements of each film. Nevertheless, these fundamental components provide a strong base for creating visually captivating stories that make a lasting impact on the audience.

What is compositing?

Compositing is the act of merging two or more pictures, either physically or digitally, to create a single image.

Prior to the advent of digital technology, photographers and videographers would manually manipulate film by physically cutting and combining different frames to produce a composite image. In addition, they utilized techniques such as partial models and glass paints to superimpose pictures and achieve the required visual effect while filming.

In the present day, you have the choice to digitally include or eliminate picture layers. This not only simplifies the entire process but also enables the integration of **computer-generated imagery** (**CGI**) and visual effects into your compositing workflow.

Compositing technique – a breakdown

The editing process for demonstrating the compositing method often consists of many essential steps, each of which contributes to the final unified image. Let's look at a breakdown of the procedure:

1. **Pre-production planning**

   This process begins with **storyboards**, which are pictorial representations of sequences that establish the overall shot composition. A **shot list** is then developed, outlining each exact shot needed for the production. The pre-production planning process for this project involves the following key stages:

   - *Collaboration*: Pre-production planning involves collaboration between VFX supervisors, compositors, directors, and cinematographers. This involves deciding which pieces need to be recorded or developed for compositing.

   - *Storyboarding*: Visualizing the scenes assists in determining the essential visual components and how they will be incorporated.

2. **Element gathering**

   This stage entails gathering the appropriate components. **Live-action footage** is captured, including actors and locations. **CGI elements**, **3D models**, and **animations** made with applications such as Maya or Blender are developed. **Matte paintings** offer digital or conventional backdrops.

Practical effects footage captures actual effects such as explosions and smoke. **Stock footage** can be used to replace pre-existing video pieces. **Particle simulations** use software such as Houdini to create effects such as smoke or fire. The element-gathering phase involves collecting the following resources:

- *Capture footage*: During production, a live-action video is recorded, as well as any practical effects or green/blue screen pictures that will be utilized for compositing

- *Create assets*: CGI, matte paints, and stock footage are ready for integration

3. **Keying**

Keying is the technique of distinguishing the foreground and background. **Green or blue screens** are utilized during filming to aid with this. **Keying software** such as Nuke or After Effects is used to separate the foreground. To isolate the desired elements from the background, we will use these keying techniques:

- *Keying backdrop removal*: Keying techniques remove foreground items from a solid-colored backdrop (usually green or blue). This enables the extraction of subjects from the film.

- *Refinement*: Advanced keying techniques are employed to handle complicated features such as hair or translucent objects, resulting in crisp edges.

4. **Rotoscoping**

Rotoscoping involves tracing an object's edges frame by frame using Nuke or After Effects. Rotoscoping equipment and reference film are utilized to guide this procedure. Building upon the keying process, we will now focus on rotoscoping, which involves *manual isolation*. When keying is insufficient, rotoscoping is employed to trace components frame by frame. This is especially handy for complex movements or when working with non-uniform backdrops.

5. **Tracking and match moving**

This process ensures that all items are aligned appropriately. **Tracking markers** are put across the area, and **tracking software** such as **Mocha** or **PFTrack** analyzes camera movement. To ensure accurate alignment and movement, we will use tracking and match-moving techniques, such as *camera movement*, in which tracking methods are used to match the movement of the camera or other objects in the scene. This ensures that the CGI elements flow organically and are consistent with the live-action footage.

6. **Color correction and grading**

Color correction and **grading** affect color and tone. Color grading tools such as **DaVinci Resolve** or **Premiere Pro** are utilized, as well as color reference charts tools such as **X-Rite ColorChecker**, to ensure correct color representation. You can achieve this with *cohesive look*, where compositors change the color, contrast, and tone of numerous components to complement the overall aesthetic of the shot. This step is critical for preserving visual uniformity.

7. **Lighting integration**

    Lighting integration creates and changes lighting effects with **digital lighting tools** and **reference photos**. You can achieve this with *realistic lighting*, where compositors use digital lighting effects, alter shadows, and produce reflections to make all components appear to be in the same area and lighting conditions. Here's an example:

Figure 10.9 – Before and after lighting compositing

8. **Lens effects and atmosphere**

    Lens effects and environment produce realistic visual aspects. **Lens artifacts** represent camera lens flaws, whereas **atmospheric effects** include factors such as dust, haze, or rain. Adding lens imperfections like flares and chromatic aberration, as well as atmospheric effects like dust or rain, unifies the image and enhances its reality.

9. **Final touch-ups**

    Final touch-ups improve the composite. Edge blending and motion blur may both be achieved using **detail enhancement tools**. Directors and VFX supervisors provide feedback that guides revisions. This includes *detail refinement*. The last stage entails fine-tuning features such as edge blending, motion blur, and ensuring that all elements interact convincingly (for example, character shadows on CG landscapes).

10. **Rendering**

    Rendering combines the pieces to create a final image. **Rendering software** such as Nuke or After Effects is used to produce the final result in formats such as **EXR or TIFF**. These methods include *final output*. After combining and refining parts, the final image is generated. This procedure merges all layers and effects into a single, unified frame.

11. **Review and feedback**

Review and **feedback** guarantee that the finished output fulfills expectations. Review sites and feedback forms are used to collect opinions and ideas. This could take the form of the director and VFX team analyzing composited shots and integrating input to make required improvements before final delivery.

This editing method demonstrates how compositing techniques are used to generate visually appealing and convincing pictures for cinema and television. Each stage is crucial to ensure that the finished output fulfills the creative vision and technical standards demanded by the VFX industry. In the following section, we will explore the relationship between VFX and compositing.

Is VFX the same as compositing?

Compositing is a specific technique within the broader field of VFX. While these terms are often used interchangeably, VFX encompasses a wider range of effects created using computers. VFX aims to enhance the realism and storytelling of a film.

Compositing, on the other hand, is a particular step in the VFX process. It involves combining multiple elements, such as live-action footage, 3D models, and digital matte paintings, into a single, seamless image. In Jurassic Park, for example, the dinosaurs were created using 3D animation and then composited into the live-action scenes.

What are the most effective compositing techniques in video editing?

Video editing software supports a wide range of compositing techniques. Here's a quick review of some of the most popular compositing techniques:

- *Blue or green screen?*: A common technique for preparing live-action footage for compositing is to use a blue or green screen. These brightly colored backgrounds allow actors to perform in front of a solid color. VFX artists then use chroma keying to remove the blue or green color from the footage. This creates a transparent area where new elements, such as digital backgrounds or special effects, can be added.

  This technique is frequently used in films, even those with seemingly ordinary and natural settings. For instance, in the movie Zodiac, set in San Francisco, many of the city streets were digitally created using blue screen technology. Actors performed in front of a blue screen, and the desired backgrounds were added later in post-production. Here's a real-life example of green screen being used in a studio:

Figure 10.10 – Green screen application in the studio

Video editing software frequently provides simple tools for cutting out specific shapes, such as squares and circles. You may also use drawing tools to precisely trace around certain items.

- *Blending modes*: Also known as transfer modes, these are effects that may be used on a single layer in a visual effects composition to change the colors of the layers underneath it. This can involve color effects, color keying, and silhouette creation. Here's an example:

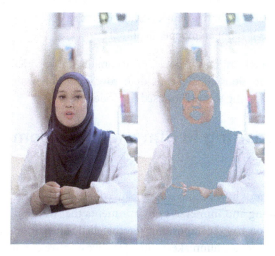

Figure 10.11 – Applying blending mode as part of compositing

There are other options for adjusting the roughness of the mask edges and the mask's opaqueness. Masks will move and change in sync with the layers they are on. However, there are tools that can be used to lock a mask in place or move it on its own.

Which compositing programs are good for editing videos?

There are several video editing software applications. Some are free, while others have limited free trial periods. To achieve the greatest tools and effects, use a high-end software application such as Adobe After Effects.

Here are some of the most popular video editing software applications:

- *Adobe After Effects* frequently works in tandem with other Adobe products, such as Photoshop for image processing and Premiere Pro for video editing. With this adaptable tool, editors and artists may produce intricate and beautiful visual effects for various projects.

- *Nuke*'s node-based compositing creates powerful and believable visual effects. It works with modern technology such as OpenColorIO to provide fantastic color control.

- *Wondershare Filmora* is a budget-friendly program. It has a user-friendly interface and a large selection of overlays and effects.

- *Blender* is a popular video editing application used for compositing. It provides powerful rendering, modeling, and sculpting techniques. Blender is suitable for both new and expert designers.

- *Autodesk Flame* is a powerful video editing software application. It has a hefty monthly cost yet produces professional-grade outcomes. It incorporates all compositing features for speedy video editing.

- *Fusion Studio* specializes in 3D compositing with its **node-based compositing** (**NBC**) solution. Its design is simple to understand for novices and has a variety of functions. Fusion is integrated into DaVinci Resolve; it is not an independent tool.

You will make mistakes as you learn how to accomplish compositing in video editing. However, with consistent practice, your compositing abilities should improve. In the following section, we will explore some of the advanced compositing techniques used in modern films.

Advanced compositing in film – Modern compositing techniques

Advanced compositing methods have become essential in contemporary cinema, allowing filmmakers to construct visually striking and immersive environments that were previously inconceivable. Techniques such as simulation-based compositing, photorealistic integration, real-time compositing, and AI-driven compositing provide filmmakers with extensive creative opportunities and assist them in maintaining competitiveness in the dynamic film business. By comprehending and mastering these strategies, filmmakers may elevate visual storytelling, cooperate more efficiently, and get superior quality outcomes, contributing to the continuous advancement of the filmmaking art. The integration of real-time elements will be achieved through the following techniques.

Real-time compositing and virtual production

Led by Epic Games Unreal Engine and other real-time engines, this technique involves combining live-action film with real-time produced scenery and characters:

- *The Mandalorian*: Using LED walls to create immersive virtual sets, performers may interact with artificial worlds in real time. To delve deeper into real-time compositing and virtual production, visit `https://www.unit-led.com/mandalorian-led-wall`.

  The design team projected the scene onto the Mandalorian LED displays to create a realistic setting. With huge forests, a wide interplanetary space, and infinite deserts, the Mandalorian LED wall can simply adapt the scenery to the filming requirements. Building such intricate scenery takes time and effort. The Mandalorian LED wall makes the scenery more efficient.

- *The Batman*: Using real-time rendering for complex settings and characters reduces post-production time. The Batman employs *Mandalorian* virtual production techniques. Virtual production, a phrase used to describe processes that allow real-time visual effects production, has grown in prominence, notably by Jon Favreau in *The Lion King* and *The Mandalorian*.

AI-driven compositing

Using artificial intelligence for tasks such as rotoscoping, object tracking, and automated matte production can create realistic younger copies of performers, as shown in films such as *The Irishman* and *Captain Marvel*. Unwanted items are automatically removed from film utilizing AI-powered technologies.

In Captain Marvel, set in the 1990s, Nick Fury (Samuel L. Jackson) and Agent Coulson (Phil Coulson) are both de-aged by around 25 years. The effects are extremely well done, making it one of the most effective de-aging attempts in the MCU. For more examples and in-depth information, visit `https://academyofanimatedart.com/the-youthening-of-samuel-l-jackson-for-captain-marvel/`.

Digital humans and facial capture

Advanced facial capture and animation techniques enable the creation of incredibly realistic artificial people. An example is *Avatar: The Way of Water*, which pushed the boundaries of digital character development with realistic avatars. Several ads and music videos include hyper-realistic digital influences. Visit `https://www.motionpictures.org/2022/12/how-avatar-the-way-of-water-visual-effects-wizards-conjured-underwater-magic/` for more information.

Wētā FX completed its greatest VFX job, *Avatar: The Way of Water*, consisting of 4,001 shots, including 3,289 in the finished film. Wētā FX handled 3,240 VFX shots, including 2,225 with water. Interestingly, just two scenes in the film lack visual effects.

The studio worked closely with Lightstorm Entertainment from the start to create new technologies and approaches to realize filmmaker James Cameron's vision. This partnership resulted in various advancements, including a novel water simulation toolset that was critical to the picture and earned a Visual Effects Society Award. This toolkit enabled realistic underwater motion and interactions with numerous aspects, such as skin, hair, and objects.

Wētā FX developed a strain-based facial performance system for improved representation and modulation of performers facial expressions during post-capture, resulting in lifelike digital representations of actors such as Stephen Lang and Sigourney Weaver.

In addition, a cable-cam eyeline system was created to let live performers interact effectively with computer-generated characters, and a depth compositing approach based on machine learning enabled the director to view real-time, blended images of live action and CG parts.

The project produced an astonishing 18.5 petabytes of data, substantially more than the original *Avatar*, and required lengthy rendering periods, with the longest shot requiring 13.6 million threaded hours to process. Overall, the picture demonstrated ground-breaking advances in visual effects technology.

Dynamic simulation and fluid effects

The dynamic simulation and fluid effects technique accurately simulate natural phenomena such as water, fire, smoke, and people. Here are some examples:

- *Avengers*: Endgame's epic fight sequences use detailed crowd simulations and deadly energy effects
- *Tenet*: Featuring mind-bending time inversion effects, such as the reversal of water and fire

In the Avengers movie, dynamic simulations and fluid effects are developed utilizing complex fluid simulation platforms that employ true fluid physics concepts such as the Navier-Stokes equations. These simulations aid in developing realistic effects for a variety of components, including water, smoke, and other fluid-like phenomena. Notably, VFX teams employ proprietary tools such as Unagi to mimic events such as explosions, character motions, and ambient interactions. It's important to recognize that these simulations have substantially advanced, allowing filmmakers to generate lifelike representations of complicated effects, which improve the overall visual storytelling.

Immersive environments and virtual reality

Creating truly immersive environments for narrative and interactive activities. For example, VR experiences such as *The Witness* and *Lone Echo* provide immersive and interactive settings. Presented here are further comprehensive examples of VR experiences that offer immersive and interactive environments:

- *The Witness*: This puzzle game places players on an enigmatic island, compelling them to resolve complex environmental riddles while navigating the stunning and eerie terrain. The VR version provides an immersive experience, enabling players to physically engage with the surroundings and enhance their connection to the planet.
- *Lone Echo*: This adventure game, set in deep space, assigns players the role of an astronaut stationed on a space station. Players may navigate the station at will, engage with things, and experience microgravity conditions. Virtual reality technology imparts a sensation of weightlessness and enables users to navigate and engage with the environment intuitively.

Music videos and advertising use virtual reality to create distinctive and compelling visual experiences.

Advanced compositing is rapidly evolving, with an increasing dependence on real-time processes to expedite production and decrease costs. The incorporation of artificial intelligence automates complicated operations, considerably increasing the realism of visual effects. There is a strong emphasis on producing hyper-realistic digital individuals and settings, while the limits of simulation and physics-based effects are constantly pushed. Furthermore, the industry is looking toward new storytelling opportunities through immersive experiences. These advancements reflect the bleeding edge of compositing and, as technology advances, we should expect even more jaw-dropping visual marvels in the future.

Summary

We have looked at the complex field of film composition in this chapter. We started by charting the development of cinematic composition from silent films of the past to contemporary blockbusters. After that, we got into the technical details of composition, talking about the significance of the aspect ratio and how it affects framing. We examined several compositional techniques, such as the use of space, leading lines, and the rule of thirds, to enhance your editing skills

Next, we looked at how various camera types, such as close-ups, medium shots, and wide shots, affect the narrative and the overall visual impression. We also examined balance, contrast, and unity—three essential components of a powerful composition.

Ultimately, we focused on the post-production phase, going over the idea of compositing and how it helps produce visually striking results. We investigated a variety of compositing approaches, ranging from straightforward layering to sophisticated strategies including simulation-based and real-time compositing. You will improve your filmmaking abilities and produce more captivating and eye-catching movies by getting to grips with these ideas.

In the next chapter, you'll learn how to adjust and correct colors in your videos like a pro. Discover essential techniques for balancing colors, correcting color casts, adjusting saturation and vibrance, working with color temperature, and using color grading. By mastering these techniques, you'll be able to transform your videos into stunning works of art with colors that truly pop.

11

Adjusting and Correcting Colors Professionally

Color correction and grading are crucial processes in converting unprocessed film into refined, cinematic works of art. Adobe Premiere Pro provides a comprehensive range of tools such as curves, color wheels, and Lumetri scopes for high-quality color modification, enabling you to enhance your films and convey your narrative through appealing graphics. Curves are utilized for making precise adjustments to specific color ranges within the image. Wheels provide a visual method for adjusting color balance, saturation, and various other properties. Qualifiers enable precise adjustments to particular parts of the image using color, luminance, or other criteria.

This chapter will delve into additional features found in the Lumetri Color panel, including primary and secondary color correction tools, color match, and various effects. You'll learn how to navigate its various features, including curves, wheels, and qualifiers, to achieve precise and professional color adjustments. You'll discover a step-by-step approach to color correction, starting with fundamental adjustments such as white balance and exposure, and progressing to more advanced techniques such as color balancing, creative color grading, and selective color correction. You will learn how to achieve consistent and stylistic looks by creating and saving custom color presets, allowing you to effortlessly apply consistent color styles across your entire project or even future projects.

This chapter provides an in-depth exploration of color correction in Premiere Pro, imparting you with the expertise and methodologies to enhance the quality of your videos significantly.

In this chapter, we're going to cover the following main topics:

- Introduction to color correction and color grading
- Changing object colors in video
- Color-correcting skin tones to near perfection
- Introduction to advanced color grading

Introduction to color correction and color grading

In filmmaking, both color correction and color grading play vital roles in shaping the visual narrative and enhancing the overall viewing experience.

While color correction ensures technical accuracy and consistency, color grading allows for creative freedom. This distinction is crucial in filmmaking as it allows the colorist to do the following:

- Maintain natural-looking visuals for documentaries or realistic dramas while utilizing expressive color palettes for fantasy or stylized films

- Subtly enhance emotions in a scene without distracting from the narrative through color grading

- Create a cohesive visual style throughout the film, contributing to the overall storytelling process

By understanding and applying both color correction and color grading techniques, filmmakers can craft visually stunning and emotionally impactful stories on screen.

Analyzing the distinctions between color correction and color grading

Prior to delving into the tools, it is important to distinguish between color correction and color grading:

- **Color correction:** This primarily addresses technical imperfections, such as white balance, exposure, and color casts, guaranteeing precise color depiction. Consider it as the process of rejuvenating the authentic appearance of your film.

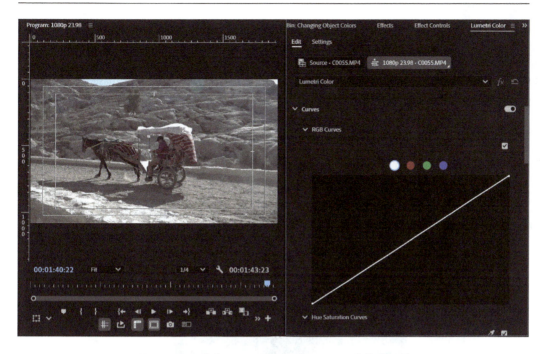

Figure 11.1 – Color correction in the Lumetri Color panel

- **Color grading**: This surpasses mere correction by applying artistic modification to generate a distinct mood, style, or ambience. This is the place where artistic expression becomes significant, as it shapes the emotional influence of your visuals.

Figure 11.2 – Color grading in the Effects panel

Color correction and color grading are often confused but serve distinct purposes. Color correction acts as the technical foundation, fixing color imbalances and achieving a natural look. In contrast, color grading is the artistic flourish, adding style and mood by manipulating colors beyond realism. Imagine color correction like prepping a canvas, while color grading is where you paint your masterpiece. They work together to bring your video to life.

Exploring the Lumetri Color panel – a tool for mastering color

The **Lumetri Color** panel in Premiere Pro is a powerful tool for color correction and grading. This platform serves as a convenient and comprehensive resource for all color-related needs, providing a wide range of tools to meticulously adjust every element of your image.

The **Lumetri Color** panel consists of several crucial sections:

- **Basic Correction**: Fine-tune the white balance, exposure, contrast, and highlights/shadows to provide a strong base.

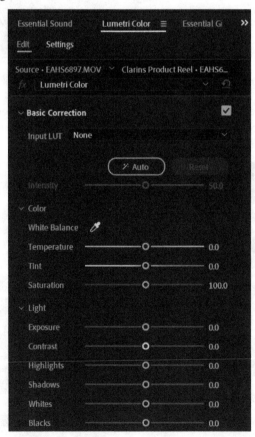

Figure 11.3 – The Basic Correction settings in the Lumetri Color panel

- **Creative**: Utilize curves, wheels, and sliders as creative tools to precisely modify individual colors, saturation, and hue, allowing for artistic expression.

Figure 11.4 – The Creative tools in the Lumetri Color panel

- **HSL Secondary**: Secondary color wheels allow for precise adjustment of individual colors in an image while preserving the integrity of other colors, making them perfect for isolating and highlighting specific components.

Figure 11.5 – Secondary color wheels in the Lumetri Color panel

- **Color Wheels & Match**: Utilize waveform, vectorscope, and parade scopes to monitor color modifications with technical precision and ensure consistency; this will be explained further in this chapter.

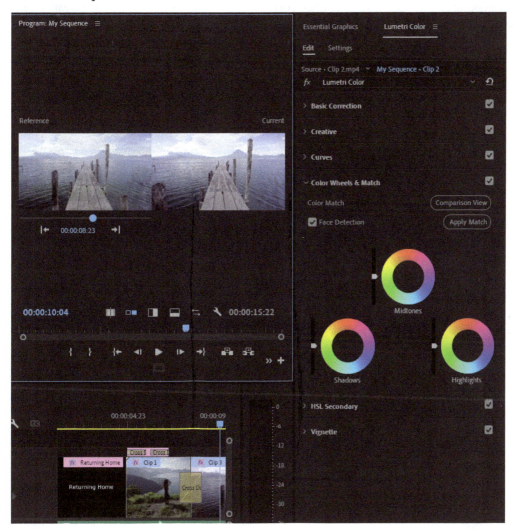

Figure 11.6 – Color Wheels & Match in the Lumetri Color panel

Understanding color theory allows you to expertly match colors and achieve precise adjustments. But why is this so important? Mastering color correction goes beyond technical accuracy. It empowers you to set the mood, evoke emotions, and create a visually cohesive film. With this foundation in place, get ready to dive deeper in the next section, where we'll explore how to truly enhance your visuals with creative color-grading techniques!

Enhancing visual aesthetics with color grading in narrative expression

After making precise adjustments to color correction, you may freely express your creativity by applying color grading.

The following are a few widely used methodologies:

- **Warm versus cool looks**: Choose warmer tones to create an appealing and nostalgic atmosphere, or opt for colder tones to achieve a contemporary and modern ambience. Here's an example:

Figure 11.7 – Warm versus cool looks in color grading

- **Color palettes**: Create a uniform color palette in your video to strengthen the storyline and elicit particular emotions.

Figure 11.8 – Color palette sample in film

Imagine a film set in a bustling city. The color palette might be dominated by cool blues and grays, reflecting the steely skyscrapers and the fast-paced urban environment. This creates a sense of detachment and anonymity, mirroring the experience of being just one person in a vast city.

Now, picture a scene set in a cozy farmhouse kitchen. Warm yellows and oranges likely dominate the palette, mimicking the glow of sunlight streaming through the window and the inviting warmth of freshly baked bread. This evokes a sense of comfort and togetherness, reflecting the feeling of a family gathering.

These are just two examples, but film color palettes work similarly to the real-world color schemes we encounter daily. Here's how you can correlate the concept:

- Think about your favorite restaurant. Does it use warm reds and oranges to create a feeling of warmth and appetite appeal? Perhaps it has a more calming atmosphere with cool blues and greens to promote relaxation.

- Consider a brand logo. Companies often choose specific color palettes to evoke certain emotions and brand associations. For example, a tech company might use cool blues and grays to convey a sense of innovation and professionalism, while a children's toy brand might use bright and playful colors to attract young audiences.

By understanding how filmmakers use color palettes, you can become more aware of the subtle ways color influences your emotions and perceptions in the real world. You can analyze the color schemes in your own environment – homes, workplaces, and advertisements – and understand the intended mood or message being conveyed.

This knowledge empowers you to make conscious choices when creating your own visuals, whether it's editing photos, designing presentations, or even decorating your living space. Choosing a specific color palette can help you achieve the desired effect and evoke the right emotions in your audience or viewers.

- **Selective color adjustments**: These can be used to intensify particular colors or diminish undesired ones, so directing focus toward important features or generating striking visual effects.

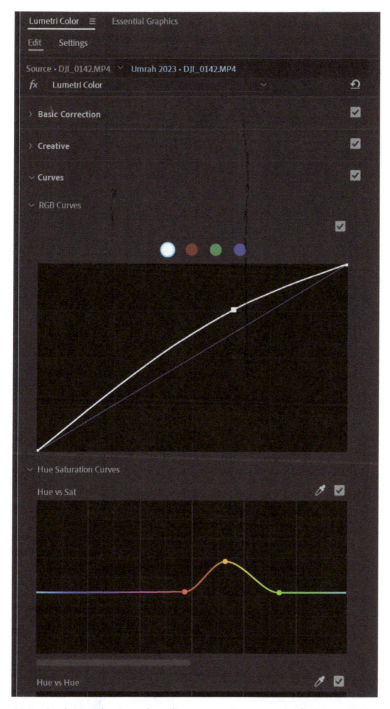

Figure 11.9 – Applying selective color adjustment using curves in the Lumetri Color panel

- **LUTs**: Also known as **Lookup Tables**, these allow for the immediate application of pre-existing color grading profiles, resulting in instant and impactful stylistic changes.

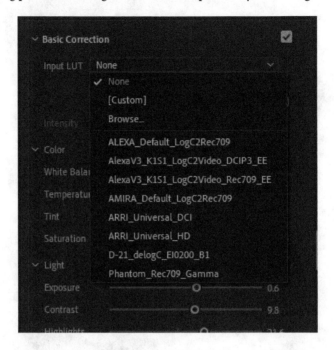

Figure 11.10 – Applying LUTs in the Lumetri Color panel

LUTs are powerful tools in Premiere Pro that allow you to quickly apply a specific color grade to your footage. Here's a simplified breakdown of how to use them:

- **Find your LUT**: You can download free LUTs online or purchase them from professional creators. Ensure that they're compatible with Premiere Pro.

- **Import the LUT**: There are two ways to do this:

  - **Drag and drop**: In the **Color** workspace, navigate to the **Lumetri Color** panel for your clip. Under the **Creative** tab, there's a **Look** drop-down menu. Click it and choose **Browse**. Locate your LUT file and import it.

Figure 11.11 – Importing LUTs in the Lumetri Color panel

- **Manual placement**: For frequent use, find the LUT folder on your computer (consult your software's documentation for the specific location). Copy and paste the LUT file(s) into the designated **Creative** folder within the LUTs folder of Premiere Pro. Restart the software for the LUTs to appear in the **Look** drop-down menu.

- *For macOS users*: Go to the **Application** folder | **Premiere Pro CC**. Right-click on the **Premiere Pro CC** app and select **Show package contents**. Then, go to **Content | Lumetri | LUTs | Technical**.

- *For Windows users*: Go to **Program Files | Adobe | Common | LUTs | Technical**.

Figure 11.12 – Finding LUTs in the local drive and importing into the Creative tab

- **Apply and fine-tune**: Select the desired LUT from the **Look** menu. It will instantly transform your footage with the predefined color grade. Remember, LUTs are a starting point, not a one-click solution. You can still use the **Lumetri Color** panel's other tools to further refine the look and achieve your creative vision.

Now, let's look at the before and after results of applying LUTs to an image:

Figure 11.13 – Before and after applying LUTs

Now that you've witnessed the dramatic transformation LUTs can bring, let's recap. We explored how to import and apply LUTs in Premiere Pro, transforming your footage with a single click. But remember, LUTs are just the beginning! The **Lumetri Color** panel remains your canvas for further refinement.

So, why are LUTs important? They offer a quick and efficient way to achieve a specific color style, saving you time and effort in color grading. Whether you're aiming for a vintage film look, a vibrant cinematic style, or a subtle color correction, LUTs provide a versatile starting point to elevate your video's visual aesthetics.

In the next section, we'll delve deeper into the art of color grading, empowering you to go beyond presets and create unique color palettes that tell your story through the power of color.

Changing object colors in video

If you need to replace a solid block of color in a background or graphic element, the **Change to Color** effect can be a fast option. For instance, imagine a video with a red banner throughout. If you need to quickly change that banner to blue for branding purposes, this effect could work in a pinch. However, be aware that if the red banner has any texture or detail, the effect might replace those details unintentionally as well. Follow these steps:

1. **Apply the effects**: Access the **Effects** panel by pressing *Shift + 7*. In the search bar, type change to color and locate the **Change to Color** effect. Drag and drop this effect onto the desired clip.

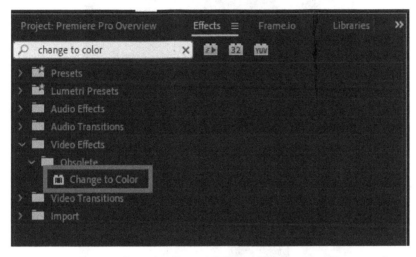

Figure 11.14 – Applying the Change to Color effect from the Effects panel

2. **Select a base color**: Access the **Effect Controls** panel by pressing the *Shift* key and the number 5 simultaneously. In the **Change to Color** box, utilize the **From** eyedropper tool to select and sample the specific color that you wish to substitute.

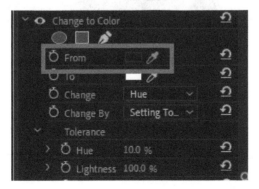

Figure 11.15 – Changing the base color in the Effect Controls panel

3. **Refine the color selection**: Refine your color selection by making subtle modifications to the **Tolerance** (**Hue**) and **Softness** settings.

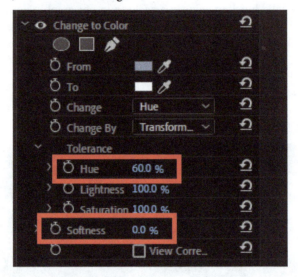

Figure 11.16 – Changing Hue and Softness in the Effect Controls panel

4. **Pick a new color**: Select the **To** color chip and designate a different desired color. To set the starting point of the clip, click the *stopwatch* icon located next to the **To** option while the playhead is at the beginning. This generates the first animation keyframe.

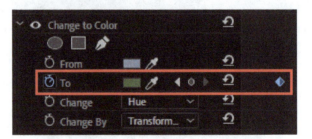

Figure 11.17 – Picking a new color and adding a keyframe value

5. **Animate the color**: Move the playhead forward and select a different color to establish a new keyframe. Proceed with advancing the playhead and establishing a fresh color at different time intervals in order to animate the progression of colors within the shot. Depress the *spacebar* to observe a glimpse of the ultimate outcome.

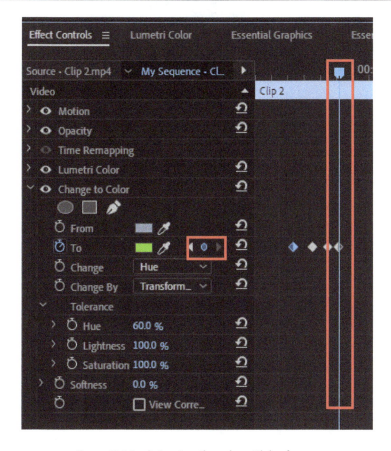

Figure 11.18 – Animating the color with keyframes

The following is the result:

Figure 11.19 – Result of animating the color with keyframes

Experiment with these techniques for altering color and observe the results you obtain! Mastering color correction and matching requires extensive practice. Each piece of video necessitates a distinct amalgamation of tools and a unique methodology. However, as you acquire more knowledge, you will become better equipped to make intelligent adaptations.

Once you grasp the functionality of the tools, you will possess the ability to modify even the most difficult film. We trust that these instructions have facilitated your progress in creating a project that you would be pleased to include in your showreel.

Color-correcting skin tones to near perfection

Accurate adjustment of skin tone is a meticulous skill in video editing, frequently distinguishing inexperienced colorists from experts. Accurately capturing and enhancing natural, pleasing skin tones enhances the overall visual excellence of your footage, but incorrect modifications can be jarring and unconvincing.

Thankfully, Premiere Pro provides a robust set of tools to achieve almost flawless skin tones, accommodating both slight improvements and drastic changes.

Understanding skin tone variations

Prior to delving into the tools, it is important to understand the extensive range of skin tones. The perception of perfection might vary from one individual to another. Hence, a fundamental idea is to maintain the inherent attractiveness and distinctiveness of the subject's skin tone while rectifying any technical flaws or unwanted coloration.

Basic color correction for natural skin

Here's a step-by-step guide to tackling the fundamentals of **skin tone correction** in Premiere Pro:

1. Navigate to the **Lumetri Color** panel, and go to the **Window** menu | **Lumetri Color**.

2. Go to **Basic Correction**. This provides essential tools for achieving accurate color representation and addressing technical issues within your footage:

     I.   **White Balance**: Use the *eyedropper* tool to click on a neutral white or gray area in the shot for more accurate white balance.

II.   **Shadows** and **Highlights**: Adjust these to reveal natural details without crushing blacks or blowing out whites, ensuring that skin tones maintain their depth and range.

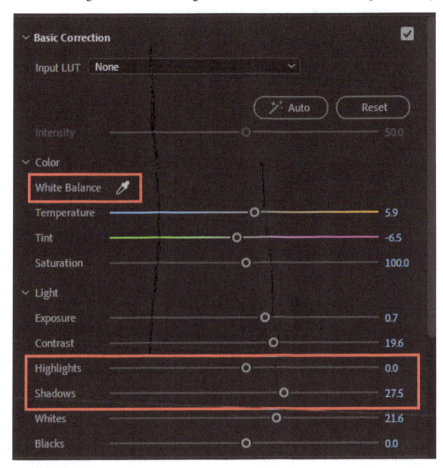

Figure 11.20 – Applying White Balance using the eyedropper tool and adjusting Highlights and Shadows in the Lumetri Color panel

3. Address **color casts**. If your footage has unwanted color casts (greenish, orangey, etc.), use the color wheels or **Curves** tools to neutralize them subtly.

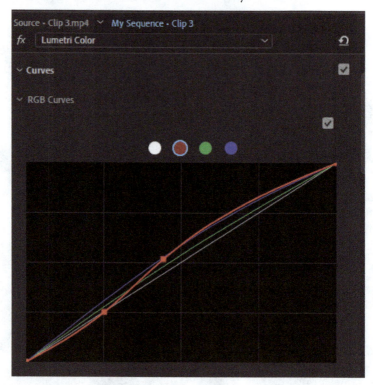

Figure 11.21 – Adjusting curves in the Lumetri Color panel

RGB Curves allow for precise manipulation of the luminance and tone ranges of a video clip through curves. The master curve governs the luminance. At first, the master curve is depicted as a white diagonal line. Modifying the master curve concurrently modifies the values of all three RGB channels. In the world of color correction and grading, *Curves* refers to a powerful tool that allows for precise adjustments to specific color ranges within an image. Imagine a graph where the x axis represents the original colors in your video and the y axis represents their output. By manipulating points on this curve, you can selectively brighten or darken specific colors, enhance saturation in certain areas, or even create subtle color shifts. This level of control goes beyond basic color balance adjustments and empowers you to achieve nuanced and professional-looking color corrections in your videos.

Let's learn more about the use of curves before proceeding with the next steps.

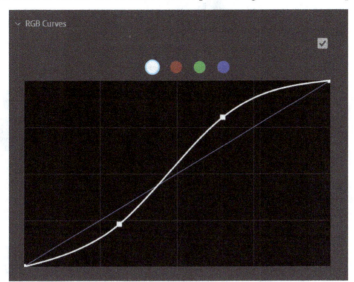

Figure 11.22 – Sample to manipulate points in RGB Curves

Premiere Pro provides a selection of color hue saturation curves that let you apply several types of curve-based color modifications to your clip. Here's a breakdown of the key terminology and how they differ in color correction:

- **Hue versus saturation**: Hue represents the *what* (red, green, blue), while saturation represents the *how much* (vibrant or muted) of that specific color. Adjusting the hue changes the fundamental color, whereas adjusting the saturation changes its intensity without changing the color itself.

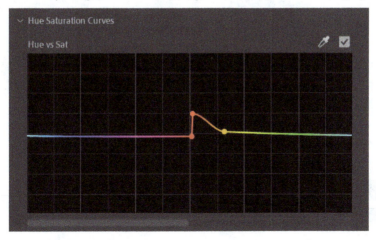

Figure 11.23 – Hue versus saturation in Hue Saturation Curves

- **Hue versus hue:** Think of hue as the color itself. It's the basic characteristic that distinguishes one color from another (e.g., red, green, blue). In color correction, manipulating the hue allows you to shift a specific color to a different one. For example, you could adjust the hue of a red shirt to make it appear more orange.

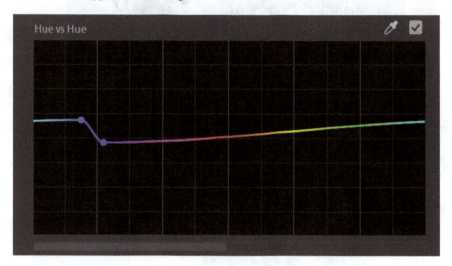

Figure 11.24 – Hue versus hue in Hue Saturation Curves

- **Hue versus luma:** While hue and saturation define the color itself (its *what*), luma focuses on the color's *how bright* aspect. Adjusting the hue changes the color entirely, whereas adjusting the luma changes its brightness without affecting the actual color.

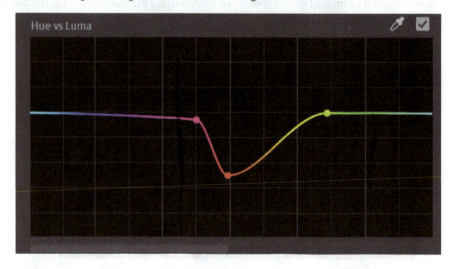

Figure 11.25 – Hue versus luma in Hue Saturation Curves

- **Luma versus saturation**: Luma represents the brightness or luminance of a color. It's independent of hue and saturation, focusing solely on how light or dark a color is in color correction; adjusting luma allows you to control the brightness of specific colors without affecting their hue or saturation. For example, you could brighten the luma of a red object without changing its red hue or saturation.

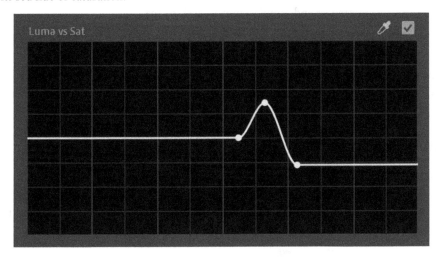

Figure 11.26 – Luma versus saturation in Hue Saturation Curves

- **Saturation versus saturation**: It would be more common to say *adjusting multiple saturations* to imply working with the intensity of several different colors. Colors can be modified by manipulating control points. When you manipulate a control point, a vertical band materializes to assist you in evaluating your ultimate outcome.

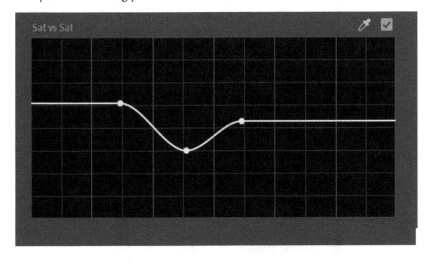

Figure 11.27 – Saturation versus saturation in Hue Saturation Curves

Now that you have learned about manipulating points in the **Hue Saturation** curve, let's revisit our step-by-step guide to addressing the fundamentals of skin tone correction:

1. **Fine-tune skin tone with HSL Secondary color wheels**: This powerful tool allows you to isolate and adjust specific color ranges within your image. Here's how to use it for skin:

    I.   Click the *eyedropper* and sample a mid-tone skin area.

    II.   Adjust the **Hue**, **Saturation**, and **Lift** sliders to refine the hue of your skin tones without affecting other colors in the shot.

2. **Monitor your adjustments**: Utilize the **color scopes** (**Waveform**, **Vectorscope**, and **Parade**) to ensure that your color changes are technically accurate and avoid clipping (loss of detail).

We'll discuss these in more detail in the next section.

Exploring the Lumetri Scopes panel

The **Lumetri Scopes** panel, accessible through the **Window | Lumetri Scopes** menu, showcases a collection of adjustable pre-installed video scopes, including **Vectorscope YUV**, **Histogram**, **Parade (RGB)**, and **Waveform (RGB)**. These scopes assist in the assessment and adjustment of your video clips' color accuracy.

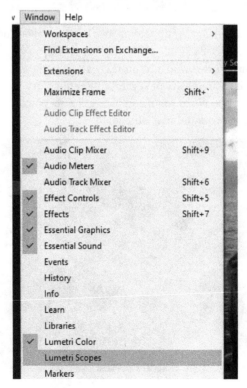

Figure 11.28 – Opening the Lumetri Scopes panel from the Window menu

To showcase a scope, simply perform a right-click action within the **Lumetri Scopes** panel and choose a scope from the available drop-down menu.

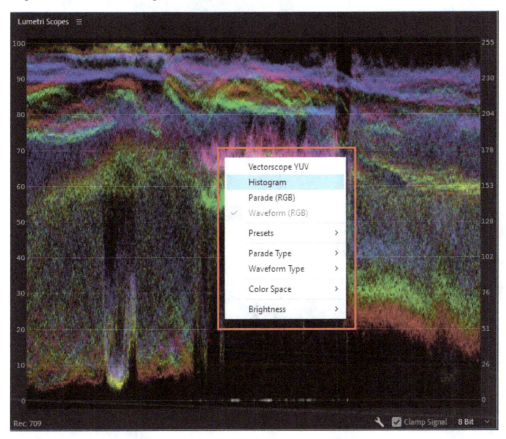

Figure 11.29 – Right-click action within Lumetri Scopes

To analyze the scopes in the **Lumetri Scopes** panel, you have the option to choose **8 Bit**, **10 Bit**, **float**, or **HDR**. This selection can be made from the drop-down list located in the lower-right corner. Choosing the **HDR** option will cause the scopes to display high dynamic range data, with the scale ranging from *0* to *10000* nits.

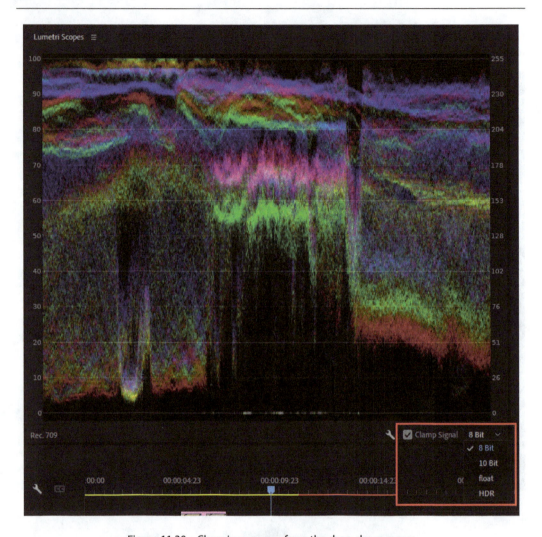

Figure 11.30 – Choosing a scope from the drop-down menu

If you wish to limit any signal displayed in the scopes to a range between *0* nits and *100* nits, choose the **Clamp Signal** option. The clamping signal solely affects the output within the **Lumetri Scopes** window. Applying clamping to the scope does not affect the frame being displayed on the timeline or the output generated during the export.

> **Tip**
>
> You have the ability to view all the scopes available in the **Lumetri Scopes** panel at any one moment. To access the **Lumetri Scopes** panel, right-click on it and choose either **Presets | All Scopes RGB** or **Presets | All Scopes YUV/YC** (see *Figure 11.31*).

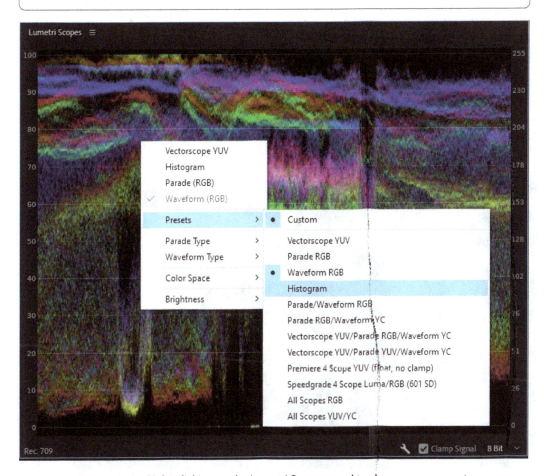

Figure 11.31 – Right-clicking on the Lumetri Scopes panel to choose scope presets

Having explored the fundamentals of color correction and the powerful tools within the **Lumetri Color** panel, let's delve deeper into another valuable tool: the histogram. This visual representation of your video's color distribution will provide further insights into color balance and guide you toward even more precise adjustments.

Histogram

The Premiere Pro histogram shows how light is distributed in your video (shadows, highlights, midtones) using *CIN* code values (*95-685*) - a default range suitable for broadcast to ensure legal levels (no clipping or crushed blacks). You can change this range to better suit your project's needs (e.g., Rec. 709 for another broadcast standard, or Video *0-1000* for broader editing).

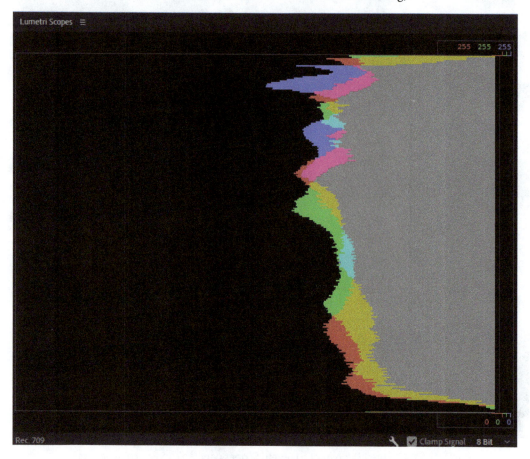

Figure 11.32 – Histogram in Adobe Premiere Pro

The **Histogram** option utilizes the **red, green, and blue** (**RGB**) values. Numerical feedback indicating the minimum **Luma** values for each channel is displayed at the bottom. The highest values are shown at the top. The output range is indicated by two horizontal lines.

Parade

The **Parade** scope exhibits distinct waveforms for the various elements of an image. The waveforms are presented in parallel, facilitating the comparison of color intensity in an image and enabling necessary modifications. This scope facilitates the identification of color casts in your image.

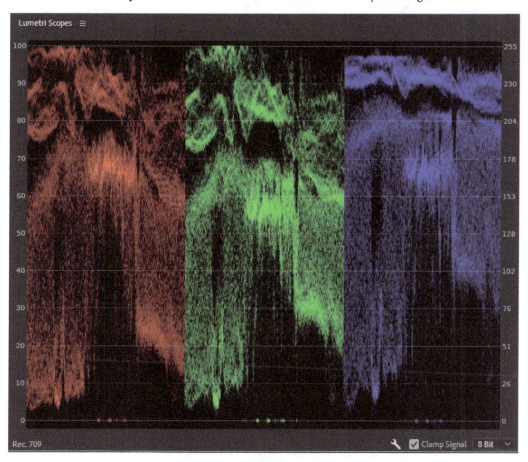

Figure 11.33 – Parade in Adobe Premiere Pro

The display showcases waveforms that depict the levels of brightness and color difference channels in the digital video signal.

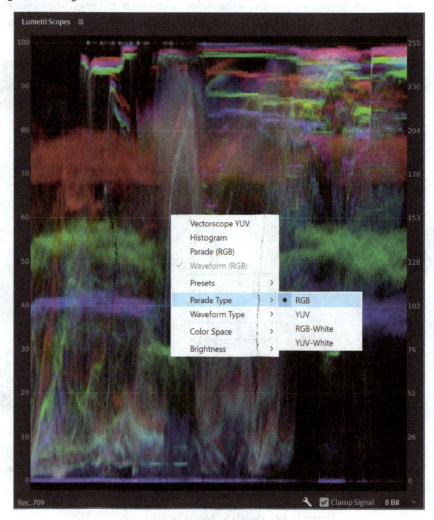

Figure 11.34 – Parade in Adobe Premiere Pro

The **Parade Type** options for selection are **RGB**, **YUV**, **RGB-White**, and **YUV-White**.

Waveform

Waveforms are frequently utilized in scope, including during on-set monitoring. This display represents the luminance levels existing in your scene. It is intriguing since it displays readings throughout the entire frame. The left side of the waveform corresponds to the left half of the frame. The range spans from *0* to *255*, representing the spectrum from absolute black to absolute white.

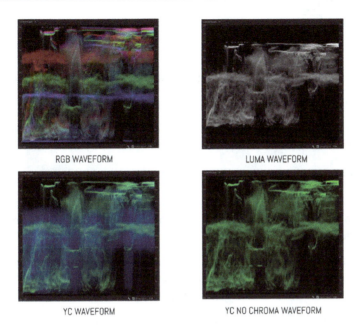

RGB WAVEFORM   LUMA WAVEFORM

YC WAVEFORM   YC NO CHROMA WAVEFORM

Figure 11.35 – Waveforms in Adobe Premiere Pro

In the **Lumetri Color** panel of Premiere Pro, you'll encounter four main types of waveform:

- **RGB waveform**:

  - This portrays the individual red, green, and blue channel levels of your video.

  - Each color channel has its own line on the graph, revealing its distribution across the brightness range.

  - It helps you identify and correct color imbalances where one color channel might be dominating or lacking in specific areas.

- **Luma waveform**:

  - This displays the brightness distribution of your video.

  - The x axis represents the brightness level from black (left) to white (right).

  - The y axis represents the number of pixels at each brightness level.

  - It helps you visualize overexposure (clipped whites on the right) and underexposure (clipped blacks on the left), allowing you to adjust exposure and shadows/highlights accordingly.

- **YC waveform:**

  - This combines **luma (Y)** and **chroma (C)** information into a single waveform.

  - The *luma* component is similar to the Luma waveform, displaying brightness.

  - The *chroma* component shows the color saturation and hue information.

  - It allows you to assess overall color balance while keeping an eye on saturation levels to avoid washed-out or overly saturated colors.

- **YC No Chroma waveform:**

  - The YC No Chroma waveform in Premiere Pro displays the luma (brightness) information of your video footage, similar to the regular Luma waveform. However, it excludes the chroma (color) information.

  - By removing color information, it can be easier to identify overexposure or underexposure solely based on brightness levels. This can be helpful in situations where complex colors might obscure the issue in the regular Luma waveform.

When editing black and white footage (which inherently lacks color), the YC No Chroma waveform becomes identical to the Luma waveform, as there's no chroma information to display.

This is advantageous as it allows you to observe the distribution of brightness ranges throughout the frame. To enhance its utility, you can employ a mask to only choose a limited region within the frame. By choosing skin tones, you can accurately assess their level of brightness.

The consensus for skin tones is to maintain a brightness level of approximately 70%. By examining the waveform and making appropriate modifications to the image, you can increase or decrease the brightness until the skin tones are about 70%. For darker skin tones, the percentage will vary between around 40% and 60%, depending on the specific shade of their skin.

With the issue of brightness resolved, you can now direct your attention to color. Replace your waveform with a vectorscope. The color wheel showcases all the hues present in the frame. Increasing the saturation will result in a broader distribution of colors on the color wheel. By applying a mask, you can specifically isolate and examine the skin tones.

Vectorscope

A **vectorscope** is a circular graph that monitors the chromatic information of an image. The measurement assesses the level of saturation starting from the center and evaluates the hue in a circular manner.

Premiere Pro provides **YUV Vectorscope**, which looks like this:

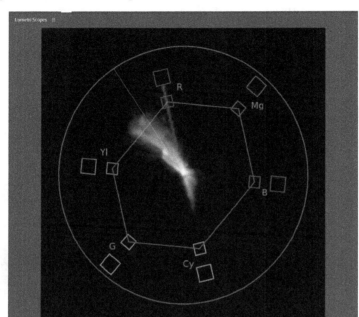

Figure 11.36 – YUV Vectorscope in Adobe Premiere Pro

Next, let's understand **YUV Vectorscope** in Premiere Pro:

This is the most common type used in video editing and is particularly well-suited for adjusting color balance and saturation.

- It displays a circular graph with primary and secondary color hues positioned around the circumference.

- The x axis represents hue, with red at 0 degrees and green and blue at 120 and 240 degrees, respectively.

- The y axis represents saturation, with the center of the circle indicating low saturation (desaturated colors) and the outer edge representing high saturation (vibrant colors).

- **Color balance adjustments**: By dragging the white vector point (representing your overall color balance) closer to a specific color section, you can increase the saturation of that color and decrease the saturation of its complementary color.

- **Saturation adjustments**: The overall spread of the color points from the center reflects the image's overall saturation level. A tight cluster indicates a desaturated image, while a wider distribution signifies a more vibrant image.

One useful feature of the vectorscope is a reference line in the top-left corner that specifically indicates skin tones. Subsequently, you can employ your color wheels to adjust in order to align your skin tones with this reference point.

Once you've mastered the correction and color grading, you can explore advanced techniques such as such as **mask-based grading**, in which you apply targeted color adjustments to specific skin areas such as cheeks, forehead, or shadows for precise sculpting.

Figure 11.37 – Mask-based grading in Adobe Premiere Pro

Armed with this limited amount of knowledge, you should be capable of achieving improved skin tones at a quicker pace and with greater consistency.

Introduction to advanced color grading

After acquiring proficiency in the basics of color correction and skin tone modifications, you are now prepared to delve further and explore the artistic aspects of color manipulation. This section explores advanced techniques and innovative ideas that will elevate the visual appeal of your videos, taking them from technically proficient to captivating.

Creative color-grading techniques

Advanced color grading transcends mere correction, embracing artistic license to shape the mood, tone, and style of your visuals. Here are some exciting techniques to unleash your creativity:

- **LUTs**: These customizable profiles apply predefined color palettes and grading styles in a single click. While convenient, use them as a starting point and fine-tune them for a personalized touch.

- **Color wheels and curves**: Master these powerful tools to manipulate specific colors, adjust saturation, and create custom curves for targeted color shifts and artistic effects.

- **Masking and trackers**: Refine your adjustments by applying them to specific regions of your image using masks. Trackers follow objects in motion, allowing you to isolate and highlight their color throughout the scene.

- **Color grading for different genres**: Understand and apply genre-specific color palettes. Using warm, desaturated tones for documentaries, cooler palettes for sci-fi, and rich, vibrant colors for fantasy can enhance the narrative and emotional impact of your visuals.

Now that you've explored the art of creative color grading and unlocked the power to transform your visuals with unique color palettes, let's delve into a powerful tool that can streamline your workflow: LUTs. These predefined color styles offer a one-click solution to achieve stunning looks, saving you time and effort in the color-grading process.

LUTs

Utilizing LUTs is an excellent method to commence the process of color grading video material. Nevertheless, it is worth noting that LUTs often produce inconsistent outcomes upon initial application. There are several possible causes for this phenomenon. In this section, we will examine these topics and go into the distinctions between **Basic Correction** LUTs and **Creative** LUTs. Additionally, we will cover the process of exporting personalized LUTs in Premiere Pro.

Adjusting your settings in the Lumetri Color panel

While LUTs offer a great starting point, you can further refine the look by adjusting individual settings within the **Lumetri Color** panel, such as the color wheels, curves, and qualifiers. Here's how:

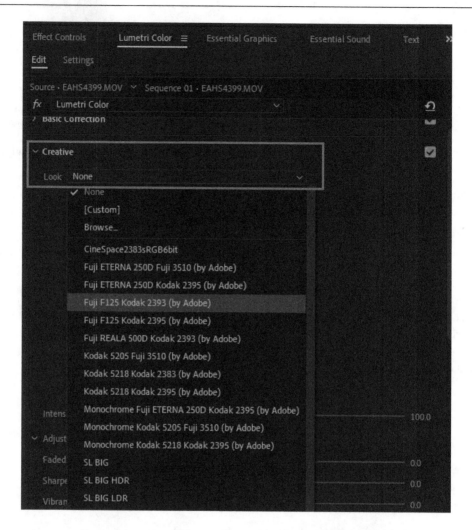

Figure 11.38 – Applying Creative LUTs in the Lumetri Color panel

The optimal **Basic Correction** settings to modify in the **Lumetri Color** panel, subsequent to the use of a **Creative** LUT, include **White Balance**, **Tint**, and **Exposure**. I suggest exploring the **Vibrance** and **Saturation** settings in the **Creative** section of **Lumetri Color**.

Exporting your own LUTs

Ultimately, you may effortlessly generate and save your own LUTs derived from your **Lumetri Color** configurations. Prioritize working in the **Color** workspace in Premiere Pro. Located at the upper section of the **Lumetri Color** panel, there is a *menu* button positioned adjacent to the **Lumetri Color** text. The *menu* button is represented by a symbol consisting of three horizontal lines (or a hamburger menu). By selecting the menu, you will be presented with the **Export .cube…** option. Subsequently, you can import the aforementioned LUT into Premiere Pro, or utilize it with any other software that employs LUTs in the `.cube` format. The `.cube` format is widely recognized as one of the most versatile LUT formats.

Here's where you can find **Export .cube…** in the **Lumetri Color** panel:

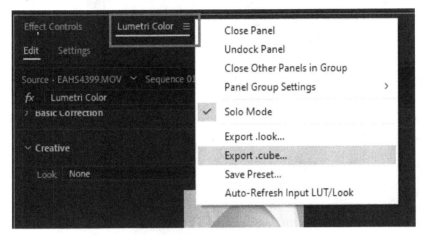

Figure 11.39 – Exporting Creative LUTs in the Lumetri Color panel

Now that you've explored the creative possibilities of LUTs and discovered how to unlock unique color palettes with the **Lumetri Color** panel, let's delve deeper into the fundamental tools within your color correction arsenal: color wheels and curves. These powerful tools offer precise control over individual colors and tonal ranges, empowering you to achieve nuanced and professional-looking color adjustments in your videos, going beyond the predefined styles of LUTs and tailoring the color to your specific vision.

Color wheels and curves

The **Lumetri Color** panel used in Adobe's Premiere Pro video editing software serves as the inspiration for the new **Color Grading** panel, which replaces the existing **Split Toning** panel. In contrast to **Split Toning**, which solely permits adjustments to the highlights and shadows, the innovative **Color Grading** panel goes a step beyond by enabling modifications to the coloring of the midtones as well.

Here's where you can find the color wheels in the **Lumetri Color** panel:

Figure 11.40 – Color wheels in the Lumetri Color panel

Furthermore, the panel has a facelift in addition to the inclusion of midtones. It now employs a tri-wheel mechanism, similar to the color wheels commonly used in professional video editing software. The sliders and each wheel function in tandem offer comprehensive control over highlights, midtones, and shadows in the HSL spectrum.

Additionally, there is a universal color wheel available for making broader modifications, along with a mixing slider that can amplify or diminish your edits, depending on the desired aesthetic.

File type and export settings

File type and export settings can definitely impact the colors in your final video export. Here's a breakdown of how:

- **Color profiles**: Different file types and devices use various color profiles. These profiles define how colors are represented by numbers. A mismatch between the profile used for editing and the export profile can lead to color shifts.

- **Compression**: Compressed video formats such as MP4 use compression techniques to reduce file size. This compression can sometimes affect color accuracy, especially in high-compression settings.

- **Gamma**: Gamma refers to the tonal response of an image or video. Different display devices have different gamma curves. Exporting without considering gamma can result in washed-out or overly dark videos on certain devices.

Here are some ways to maintain color accuracy during export:

- **Match color profiles**: Ensure that your editing software and export settings use the same color profile. Common profiles include Rec.709 for HDTV and Rec.2020 for HDR.

- **Use less compression**: If color accuracy is critical, consider using a less compressed format such as ProRes or DNxHD, though these files will be larger.

- **Apply LUTs**: LUTs are mathematical tables that can be used to adjust the color space of your video during export. This can help compensate for gamma shifts and ensure consistent colors across devices.

Video file types and export settings can influence your final colors. Different file formats use varying color profiles, and compression in some formats can affect accuracy. Mismatched profiles or high compression can lead to color shifts. To maintain color fidelity, use the same color profile for editing and export, opt for less compressed formats when needed, and consider applying LUTs to adjust for gamma shifts and ensure consistent colors across devices.

Technical refinement for professional results

While embracing artistic freedom, remember the technical foundation for flawless color grading:

- **Calibrated display**: Ensure that your monitor accurately represents the colors you're manipulating.

- **Color scopes**: Monitor your adjustments using **Waveform**, **Vectorscope**, and **Parade** scopes to avoid clipping and maintain technical accuracy.

- **Secondary color wheels and Parade scopes**: Use these powerful tools in tandem to isolate and adjust specific color ranges within your image for precise and targeted grading.

- **HDR grading**: For high dynamic range footage, utilize HDR tools and scopes to ensure optimal contrast and detail without losing information in highlights or shadows.

- **Color spaces**: Rec.709 is the standard color space for most TVs, offering a familiar viewing experience but with a limited range of colors and contrast. Rec.2100 HLG, an HDR format, boasts a wider color gamut and increased dynamic range, displaying richer colors and more detail in highlights and shadows, but requires an HDR-compatible display to truly shine.

Utilizing advanced color grading techniques in Premiere Pro expands the range of creative opportunities available. Embrace the artistic implements, refine your technical aptitude, and consistently acquire knowledge and engage in experimentation. By committing yourself to this art form, you will elevate your videos from being technically proficient to visually breathtaking works of art, captivating people with your distinctive sense of color.

Summary

In this chapter, we've dived into the fascinating world of color correction and Lumetri Color in Premiere Pro. Understanding how to manipulate color effectively is fundamental for creating visually compelling videos. Lumetri Color provides a robust set of tools, from basic adjustments such as white balance and exposure to advanced techniques such as curves and qualifiers. By mastering these tools, you can not only achieve accurate color representation but also craft unique and artistic looks to elevate your storytelling.

We established a clear distinction between color correction, which focuses on fixing imbalances and achieving neutrality, and color grading, the artistic process that injects creative intent and stylistic flourishes. We delved into practical techniques for meticulously adjusting the colors of specific objects or transforming the entire visual atmosphere of your scene. A significant portion of the chapter was dedicated to achieving near-flawless skin tones, a cornerstone of polished and professional video productions. By using the tools and strategies outlined in this chapter, you can effectively overcome the task of correcting skin tones in Premiere Pro and enhance the quality of your videos to achieve a higher degree of professional refinement.

Moving beyond the basics, we explored the depths of advanced color correction tools. The mighty **Lumetri Color** panel took center stage, offering meticulous control through a combination of **Color Wheels** and **Curves**, selective color wheels for targeted tweaks, and **Vectorscope** for visualizing color relationships. To further refine color accuracy, we investigated the power of LUTs for applying predefined color styles. We also deciphered the language of the **Histogram** and **Waveform** monitors, uncovering the wealth of information they reveal about color distribution and intensity levels within your video. Finally, to ensure your masterpiece translates flawlessly to different viewing environments, we concluded by examining color spaces and their critical role in video export formats. By understanding these concepts, you are now empowered to export your video with the confidence that it will retain its intended look and color for audiences to enjoy.

Keep in mind that your commitment to becoming proficient in this craft will open up fresh avenues for creativity and enable you to capture the beauty and uniqueness of your subjects in each video.

In the next chapter, we'll shift our focus to the realm of titles and graphics in Premiere Pro, equipping you with the skills to add impactful visual elements and text overlays to your projects, further enhancing your video editing expertise.

12
Mastering Titles and Graphics with the Graphics Templates Panel in Premiere Pro

The inclusion of titles and graphics is essential in enhancing the quality of your films, transforming them from simple recordings to refined and professional presentations. The Graphics Templates panel in Adobe Premiere Pro enables users to generate captivating text animations, motion graphics, and dynamic visuals directly within the editing timeline. This chapter explores the complexities of the Graphics Templates panel, enabling you to fully utilize its capabilities in creating compelling titles and visuals that enrich your storytelling. Producing visually striking titles, lower thirds, and other graphic components enhances the professionalism and clarity of your video productions.

This chapter explores the capabilities of the Graphics Templates interface in Adobe Premiere Pro, giving guidance on how to effectively utilize its features to produce these vital elements. We will examine the possibilities of customizing pre-existing graphics, utilizing pre-built templates, and even constructing your own, enabling you to personalize visuals in a way that harmoniously complements the vision of the project. You will possess the ability to effectively utilize the Graphics Templates interface by the conclusion of this chapter, thereby gaining access to an extensive array of imaginative opportunities to visually enhance your narratives in Premiere Pro.

In this chapter, we're going to cover the following main topics:

- Creating dynamic titles and lower thirds with the Graphics Templates panel
- Working with motion graphics templates
- Creating MOGRTs in .aegraphic files in Adobe After Effects
- Creating MOGRTs with third-party plugins in Premiere Pro
- Troubleshooting motion graphics in Premiere Pro
- Creating captions and subtitles

Creating dynamic titles and lower thirds with the Graphics Templates panel

This powerful tool empowers you to craft captivating titles, lower thirds, and various graphics elements. Access the panel through the **Window** menu. You will see further information on how to navigate the panel in the following sections.

What is the Graphics Templates panel?

In essence, the Graphics Templates panel empowers any Premiere Pro editor with the motion graphics capabilities of After Effects. However, this feature is not just available to you but also to your entire staff and clients, all within your preferred **non-linear editing** (NLE) tool.

If you are a Premiere Pro editor who works with motion graphics artists in a collaborative setting, the Graphics Templates panel has the potential to greatly enhance your productivity. Using graphics packages not only saves time but also enhances efficiency by automating rendering processes and ensuring uniformity in visual elements.

Graphics templates – your gateway to visual storytelling

The Graphics Templates panel functions and acts as a comprehensive hub for text and graphics design within Premiere Pro. The software provides an interface that is easy for users to navigate, templates that can be personalized, and robust animation tools, enabling you to do the following:

- **Generate dynamic titles**: Craft visually captivating introductory sequences, lower thirds, and calls-to-action using animation and special visual enhancements
- **Create custom graphics**: Construct various shapes, use static photos and video clips, and utilize motion graphics templates to produce distinctive visual components
- **Effortlessly animate**: Employ user-friendly timelines, keyframes, and pre-existing animations to infuse vitality into your text and graphics
- **Ensure consistency**: Preserve and reuse your designs as graphic presets, guaranteeing effortless uniformity and aesthetics across all your projects

Whether you are producing instructional videos, promotional films, or short films, the Graphics Templates panel within Premiere Pro provides access to visually captivating narratives that captivate viewers. Next, let's see how to navigate around this panel with the help of the Properties panel to create and edit motion graphics within your video projects.

New Properties panel for Premiere Pro

The new Properties panel in Premiere Pro allows you to conveniently access frequently used features. As you choose clips from the timeline, the Properties panel will automatically display the most relevant controls and fast actions.

Do you need to resize multiple video clips and graphics or adjust the volume of several audio clips? Now, you can select multiple clips in the timeline and modify their attributes all at once. For more advanced controls, the Properties panel will guide you to the additional panels you need.

To enable the **Properties** panel in Premiere Pro, select the **Window** menu and choose **Properties**, as shown in *Figure 12.1*:

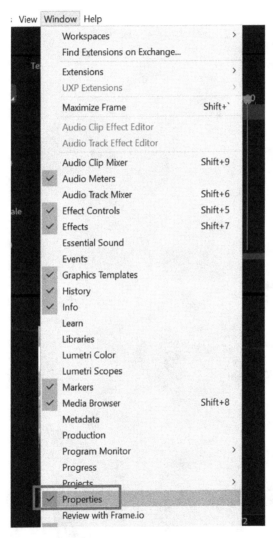

Figure 12.1 – Enabling the Properties panel from the Window menu in Adobe Premiere Pro

You can add the **Properties** panel to your existing workspace by docking it wherever you like. The **Properties** panel is now automatically docked in all default workspaces and will be visible when you click **Reset to Saved Layout**.

Changes in the latest update (2025)

The latest update introduces significant changes to the editing workflow. Controls for editing graphics and captions have been entirely relocated to the **Properties** panel, streamlining the process. Additionally, **motion graphics templates** (**MOGRTs**) are now accessible from the **Graphics Templates** panel, providing a more organized workspace. The **Properties** window for source clips has been renamed to **Media File Properties**, reflecting its broader functionality.

Figure 12.2 – The Properties panel in Adobe Premiere Pro

These updates to the editing workflow are intended to improve productivity and streamline the creative process. The latest version improves the user experience by streamlining editing controls and giving a more organized workspace.

Available controls in the Properties panel

The **Properties** panel offers a range of controls depending on the type of clip selected in the timeline. For video clips, you can adjust transform properties such as **Position**, **Scale**, **Anchor point**, **Rotation**, and **Opacity**. Audio clips can be modified with volume and pan controls. For graphics, all graphic controls are available, including those for captions. Additional quick actions such as **Speed**, **Fill Frame**, and **Fit to Frame** are also accessible, enhancing your editing capabilities

Now that you're familiar with the **Properties** panel, let's put that knowledge to use by creating eye-catching lower thirds for your videos.

Creating lower thirds

One notable application of the Graphics Templates panel is its ability to create lower thirds. An After Effects user can create a graphic and save it as a MOGRT (`.mogrt`) file (often pronounced *mo-gurt*). Subsequently, any editor proficient in Premiere Pro can import the `.mogrt` file and effortlessly modify the text and other attributes, while preserving the seamless animation crafted in After Effects.

The Graphics Templates panel can integrate a significant number of After Effects characteristics, but not all of them, and it can also utilize third-party plugins from After Effects, such as Video Copilot's Element 3D. Often, the installation of After Effects is unnecessary on the Premiere Pro system when utilizing the `.mogrt` file. This is a revolutionary development when designing Premiere Pro templates for clients.

While Adobe After Effects offers unparalleled power for motion graphics creation, its installation isn't required when solely working with `.mogrt` files in Premiere Pro. Here's why:

- **MOGRTs are self-contained packages**: Imagine them as streamlined versions of After Effects compositions, containing all the necessary elements such as animations, visuals, and effects. These elements are encapsulated within the `.mogrt` file, eliminating your need for the full After Effects project.

- **Premiere Pro offers user-friendly controls**: Instead of the After Effects complex interface, MOGRTs expose simplified controls directly within Premiere Pro's Graphics Templates panel. These controls offer intuitive adjustments for aspects such as text content, colors, basic animations (depending on the template design), positioning, and scaling. This streamlined approach empowers editors without requiring them to delve into After Effects.

- **Performance efficiency plays a role**: Premiere Pro is optimized for efficient playback and rendering of MOGRTs. Accessing the full After Effects project within Premiere Pro would increase resource demands and potentially hinder workflow smoothness. MOGRTs maintain this performance efficiency while offering flexibility, allowing you to make essential adjustments directly within your video timeline.

However, if you're interested in creating MOGRTs from scratch, you'll need After Effects to build your own custom templates. For fundamental changes to a MOGRT's structure or animations beyond the provided controls, After Effects is necessary to open and edit the source project.

In essence, if your focus lies solely on using pre-existing MOGRTs within Premiere Pro, installing After Effects is unnecessary. Premiere Pro provides all the tools you need to seamlessly integrate and customize MOGRTs within your projects. Now, let's take an in-depth look at how we can get started with using MOGRTs.

Working with MOGRTs

As a Premiere Pro editor, you may be enthusiastic about the prospect of producing visually appealing graphics directly within Premiere Pro. However, it is possible that you lack expertise in After Effects or are not collaborating with a motion graphics artist. There is no need to be concerned. Adobe and other companies continue to provide assistance or support for your needs.

Accessing the **Graphics Templates** panel (*Figure 12.3*) in Premiere Pro (**Window | Graphics Templates**) unveils a diverse array of pre-existing templates that are included with Premiere Pro by default:

Figure 12.3 – Browsing MOGRTs in the Graphics Templates panel

These templates encompass many elements such as titles, lower thirds, captions, credits, and additional components. If you encounter a circumstance where you need to quickly produce clean and elegant graphics, this resource is a convenient option to use. However, it is important to note that these templates are accessible to all individuals who possess an active Creative Cloud subscription. Consequently, you or your clientele may observe a significant number of other individuals utilizing comparable or indistinguishable visuals.

There is no need to be concerned. There are alternative choices available. In addition to offering a wide range of possibilities through Adobe Stock, Adobe also provides access to several paid and free templates on platforms such as PremiumBeat and VideoHive. In the upcoming subsections, you will learn how to create custom MOGRTs in Premiere Pro, including the steps to design, animate, and export these templates for use in various video projects.

Creating MOGRTs in Premiere Pro

Adobe Premiere Pro allows users to design their own visual templates, which can include motion effects or be static. Follow the next steps to create your own template:

1. To begin, you must generate your title or motion graphic. Include any text or shape layers. Modify the style, dimensions, or placement. Apply keyframes to incorporate animations.

Figure 12.4 – Creating assets for .mogrt files in Premiere Pro

2. After creating your text graphic, simply right-click on it in your timeline and select the **Export As Motion Graphics Template…** option, as shown in *Figure 12.5*:

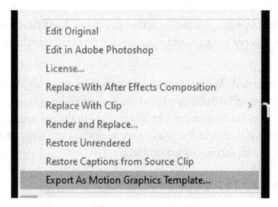

Figure 12.5 – Installing the .mogrt file in the Graphics Templates panel

3. Save it in the **Local Templates Folder** directory to ensure its visibility in the panel.

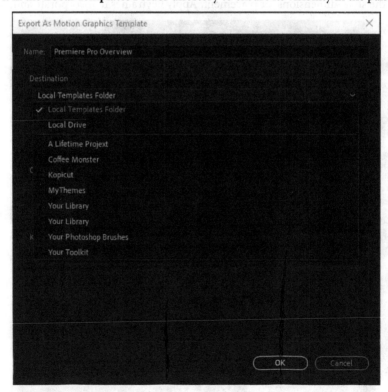

Figure 12.6 – Saving the .mogrt file in the Local Templates folder

4. After being saved, it will be visible on the **Graphics Templates** panel (see *Figure 12.7*), namely, in the **My Templates** tab. You are now able to categorize your generated visuals into folders inside the **Local Templates** and **Libraries** sections. To return to the main Premiere Pro interface, click the Premiere Pro logo in the top-left corner.

Figure 12.7 – Browsing .mogrt files in the Graphics Templates panel

These templates are applicable across various projects. You have acquired knowledge on how to generate and modify titles using the recently introduced Graphics Templates panel in Adobe Premiere Pro CC. In my opinion, this is a progressive advancement toward transforming Premiere Pro into a comprehensive software that enables users to generate intricate graphics and perform color correction using the Lumetri Color panel. Next, we will learn how to use MOGRTs in Adobe Premiere Pro.

Using MOGRTs in Premiere Pro

When the moment arrives to utilize a personalized MOGRT in Premiere Pro, there is no need to be alarmed. The **Graphics Templates** panel simplifies the process.

To begin, access the **Graphics Templates** panel by navigating to **Window | Graphics Templates**.

Then, proceed to select the **Install Motion Graphics template** option icon highlighted in the red box in the following screenshot:

Figure 12.8 – Installing the .mogrt file in the Graphics Templates panel

The **Graphics Templates** panel in Adobe Premiere Pro offers a quick and easy way to add pre-made animations to your videos. Simply drag and drop MOGRTs into the panel to import them and save time. This action imports the graphics template into the **Graphics Templates** panel of Premiere Pro. Simultaneously, the file is placed in the chosen **Motion Graphics Template Media** area of the project, which can be accessed using the **File** menu and then selecting **Project Settings** followed by **Scratch Disks**.

Once you have imported a .mogrt file, you are ready to utilize it. It is that simple.

Simply drag the .mogrt file right onto a timeline (as shown in *Figure 12.9*). Premiere Pro automatically includes a **Motion Graphics Template Media** bin in the project and places the graphic in that bin when editors require its use. By simply clicking a few times within a matter of seconds, editors are able to access and utilize the visual capabilities of After Effects directly within Premiere Pro, without the need to switch between the two programs.

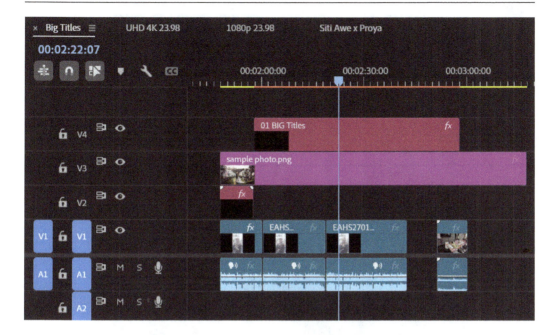

Figure 12.9 – Dragging the .mogrt file onto the timeline

Imagine simply dragging and dropping a pre-designed template directly onto your video clip in the timeline. No lengthy exports or time-consuming project setup in After Effects are required. From there, the intuitive Graphics Templates panel within Premiere Pro opens the door to customization. Change text content, experiment with colors, adjust positioning and scale, and even modify basic animation parameters (depending on the template design) – all within a single, user-friendly workspace.

Editing properties

Modifying the artwork is even simpler than importing it. The wording can be modified and the monetary value can be updated in terms of its magnitude either through the **Graphics Templates** panel or the **Effect Controls** panel. A useful technique is to utilize sliders to manipulate .mogrt variables, whenever feasible. This prevents the end user from keying in input values beyond the constraints of the input field. *Figure 12.10* shows how to modify a MOGRT file in the **Graphics Templates** panel:

Figure 12.10 – Modifying the .mogrt file in the Graphics Templates panel

Premiere Pro generates numerous iterations of a graphics template when it is employed more than once within a singular timeline. Consequently, modifying the contents of one does not have any impact on another. Multiple distinct images can be created within a single video sequence by employing an identical template.

Custom Premiere Pro MOGRTs

Premiere Pro possesses the capability to generate personalized MOGRTs. The capability is somewhat less extensive compared to After Effects, yet the method is analogous. Initially, you must generate a visual representation and then animate its components in a specialized timeline. Subsequently, you can export it by means of the Graphics Templates panel. That is the entirety of it.

An advantage of generating templates in Premiere Pro is the capability to incorporate direct uploads within the MOGRT, similar to a video or an image. This feature is not supported by MOGRTs generated in After Effects. However, Adobe releases updates often, so remain vigilant.

Sharing custom graphics templates

Custom templates can be shared using two methods. You have the option to distribute .mogrt files, as previously mentioned, or you can distribute .aegraphic files (which we will now explain in detail).

The .aegraphic file is generated upon importing a .mogrt file into Premiere Pro. Strictly speaking, Premiere Pro is the only software capable of opening this After Effects file through the Graphics Templates panel. It is a type of file used for exchanging information, and it was first introduced in the 2017 version of Adobe Creative Cloud. In the upcoming subsections, you will learn how to create .mogrt files within .aegraphic files using Adobe After Effects, including the process of designing, animating, and exporting these MOGRTs for seamless integration into video projects.

Creating MOGRTs in .aegraphic files in Adobe After Effects

Typically, providing a .mogrt file is satisfactory for a client or collaborator to import and utilize. However, .aegraphic files are crucial when you either need to merge a Premiere Pro project (**File | Project Manager**) or when you need to generate a Premiere Pro template that utilizes graphics templates.

For the graphics template to load correctly in another Premiere Pro project on a different system, it is necessary to include the .aegraphic file (not the .mogrt file) along with the project. Ensure that the .aegraphic file is included if you or the client anticipate the likelihood of its use.

Although Premiere Pro is a robust video editing application, it is frequently more effective to create intricate MOGRTs with After Effects. This results from After Effects-specific tools and functionality for crafting animations, effects, and compositions. In the upcoming subsections, we will look at a breakdown of the typical workflow.

Creating MOGRTs in After Effects

Once you have a composition set up, begin designing your graphics. Use tools such as the Pen tool or Shape tools to create shapes, add text using the Type tool, and apply effects to enhance the visual appearance. You can also import images, videos, or audio files to incorporate into your design.

In the upcoming subsections, you will learn how to design compelling graphics in After Effects, covering essential techniques for creating visually engaging and dynamic elements for video projects.

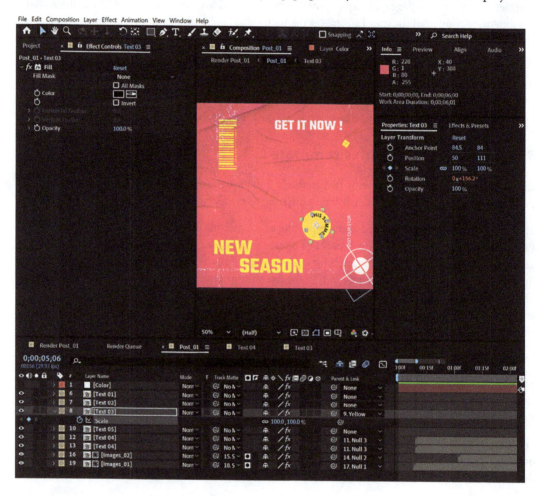

Figure 12.11 – Designing graphics in After Effects

To create a MOGRT in After Effects, go to the **Essential Graphics** tab, change the **Primary** value to **Main comp**, and name the template. Refer to the following screenshot:

Figure 12.12 – Creating a MOGRT file in the Graphic Templates panel in After Effects

Then, select **Solo Supported Properties** to filter and show properties that may be modified in the timeline. Next, right-click on the **Text** layer's **Source Text** property and choose **Add Property to Essential Graphics** Refer to the following screenshot:

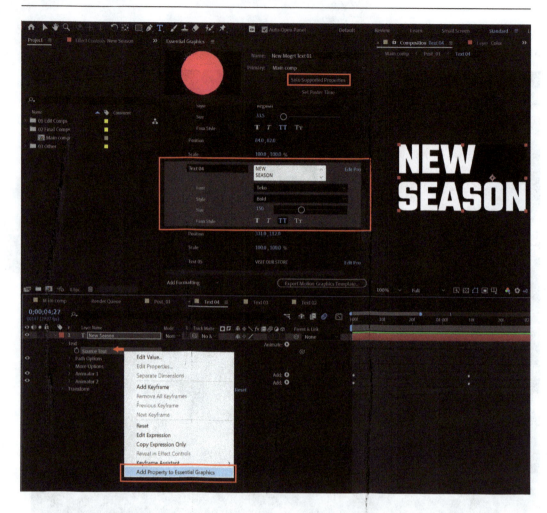

Figure 12.13 – Enabling Solo Supported Properties in the Graphics Templates panel in After Effects

To arrange properties, create groups and drag and drop relevant properties into them. This creates a MOGRT with only the customizable parts you've chosen, making it easier to use and maintain in Premiere Pro.

Exporting the MOGRT file

Once you're pleased with your design, select all of the parts that comprise your template and export them as a MOGRT file. Specify the template's name, location, and any other preferences. Save the template and use it in Premiere Pro. In the **Project** panel, select all the elements that make up your template. In the **Essential Graphics** panel, click **Export Motion Essential Graphics**:

Figure 12.14 – Exporting MOGRT file in the Graphic Templates panel in After Effects

Creating your own MOGRT files streamlines your workflow, increases productivity, and ensures excellent quality and consistency in your video projects. Next, get ready to transform your videos into truly inclusive experiences by adding captions and subtitles.

Creating MOGRTs with third-party plugins in Premiere Pro

In Premiere Pro, you may use third-party plugins to build a MOGRT; however, the process usually begins with After Effects. You'd need to pre-render some components in After Effects before importing them into Premiere Pro as part of the MOGRT file. For comprehensive details, refer to the plugin's individual instructions. These plugins often provide specialized tools and effects that aren't available natively in Premiere Pro.

Here's a general outline of the process:

1. **Install and activate plugins**: Ensure the third-party plugins you want to use are installed and activated within Premiere Pro. If you are installing an `.aex` plugin, there is a plugin folder in your Adobe installation path where you may place the AEX. The file path may look like this (`C:/Program Files/Adobe/Common/Plug-ins/PREMIERE VERSION NUMBER [will be 14 for 2020 or 15 for 2021]/MediaCore/`)

2. **Apply plugin effects**: Use the plugin's interface to apply the desired effects or create animations. Adjust the plugin's settings and parameters to achieve your desired look.

3. **Create the MOGRT**: Select the clip of the element in the timeline, right-click, and select **Export As Motion Graphics Template….** Refer to the following screenshot:

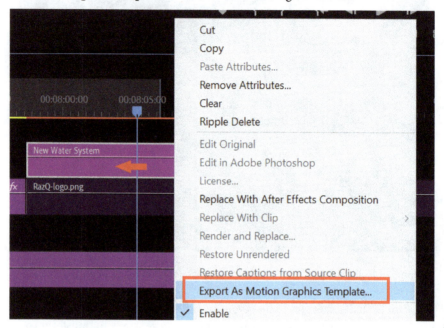

Figure 12.15 – Exporting as a MOGRT file in Premiere Pro

By creating a reusable template such as a MOGRT, you can significantly speed up your workflow. Instead of spending hours animating each individual element of your project, you can simply apply the template and customize it as needed. This saves time and ensures consistent branding across your work.

Popular third-party plugins for motion graphics in Premiere Pro

Premiere Pro has a comprehensive set of tools for generating motion graphics, but third-party plugins may dramatically increase your creative options and improve your workflow. These plugins add specific capabilities, effects, and tools to Premiere Pro that are not accessible natively. Here are some of the most popular third-party plugins for motion graphics:

- **Red Giant**:

  - *Trapcode Particular*: Generates beautiful particle effects for explosions, rain, snow, and more

  - *Optical Flow*: Detects motion in film and uses it to stabilize, track objects, and add effects

  - *Universe*: A suite of tools for producing titles, transitions, and effects

- **Boris FX:**

  - *Sapphire*: Provides complex compositing and visual effects capabilities including keying, rotoscoping, and 3D effects

  - *Continuum*: Offers motion tracking, stabilization, and other video post-production technologies

  - *Title Studio*: Generates dynamic and configurable titles and text animations

- **Trapcode:**

  - *Particular*: Generates particle effects comparable to Red Giant's *Trapcode Particular*

  - *Mirrored*: Creates mirrored or duplicated items to achieve symmetrical effects

- **Cineware:**

  - *3D integration*: Lets you import and render 3D models and animations straight into Premiere Pro

- **Plugin Alliance:**

  - *Video Copilot*: Provides a variety of plugins for effects, titles, and transitions

  - Many of *Red Giant*'s plugins are also accessible through the Plugin Alliance

Other notable plugins

Assimilate is well-known for its color-correcting and grading capabilities. *GenArts* provides a range of plugins for effects, titles, and transitions. You may refer to this site for the official list of compatible plugins: `https://helpx.adobe.com/premiere-pro/plug-ins.html`.

Third-party plugins provide several benefits for motion graphics artists working with Premiere Pro. With third-party plugins, you can create eye-catching motion graphics that elevate your work to the professional level. Furthermore, many plugins interact easily with Premiere Pro's interface, resulting in a smooth and straightforward user experience.

Troubleshooting motion graphics in Premiere Pro

When working with motion graphics in Premiere Pro, it's not uncommon to encounter various challenges that can disrupt your workflow. These issues can range from performance slowdowns to unexpected glitches in your graphics. Understanding how to troubleshoot these problems effectively is crucial for maintaining a smooth and efficient editing process.

In the following sections, we'll explore common troubleshooting techniques and solutions to help you resolve motion graphics issues in Premiere Pro.

- **Performance**:

  - *Overly complicated templates*: Simplify your templates by lowering the number of effects, layers, and animations

  - *Insufficient system resources*: Ensure that your machine fulfills Premiere Pro's minimal system requirements, including enough RAM and computing power

  - *Large media files*: Use lower-resolution or compressed media files to boost performance

- **Rendering errors**:

  - *Corrupted media files*: Look for faults or inconsistencies in your media files

  - *Plugin conflicts*: To avoid rendering issues, disable any unwanted plugins

  - *Insufficient disk space*: Make sure you have enough free disk space to render

- **Template customization**:

  - *Incorrect placeholders*: Make sure you're using the proper placeholders for text, photos, and other media

  - *Conflicting options*: Check that the settings in your template match those in your Premiere Pro project

  - *Corrupted templates*: If a template isn't operating properly, try starting from scratch

- **Animation**:

  - *Keyframe issues*: Check for missing or misplaced keyframes, and make sure the animation curves are smooth

  - *Expression errors*: Make sure your expressions are syntactically correct and error-free

  - *Timeline conflicts*: Avoid overlapping animations or competing effects, which might result in unexpected behavior

- **Plugin-related errors**:

  - *Incompatible plugins*: Check that the plugins you're using are compatible with both Premiere Pro and your system

  - *Plugin conflicts*: Disable any superfluous plugins to minimize potential complications

- *Plugin errors*: Check the plugin manual for troubleshooting advice, or contact the developer for assistance

- **Audio synchronization**:

  - *Frame rate mismatch*: Make sure the frame rates of your video and audio tracks match

  - *Audio offset*: To synchronize the audio with the video, adjust its start and finish times

  - *Audio effects*: Turn off any audio effects that may be creating synchronization issues

By tackling these frequent concerns, you will be able to diagnose and repair most of the problems you may find while working with motion graphics in Premiere Pro. If you continue to have problems, refer to the Premiere Pro user manual or online resources for more help. Next, we'll delve into creating captions and subtitles to make your videos accessible to a wider audience.

Creating captions and subtitles

Incorporating captions and subtitles into your films serves not only as an accessibility function but also as a potent storytelling element. They improve comprehension, cater to a wide range of audiences, and even extend the reach of **search engine optimization** (**SEO**). Adobe Premiere Pro provides a wide range of advanced options for producing high-quality captions and subtitles, guaranteeing that all viewers can fully appreciate your visual storytelling. This section provides an in-depth exploration of captioning and subtitling in Premiere Pro, imparting the necessary information and skills to become proficient in this crucial discipline.

Prior to delving into the tools, let us distinguish between captions and subtitles:

- **Closed captions**: Primarily intended for individuals with hearing difficulties. They provide a textual representation of spoken dialogue and other auditory information.

- **Subtitles**: Refer to the translation or modification of spoken conversation for individuals not fluent in the language or those watching in noiseless settings.

Gaining a clear comprehension of their designated responsibilities enables you to customize your approach and guarantee efficient communication.

Differences between subtitles and closed captions

Upon initial observation, closed captions and subtitles may seem indistinguishable as they both involve textual content displayed on the screen to inform the audience about the spoken words. Nevertheless, there exist nuanced distinctions, with the primary distinction lying in their intended recipients.

Subtitles exhibit all spoken content, including character dialogue, voice-over, and narration. Subtitles are designed to provide a written transcript of your film and are extremely beneficial for language translation and accessibility for anyone who cannot hear the audio. Currently, the majority of social sites automatically generate subtitles for your uploaded videos, allowing viewers to choose whether to display them or not.

Closed captions are subtitles that provide additional information beyond transcribing spoken words. They provide facts about other significant audio elements, such as music, sound effects, and background noises. Closed captions are designed for individuals who lack auditory input, such as individuals with hearing impairments.

Closed captions provide an interpretation of the audio content in your video, conveying not just the spoken words but also the tone, emotion, and rhythm. Subtitles are frequently modified from the spoken language to enhance the lucidity of the communication, by eliminating stutters, *umms*, and *errs*. Closed captions frequently incorporate instances of conversational stumbles to assist individuals who may rely on lip reading in comprehending the content. In the following section, let's see how we can add subtitles in Premiere Pro.

How to add subtitles in Premiere Pro

Premiere Pro provides an extensive and powerful set of capabilities for creating subtitles and closed captions, surpassing those found in other professional editing software. Indeed, Premiere Pro simplifies the process of subtitling to such an extent that it automatically completes an entire track for you.

The **Text** panel in Premiere Pro functions as the central location for all text-related tasks, such as captions and subtitles. Here is how to add captions to your video:

1. Edit your video then incorporate the subtitles as the final step.
2. Navigate to the window labeled **Text** and locate the section labeled **Captions file**. Within this section, select the option labeled **Transcribe Sequence**.

9.   Emphasize all of your headings and utilize the **Properties** panel to modify the font, boldness, size, and color of the subtitles.

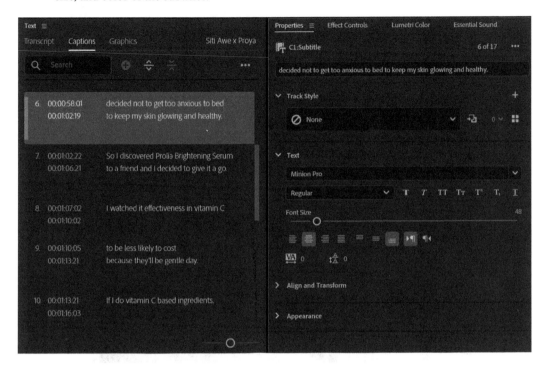

Figure 12.23 – Editing the caption style in the Properties panel

The **Text** panel allows you to transcribe audio into text, create caption tracks, and access the Graphics Templates panel for customization. Within the Graphics Templates panel, you can modify the appearance of your captions by adjusting font styles, sizes, colors, and various other visual elements. This customization ensures your captions are not only accurate but also visually appealing and complement your video's overall aesthetic.

How to add closed captions in Premiere Pro

Fortunately, incorporating closed captions into your videos in Premiere Pro follows the same procedure as subtitles, but additional editing may be required. Premiere does not support 2-caption tracks. Additionally, the transcription will solely consist of the spoken words. Therefore, you will have to manually insert any additional audio information that you consider essential.

There are two methods to include a new caption that was not generated by transcription: as an addition to the old subtitle or as a whole new title.

Method 1 – adding a caption to an existing subtitle

To add a caption to an existing subtitle, follow these steps:

1. Locate the desired subtitle in the **Titles** panel for which you wish to include an audio description.

2. To add a new text box to caption, simply right-click on the title and select the **Add new text block to caption** option.

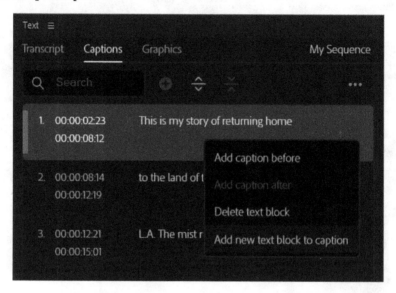

Figure 12.24 – Adding a new caption to an existing caption

3. Enter your audio description in the provided area. It will be included in the transcribed titles.

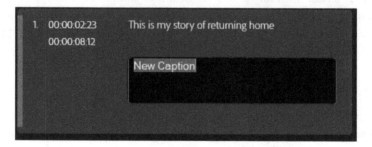

Figure 12.25 – Typing a new caption in the box

That is one way to add new captions. Next, let's look at another way to add a new caption to your video.

Method 2 – adding a new title

Adding a new title to your video is easy. Just follow these steps:

1. Prior to adding a new title, it is imperative to verify the availability of sufficient space for its inclusion.

2. Adjust the duration of your subtitles by extending or reducing their length in the timeline.

3. Move the title element along the timeline if necessary.

Figure 12.26 – Empty space between caption block

4. If you possess adequate space, right-click on **Subtitle** located within the **Titles** panel.

5. Select either **Add caption before** or **Add caption after** based on your requirements. If the title remains grayed out, it indicates that additional space is required to include a caption.

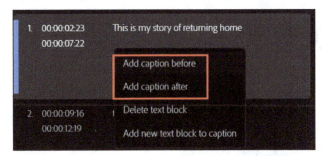

Figure 12.27 – Add caption before or after in existing caption block

6. It is important to note that relocating your titles may result in timing issues with your dialogue or subtitles.

The implementation of closed captions in Premiere Pro is crucial for a multitude of reasons. To begin with, it facilitates accessibility by offering a textual rendition of the aural content to individuals who are deaf or hard of hearing, thereby allowing them to completely understand the video. Additionally, it accommodates global audiences by providing the capability to subtitle videos in various languages, thereby broadening your outreach beyond linguistic constraints. In addition, comprehension can be improved by means of captioning, even for those without hearing impairments, by reinforcing the spoken message, particularly in noisy environments or when complex information is presented. In addition, by permitting search engines to index the video content according to the transcribed text, captioning can enhance SEO. In general, the integration of closed captions into Premiere Pro showcases a commitment to inclusivity, expands the scope of your audience, and enhances the overall viewing experience.

How to download the subtitles file

When you export your video with subtitles, they are permanently integrated into the composition and cannot be toggled on or off by the viewer. Furthermore, due to the availability of an automatic subtitling tool on platforms such as YouTube improves accessibility by providing closed captions for videos, assisting viewers who do not comprehend the spoken language or are hard of hearing. This feature makes content more inclusive and allows language learners to practice their abilities with visual text accompaniment.

YouTube accepts a variety of subtitle formats, including **SubRip Text** (.srt), **Timed Text Markup Language** (.ttml), **YouTube Captions** (.yt), **Web Video Text Tracks** (.vtt), and **Scenarist Closed Caption** (.scc). However, for the widest compatibility, it's advised to utilize .srt files.

Here's how you can export the caption in the **Text** panel:

Figure 12.28 – Exporting the caption in the Text panel

Fortunately, most services also provide the option to upload the subtitles file together with your video. In this manner, you attain absolute authority over the titles while ensuring that they remain discretionary for the audience. Each platform will have a slightly varied procedure for uploading these files; however, Premiere Pro facilitates their download in a highly convenient manner. To export the **Titles** panel to an SRT file, click on the three dots located in the upper-right corner and select the **Export to SRT file…** option.

Pro tips on using captions

There are three primary justifications for why you should consider incorporating subtitles into your upcoming video:

- Utilize subtitles to enhance the accessibility of your video for individuals with hearing impairments who are unable to hear the audio while viewing the video (thanks to considerate colleagues in the office!)

- Expand the reach of your video by converting the audio into captions in several languages, making it accessible to a broader audience

- Search engines can enhance the indexing and ranking of your video material by incorporating searchable subtitles that are visible to the crawler

Incorporating subtitles is an excellent method to enhance the accessibility of your films to a wider range of viewers. Numerous internet consumers consume video content without audio; therefore, if your project includes spoken words, subtitles are essential. Premiere Pro offers extensive control over the appearance and formatting of subtitles, and its convenient AI Transcription tool simplifies the process. If you require additional assistance in manipulating audio within Premiere Pro, I recommend consulting this useful guide. Visit this link for reference (`https://helpx.adobe.com/premiere-pro/using/bestpractices-audio.html`).

Summary

In this chapter, we went further into the realm of motion graphics in Premiere Pro, building on the core knowledge you've already gained. We looked at the new Properties panel and its control, then at how to use the Graphics Templates panel to create dynamic titles and lower thirds, how to work efficiently with motion graphics templates, how to construct complicated templates in After Effects, how to use third-party plugins, troubleshooting common issues with motion graphics in Premiere Pro, and how to add captions and subtitles to your films. We also mastered the art of working with motion graphics templates, both pre-made and custom-designed.

Furthermore, we looked at After Effects' capability for creating intricate templates and exporting them as `.aegraphic` files. We recognized the value of third-party plugins for increasing our motion graphics toolbox and identified the common issues faced by editors. Finally, we learned how to add captions and subtitles to our videos to make them more accessible.

With this solid foundation, you're ready to take your motion graphics abilities to the next level. Consider experimenting with more sophisticated approaches, discovering new plugins, or delving into other video editing disciplines such as color correction or audio post-production.

In the next chapter, we'll shift gears and dive into the world of multi-camera editing in Premiere Pro, where you'll learn how to seamlessly combine footage from multiple cameras into a cohesive and compelling final video.

13
Multi-Camera Editing in Premiere Pro

Premiere Pro enables the creation of a multi-camera source sequence by utilizing clips from many camera sources. Alternatively, you can utilize audio-based synchronization to precisely align segments in a multi-camera sequence. This chapter is your comprehensive guide to conquering multi-camera editing in Premiere Pro. We'll take you on a journey through the entire workflow, from importing your multi-camera footage to creating a dynamic final product. Whether you're editing a concert performance, a captivating interview, or any scenario with multiple camera angles, Premiere Pro offers powerful tools to streamline your process.

We'll break down the key steps involved, including automatic synchronization and angle switching, to build a refined multi-camera sequence that flows effortlessly. But for those who crave even more control, we won't leave you hanging – we'll also explore the process of creating a multi-camera sequence manually. By the end of this chapter, you'll be a multi-camera editing master, wielding the power of Premiere Pro to seamlessly switch between camera angles and create polished videos that truly captivate your audience.

In this chapter, we're going to cover the following main topics:

- Working on multi-camera editing
- Refining a multi-camera sequence in Premiere Pro
- Creating a manual multi-camera sequence
- Tips for troubleshooting common issues in multi-camera editing
- Optimizing performance with large multi-camera projects
- Utilizing multi-camera angles to enhance storytelling
- Alternative editing techniques or multi-camera workflows
- Software variations and troubleshooting tips

Working on multi-camera editing

Envision the act of recording a live event from various viewpoints, each offering a distinct outlook, a convergence of visual experiences awaiting synchronization. With multi-camera editing in Adobe Premiere Pro, you can effortlessly integrate multiple camera angles to create a cohesive and engrossing storyline. This section reveals the techniques of multi-camera editing, enabling you to convert multi-camera video into refined productions that immerse your audience in the action.

In this section, you'll discover the art of swiftly editing multiple angles of footage captured simultaneously. With the ability to seamlessly transition from one angle to another, Adobe Premiere Pro allows for a smooth and uninterrupted viewing experience.

The intricacies of multi-camera production and post-production processes far surpass the simplicity of setting up and managing media from a single camera. The techniques explored in this lesson are not to be used. However, it is important to grasp the method by which Premiere Pro handles multi-camera source material and automated synchronization. We will also delve into the art of creating a multi-camera sequence manually, giving you the reins to tailor the editing process to your specific vision.

What is multi-camera editing?

Multi-camera editing involves the manipulation of material captured from multiple cameras and viewpoints to create a cohesive and visually dynamic final product. Presenting an identical scenario or subject from various perspectives enhances the video's dynamism and visual allure for your viewers. Employing this strategy additionally facilitates the depiction of the identical picture from various viewpoints. Multiple cameras are frequently employed in music videos, soap operas, reality TV shows, live performance records, corporate videos, and weddings.

Creating a multi-camera sequence in Premiere Pro

Playing multiple camera angles simultaneously is only limited by the computing power needed to play back your clips. If your computer and storage drives possess sufficient speed, you should be able to effortlessly play back multiple streams in real time. Creating a multi-camera source sequence is a straightforward task.

Here is a step-by-step guide on how to perform multi-camera editing:

1. Begin by choosing all the footage. Simply right-click and select **Create Multi-Camera Source Sequence…**:

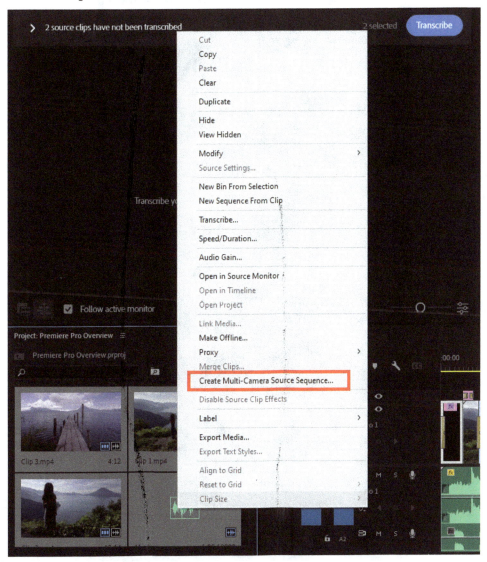

Figure 13.1 – Choosing Create Multi-Camera Source Sequence…

Within the pop-up window, we can configure our multi-camera sequence. You have the option to name it based on the main video clip or the audio, or you can come up with a completely new name:

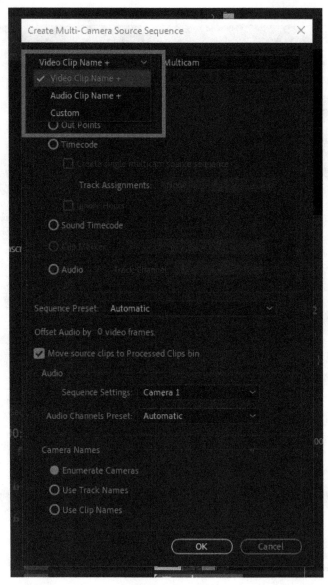

Figure 13.2 – Create Multi-Camera Source Sequence window

Next, it is important to specify a synchronization point. This determines the method by which Premiere Pro will synchronize our various cameras.

2. Consider utilizing in and out points as a potential solution. In order to accomplish this, it is necessary to designate the starting and ending points in each of your clips prior to generating a multi-camera sequence.

3. Another alternative is to utilize a timecode, which requires either setting it up during recording or manually adjusting the timecode of your clips.

4. Additionally, you have the option to synchronize your clips based on their audio. In order to accomplish this, it is important to ensure that all of your clips have audio recorded. Once this is done, you can proceed to choose audio that will be primarily utilized for syncing purposes:

Figure 13.3 – Audio synchronization option

5. You have the option to choose between using audio from all the clips or selecting a specific camera angle's audio during the editing process. This option is also applicable if you have separate audio files:

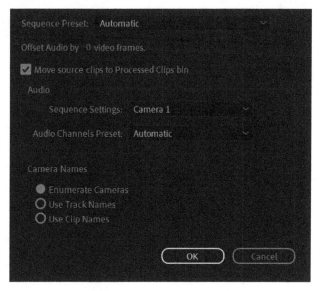

Figure 13.4 – Selecting audio preset options and clicking OK

6. Within the **Audio Channel Presets** menu, the audio can be adjusted to either **Mono** or **Stereo**. Within **Camera Names**, there is an option to showcase either clip or track names, or alternatively, utilize **Enumerate** to assign numbers to the cameras.

7. After you've made your selection, simply click **OK** to create your new multi-camera source sequence.

8. After analyzing the clips, Premiere Pro works its magic and generates a brand new multi-camera source sequence that conveniently shows up in the **Project** panel:

Figure 13.5 – Audio and multi-clip processing

And there it is! This sequence functions just like any other nested sequence. It encompasses all the footage but behaves as a single clip:

Figure 13.6 – Multi-camera sequence in the Project panel

9. When you double-click on the clip, you'll be able to see the various camera angles in the source window. You have the option to incorporate it into an existing sequence or establish a fresh sequence using it. Drag it over to the **New Item** icon in the bottom-left corner of the project window. It's the one that resembles a folded piece of paper. See the highlighted icon in the following screenshot:

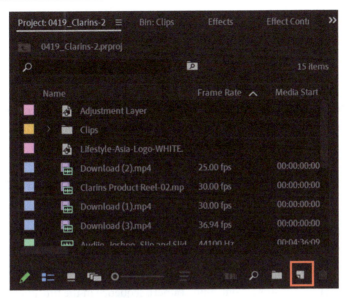

Figure 13.7 – New item icon in the Project panel

The following screenshot shows what you will see in your source monitor:

Figure 13.8 – Multi-camera sequence in source monitor

Premiere Pro dynamically adapts the multi-camera grid to fit the number of angles being utilized. For instance, if you own a maximum of four clips, you will observe a grid with dimensions of 2x2. Using a quantity of clips ranging from five to nine would result in a grid with dimensions of 3x3. Similarly, employing 16 angles would yield a grid with dimensions of 4x4. Now that you've mastered the art of building a multi-camera sequence in the **Project** panel, let's dive deeper! This next section will equip you with the skills to fine-tune and polish your multi-cam masterpiece. We'll explore techniques for adjusting cuts, refining synchronization, and optimizing your sequence for a seamless and captivating final edit.

Refining a multi-camera sequence in Premiere Pro

After you have learned about bringing together footage from multiple cameras, it's now time to elevate your edit by adjusting, refining, and polishing your multi-camera sequence. This section will equip you with essential tools and techniques to transform your raw footage into a captivating final product. You now have a ready-to-use multi-camera target sequence.

See the following screenshot; it shows your multi-camera sequence in the timeline:

Figure 13.9 – Multi-camera sequence in timeline

Once you're inside the multi-camera clip, you have the flexibility to manually tweak the size, color, or audio settings for each individual file. Changes made will be saved and updated across all instances where the multi-camera source clip is utilized.

Perform a right-click on the nested multi-camera sequence located in the **Timeline** panel and examine the **Multi-Camera** settings:

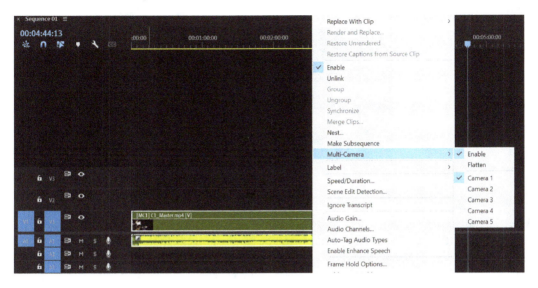

Figure 13.10 – Multi-Camera options in Timeline panel

For a multi-camera sequence clip to function properly, the **Multi-Camera | Enable** option must be chosen. The **Multi-Camera** mode is activated automatically for this clip due to the manner in which it was generated.

You can toggle this feature on or off whenever you choose. When the option is disabled, the nested sequence will function in the same way as any other nested sequence:

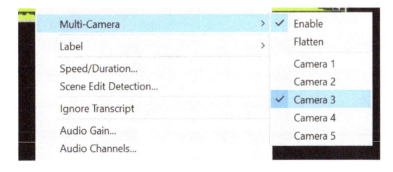

Figure 13.11 – Selecting different camera angle options in the Timeline panel

The camera angle has already been chosen. Explore a different perspective from the menu options and see the **Program Monitor** come to life with real-time updates. The name of the clip also updates in the sequence:

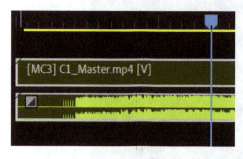

Figure 13.12 – The Master multi-camera sequence in the Timeline

After constructing the multi-camera source sequence and incorporating it into the multi-camera target sequence, the time has come to commence the editing process. In the next section, discover the incredible power of the **Multi-Camera** view in the **Program Monitor**, allowing you to witness your creation unfold in real time. Switching between different angles is easily done by either clicking in the **Program Monitor** or using a keyboard shortcut.

Creating a multi-camera view in Premiere Pro

In the fascinating world of multi-camera editing, one can effortlessly choose the perfect camera angles for each clip on the timeline. This is made possible through the ingenious **Multi-Camera** mode, which can be found in the **Program Monitor**.

When playback comes to a halt, simply click on an angle located on the left side of the **Program Monitor**. This action will cause the current clip in the sequence to seamlessly synchronize.

As you engage with the playback, a simple click on an angle in the **Program Monitor** triggers a seamless update in the sequence clip. This results in a smooth transition between the previous camera angle and the newly selected one, as an edit is gracefully applied to the clip. The changes you make won't appear in the **Timeline** panel until playback comes to a halt.

It would be beneficial to modify the view to have a comprehensive display of the camera angles in the **Program** window, so let's do that:

1. Click on the wrench icon and choose the **Multi-Camera** option:

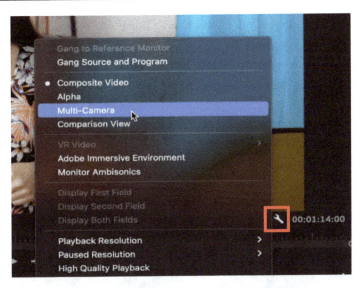

Figure 13.13 – Multi-Camera view in Program Monitor

2. To add a button to the toolbar for easy access to this view, start by clicking the + sign located in the bottom left-hand corner. Now, simply click on the icon to switch to the **Multi-Camera** view and effortlessly move it to the toolbar:

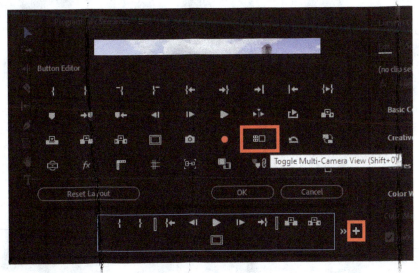

Figure 13.14 – Toggling Multi-Camera view in Button Editor

3. Alternatively, you can open up this view by using the *Shift + 0* shortcut.

4. After completing a multi-camera edit in the **Multi-Camera** view, the next step is to polish and ultimately complete it. The resulting sequence resembles any other sequence you have constructed, allowing you to employ the editing or trimming techniques you have acquired thus far. However, there are a few more options at your disposal.

5. Use these options to help you with multi-camera editing:

- **Camera Monitors**: Experience the convenience of effortlessly viewing all your camera angles at once, allowing for seamless switching between them.

- **Program Monitor**: Observe the current *live* output and the seamless sequence as you make edits.

- **Record Button**: Preserve your edits in the main timeline while still having the flexibility to switch between multiple camera angles.

- **Sync Lock**: Ensures all cameras remain synchronized using a selected *master* audio or video source.

6. Locate the small wrench icon situated at the lower-left corner of the **Program** window. Feel free to scroll down and make any necessary adjustments to your cameras. You have the option to reorganize clips order and enable or disable them as needed:

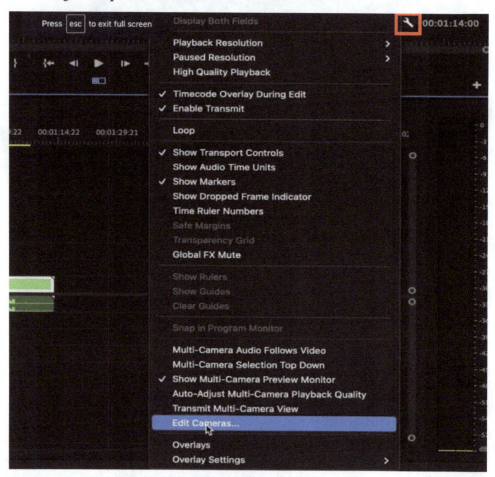

Figure 13.15 – Enabling Edit Cameras… in sequence

Each clip from the program window can be easily clicked on. By making this adjustment, the larger preview image on the right will be altered. This feature provides information about the clip that will be shown.

7. To preview the video, simply press **Play** (or you can use the spacebar).

How to cut and switch cameras

If you are satisfied with the timing of an edit but not the perspective you have chosen, you have the option to exchange the perspective for a different one. There are several methods to accomplish this task to switch camera angles:

1. When you're playing the clip on the timeline, feel free to click on any of the camera angles to switch up the perspective.

    Premiere Pro effortlessly generates cuts on the clip timeline to indicate shifts in camera angles. You will discover them once you take a moment to pause.

    The following screenshot shows you can start the playback of the clip and trim the camera angles:

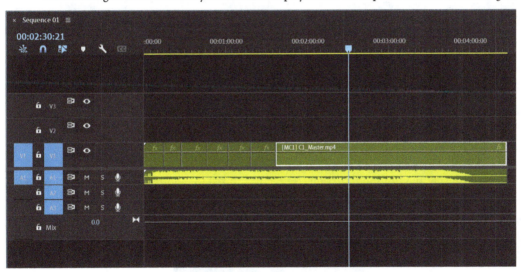

Figure 13.16 – Starting to trim the multi-camera in timeline sequence

2. Additionally, you have the option to use the numbers on your keyboard to switch between different camera angles while viewing your clip. If your keyboard is equipped with the necessary keys, you have the option to conveniently press one of the shortcuts (in this case, *1-5*). Alternatively, you can effortlessly click on your desired angle in the **Multi-Camera** view of the **Program Monitor**.

3. If you decide to alter your perspective and opt for a different camera angle at a particular moment, just navigate the playhead to the desired clip where the angle adjustment is desired. It will be brought to your attention automatically:

Figure 13.17 – Switching camera angles in timeline sequence

4. Then, choose a new angle that suits your preference or enter the number of the camera angle you desire. From here, you can treat them as separate clips and edit them in your usual manner.

Additionally, the **Rolling Edit Tool (N)** can be utilized to modify the beginning and ending points of each cut. To perform the desired action, you can either press the *N* key on your keyboard or click on the designated icon located in the toolbar:

Figure 13.18 – Rolling Edit Tool in toolbox

5. Next, locate the point where the two clips meet and make the necessary adjustments to the cut.

6. When eliminating unnecessary background noise, it's important to remember that any cuts made to a multi-cam sequence only affect the visual aspect. To ensure a seamless audio experience, be sure to make corresponding cuts to the audio as well. Make sure you're in the right spot by clicking *Shift*, then use the *C* key to cut the audio.

7. There are a couple of ways to activate the **Ripple Edit Tool (B)**. This tool allows you to effortlessly modify the starting or ending point of a clip, seamlessly integrating it into the rest of your timeline. One option is to use the tool directly, while another is to simply press the *B* key:

Figure 13.19 – Ripple Edit Tool in toolbox

The **Ripple Edit Tool (B)** feature enables you to effortlessly connect and align clips, ensuring a seamless viewing experience without any gaps.

8. And of course, if you want to remove a whole section of gaps between clips, simply select it and press *Option + Delete*. By performing this action, the section will be removed and the clips will seamlessly connect.

Ripple edits ensure that the synchronization of multi-camera clips remains intact. As you adjust the duration of a clip, Premiere Pro seamlessly modifies the surrounding clips in the multi-camera sequence to maintain smooth transitions.

While Premiere Pro offers a convenient way of using buttons and tools to create a multi-camera source sequence option, you might prefer the granular control of building a multi-camera sequence manually. In the next section, let's see how to achieve that.

Creating a manual multi-camera sequence

Within Premiere Pro, you have the option to create multi-camera sequences using either automatic or manual methods. Although the automatic option is undeniably fast and convenient, certain users may find themselves inclined toward the manual approach for a variety of reasons. Editors who desire greater control over synchronization can utilize the manual method, which provides the opportunity for meticulous adjustments using audio waveforms, timecodes, or visual cues.

Seasoned editors may find the manual workflow to be a familiar and efficient method that aligns with their established techniques. The manual method provides a wide range of possibilities for tailoring the sequence to your liking. You have the freedom to include specific clips, organize them by nesting, or even enable multi-camera functionality on selected elements. For intricate projects or those with specific editing needs, this can prove to be quite valuable. Ultimately, if automatic synchronization falls short, the manual approach grants editors the ability to identify and resolve any issues firsthand, guaranteeing seamless synchronization prior to delving into the editing process. In the end, the decision between automatic and manual creation is determined by the specific requirements of the project and personal editing preferences.

If you'd like to have a bit more control, you also have the option to manually create a multi-camera sequence. Here's how to achieve that:

1.   Organize your video clips on separate tracks:

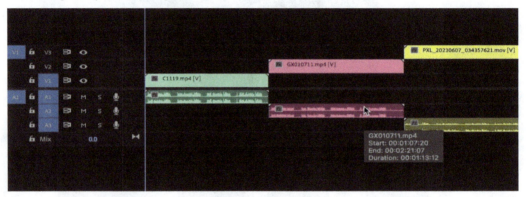

Figure 13.20 – Creating multi-cam sequence manually in timeline

2.   Highlight all the clips, right-click, and choose the option to **Synchronize** them:

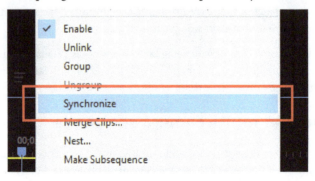

Figure 13.21 – Synchronizing the clips in timeline

3. When presented with a pop-up window, you will have the option to select your preferred method of file synchronization. Please click **OK**. Now, all of your clips are synced.

4. Let's choose all of them once more, right-click, and select **Nest...** to nest the sequence:

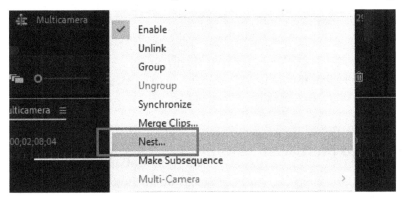

Figure 13.22 – Nest sequence in timeline

5. Choose a name and then click **OK**. Next, simply right-click on the newly created nested sequence and choose the **Multi-Camera** option, followed by selecting **Enable**:

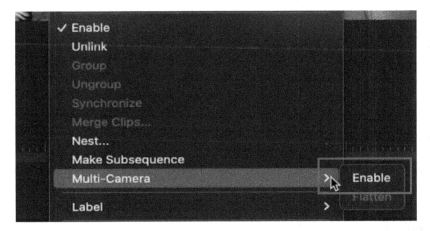

Figure 13.23 – Enabling Multi-Camera option from the nested sequence

6. Now, this sequence will function as a multi-camera clip.

Ensure that the sequence you are using to create a multi-camera sequence has the correct video and audio output settings to ensure a smooth workflow. Select the appropriate option based on whether you have stereo or mono audio.

Editing multi-camera timelines is a breeze in Premiere Pro. Switching between different angles and making cuts with a single keystroke can greatly enhance your workflow, making it faster and more efficient. It's also worth noting that using this method does not result in nested audio tracks. This feature enables you to modify audio directly in the timeline, eliminating the need to access a nested sequence.

It's important to note that automatic multi-camera sequence creation in Premiere Pro is generally very efficient and accurate. For most users, it will be the quickest and easiest way to get started. The manual method offers more control and flexibility, but it comes at the cost of additional time and effort. Ultimately, the best choice depends on the specific needs of the project and the editor's personal preferences.

Handling nested multi-cam sequences

The inability to edit a nested multi-cam sequence directly within the timeline can be a hurdle for new users. The following section explains this point effectively.

Challenge – limited editing in nested multi-camera sequences

When it comes to nesting multi-camera sequences, there are a few challenges that you might encounter:

- While nested multi-cam sequences offer a clean timeline, they have one key limitation: you can't directly switch camera angles or apply Lumetri effects within the timeline itself. To make these edits, you'll need to access the multi-cam editing window.

- Think of it like this: imagine the nested multi-cam sequence as a pre-assembled video clip. You can see it on your timeline, but you can't directly manipulate the content inside it. To make changes, you need to open the *master box*, which reveals the individual camera angles.

Here's the analogy

Think of a toolbox. The nested sequence is like a pre-built tool, ready to use. But if you need to adjust individual components (such as a screwdriver or wrench), you need to open the toolbox (multi-cam editing window) to access them.

This opens the multi-cam editing window, allowing you to do the following:

- Switch between camera angles using keyboard shortcuts (numbers *1*, *2*, *3*, and so on) while the sequence plays

- Apply Lumetri color grading to individual camera angles

Making any other edits specific to each camera angle

Premiere Pro doesn't allow directly accessing Lumetri colors within a nested multi-cam sequence. However, you can achieve color grading for individual clips within the nested sequence. Next are two methods for doing this.

Accessing the original clips

Here's how you can access the original clips from the nested multi-camera clip:

1. Right-click the nested multi-camera clip in your timeline and select **Reveal in Project**:

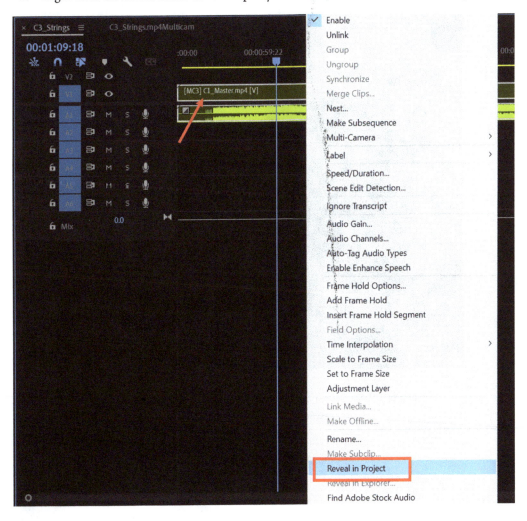

Figure 13.24 – Reveal in Project multi-camera sequence in timeline

2. This will open the **Project** panel and highlight the nested sequence.

3. Right-click the nested sequence and choose **Open in Timeline**:

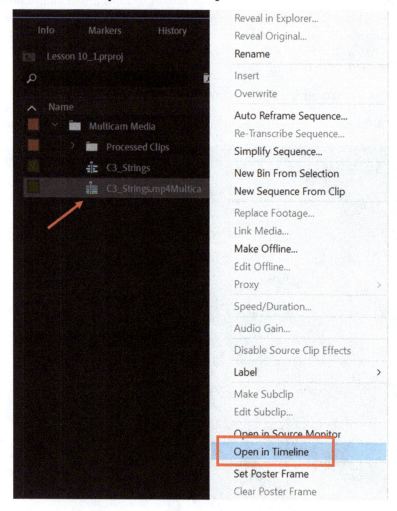

Figure 13.25 – Opening multi-camera sequence in timeline

4.   This reveals the original clips used to create the multi-cam sequence:

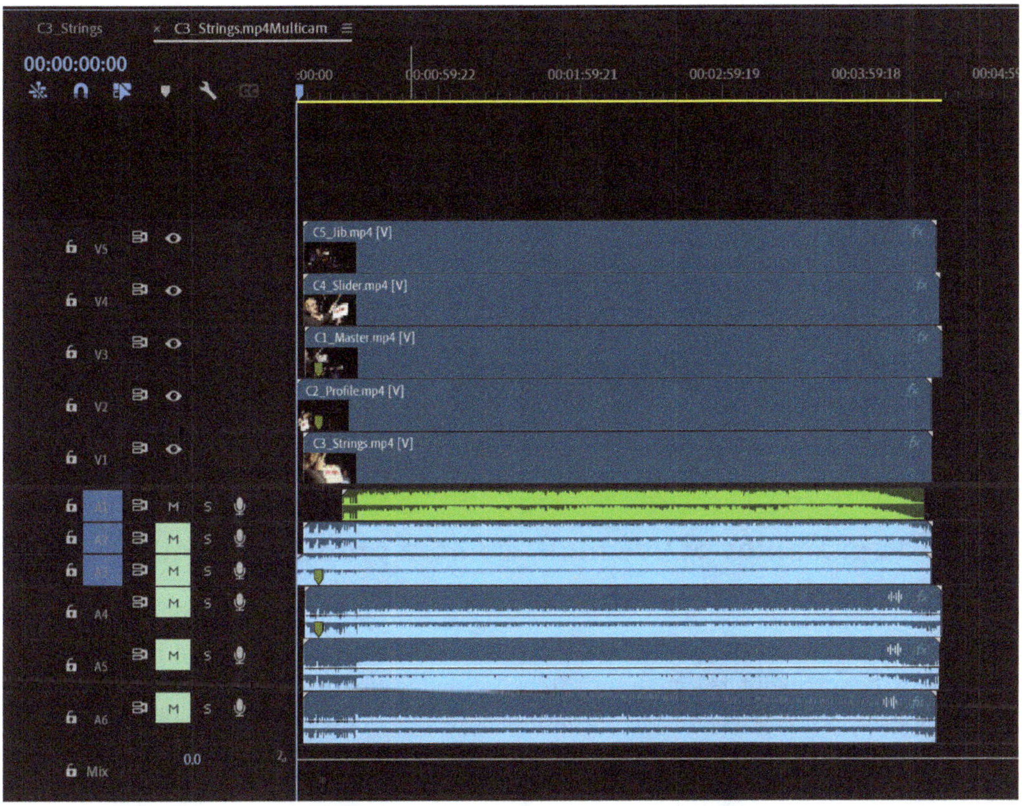

Figure 13.26 – Revealing the original clips of multi-camera sequence in timeline

5.   Now, you can select individual clips and apply Lumetri effects in the **Color** panel as usual.

Additional tips and resources

Here are some tips to remember:

- Any changes you make in the original clips will affect all instances of that clip throughout your project, not just the nested sequence

- Consider using adjustment layers within the nested sequence for broader color corrections that affect multiple clips

For a more visual explanation, you can refer to these resources:

- YouTube: `https://m.youtube.com/watch?v=hYNFD2jBh24` on color correction on a multi-camera edit

- YouTube: `https://m.youtube.com/watch?v=93Jlcf1tmCM` on how to color grade multi-cam footage in Adobe Premiere with Lumetri

> **Important note**
>
> Once you've made your edits, the changes will be reflected in the nested sequence within your main timeline. This nested sequence approach keeps your timeline clean while providing flexibility for edits.

By using this explanation and analogy, you can help readers understand the rationale behind nested multi-cam sequences and guide them through the process of accessing the editing window for further control.

Real-world examples of live multi-camera production with talkback recording

When planning a multi-camera production, there are several factors to consider. A multi-camera production in the studio differs significantly from one on location. For starters, power is already available in a studio, whereas on location, you must consider how much power is required for lighting, cameras, sound, special effects, and so on. This would entail working with various companies such as stage designers and stage builders to plan where your cameras will be located and how much power they will require. Another distinction between studio and location is illumination. Here is an example:

Figure 13.27 – Multi-camera production setup in a studio

In a studio, you have considerably greater control over the lighting, whereas on location, you have to account for natural illumination. Not only that, but you would need to consider the weather and how it affects overall production. For example, if it begins to rain, cameras, lighting, microphones, wiring, and other equipment will all become wet. To avoid damage or electric shock, you should plan ahead of time to ensure that all equipment is weatherproofed. Another logistical problem would be having a mobile studio on-site to switch between cameras and control graphics, lighting, and sound. This would already be established in a studio environment; it is commonly referred to as a gallery. See the following photo for an example:

Figure 13.28 – Multi-camera production room

Next, let's see some advanced techniques and tips for editors to handle common issues in multi-camera editing.

Tips for troubleshooting common issues in multi-camera editing

Beyond the basic troubleshooting of multi-camera editing, the following sub-sections show some advanced techniques and tips for editors to handle common issues.

Color and exposure consistency

Here is a list of techniques to improve your multi-camera editing workflow:

- **Matching white balance:**

  - Use a color chart or reference monitor to ensure consistent white balance across all cameras during filming.

  - In post-production, advanced color grading techniques such as secondary color correction can be used to fine-tune specific areas and achieve a seamless look.

- **Audio synchronization and timecode synchronization:**

  - Utilize an external audio recorder with timecode synchronization capabilities to ensure perfect audio alignment during post-production.

  - Advanced multi-cam audio synchronization tools within your editing software can further refine the process and handle minor discrepancies.

- **Frame rate and resolution mismatches:**

  - **Project settings:** Double-check project settings to ensure all footage matches the frame rate and resolution of the primary camera.

  - Utilize software tools for scaling or frame rate conversion if necessary, but be mindful of potential quality loss.

- **Advanced editing techniques:**

  - **Nested sequences:** For complex multi-camera edits, consider nesting sequences of specific camera angles. This allows for more precise control over individual cuts and transitions within the overall sequence.

  - **Ripple editing:** Utilize ripple editing to efficiently adjust the timing of multiple camera angles simultaneously, maintaining synchronization across the entire sequence.

Troubleshooting tips

Here are some suggested practical tips:

- **Review camera settings**: Before diving into editing, double-check individual camera settings for potential inconsistencies in frame rate, resolution, or audio recording format.

- **Utilize software tools**: Modern editing software offers advanced tools such as multi-cam editing panels and automatic sync functions. These can significantly streamline the editing process and help identify and resolve syncing issues.

- **Test and preview**: Regularly test and preview your edits to catch any discrepancies early on. Pay close attention to audio and visual continuity across camera angles.

- **Experiment and refine**: Don't be afraid to experiment with different editing techniques and find what works best for your specific project.

Remember – achieving seamless multi-camera editing often requires a combination of technical expertise and creative problem-solving.

By mastering these advanced techniques and troubleshooting tips, editors can overcome common multi-camera editing challenges and produce polished, professional-looking final products.

Optimizing performance with large multi-camera projects

Optimizing performance with large multi-camera projects and integrating third-party plugins requires a multi-pronged approach. You can significantly improve performance during high-performance video editing, especially in Premiere Pro with large multi-camera projects. Here's how:

- Hardware optimization:

  - **High-performance computer**: Invest in a computer with sufficient processing power, RAM, and storage space to handle demanding multi-camera editing tasks. Consider upgrading your CPU, RAM, and storage to SSDs for faster processing and data access.

  - **Dedicated graphics card**: A dedicated graphics card with ample video memory significantly improves rendering performance, especially when working with high-resolution footage and complex effects.

- Software optimization:

  - **Proxy editing**: Utilize proxy editing to work with lower-resolution versions of your footage during the editing process. This reduces strain on your system while maintaining the ability to switch back to high-resolution footage for final rendering.

  - **Optimize project settings**: Adjust project settings to match your footage specifications. This includes frame rate, resolution, and color space.

- **Close unused applications**: Closing unused applications can significantly improve performance during high-performance video editing. During high-performance editing, especially with demanding multi-camera projects in Premiere Pro, closing unused applications frees up crucial processing power and RAM (memory). With fewer programs competing for these resources, Premiere Pro can run smoother, render faster, and experience less lag by having more breathing room to handle your video editing tasks.

- Third-party plugins:

  - **Research compatibility**: Before integrating third-party plugins, ensure compatibility with your editing software and hardware specifications. Check for potential performance bottlenecks or conflicts with other plugins.

  - **Utilize plugins strategically**: Only use plugins when necessary for specific tasks. Overusing plugins can significantly impact performance. Consider alternative editing techniques or built-in functionalities whenever possible.

  - **Plugin updates**: Keep your plugins updated to the latest versions to benefit from performance improvements and bug fixes.

Additional tips

You can use the following tips to optimize Premiere Pro's performance:

- **Organize footage**: Maintain a well-organized project structure with clear naming conventions for your footage and project files. This helps minimize confusion and speeds up the editing process.

- **Regular backups**: Regularly back up your project files to prevent data loss in case of system crashes or unexpected issues.

- **External storage**: Consider utilizing external storage solutions such as high-speed external drives or RAID systems for storing large media files, especially if your internal storage is limited.

By implementing these optimization techniques and using third-party plugins strategically, you can significantly improve performance and handle large multi-camera projects with greater efficiency. Remember to constantly evaluate your workflow and adjust your approach based on the specific demands of your project.

Utilizing multi-camera angles to enhance storytelling

Utilizing several camera perspectives in storytelling is essential as it provides a more intricate and dynamic visual vocabulary. Editors can manipulate emotions, regulate scene tempo, alter audience viewpoint, highlight important elements, and deviate from conventions to create a distinctive visual aesthetic by utilizing different camera angles. This versatile method enables a more profound involvement with the storyline, fully immersing viewers in the narrative and transmitting information through many means, ultimately resulting in a more powerful and captivating experience.

Here's how to expand on creative approaches to storytelling using multiple camera angles, incorporating exercises and challenges for you:

- Creative storytelling with multi-camera editing:

  - **Emotional impact**: Discuss how different camera angles can evoke specific emotions in the viewer. Explore techniques such as close-ups for intimacy, wide shots for establishing shots, and Dutch angles for tension or unease.

  - **Pacing and rhythm**: Explain how camera angle choices can influence the pace and rhythm of a scene. Utilize fast cuts and shot changes for action sequences and slower, more deliberate cuts for dramatic moments.

  - **Point of view**: Explore how camera angles can shift the audience's perspective and create a sense of subjectivity. Utilize subjective camera angles to place the viewer directly in the character's shoes.

  - **Focus and emphasis**: Highlight how camera angles can direct the viewer's attention to specific elements within the scene. Utilize close-ups to emphasize details or wide shots to showcase the environment.

  - **Breaking the rules**: Encourage experimentation with unconventional camera angles and editing techniques to create a unique visual style.

- Exercises and challenges:

  - **Storytelling exercise**: Provide a short script or scenario and challenge readers to create a multi-camera edit that emphasizes specific emotions or narrative elements using different camera angles.

  - **Genre challenge**: Assign specific genres (for example, comedy, thriller, documentary) and challenge readers to utilize multi-camera editing techniques to create a short film within that genre, focusing on conveying the appropriate tone and atmosphere.

  - **Technical experimentation**: Encourage readers to experiment with advanced editing techniques such as split-screen editing, jump cuts, or time-lapses to create visually engaging sequences within their multi-camera projects.

  - **Reimagining scenes**: Provide a scene shot with a single camera and challenge readers to reimagine it using multiple camera angles, considering how the story changes with different perspectives.

  - **Collaboration project**: Encourage readers to collaborate on a multi-camera project, assigning different camera positions and editing responsibilities to showcase the power of teamwork and diverse perspectives.

By incorporating these creative approaches and practical exercises, readers can develop their storytelling skills and gain a deeper understanding of how to utilize multi-camera editing to create impactful and engaging narratives.

Alternative editing techniques or multi-camera workflows

Exploring alternative editing processes and workflows tailored to particular genres or industries can dramatically improve your understanding and skill set. Each genre has set conventions and expectations. You will learn how to customize your approach to maximize the effect of your writing. For example, documentaries frequently use voiceover narration and slow pans to impart information, whereas action films may use fast cuts and rapid camera movements to generate a sense of urgency. Similarly, understanding industry-specific workflows, such as the fast-paced editing style of news broadcasts or the painstaking precision required for medical video editing, enables you to use your abilities in a variety of professional contexts. This exploration broadens your creative horizons and provides you with the tools you need to thrive in various editing assignments.

Here are some examples of alternative editing techniques or multi-camera workflows for specific genres or industries:

- Documentaries:

    - **Voiceover narration**: This technique provides context and information alongside the visuals, often used for historical explanations or expert commentary

    - **Slow pans and zooms**: These emphasize specific details or create a sense of exploration and discovery

    - **Interviews**: Multi-camera setups with close-ups and cutaways between speakers enhance the interview flow and capture reactions

- Action films:

    - **Fast cuts and rapid camera movements**: These create a sense of urgency and excitement, keeping the audience engaged in the action sequences

    - **Jump cuts**: These create a disorienting or jarring effect, often used to emphasize tension or a shift in time

    - **Slow motion**: This emphasizes specific moments within the action, adding drama and impact

- Comedies:

    - **Reaction shots**: These capture the audience's laughter and emphasize comedic timing

    - **Rule of thirds**: Framing jokes or characters slightly off-center can add a touch of comedic awkwardness

    - **Musical montages**: These can be used for quick transitions or comedic effect

- News broadcasts:

  - **Fast-paced editing**: This keeps the pace of the news flow and delivers information quickly

  - **Lower-thirds and graphics**: These provide additional context and information alongside the visuals

  - **Live multi-camera setup**: This allows for seamless switching between anchors, reporters, and studio elements

- Medical video editing:

  - **Precise cuts and transitions**: These ensure clarity and accuracy in conveying medical procedures or information

  - **Close-up shots**: These showcase specific anatomical details or surgical techniques

  - **Animation and overlays**: These can be used to visualize complex medical processes or concepts

- Sports broadcasting:

  - **Instant replay**: This allows viewers to re-watch key moments from different angles

  - **Split-screen editing**: This showcases multiple events or players simultaneously.

  - **Slow motion and close-ups**: These emphasize the athleticism and skill of the players

These are just a few examples, and the possibilities are vast. By understanding the specific conventions and expectations of different genres and industries, editors can tailor their editing techniques and workflows to create the most impactful and engaging content.

Software variations and troubleshooting tips

While the core principles of multi-camera editing remain consistent, specific software versions and system configurations can lead to variations in the implementation process. This section addresses potential discrepancies and offers troubleshooting tips:

- Software variations:

  - **Multi-camera editing features**: Different editing software might offer distinct multi-cam editing functionalities. Familiarize yourself with the specific tools and features available within your chosen software. For example, Adobe Premiere Pro offers a dedicated **Multi-camera** workspace with features such as automatic syncing based on audio waveforms or timecode, while Final Cut Pro X utilizes a **Syncing** inspector with manual adjustment options.

- **Keyboard shortcuts and workflows**: Keyboard shortcuts and editing workflows can vary between software. While the general principles of multi-camera editing apply, adapting to the specific software's shortcuts and workflow will optimize your efficiency. In Premiere Pro, the *C* key toggles the camera angle view, while in DaVinci Resolve, users might need to access **Multi-camera View** from the menu bar.

- Troubleshooting tips:

  - **Consult software documentation**: If you're using Premiere Pro and encounter syncing issues, the official documentation provides detailed troubleshooting steps for analyzing audio waveforms and adjusting timecode settings.

  - **Search online forums and communities**: Search online forums for *Premiere Pro multi-cam audio sync problems* to see if other users have encountered similar issues and discovered solutions specific to that software.

  - **Experiment and adapt**: While some software might offer automatic syncing options, you might discover that manually adjusting specific camera angles in your project based on visual cues provides a more precise synchronization.

  - **Seek professional help**: If you're working on a complex multi-camera project in Adobe Premiere Pro and encounter performance issues, consider seeking assistance from experienced Premiere Pro editors or contacting the software support team for advanced troubleshooting.

By acknowledging software variations and providing troubleshooting tips, you empower readers to navigate potential discrepancies and adapt their approach based on their specific tools and system configurations. This ensures a more inclusive and adaptable learning experience for readers using different software versions.

Summary

This chapter delved into the world of multi-camera editing, equipping you with the skills to effectively manage and weave together footage captured from multiple angles. We began by exploring the fundamentals of refining existing multi-camera sequences in Premiere Pro, followed by a step-by-step guide on creating your own manual multi-camera sequence from scratch. To ensure smooth operation, we addressed common troubleshooting issues that may arise, offering practical tips and alternative methods.

Further, we explored how optimizing performance becomes crucial with large multi-camera projects, discussing strategies for maximizing efficiency through hardware and software optimizations. The chapter then dove into the power of storytelling using multiple camera angles, highlighting how different angles can be used to evoke emotions, control pacing, and create a more dynamic and immersive narrative.

Recognizing the diverse software landscape, we acknowledged potential variations across different editing platforms and provided troubleshooting tips to address discrepancies encountered with specific software versions or system configurations. This comprehensive approach will empower you to confidently navigate the multi-camera editing process, regardless of your software or project specifics.

With this chapter, you have triumphed over the vast realm of multi-cam editing in Premiere Pro! We embarked on a captivating journey that turned you into a master of harmonizing footage, leaving behind your days as a mere wrangler of multiple clips. We delved into the entire process, starting with importing a multitude of camera angles and culminating in the creation of a refined final cut.

In the next chapter, we will delve into the exciting realm of social media and explore how to craft content that captivates this fast-paced digital landscape. Prepare yourself for a journey into the art of enhancing your edits to captivate your audience and navigate the ever-changing world of online video.

14

Creating and Editing Trendy Videos for Social Media

The internet is constantly buzzing with the popularity of social media, and video content is at the forefront of it all. In this ever-changing world, fads come and go like fleeting moments, requiring creators to adapt to the transient nature of the digital landscape.

This chapter provides you, the adventurous video editor, with the necessary tools and techniques to create captivating social media videos in Adobe Premiere Pro that captivate your audience and gain traction on the algorithm. This chapter equips you with the knowledge and tools to navigate the ever-evolving social media landscape, ensuring your videos stay fresh and relevant. From crafting titles that act as irresistible hooks to mastering the nostalgic charm of light leaks and eye-catching lens flares, you'll unlock a treasure trove of creative techniques. Don't worry about mastering complex editing software – we'll show you how to effortlessly manipulate split-screen sizes and positions, adding a whole new dimension to your storytelling. By seamlessly integrating these techniques into your videos, you'll not only grab attention but also forge a connection with your audience, propelling your social media presence to new heights. The ultimate goal? To transform you from a social media bystander into a content creator extraordinaire.

In this chapter, we're going to cover the following main topics:

- Understanding the social media landscape
- Creating titles that pop for your videos
- Choosing a video font
- Adding light leaks, film burns, and lens flares to videos
- Adjusting the size and position of split screens
- Success story – the MrBeast blueprint!

Understanding the social media landscape

Let's explore the wide range of social media platforms. Every platform has its own unique style and caters to different types of readers. **Instagram** values polished aesthetics and concise narratives, while **TikTok** thrives on quirky dares and contagious enthusiasm. **YouTube** is fueled by captivating stories and in-depth investigations.

It is vital to understand the platform you're on, the audience it attracts, and the popular trends that dominate its digital landscape.

Creating titles that pop for your videos

In this section, you'll discover valuable techniques for enhancing your titles in Premiere Pro, ensuring that they capture attention and leave a lasting impression. Discover the fundamentals of typography, the significance of selecting the right font, and techniques for ensuring that it complements the mood of your video. You'll even discover some techniques to add a touch of ingenuity to your titles, ensuring that the text in your upcoming video goes beyond mere information and truly elevates the entire production.

The following subsections will show us five effective strategies to make your text truly captivating.

Method 1 – contrast

First and foremost, it is essential to ensure that your text has sufficient **contrast** to ensure readability. For instance, if you are editing the background of a video and using a yellow background with white text, it can become challenging to read. If you're struggling to make your text more engaging, here are some suggestions to make it more captivating:

- Firstly, select a text color and position within the frame that will make it stand out against any background. A contrast of darkness and light, strategically placed for optimal readability throughout the text, is best. It may seem straightforward, but it's worth reviewing because it's an easy solution.

- Another easy solution is to apply a **Gaussian blur** to the background. In this way, the text becomes more prominent as it is the sole element in focus. Another way to achieve this effect is by applying a color wash to the footage while keeping the text in a neutral color (such as white) to make it stand out.

- You may add strokes. Create a solid edge around your text and add a visual element. This is especially handy for attention-grabbing headlines and calls to action.

- Drop shadows provide the idea that your text is slightly elevated from the backdrop, providing depth and dimension. This is especially useful for enhancing readability against complicated graphics such as for subtitles or captions.

Here's a step-by-step guide on how to add a background in Premiere Pro:

1. Add a solid color to your Project Manager by right-clicking and selecting **New Item | Color Matte....**

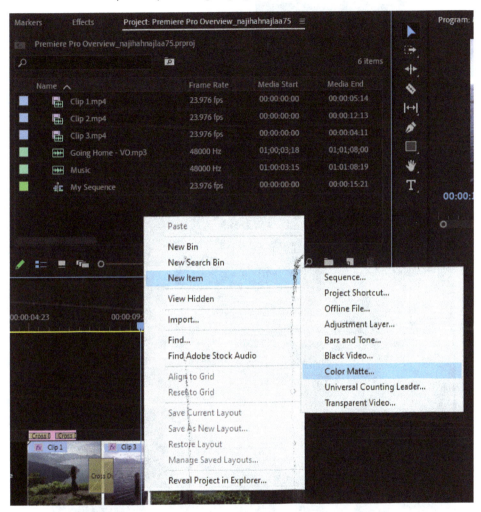

Figure 14.1 – Adding Color Matte in Project Panel

2. Select your preferred color, choose a name for your background and apply it to your footage, positioning it below your text. This will generate a solid color as a backdrop for your text.

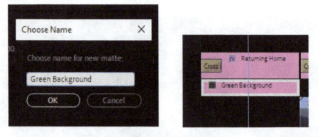

Figure 14.2 – Choosing name for new matte (left); Adding new background below text (right)

3. Experiment with adjusting the **Opacity** of the color matte and exploring different types of **Blending Mode** in the **Effect Controls** panel.

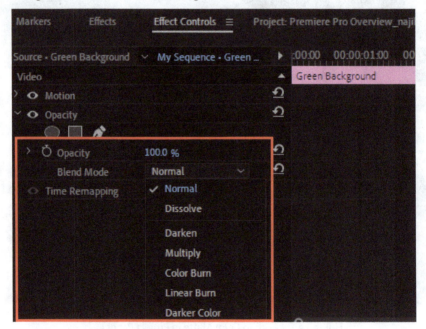

Figure 14.3 – Adjusting opacity and Blending Mode in Effect Controls panel

4. Premiere Pro offers a wide range of blending modes within the Opacity settings. Here's a breakdown of the categories instead of listing every single option (there are many!):

    • **Normal**: This is the default mode, showing the top clip regularly without any blending effects.

    • **Subtractive** (Darken the bottom clip): Darken, Multiply, Color Burn, Linear Burn generally darken the image by reducing the light passing through the layer.

- **Additive** (Brighten the bottom clip): Screen, Lighter Color, Color Dodge, Linear Dodge increase the light passing through the layer, resulting in a lighter image.

- **Complex**: This offers the **Overlay**, **Soft Light**, **Hard Light**, **Vivid Light**, and **Clear, Exclusion** options. It's used to produce more complex interactions based on pixel values in both clips.

- **Difference**: This contains the **Difference**, **Subtract**, and **Exclusion** options. It's used to create new colors based on the contrasting colors between the clips.

- **Hue**, **Saturation**, and **Lightness**: The **Hue**, **Saturation**, **Color**, and **Luminosity** options target specific color aspects (hue, saturation, and brightness) of the source clip and blend them with the base clip.

- **Dissolve**: This is used to create a fade between clips based on the opacity value. You can add this color layer to bring your animation to life. The footage remains unchanged until the text appears, at which point it becomes more visually striking.

Method 2 – typography

If you lack confidence, it's best to avoid mixing fonts. In the world of **typography**, it's generally advised to stick to a maximum of three different fonts. However, it is entirely feasible to utilize a maximum of three ingredients and still achieve an unappealing appearance. So, what's the solution?

If you're not familiar with combining different fonts, it's best to stick to using just one font and gradually expand from there. It's quite simple to achieve variation while using just one font. With just a few adjustments to elements such as size, font style, and spacing, you can create attractive titles, subtitles, or any other text your video requires.

Figure 14.4 – Adding lower-third text to a clip

Begin with a font and experiment with different styles to achieve a stylish and cohesive look.

Method 3 – placement

When is it appropriate to center text? When would it be appropriate to use a lower third?

The significance of whatever is being displayed is often determined by its size and location. If you enlarge your text and position it in the center, it will appear highly significant. Lower thirds and titles are both text elements used in video editing, but they serve different purposes and typically appear in distinct locations on the screen. The title is a clear illustration of this.

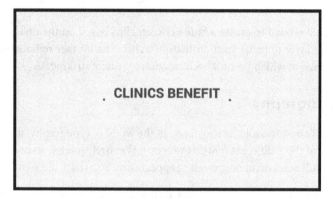

CLINICS BENEFIT

Figure 14.5 – Positioning text in the middle

The lower thirds, on the other hand, should be positioned in the lower third of the screen and should be smaller in size compared to the title. They are often found in the lower third of the video frame (hence the name!). This location guarantees that they do not obscure the primary material while staying easily visible. You can make modest adjustments based on your video but avoid blocking crucial sections. It's used to display informative text, such as the following:

- Names and titles (e.g., John Smith, CEO)
- Locations (e.g., Paris, France)
- Dates and times (e.g., May 10th, 2024)
- Other relevant details

Lower thirds help viewers understand the context of the video by providing clear and concise information. Keep them on the screen long enough for people to easily read the content. The usual norm is to display them for at least 2-3 seconds; however, this may be adjusted depending on the amount of content.

Here's an example of where you can place the lower third in your video:

Figure 14.6 – Positioning a smaller lower third at the bottom of the screen

Furthermore, when portraying someone on screen, their name and description are less significant than what they look like. The individual's personal experiences and perspectives are of the utmost importance. It's important to exercise caution when positioning text over subjects or objects in your shot. If what's happening holds significance, ensure its visibility.

Make sure that the writing in your lower third is plainly visible against the backdrop of the video. If necessary, put a somewhat translucent backdrop box behind the text to boost contrast. Avoid using lower thirds on distracting or busy areas of the video. Position them on a clean backdrop for the best legibility.

When adjusting your text's position, be mindful not to let it extend to the very edge of the frame. It's highly recommended to enable safe margins when working with text.

Here's where you can find the safe margins button to enable it:

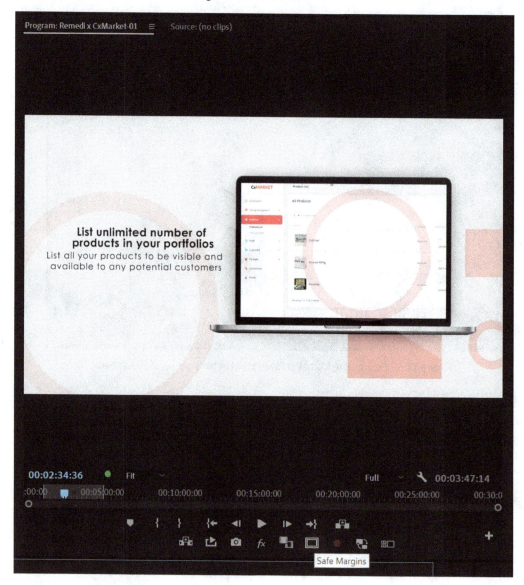

Figure 14.7 – The safe margins icon in the Program Monitor

Access the Program Monitor, locate the + icon, and choose the option for safe margins. You will find an outline of placements that your text should stay within. These margins guarantee that regardless of the device or circumstance in which your video is being watched, your text will not be truncated at the edges.

Here's how you can tell which is **title safe** and which is **action safe**:

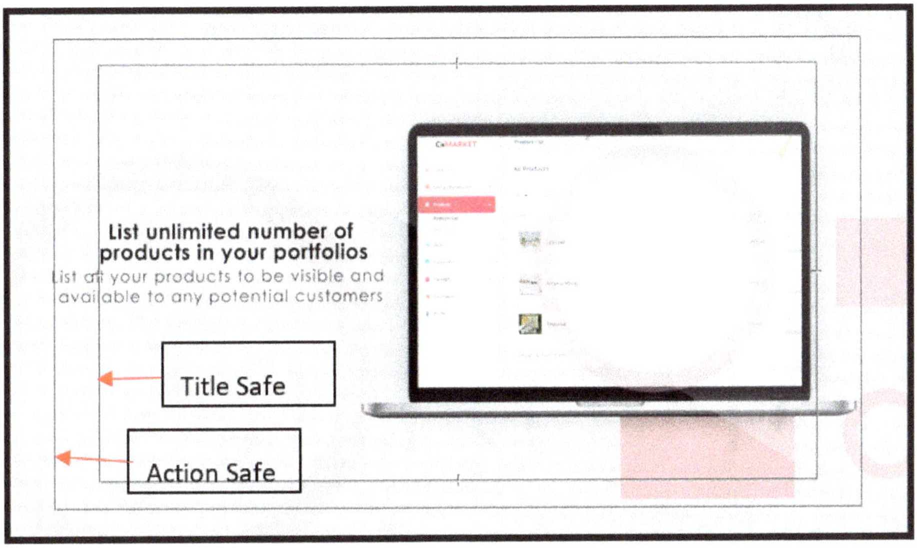

Figure 14.8 – Title safe and action safe margin icons in the Program Monitor

In the past, it was common for older TVs to display text within the inner box known as title safe. It was beneficial in ensuring that your text would be displayed correctly on the screen. However, in today's era, it is generally advisable to keep it within the second box, known as action safe. The corner of the action-safe box is a comfortable place to hold your lower thirds, too.

Method 4 – be creative

Consider incorporating your text into the scene by using masking techniques to create the illusion that the text is positioned behind the object. Masking in Premiere Pro is a powerful technique that lets you control the visibility of specific areas within a video clip.

Remember to keep your writing concise and straightforward. People should be more inclined to watch your video than to read it. Keep your titles concise, perhaps even having them consist of just a single word. If you have a complex line that needs to be displayed on the screen, there is always a way to simplify it. Condense your message into its essence, using as few words as you can.

One interesting exception to this is **kinetic typography**, as its movement adds a visually stimulating element to the overall experience. See this link for an example: `https://media.giphy.com/media/v1.Y2lkPTc5MGI3NjExMHVnM2N5NHZmbzRicG91MXp2N25pZmN4b2k0YnRlaW15a2cwOXI1ZCZlcD12MV9pbnRlcm5hbF9naWZfYnlfaWQmY3Q9Zw/iWXGykBsB8NxJqKecc/giphy.gif`.

Method 5 – tone

Always be mindful of the **tone** of your video! Ensure that your writing aligns with the desired tone for each individual project you undertake. If you're creating a professional, corporate video about a manufacturing plant, using a playful font such as Comic Sans would not be appropriate, nor would Impact or Papyrus.

When selecting a font for professional videos, it's best to avoid zany or flashy options. Choose styles that exude a sense of tranquility, composure, and poise. If your video showcases the creation of significant products, it is essential to highlight the text using a contemporary font.

Here's an example of a modern typeface you might use in your film:

Figure 14.9 – An example of contemporary fonts

When it comes to giving your text a contemporary feel, opting for a **sans serif** font is a wise choice. These fonts have a sleek and modern design, with clean lines and no decorative elements. Consider using a **serif** font, with all its flares, to achieve a different video tone.

It is important to exercise caution and avoid making impulsive decisions. Experiment with various fonts, styles, and applications to determine which ones resonate with you the most. Keep in mind that taking a more unconventional approach may lead to more mistakes compared to sticking with a more conventional method.

Choosing a video font

When you start looking through typefaces, pay great attention to these five factors. The appropriate typeface may take your video from decent to amazing. It serves as a visual indication, highlighting the tone and style of your project. Here's a guide to choosing the ideal font:

- **Prioritize legibility**: Prioritize easy-to-read typefaces. The golden rule is that your audience should be able to read your work without difficulty. Avoid using extremely ornamental or thin typefaces, especially with lower text sizes or crowded backgrounds. Sans-serif fonts, such as Open Sans or Lato, are typically legible and suitable for most videos.

- **Leading**: Leading, in the context of typesetting, refers to the vertical distance separating two lines of text. In written language, this is commonly conveyed through single-spaced, one-and-a-half-spaced, or double-spaced text. When editing a video, you may optimize the vertical space on the screen by strategically spacing out the text, making it more legible for viewers.

- **Kerning**: Kerning refers to the adjustment of the space between individual characters in a piece of text. It refers to the precise measurement of the horizontal space between two distinct letters. Word processing systems automatically use kerning to maintain uniform spacing between characters in a line, particularly when the **justified** alignment is chosen. Certain video editors employ justified text on title cards or huge caption blocks, and the video editing software often manages any kerning necessary to ensure that these justified blocks appear visually pleasing.

- **Tracking**: Tracking, often known as letter spacing, refers to the adjustment of the spacing between all characters in a text, rather than just the space between two nearby letters.

- **Consistency**: Ensure font consistency, or uniformity of fonts, across your project. Various video editing projects may necessitate the utilization of numerous fonts to fulfill the varied text demands. These fonts should be linked together. For instance, if you utilize a typeface with serifs (the strokes or decorative elements on the ends of letters; an example is Times New Roman), be sure to incorporate other typefaces with serifs in your graphic design. The same principle applies to projects that utilize sans-serif typefaces (fonts without decorative strokes, such as Arial and Helvetica Neue). The main idea is that you want a consistent visual design as you edit. Your viewers may not notice it, but a consistent visual design is one of the many elements that help unify a film.

- **Consider the tone**: Fonts have distinct personalities. Serif typefaces, characterized by their subtle embellishments, give a feeling of heritage or sophistication. Sans-serif fonts possess a more refined and contemporary aesthetic, exemplified by typefaces such as Helvetica. Script typefaces exude a hint of stylishness or casualness (see Pacifico for an example). Select a typeface that enhances the desired atmosphere you wish to establish.

- **Match your video's style**: Is your video fun and lighthearted? A whimsical, hand-drawn typeface could be ideal. Are you developing a corporate explainer video? A professional sans serif font would be more appropriate. Consider the overall look and select a typeface that reinforces it.

- **Limit your font choice**: While it's tempting to experiment, combining too many typefaces might result in a crowded appearance. Use no more than two fonts: one for headers (bigger and bolder) and another for body text (clearer and simpler to read).

- **Utilizing font pairing**: Combining two typefaces can provide a visually appealing result. A frequent method is to use a serif font for headers and a sans-serif font for body content. Experiment with different combinations while prioritizing readability.

Here are some tips on font selection:

- **Educational video**: For titles and body text in educational videos, use Open Sans (sans-serif). This is clear and simple to read.

- **Travel vlog**: Pacifico (script) is great for headlines and Lato (sans-serif) is ideal for body text in a travel blog. Pacifico adds a hint of quirkiness, while Lato stays straightforward.

- **Corporate presentation**: Corporate presentation uses Montserrat (sans serif) for headers and Open Sans (sans serif) for body text. Both typefaces have a professional, contemporary appearance.

Do not be afraid to experiment! Adobe has a variety of pre-loaded typefaces. Try them out and discover what works best for your film. Remember to prefer clarity over flamboyance.

Adding light leaks, film burns, and lens flares to videos

Light leaks, film burns, and lens flares hold a certain allure, as they carry the essence of celluloid cinema into the digital realm. They bring a sense of richness, complexity, and a hint of nostalgic charm to your videos, captivating viewers and immersing them in your visual narrative:

- **Light leaks**: These delicate streams of light, reminiscent of sunbeams gently filtering through a slightly ajar window, infuse your scenes with a whimsical and otherworldly ambiance

- **Film burns**: These organic scorch marks, reminiscent of vintage projectors, add a touch of nostalgia and genuine character to your footage

- **Lens flares**: These mesmerizing bursts of light, reminiscent of the way real lenses respond to intense sources, add a hint of cinematic splendor and excitement

If you ever find yourself wanting to enhance or add depth to a sequence, there's a high probability that you'll utilize light leaks to achieve that effect. In today's film industry, light leak overlays have become increasingly popular among filmmakers for a variety of purposes. At times, they serve as a way to indicate that the scene unfolding is a recollection, foreshadowing, or illusion. However, it is also quite common to observe the utilization of light leak overlays for stylistic purposes, adding a wistful or vintage atmosphere to a scene, as exemplified here:

BEFORE   **AFTER**

Figure 14.10 – The difference between not using light leaks (left) and using light leaks (right)

Here is how to add light leaks to your clip:

1. Download any free light leaks to your device.

2. Import the light leaks into the Adobe Premiere Pro timeline and place them on top of your clip, as shown here:

Figure 14.11 – Adding light leaks on top of the clip in the timeline

3. Pick the **Screen** option under **Blend Mode** and adjust the **Opacity** accordingly:

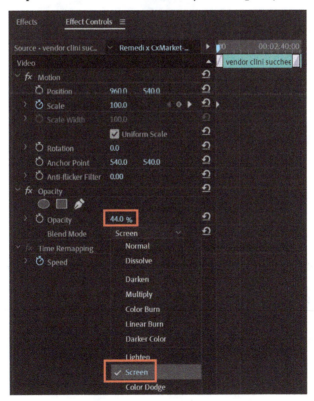

Figure 14.12 – Blend Mode and Opacity in Effect Controls

4. Select **Screen** from the drop-down menu and see the result on the clip.

5. The resulting color is always lighter than both input colors. Imagine a scenario where multiple photographic slides are projected onto a single screen all at once. This is exactly what happens when you use the **Screen** mode.

    Keep in mind that sometimes, simplicity is key. The light leaks are powerful additions, not the main focus. Excessive utilization of them can cause your video to be overwhelmed by a multitude of digital imperfections.

Here's when you should consider using the light leaks in your videos:

- **Focusing on particular scenes**: Add a touch of magic to ethereal landscapes, infuse nostalgia into vintage settings, and enhance dramatic moments with captivating visual effects.

    Here's an example of how to use light leaks in a particular scene:

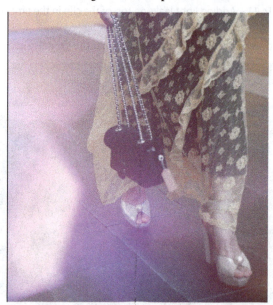

Figure 14.13 – Adding light leaks to give a more dramatic effect to the scene

- **Adjusting opacity and blend modes**: Refine the intensity and blending of your effects to create a seamless, cohesive appearance, as seen in *Figure 14.13*.

- **Experiment with animation**: Add a **Cross Dissolve** effect to ensure seamless transitions.

Figure 14.14 – Adding a Cross Dissolve effect to the clip

One fantastic aspect of light leak overlays is how effortlessly they can enhance your videos, giving them a stunning visual appeal. One of the downsides is that they can be quite elusive to locate – for a bargain price, that is.

There are two sorts of websites that provide free, downloadable light leaks for video editing:

- **Stock footage websites**: These sites provide royalty-free video clips, which include light leak overlays. Pixabay and Pexels are popular possibilities. Look for *light leaks* or *light leak overlays* to get free printable sets.

- **Video editing resource websites**: These websites offer materials tailored exclusively to video editors, such as free light leak packs. Look for websites that cater to your editing program (for example, Adobe Premiere Pro). A short online search for *free light leaks for Premiere Pro* should provide several results.

Indeed, the vast expanse of the Internet is teeming with an abundance of light leak overlays, patiently awaiting their moment to be acquired through a simple download. However, the cost of these items can quickly accumulate when you're working on numerous projects.

Adjusting the size and position of split screens

Video trends often lead to many people and corporations adopting a similar style. We've seen whiteboard animations, fast-paced abstract films, and even star wipes, which were briefly fashionable. Split screens remain popular. This video effect is remarkable, and Adobe Premiere Pro makes split screens easy.

How to create a split screen

When you create a split screen, the screen space is divided to allow multiple clips to be viewed simultaneously. For those interested in split screens, it's important to understand the process of cropping. Discover how to apply the crop effect in this comprehensive guide:

1. Arrange all the clips you want to be shown on screen in the desired sequence.

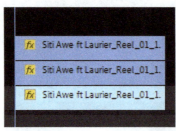

Figure 14.15 – Arranging the clips in a timeline

2. Adjust the clips to ensure that they have a consistent duration.

3. Disable the highest-ranking tracks to focus solely on the lowest one.

Figure 14.16 – Disabling the highest tracks visibility

4. Head over to the **Effects** panel and incorporate the **Crop** effect.

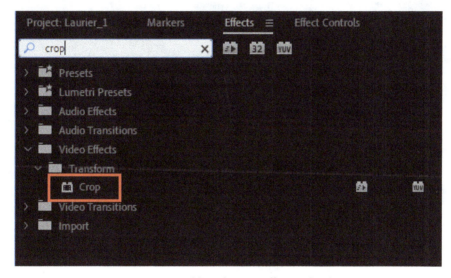

Figure 14.17 – Adding the crop effect to the clips

5. Fine-tune the **Crop**, **Position**, and **Scale** effects of the clip until you are satisfied with its visual appearance. From the **Effect Controls** panel, cropping allows you to specify the viewable section of your clip using a rectangular selection tool. Positioning regulates clip placement in the frame regardless of size. Imagine shifting a desk picture.

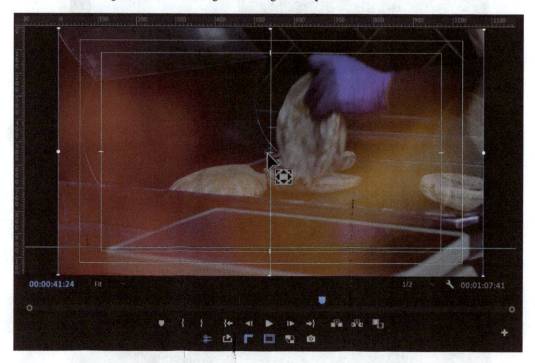

Figure 14.18 – Adjusting the clip's position using the anchor point

6. Finally, scaling scales the clip on the screen. You can change these parameters graphically in the Program Monitor or via sliders or values. You may fine-tune how your clips are changed in your project using the Anchor Point as a reference point.

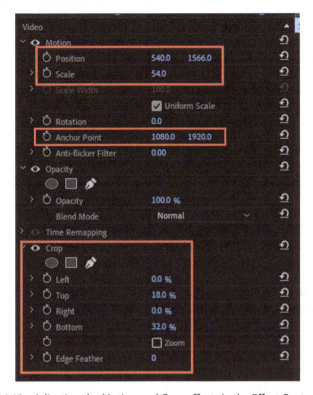

Figure 14.19 – Adjusting the Motion and Crop effects in the Effect Controls panel

Here's the result:

Figure 14.20 – A top-and-bottom split screen (vertical)

As shown in *Figure 14.20*, there are multiple video clips displayed simultaneously within a single frame. The top-and-bottom layout displays two clips vertically, one above the other. Social media thrives on grabbing attention and conveying information quickly. The split-screen technique can be a powerful tool in this context by allowing you to showcase two things simultaneously.

Here are some prime scenarios for using split screens:

- **Comparisons**: Put two contrasting products, ideas, or situations side-by-side to highlight differences or spark debate

- **Before and after**: Show the dramatic transformation of something, such as a workout routine or a DIY project, by displaying the *before* and *after* states on a split screen

- **Reacting and watching**: Capture genuine reactions alongside the original content; this is perfect for reviews or funny commentary videos

- **Multitasking and efficiency**: Demonstrate how your product or service helps manage multiple tasks at once by splitting the screen between a person using it and the benefits achieved

- **Live and recorded footage**: Combine a live host commenting on a pre-recorded video or event, keeping viewers engaged with both elements

This technique lets you showcase two things at once, making it perfect for scenarios such as comparisons (think product reviews), before-and-after reveals (such as makeup tutorials), or even reactions to videos. It can also boost engagement by demonstrating multitasking benefits or combining live commentary with pre-recorded footage. With its ability to present information in a visually dynamic way, the split-screen technique is a powerful tool for social media creators.

Choosing your split screen layout

Before delving into the split screen techniques, allow your imagination to be your compass. What narrative are you attempting to convey? Are you interested in comparing two different scenes, creating a sense of simultaneous action, or presenting multiple perspectives at once? The layout you choose should prioritize the narrative, rather than the other way around.

Let's look at the different types of split-screen layouts:

- **Classic side-by-side**: A timeless option for displaying two equal elements, ideal for comparisons or contrasting viewpoints

The side-by-side layout looks like this:

Figure 14.21 – The side-by-side layout (horizontal)

Here's how to do the side-by-side layout:

I.   After importing your clips into the project, seamlessly position one file over another on
       the timeline to craft a fresh and captivating sequence. In order to achieve a split-screen
       effect in your video, it is crucial that both videos have the same duration. Ensuring that
       the videos have a consistent period requires making adjustments to their alignment.

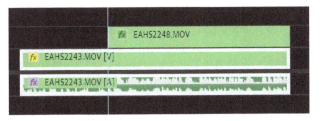

Figure 14.22 – Placing one clip over another on the timeline

II. Now, let's focus on your first clip in the timeline and proceed to the **Effect Controls** panel. Within this menu, you will discover the **Motion** option. Here, you can fine-tune the settings to precisely control the positioning of your videos. If you want to evenly distribute them, just change the number **960** to **1920** in the position category.

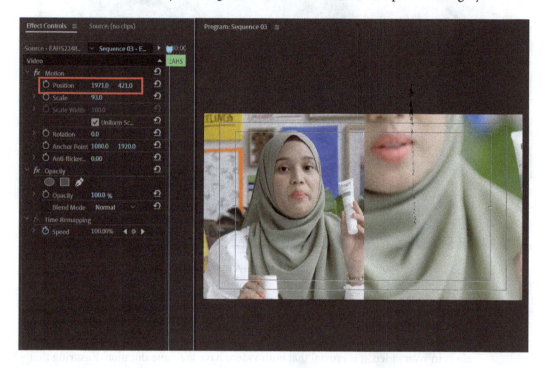

Figure 14.23 – Adjusting a clip's position in Effect Controls

III. Go to the preview window and carefully examine the modifications you have made in the recent past. The videos are displayed side by side, each taking up 50% of the screen. The screen is neatly divided in half. However, it's important to keep in mind that these settings may not accurately showcase your video information. This is because a significant portion of the objects will be concealed, as the screen coverage is limited to 50%.

IV. Next, navigate to the **Effects** panel and locate the crop effect using the search bar. You can find it under the **Video Effects** option, specifically under **Transform**. With a simple drag, you can effortlessly move the **Crop** option to the timeline window and position it above the first clip.

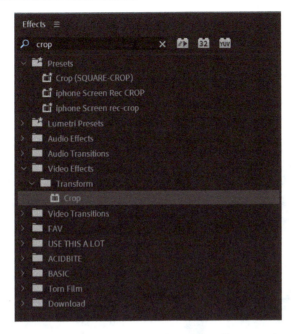

Figure 14.24 – Adding Crop effects from Effects panel

V.   Go to the crop effect settings and carefully adjust the cropping on the video's right and left sides. Make sure to position it just right so that it fits perfectly within the split screen. Adjust the position slider to your liking and save the results once you are satisfied with the alignment.

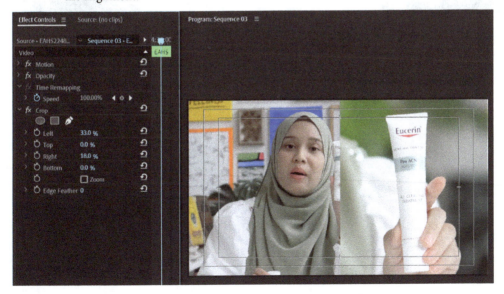

Figure 14.25 – Cropping a clip in Effect Controls

Next, proceed with the identical process to fine-tune the placement of the second video and implement the desired crop settings for optimal display. By examining the outcome in the preview window, one can fine-tune the settings to achieve a more impressive split-screen effect in the video. More examples of split-screen ideas are as follows.

- **Picture-in-picture**: This is an adaptable choice for emphasizing a crucial element while preserving the overall context within the larger frame.

Figure 14.26 – The picture-in-picture layout

- **Grid layouts**: Explore the possibilities of multiple frames; this is perfect for displaying a range of perspectives or crafting captivating montages.

Figure 14.27 – The grid layout

- **Creating unique shapes and overlays:** Escape the confines of the rectangle! Explore the creative possibilities of masks and shapes to craft captivating split-screen arrangements.

Figure 14.28 – Using shapes and overlays

Crafting exquisite split-screen videos requires dedication, but the end result is truly worth the effort. Now that you have mastered the fundamentals of Adobe Premiere split-screen video editing, it's time to unleash your creativity and take your skills to new heights.

Success story – the MrBeast blueprint!

MrBeast, whose actual name is Jimmy Donaldson, is the current king of YouTube. When Jimmy Donaldson established his YouTube channel in 2012, he used the moniker MrBeast. MrBeast originally struggled to build a fan base, delivering uninspiring gaming videos with random thumbnails and titles. However, he quickly shifted his channel's attention to themes such as calculating YouTuber's Adsense revenue, thus introducing his first viral format.

MrBeast's channel had a significant surge in popularity due to the *#TeamTrees* campaign, after his initial success with the *Counting to 100,000* video. The effort aimed to generate $20 million in funds to facilitate the planting of 20 million trees by 2020. However, MrBeast surpassed this goal by garnering over $22 million in contributions and successfully planting more than 23 million trees within a year. MrBeast's philanthropic activities and popularity among his vast audience were solidified by this highly successful campaign. He is renowned for creating movies in which he generously distributes substantial amounts of money, facilitates the restoration of vision for 1,000 blind individuals, and accomplishes intricate challenges such as those shown in the fictional series *Squid Game*.

In addition to his philanthropic pursuits, MrBeast has expanded his brand by venturing into entrepreneurship. He has initiated the establishment of a merchandising store named *Shop MrBeast*, an online-only restaurant called *MrBeast Burger,* and collaborated in the creation of *Finger Lime*, a brand that offers healthier snack options. MrBeast is a very influential content producer with a worldwide fanbase. He currently holds the title for the most-watched YouTube channel in 2021 and was honored with the prestigious Streamy Producer of the Year award in 2023. In November 2022, MrBeast surpassed PewDiePie as the individual YouTuber with the highest number of subscribers, taking up a position that PewDiePie had held for almost ten years.

I acquired some fascinating and important ideas from watching multiple interviews with him. Here's a look at his path to popularity and how he achieved success:

- **Quality content always surpasses quantity**. Investing that additional effort into a video ultimately yields rewarding results. Attempting to adhere to a strict timetable and hastily producing videos does not contribute to the rapid growth of your channel.

- **Tags may not hold as much significance as one might assume**. His response was brief, as if he had little to say on the matter. However, it was evident that there came a point when he made the decision to cease including tags in his videos. This was before he became wildly successful. I would still highly recommend it, as it provides a modest boost of around 5% to the algorithm, based on his viewers.

- **Titles and thumbnails are crucial for success**. It is advisable to avoid placing your thumbnail at the end. Curating your content should be one of your top priorities from the very beginning, just like crafting the perfect title for your work. It is crucial to have a clear understanding of your title, or at the very least, a well-defined concept of it before you begin filming. By dedicating ample effort to crafting captivating thumbnails and titles, you can expedite your journey toward becoming a full-time YouTube content creator.

- **Keep the audience engaged and captivated**. Captivating your audience while they are immersed in your content on their smartphones or computers can be quite challenging, yet it holds immense significance. It is crucial to strive for a viewer retention rate of at least 70% on every video. Discovering the precise number for each video is made possible through powerful analytics tools.

- **The size of the channel is inconsequential**. Having a mere 10 subscribers should never discourage you from achieving a staggering million (or more) views on a single video. It simply implies that it's a tad more challenging. However, it is indeed possible to garner a substantial following on a lesser-known channel. I have witnessed such instances numerous times over the course of my career. *Let's cut to the chase*. When you begin your video, it's important to provide the audience with exactly what they're looking for. Craft it with brevity and infuse it with exhilaration. Crafting a captivating introduction is crucial. In those initial 10 seconds, you have the opportunity to captivate your audience and draw them into your video. It's during the first 45 seconds that you must skillfully hook viewers and entice them to stay engaged with your content. This is where the magic happens. As you engage in this activity, it is also advisable to keep things interesting.

- **Make it interesting**. It is becoming increasingly common to find high-quality videos, especially in the realm of entertainment, that incorporate multiple storylines. Imagine yourself engrossed in a captivating television series. Imagine a vivid scene that unfolds before your eyes, filled with unexpected twists and turns. Just when you think you have a grasp on what's happening, the story takes a sharp turn and transports you to a completely different setting, seemingly unrelated to the previous one. That's absolutely captivating. Alternating between different storylines adds a dynamic and captivating element to the narrative. **SNEAKO** effortlessly captures the essence of his thoughts in his concise one-minute podcasts. This is an incredibly effective method. If this idea doesn't align with the type of content you create, that's perfectly alright! Ensure that your video captivates the audience from start to finish.

- **Craft a compelling conclusion**. Something that captivates the audience, building anticipation for what lies ahead, is a great idea. Take MrBeast, for instance. He never fails to deliver mind-boggling surprises or to pull off jaw-dropping stunts toward the conclusion of his videos. However, you'll have to stick around and watch the whole thing to experience the full impact! There is a satisfying reward awaiting! Craft a compelling incentive for viewers to stay engaged until the very end of your video.

- **Ideas hold immense significance**. Your video concept has the potential to set you apart from the rest. MrBeast has an immense appreciation for brilliant ideas. He would go to great lengths to stimulate his mind, even attempting to generate ideas while in the depths of REM sleep. His unwavering dedication to crafting a captivating video is truly remarkable.

It's important to keep in mind that even if your video idea has the potential to go viral, poor execution can still prevent it from gaining traction. During an interview, he casually discussed with a few friends how another YouTuber's video of creating an icehouse out of Orbeez could have gone viral with some improvements in video production.

Summary

This chapter equipped you with a toolbox of visual effects to elevate your Premiere Pro edits. We started with understanding the power of overlays. These versatile graphics can be used to create lower thirds that display essential information such as names, locations, dates, or titles to introduce, conclude, or separate sections of your video – all without overwhelming viewers. Additionally, we introduced light leaks, a popular effect that adds a vintage film-like feel to your edits. We then explored the split-screen technique. By strategically using the crop effect, you can divide your screen and showcase two things simultaneously. This is perfect for product comparisons, before-and-after reveals, or even live reactions to videos.

This chapter also explored the meteoric rise of MrBeast (Jimmy Donaldson), the king of YouTube. We delved into his journey, from early gaming videos to outrageous stunts and challenges that dominate the platform. By examining MrBeast's blueprint, aspiring YouTubers gained valuable insights into capturing audience attention and building a loyal following.

The next chapter focuses on optimizing your workflow and maximizing performance in Premiere Pro. We'll explore practical tips and tricks to help your editing software run more smoothly, navigate shortcuts that streamline your process, and discover techniques for keeping your project files organized. By mastering these optimizations, you'll be well on your way to becoming a more efficient and effective video editor.

15

Optimizing Premiere Pro's Performance Settings for Smooth Workflows

Working with video demands technical understanding and data management due to high bitrates, project-sharing requirements, and diverse codecs.

Mastering the art of video production requires a deep understanding of the technical aspects involved, as well as the ability to manage data effectively. This is because video files often have high bitrates, necessitating careful handling, and projects often require collaboration and sharing, which comes with its own set of requirements. Additionally, the use of diverse codecs adds another layer of complexity to the process. By delving into this chapter, you will gain the necessary insights to fine-tune Premiere Pro's settings, resulting in a seamlessly efficient editing journey. In this discussion, we will explore various strategies that can greatly enhance your editing experience. These include utilizing proxy workflows to efficiently handle high-resolution footage, harnessing the immense power of your graphics card for accelerated performance, and optimizing **random-access memory** (**RAM**) allocation to ensure smooth project handling.

In this chapter, we will delve into the realm of networked storage solutions, uncovering their ability to effortlessly provide your entire team with instant access to project data. By delving into the inner workings of footage, projects, and other data stored in a centralized location, you will discover the intricate web that links workstations and storage effortlessly. These invaluable insights will guide you in crafting a collaborative editing environment. After going through this guide, you will have the knowledge and skills to maximize the performance of Premiere Pro, tap into the full capabilities of networked storage, and ultimately enhance your editing workflow so that it's more efficient and collaborative.

In this chapter, we're going to cover the following main topics:

- Pro tips for peak performance
- Exploring Premiere Pro settings for peak performance

- Understanding proxy workflows in Premiere Pro

- Rendering clips for smoother playback

- Using Render and Replace for linked elements

- Adjusting playback resolutions

- Managing project and media files on networked storage for collaboration

- Common troubleshooting issues with proxy editing

Pro tips for peak performance

Ensuring a seamless editing workflow in Premiere Pro is essential for video editors who strive for professionalism. Let's delve into how to fine-tune your software settings to unleash their maximum potential:

- **Leverage proxy workflows**: Embrace Premiere Pro's proxy editing functionality. This allows you to generate lower-resolution versions of your original footage, significantly reducing processing demands during editing. Premiere Pro seamlessly integrates these proxies for playback, ensuring a lag-free editing experience. When it's time to export your final video, Premiere Pro effortlessly switches back to the pristine high-resolution files for the best possible quality.

- **Harness the power of hardware acceleration**: Unlock the processing potential of your graphics card (GPU) by enabling hardware acceleration within Premiere Pro's preferences. Modern GPUs are specifically designed for tasks such as video editing. Leveraging hardware acceleration significantly improves playback performance, especially when working with complex effects or high-resolution footage, by offloading the processing burden from your CPU to the GPU.

- **Maximize RAM Allocation**: RAM acts as your computer's short-term memory, and Premiere Pro relies heavily on it to store project data for immediate access during editing. Allocate a larger portion of your system's RAM to Premiere Pro. This ensures more project information is readily available, minimizing the need to access slower storage drives and resulting in faster editing responsiveness.

- **Implement effective cache management**: Over time, Premiere Pro accumulates temporary media cache files. While these files can offer short-term performance benefits, they can become bloated with unused data. Regularly clear your media cache (accessible through **Preferences | Media Cache**) to remove these unnecessary files. This not only frees up valuable disk space but can also potentially improve editing performance.

- **Fine-tune playback resolution**: The playback resolution that's displayed in the **Program Monitor** window directly affects the processing power required for smooth playback. By strategically lowering the playback resolution, you can effectively reduce the workload on your system. This doesn't compromise the final video quality but allows for smoother editing, particularly on less powerful hardware or when handling complex projects. You can easily adjust playback resolution on the fly to strike the optimal balance between performance and visual fidelity.

Now, let's look at how to optimize Premiere Pro for peak performance. Premiere Pro operates better with well-organized projects, just as a car runs smoother on a clean roadway, and as we'll see, some very important things must be considered to ensure this optimized performance.

Exploring Premiere Pro settings for peak performance

Premiere Pro offers many settings that significantly impact your editing experience. Here's a breakdown of the crucial settings you should focus on for optimal performance.

System requirements

The allocation of computer resources in Premiere Pro is determined by the specific workflow being utilized. To optimize your editing workstation, it is essential to have sufficient RAM and a powerful CPU. An impressive graphics card has the potential to significantly enhance the program's performance. It is highly advisable to ensure that your editing client's hardware is equipped with the latest drivers. To ensure a seamless experience with Premiere Pro, it is essential to have a computer that boasts a considerable amount of power. For optimal performance, it is recommended to have a modern Intel 6th generation or newer CPU, or an AMD Ryzen 1000 series or newer. Additionally, 8 GB of RAM and 8 GB of available hard drive space is necessary. To ensure a seamless editing experience, particularly when working with high-resolution footage, it is recommended to have a modern Intel or AMD processor, a minimum of 16 GB of RAM, a speedy SSD for storage, and a dedicated graphics card with at least 4 GB of memory.

While Premiere Pro can technically work with various graphics cards, the NVIDIA GeForce and Quadro lines are generally recommended for optimal performance. Here's a breakdown of some good options:

- **High-end**: NVIDIA GeForce RTX 3080 (best value) and RTX 3090 (absolute best) offer top-tier performance for demanding projects with high-resolution footage and complex effects.

- **Mid-range**: NVIDIA GeForce RTX 3060 and RTX 3070 provide a good balance between power and price, suitable for most editing needs.

- **Budget-friendly**: NVIDIA GeForce GTX 1660 Ti (older but capable) offers a more affordable option for basic editing or working with lower-resolution videos.

- **Mac specifics**: Mac computers equipped with Apple silicon, such as the M1 and M2 chips, boast seamless compatibility with Premiere Pro and offer impressive editing performance.

  For those utilizing an Intel Mac, it may be worth contemplating the addition of an NVIDIA GeForce graphics card through an external enclosure (eGPU) to enhance performance.

It's important to note that AMD Radeon cards are generally not recommended for Premiere Pro due to lower optimization compared to NVIDIA.

Further reading

Adobe created this helpful guide that provides hardware recommendations and platform-optimal setups: https://helpx.adobe.com/premiere-pro/system-requirements.html.

Leveraging the GPU

Before proceeding, it is necessary to have GPU-accelerated rendering enabled in Premiere Pro. Contained within the **General** section of **Project Settings** is the following information. Ensure that **Renderer** is set to **Mercury Playback Engine GPU acceleration**. Premiere Pro is compatible with a wide range of GPUs, including NVIDIA, AMD, Intel, and Apple. Nevertheless, the level of hardware acceleration can differ.

Exclusively from NVIDIA, the recommended graphics cards for Premiere Pro are a must-have for optimal performance. While AMD does manufacture graphics cards, such as the AMD Radeon series, they are not usually at the forefront of benchmark rankings. While Premiere Pro is optimized for NVIDIA Quadro cards, the NVIDIA GeForce RTX series should be more than enough for most casual users.

It is crucial to approach the task of choosing a GPU with great care. Despite the attractive affordability of the GTX 1660 Super and other comparable graphics cards, it is disheartening to acknowledge that the current market is plagued by exorbitant price tags on most GPUs. This unfortunate situation can largely be attributed to the problem of scalping. Over a prolonged duration, the cost of the RTX 3090 remained astronomically steep.

The RTX 3070 and RTX 3080 stand out as exceptional choices in the midrange category, representing the pinnacle of NVIDIA's GeForce GTX GPUs. These models also come equipped with powerful GPU VRAM, which greatly enhances the rendering speed of Premiere Pro.

Although the RTX 3070 and RTX 3080 are excellent choices for a PC, they unfortunately cannot be used directly with a Mac because they are not compatible. Allow me to provide a detailed explanation for Mac users.

For Mac users with Apple Silicon (M1 and M2 chips):

- These Macs come equipped with integrated graphics and cannot accommodate external GPUs (eGPUs) such as NVIDIA GeForce cards.

- Fortunately, Premiere Pro has embraced the power of Apple silicon, allowing the M1 and M2 chips to shine in the realm of video editing. With their impressive performance, these chips are particularly well-suited for handling less demanding projects.

For Mac users with Intel Macs:

- For those fortunate enough to own an Intel Mac, the addition of an NVIDIA GeForce card via an external enclosure (eGPU) can truly work wonders for enhancing the performance of Premiere Pro.

- Although the RTX 3070 and 3080 are undeniably excellent options for PCs, it's worth noting that their power demands may exceed the capabilities of many eGPU enclosures.

For Mac users with eGPUs, it's worth exploring these alternative NVIDIA GeForce options:

- The NVIDIA GeForce RTX 3060 Ti is a compelling choice for those seeking a potent eGPU solution to enhance their Premiere Pro experience. This graphics card strikes an impressive equilibrium between performance and affordability, making it a worthy consideration for content creators.

- The NVIDIA GeForce RTX 3070 (lower wattage version) is a remarkable piece of technology. Seek out a variant tailored for eGPUs that boasts a lower wattage.

It is crucial to ensure that the eGPU enclosure you select is compatible with the NVIDIA GeForce card you have in mind before you make your purchase. This step will help you avoid any potential compatibility issues down the line.

Let's examine where you may change the GPU settings for your new project in Premiere Pro:

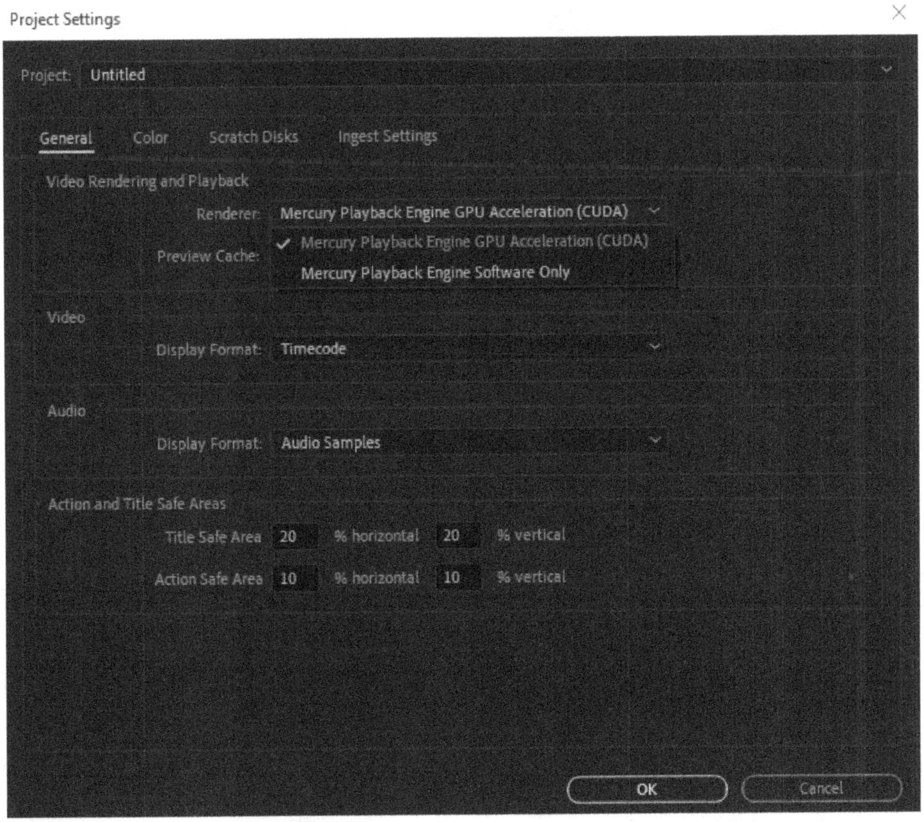

Figure 15.1 – Selecting a GPU in Project Settings

Utilizing GPU acceleration is highly recommended as it allows for efficiently transferring CPU processing tasks to the GPU. While GPU acceleration can certainly enhance the perfor mance of Premiere Pro, it is not a mandatory requirement for running the software. Perhaps turning it off and updating your GPU drivers could potentially resolve any issues you may be experiencing. Although not essential for the software's functionality, I strongly advise making use of GPU acceleration in Premiere Pro. You're faced with a crucial choice: should you focus on enhancing performance or rely solely on the processing power of the CPU? Let's take a look.

Why use GPU acceleration?

- **Enhanced performance**: GPUs are deliberately designed to excel at video editing and effects processing. By utilizing GPU acceleration, you may relieve your CPU of this difficult work. What's the result? A smooth playing experience, faster editing possibilities, and lightning-fast rendering speeds. This is especially useful when you're working with complex projects, high-resolution film, or resource-intensive effects.

- **Unlocking features**: Certain Premiere Pro effects and tools require GPU acceleration to function properly. Without it, users may see error messages or be unable to access some functions.

Can you run Premiere Pro without GPU acceleration?

Yes, it's possible. Premiere Pro has the extraordinary ability to run entirely on the processing capabilities of your CPU. Unfortunately, the experience may not live up to your expectations:

- **Expect slower performance**: Expect a noticeable decrease in speed when it comes to editing, playback, and rendering, particularly with more demanding projects. Such an impact can greatly affect the flow of your editing process and your overall productivity.

- **Limited functionality**: Some features and effects, such as color correction tools, sharpening and noise reduction, video stabilization, and text animation, may not be accessible without the use of GPU acceleration.

To make an informed choice, there are some other things you must consider. The decision to enable GPU acceleration depends on several factors:

- **Your hardware:**

  - **GPU compatibility**: Ensure your graphics card is compatible with Premiere Pro's GPU acceleration (check Adobe's documentation for supported GPUs).

  - **GPU power**: The performance that's gained from GPU acceleration will depend on the capabilities of your graphics card. A powerful GPU will offer more significant improvements.

- **Project requirements**: Complex projects with high-resolution footage or heavy use of effects will benefit the most from GPU acceleration.

- **Workflow needs**: If smooth editing and fast rendering times are crucial for your workflow, enabling GPU acceleration is highly recommended.

Although Premiere Pro may run without GPU acceleration, fully utilizing this tool's capabilities can significantly improve your editing experience. Enabling GPU acceleration is essential for better workflows, faster rendering, and realizing Premiere Pro's full editing potential, especially if you have a suitable graphics card.

Premiere supports the following GPU acceleration options:

- Mercury Playback Engine
- Hardware-accelerated encoding
- Hardware-accelerated decoding

We'll look at each of these options in the following sections.

Mercury Playback Engine

Mercury Playback Engine renders GPU-accelerated effects in real time and enhances playback and rendering speed. Select a **Video Rendering and Playback** engine option in `File/Project Settings/General`. Choose OpenCL, CUDA, or Metal for AMD, NVIDIA, or Mac GPUs on your workstation, respectively:

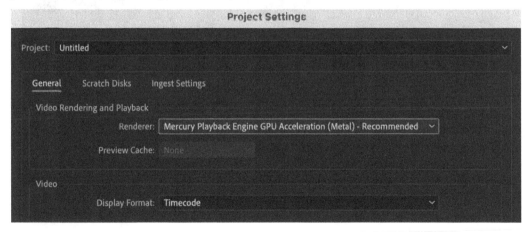

Figure 15.2 – Mercury Playback Engine

In Premiere Pro, using Mercury Playback Engine results in a smoother and quicker editing experience. Mercury speeds up effects, transitions, and even high-resolution film by using the capabilities of your graphics card. This results in real-time playback without frequent rendering delays, allowing you to edit more freely and iterate on your ideas faster. Finally, Mercury Playback Engine frees you from technological constraints, allowing you to focus on your creative vision.

Next, let's look at how hardware-accelerated encoding in Premiere Pro allows you to work more effectively. It translates to faster exports, smoother workflows, and more efficient use of system resources, allowing you to concentrate on making incredible videos.

Hardware-accelerated encoding

Hardware-accelerated encoding boosts H.264/AVC and HEVC timeline export encoding. Select H.264 or H.265 in the **Export** window and **Hardware Encoding** in the **Video** tab to enable it.

In Premiere Pro's **Export** view, activate **Hardware Encoding** under **Encoding Settings**. Sending your output to Adobe Media Encoder allows you to render **Hardware Encoding** as **Software Encoding**:

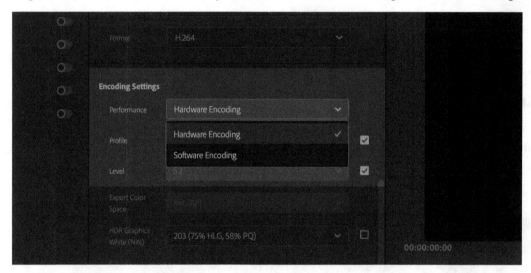

Figure 15.3 – Hardware Encoding

Premiere Pro has hardware acceleration, which uses your graphics card's processing capacity for both encoding and decoding, considerably increasing your editing experience. Hardware encoding significantly reduces export times by compressing your video into the final format using the graphics card's dedicated chip, whereas hardware decoding ensures smoother playback during editing by offloading clip decoding (uncompression) from your CPU to the graphics card. This results in faster exports, a more fluid editing process, and better use of system resources, allowing you to concentrate on making outstanding films.

In the next section, we'll cover hardware-accelerated decoding in further detail.

Hardware-accelerated decoding

Decoding involves the intricate task of transforming a compressed video file into an uncompressed format, allowing for seamless editing within Premiere Pro. By harnessing the immense processing capabilities of your computer's graphics card (GPU), hardware-accelerated decoding takes charge of this conversion.

The benefits of using hardware-accelerated decoding are as follows:

- **Faster playback**: With the help of hardware acceleration, playback performance is greatly enhanced as decoding is shifted from the CPU to the GPU. This is particularly beneficial when dealing with high-resolution or intricate video formats such as H.264 and HEVC (H.265). With this feature, editing becomes seamless and the overall experience becomes more interactive and user-friendly.

- **Minimized CPU usage**: The process of decoding can put a significant strain on your CPU. With the power of hardware acceleration, your CPU can focus on other important editing tasks, resulting in a significant boost in performance for Premiere Pro.

Now, let's look at some of the limitations of using hardware-accelerated decoding:

- **Compatibility**: It's important to note that not all GPUs can accelerate decoding for every video format. With its wide range of supported codecs and resolutions, Premiere Pro seamlessly integrates with your GPU and drivers. For more detailed information on supported configurations, I recommend referring to Adobe's comprehensive documentation.

- **Software dependence**: Although the GPU takes care of decoding, Premiere Pro still depends on software to handle the decoding process and interact with the decoded video data.

Hardware-accelerated decoding speeds up H.264/AVC and HEVC decoding when playing back the timeline. Open **Preferences | Media**, enable **H264/HEVC hardware-accelerated decoding (requires restart)**, then restart Premiere Pro. Turning on hardware decoding should improve timeline playback.

Figure 15.4 shows how to alter these settings in Premiere Pro's preferences:

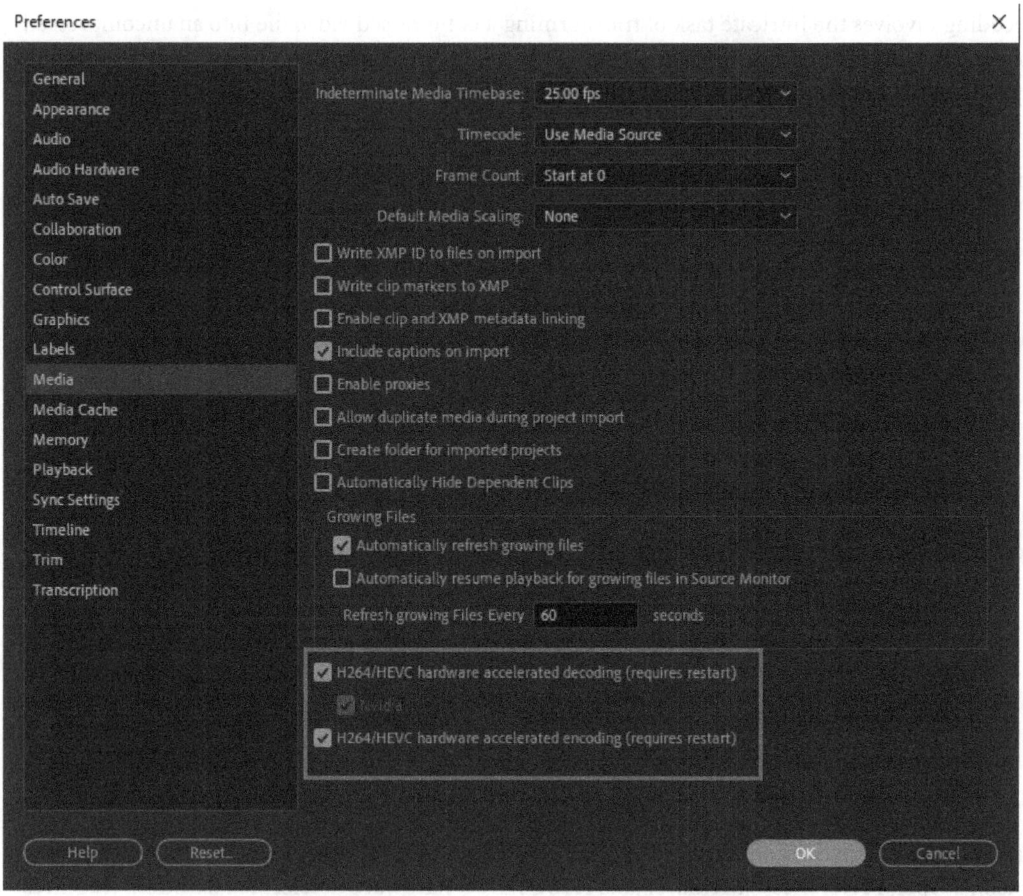

Figure 15.4 – Hardware encoding in Preferences

During the editing process, utilizing hardware-accelerated decoding truly comes to life. By harnessing the immense power of your graphics card (GPU), it effortlessly transforms compressed video files into an uncompressed format, resulting in flawlessly smooth playback. By optimizing your CPU's resources, you can enhance the responsiveness of your editing tasks. This is particularly beneficial when you're working with high-resolution footage or intricate codecs, allowing for a smoother experience.

However, when it comes to exporting your final project, software encoding becomes the main focus. By harnessing the power of your CPU, the edited video is expertly compressed into a smaller file size, making it perfect for sharing or enjoying on different devices. Although software encoding provides a higher level of control over the quality and compatibility of the final video, it may take longer to complete as it relies solely on the processing power of your CPU. We'll take a closer look at software encoding in the next section.

Software encoding

Encoding is the crucial step in transforming your meticulously crafted video project into a compressed video file ready for export. When it comes to Premiere Pro, this happens through **software encoding**, where your computer's CPU takes center stage to handle this important task.

The benefits of using software encoding are as follows:

- **Greater control**: With software encoding, you have the power to meticulously adjust the encoding parameters to achieve the exact video quality, bitrate, and file size that perfectly aligns with your unique requirements.

- **Compatibility**: When it comes to compatibility, software encoding has the upper hand. It offers support for a wide range of video formats and codecs, ensuring that your content can be played on different devices and platforms without any issues.

The following are the limitations of using software encoding:

- **Slower processing**: With software encoding, you might encounter slower processing times, particularly when dealing with high-resolution projects or demanding codecs. This is due to the heavy reliance on the CPU's processing power. Longer rendering times may be a consequence of this.

- **Increased CPU load**: With the increased CPU load, your computer's processing power is heavily utilized by the encoding process. This may impact the performance of other applications running at the same time.

This GPU acceleration speeds up timeline effects rather than the CPU. Premiere Pro can now leverage your GPU to encode and decode H.264 and H.265. In essence, hardware-accelerated decoding favors playback performance while editing by utilizing the GPU's processing capacity, whereas software encoding focuses on control and compliance with the final output video.

The most ideal workflow is as follows:

- **Editing**: Enable hardware-accelerated decoding to fully optimize your video editing experience. This will allow you to seamlessly play in numerous video formats, resulting in a smooth and uninterrupted editing workflow. This feature allows you to increase your productivity by removing irritating rendering delays.

- **Exporting**: For the final export, it is recommended to use software encoding. This method provides you with more control over the properties of the output file. By following these steps, you can ensure the exported video meets all your unique quality and compatibility requirements.

By grasping the difference between hardware-accelerated decoding and software encoding, you can enhance your workflow in Premiere Pro. By skillfully combining these methods, you can ensure a seamless editing process while retaining full control over the quality and compatibility of the exported video.

More RAM allocation

RAM serves as the computer's short-term memory. RAM plays a crucial role in Premiere Pro as it serves as a storage hub for project data, ensuring swift access while editing. By increasing the amount of RAM dedicated to Premiere Pro, you can enhance its performance and reduce the reliance on slower storage drives. This optimization leads to smoother operation and a more efficient workflow.

So, let's learn how to adjust RAM allocation.

To do this, close other applications to free up RAM. In **Premiere Pro | Preferences | Memory**, decrease the memory that's available for non-Adobe programs to increase Premiere Pro's RAM. In the selection section below, optimize rendering for performance. However, avoid giving Premiere Pro all available RAM as other essential system processes also require memory.

Figure 15.5 shows how to increase RAM allocation in Premiere Pro's **Preferences** window:

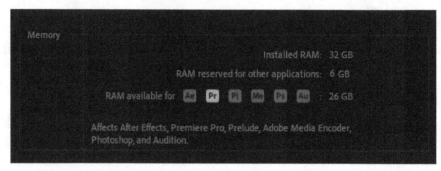

Figure 15.5 – Increasing RAM allocation for Premiere Pro

Although you'll hear that Premiere Pro needs a lot of RAM, this is only partially true. It's memory-intensive, although it depends on the project. Splicing a few 1080p clips without effects doesn't require much RAM. For example, a 2-hour film with dozens of 4K segments will require more RAM. Premiere Pro only needs 8 GB of RAM, but you should have 16 GB, and at least 32 GB for 4K video. If you're only using Premiere Pro, allow a few gigabytes for your operating system. Using other applications necessitates a precise balance. Perhaps you need to create a prototype in Photoshop or submit a video to After Effects for VFX. You may need a browser to locate stock footage or documents. In any case, you'll need enough RAM to keep the system running smoothly.

Unfortunately, there is no perfect number for everyone. It all depends on how you use Premiere and other tools. If you're experiencing slowdowns, consider adjusting your RAM allotment.

Media cache management

Temporary media cache files are generated by Premiere Pro to enhance playback performance. Over time, these files can gather unnecessary data and become bloated, which can be quite disadvantageous. By regularly clearing the media cache, you can free up valuable disk space and potentially enhance the performance of your system.

Premiere Pro caches imported clips to speed up processing. If feasible, keep these files on a different SSD from your operating system and Premiere project since they are referenced continuously. We advocate storing media cache files on a dedicated SSD drive that any editor can access in ELEMENTS shared storage. To adjust this, go to **Premiere Pro | Preferences | Media Cache**. Click **Delete Unused** to remove unnecessary cache files. Consider setting Premiere Pro to automatically delete cache files after a specific period of inactivity for long-term management.

Figure 15.6 shows how to clear the media cache in Premiere Pro's **Preferences** window:

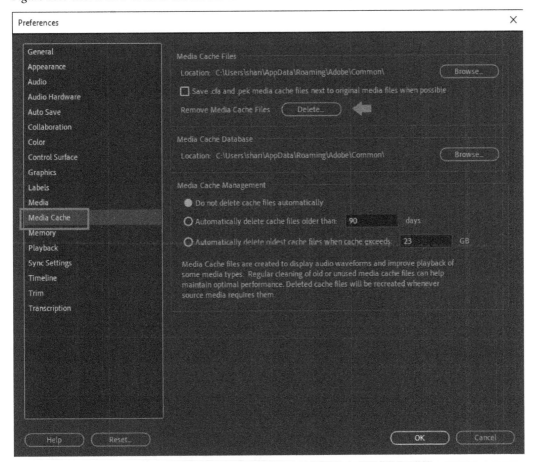

Figure 15.6 – Clearing the media cache

You may also automate cache file deletion here. After the cache reaches the given size, the oldest files might be overwritten or removed. Deleting media cache files will not delete media.

Premiere Pro generates and saves peak files simultaneously with cache files during clip import. These files contain clip audio waveforms, which slow program performance and take a long time to create. Go to **Preferences | Audio** and uncheck **Automatic audio waveform generation** to disable peak file generation.

User preferences and plugin cache reset

Resetting user preferences and purging the cache in Premiere Pro can offer several benefits for your editing workflow:

- **Improved performance:**

  - **Eliminates corrupted preferences**: As time goes on, user preferences can become corrupted for a variety of reasons, such as conflicts with plugins or updates to software. By resetting preferences, you can eliminate any corrupted settings that may be causing performance issues, such as slow playback, rendering errors, or unexpected behavior. This can help restore your system to its optimal state.

  - **Clears cache clutter**: Premiere Pro gathers cache files to temporarily store data for quicker access while editing. Over time, these files can become bloated with unnecessary or outdated information. Clearing the cache can be quite beneficial as it helps to free up precious disk space. This, in turn, can greatly enhance the overall performance of your system, particularly if you are working with limited storage capacity.

- **Enhanced stability:**

  - **Resolving plugin conflicts**: Occasionally, crashes or glitches in Premiere Pro can be attributed to incompatible or outdated plugins. When you reset your preferences, all your plugins will be disabled, and you'll have to carefully choose which ones to re-enable. By identifying troublesome plugins, you can ensure a stable editing environment, free from any potential instability.

  - **Fixing unexplained behavior**: If you happen to come across any unexplained behavior or glitches while using Premiere Pro, a corrupted preference could be the cause. By resetting preferences, you can start fresh and potentially fix these issues, bringing back the normal functionality you're looking for.

- **Streamlined workflow:**

  - **Eliminating customizations that have gone awry**: If you have meticulously tailored your settings and now find them to be overwhelming or perplexing, resetting your preferences can offer a fresh start. One option is to begin anew with the default settings or carefully choose which customizations to re-enable.

It is also important to consider the following few factors before you reset your preferences:

- **Lost customization**: When resetting preferences, all your personalized keyboard shortcuts, workspace layouts, and other custom settings will be lost. Backing up your current settings is highly recommended, especially if you frequently rely on specific customizations. This simple precaution can save you from potential headaches and ensure that your personalized setup remains intact.

- **Temporary disruption**: Resetting preferences and purging the cache can sometimes lead to a brief interruption in your workflow, although they are typically effective in improving performance. It may be necessary to reactivate your preferred plugins, adjust any custom settings, and possibly import media again if the cache stored important project data (although this is rare).

Resetting user preferences and purging the cache in Premiere Pro is a crucial troubleshooting technique that can greatly enhance performance and stability. Nevertheless, it is crucial to carefully consider the advantages in comparison to the potential disturbance it may cause to your work process. If you find yourself facing performance issues or encountering unexplained glitches, it may be worth considering resetting your preferences and purging the cache. This can often prove to be a valuable solution to investigate. It is crucial to make a backup of your custom settings before making any changes.

To reset preferences to their default settings in Premiere Pro, hold *Shift + Alt* on Windows or *Shift + Option* on Mac while starting Premiere Pro and click **OK** when you're prompted:

Figure 15.7 – Resetting preferences in Premiere Pro

Resetting preferences should be a last resort after you've tried other troubleshooting steps, such as restarting your computer, updating Premiere Pro, or checking for conflicts with other software. If you do decide to reset, be sure to back up your workspace layout and any custom presets you might lose.

Next, let's see how Mercury Transmit in Premiere Pro may enhance your editing workflow. It's a feature that sends your program's preview monitor to a secondary display; however, if you don't use a separate preview monitor, turning it off can free up resources and potentially improve playback performance. In the next section, we'll look at how to easily off Mercury Transmit so that you can improve Premiere Pro's editing experience.

Disabling Mercury Transmit

Imagine that you're working on a video project in Premiere Pro, and you want to see it playing on a bigger screen, such as a TV.

Here's why you might want to disable Mercury Transmit in Premiere Pro, especially if you're new to the program:

- **Limited impact on most setups**: Unless you have a unique configuration with dual editing monitors directly connected to your computer, disabling Mercury Transmit will have minimal impact on your video viewing experience. The video playback on your main monitor will continue to function perfectly.

- **Noticeable impact on performance**: Mercury Transmit utilizes additional computer resources to transmit the signal to another display, which can result in slower operation. When your computer lacks power, it can have a noticeable impact on the performance of Premiere Pro, particularly when working on intricate projects. By disabling it, you can liberate those valuable resources, allowing for a more seamless editing experience on your primary screen.

- **Potential for confusion**: If Mercury Transmit is enabled and you happen to click on the playback window displayed on your secondary monitor, it could inadvertently shift the focus away from your primary editing window. For those who are just starting, navigating through this process can be quite perplexing.

So, when should you use Mercury Transmit?

- **Professional editing solution**: If you find yourself in the enviable position of working in a professional editing studio, complete with a dedicated editing monitor seamlessly connected to your computer, you'll be pleased to know that Mercury Transmit can prove to be an invaluable tool. It allows you to send the video signal directly to that monitor effortlessly, ensuring a smooth and efficient editing experience.

- **Troubleshooting**: When experiencing playback difficulties with Premiere Pro, there is an uncommon but efficient debugging option that includes turning off Mercury Transmit. This strategy has been shown to solve the problem in some circumstances. Typically, this is not the first line of treatment recommended. The Adobe Premiere forums have a large number of responses that may be worth reading.

  To disable this feature in Premiere Pro, go to **Preferences** | **Playback**, then untick the **Enable Mercury Transmit** box. This may improve performance without affecting Premiere Pro's functionality if you are not utilizing an external preview monitor.

Figure 15.8 shows where you can enable or disable Mercury Transmit in Premiere Pro's **Preferences** window:

Figure 15.8 – Disabling Mercury Transmit

For most new Premiere Pro users with a single editing monitor, disabling Mercury Transmit in the preferences is a safe and potentially beneficial option. It won't affect how you see your video and can even help your computer run Premiere Pro a bit smoother.

Understanding proxy workflows in Premiere Pro

Assume you're working on a massive, gorgeous birthday cake for a celebration. Instead of normal flour, you use enormous, whole-wheat grains. It would be difficult to make, frost, and decorate the cake, right?

Premiere Pro works similarly when editing videos. The original video files are similar to those large grains of wheat; they include all of the high-quality features but can be hard to deal with, particularly on slower systems. With sluggish playback and extended wait times, editing might be annoying.

Proxy files are similar to pre-made cake batter for Premiere Pro. They are smaller, lower-resolution copies of your original video files, like how you would grind wheat into flour first. This makes them easier and faster to edit, allowing you to watch your movie, make edits, and apply effects with ease.

Modern video files are tough to edit with Premiere Pro without a powerful computer. This is because 8K, RAW, and HDR video files might slow down your workflow, but they do not require editing. Proxies may be used instead. Premiere Pro proxies allow you to edit lower-quality copies of the original video files, which increases timeline efficiency. Premiere Pro connects these proxies to the actual files, ensuring that your alteration preserves its quality when exported.

Here's a breakdown of why proxy workflows are fantastic for Premiere Pro users:

- **Enhanced editing experience**: Similar to the ease of mixing cake batter compared to whole grains, utilizing proxy files during editing ensures seamless video playback without any lag. The editing process becomes a delightful and streamlined experience.

- **Enhanced performance**: Premiere Pro experiences improved efficiency when rendering your video using proxy files. With this optimization, your computer will be able to execute the program more swiftly, particularly on laptops or older devices. Finally, bid farewell to the frustrating wait for the video to align perfectly with your edits!

- **Experimentation made easier**: With smaller proxy files, you can swiftly test out various edits and effects, saving you from enduring lengthy rendering times. For those who are just starting in the world of video editing, this is an ideal solution.

- **Zero impact on final quality**: Utilizing proxy files will have no adverse effects on the quality of your video. After completing the editing process, Premiere Pro seamlessly reverts to utilizing the original, high-resolution files for exporting. Rest assured, your birthday cake will remain delectable, even if you adorn it with batter!

Simply put, a proxy workflow in Premiere Pro allows you to edit videos with lower-resolution copies of your source files. This makes editing easier and faster, particularly for high-resolution or complicated movies. In the next section, we'll look at how to create and use a proxy workflow in Premiere Pro.

How to use proxy workflows

An offline editing workflow may be best if your project is straining your machine. Thus, Premiere Pro makes it easy to create proxy files. You just need to select your video clips and right-click. There will be an option called **Proxy** and then **Create Proxies**. Premiere Pro will help you choose settings for the smaller files and then create them for you.

Adobe Premiere Pro simplifies offline editing. During project creation, activate **Ingest** in the **Ingest Settings** tab and pick **Create Proxies**. Check the **Ingest** box and open **Ingest adjustments** in the **Media Browser** area to make the same adjustments.

Editing uses lower-resolution footage (proxies). After editing, the proxies are replaced with actual footage for color grading and export.

Let's delve into the step-by-step process of the proxy workflow:

1. Go to **Project Settings | Ingest Settings**. Select **Ingest** to enable automated ingest. Select **Create Proxies** from the dropdown. Then, select **Proxy Destination** to store them separately from your main media:

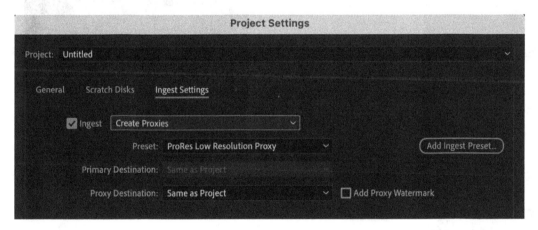

Figure 15.9 – Creating proxies in Project Settings

2. All imported clips will be automatically transcoded with the chosen codec by Adobe Media Encoder after setup. Right-clicking clips in the **Project Settings** window and selecting **Proxy | Create Proxies** creates proxies. Set a proxy file destination to store all proxies in one place.

3. Proceed as usual after creating your proxy files. In **Programme Monitor**, the + menu has a **Toggle Proxies** button. This button toggles the timeline preview between original and proxy files. Drag the **Toggle Proxies** button from the + menu into the **Programme Monitor** area's quick access bar to enable it continuously. The proxies speed up your workflow but do not influence sequence export, allowing high-quality exports at any time:

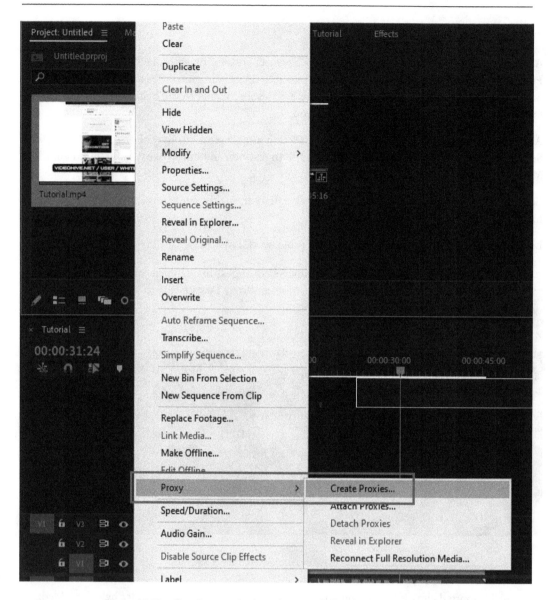

Figure 15.10 – Creating proxies by selecting all clips in the Project panel

4.   Select all imported files in Premiere Pro, right-click, and select **Create Proxies…** to make proxies quickly. Premiere sends files to Media Encoder after you choose a quality and codec. After rendering, return to Premiere Pro and click **Toggle Proxies** under your Program window. With that, you're using proxies.

5. Premiere Pro doesn't necessarily display the **Toggle Proxies** button by default. Look for it in the transport controls section at the bottom of **Program Monitor** or **Source Monitor**.

    If it's missing, you can easily add it:

    - Click the + button in the bottom-right corner of the monitor (**Button Editor**)

    - Drag the **Toggle Proxies** button from the menu to your preferred location in the transport controls:

Figure 15.11 – Adding the Toggle Proxies button from Button Editor in Program Monitor

As shown in the following screenshot, a window will expand after you locate and click on the button:

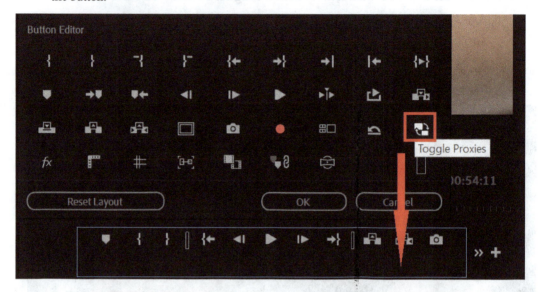

Figure 15.12 – Dragging the Toggle Proxies button into Program Monitor

The **Toggle Proxies** icon may now be dragged into **Program Monitor**. Next, click the button to make it active:

Figure 15.13 – The Toggle Proxies button in Program Monitor

The **Toggle Proxies** button acts as a switch and refers to the button color indicator to enable or disable proxies, as follows:

- Blue button ![icon]: This indicates that proxies are currently enabled. Premiere Pro is using lower-resolution proxy files for playback and editing.

- Gray button ![icon]: This indicates that proxies are disabled. Premiere Pro is using the original high-resolution files.

6. Simply click the **Toggle Proxies** button to toggle between proxies and originals. Clicking the blue button disables proxies (turns them gray) and returns to the original files. Clicking the gray button activates proxies (turns them blue) and switches to utilizing proxy files.

Remember, toggling proxies only impacts playback and editing speed. When you export your finished video, Premiere Pro will always use the original high-resolution files to ensure the highest quality.

Premiere will automatically launch Media Encoder to create proxies when importing videos. For optimal editing performance, leave proxies on and use the **Toggle Proxies** button. For focus checks and color tweaks, use the entire media file.

Proxies and preview rendering

When it comes to rendering previews in the timeline, proxies are not utilized. Also, please refrain from mistaking rendering for exporting.

It's a little-known fact among users that when rendering effects in Premiere Pro, the software utilizes the original files if they are accessible, regardless of whether proxies are attached or the **Enable Proxies** option is enabled. That's why it may require some time.

By utilizing a suitable preview codec, you can take advantage of the previews during the export process, resulting in significantly faster exports. This is particularly true when you're exporting to the same codec as your previews. If the original clip is unavailable, but the proxy remains accessible, the system will utilize the proxy instead.

In addition, when applying effects such as **Warp Stabilizer**, **Rolling Shutter Repair**, or **Morph Cut** to the clip, it reverts to the original file, regardless of whether a proxy is attached. By setting the original file to offline, it will be compelled to utilize the proxy.

Proxies and export

When you export your video project, Premiere Pro always utilizes the original, even if proxies are enabled. The sole exception to this is when the original media is unavailable but the proxy is active. In this situation, a warning message is provided, indicating that the export employs proxies.

You can override this by selecting **Use Proxies** under **GENERAL** in **Export** mode, as shown in the following screenshot:

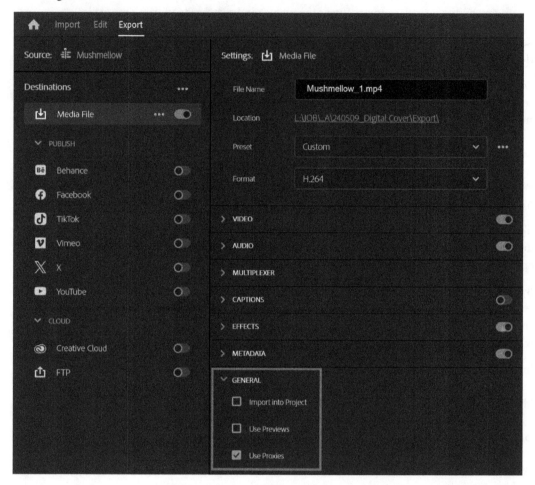

Figure 15.14 – Toggle Proxies in Program Monitor

By combining the **Use Previews** and **Use Proxies** options, you can optimize your export process. When a section of the timeline has both a rendered preview and a proxy video, the software will prioritize the rendered preview, resulting in a faster export.

Regular footage export versus proxies

The statement *Export proxies just like regular footage* is a misconception. Here's why:

- **Exporting regular footage**: This entails converting your modified timeline into a finished video file. This procedure is usually faster than playback since the editing decisions have already been made, and the program merely needs to produce the final movie according to your export settings.

- **Creating proxies**: In this step, Premiere Pro makes lower-resolution replicas of your original high-resolution film. These proxy files are intended for smoother editing playback, not for final video output.

Why are proxies not exported like regular footage?

- **Lower resolution**: Proxies are designed for quick editing, not final delivery. They often have a significantly smaller file size and poorer resolution than your original footage. Exporting them wouldn't result in a usable final video.

- **Separate workflow**: Proxy creation is a one-time activity that occurs before editing. It does not utilize your altered timeline and does not have to match the export parameters you would use for the finished video.

- Creating proxies can be time-consuming since Premiere Pro must analyze and encode each clip into a lower-resolution version. This is why it's critical to plan ahead, particularly for huge projects.

In conclusion, proxies are not exported as ordinary footage. They follow a different procedure that focuses on improving editing performance rather than generating final video outputs. Their development time might be large, so preparing ahead of time is essential to minimize delays while working on fast-paced projects.

Proxy workflows are a lifesaver for new Premiere Pro users. They make editing smoother, faster, and more enjoyable – all without sacrificing the final quality of your video. So, the next time you start a video editing project, consider using proxy files to enhance your overall experience.

Rendering clips for smoother playback

Rendering effects is a powerful way to boost Premiere Pro performance. While editing, Premiere Pro doesn't render your timeline. Playback slows down from a simple video clip to one with rich visual effects because it's all real time. Fortunately, you can render and replace these clips on your timeline to optimize playback.

In the timeline of Premiere Pro, a clever color-coded system is employed to effortlessly convey the rendering status of your project. By understanding which sections need processing, you can ensure seamless playback during the editing process. Allow me to provide you with a comprehensive analysis of the color codes and their profound influence on your workflow:

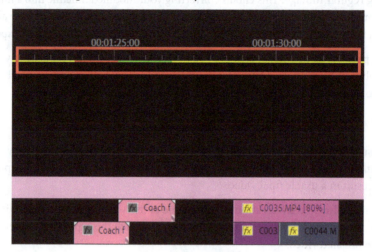

Figure 15.15 – Render bar color in the timeline

Here's a breakdown of the colors that can be shown on the render bar in the timeline:

- **Green bar**: This is the ideal scenario! A green bar signifies a rendered section. Premiere Pro has already processed all the edits, effects, and transitions within that part of your timeline. You will experience smooth playback without any lag or dropped frames.

- **Yellow bar**: A yellow bar indicates an unrendered section. Premiere Pro needs to process the edits, effects, or transitions within that section on the fly during playback. This can lead to stuttering or laggy playback, especially with complex projects or demanding effects.

- **Red bar**: A red bar indicates that Premiere Pro is having issues playing back videos with many effects. This color also signifies missing media or effects. It usually appears if you have used media files (such as videos or audio clips) or effects that are no longer linked correctly within your project. You will need to relink the missing files or effects to resolve the red bars.

Now, let's understand how to render clips for smoother playback.

To achieve smooth playback and eliminate yellow bars (unrendered sections), you have several options:

- **Render In to Out (Sequence | Render In to Out)**: This option renders the entire sequence from your chosen In point (where you want playback to start) to your chosen Out point (where playback should end). This is useful for rendering your entire project or specific scenes:

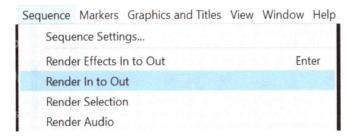

Figure 15.16 – Selecting Render In to Out in the Sequence menu

Make sure you've previously marked the In and Out clips in your timeline, as shown here:

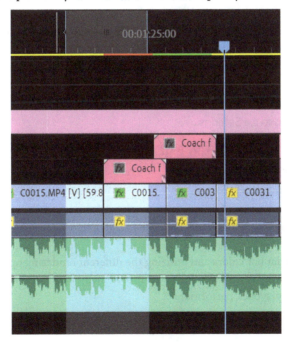

Figure 15.17 – Marking the In and Out clips in the sequence for playback rendering purposes

- **Render Selection** (**Sequence | Render Selection**): This option only renders the clips you have currently selected in your timeline. This is helpful for selectively rendering sections with complex effects or transitions that are causing playback issues. Here's where you can find the **Render Selection** option:

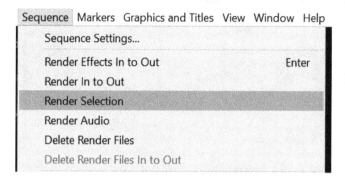

Figure 15.18 – Selecting the Render Selection option in the Sequence menu

- **Render Effects In to Out** (**Sequence| Render Effects In to Out**): This option focuses solely on rendering the effects that have been applied to your clips within the chosen In and Out points. This can be faster than rendering the entire clip if only a few effects have been applied:

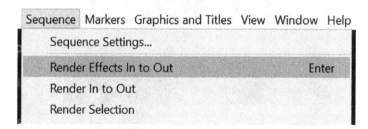

Figure 15.19 – Selecting the Render Effects In to Out option in the Sequence menu

By understanding the render bar colors and utilizing the different rendering options, you can ensure a smooth and efficient editing workflow in Premiere Pro. Remember, strive for a timeline dominated by green bars for optimal playback performance!

Using Render and Replace for linked elements

Picture yourself seamlessly integrating a sophisticated motion graphic, meticulously crafted in After Effects, into your Premiere Pro project. This connection is forged through a dynamic link, enabling you to make alterations in After Effects effortlessly and witness their immediate manifestation in Premiere Pro. Occasionally, the editing experience in Premiere Pro may be hindered by the presence of a dynamic link, particularly when dealing with intricate graphics.

Render and Replace solves this problem by generating a self-contained, pre-rendered version of the dynamically connected element (similar to an After Effects motion graphic). This means you can replace the dynamic link in your Premiere Pro timeline.

Here's the benefits of using **Render and Replace**:

- **Smoother playback**: With the substitution of a pre-rendered file, Premiere Pro can now achieve smoother playback without the need for continuous on-the-fly processing of the linked element. As a master of storytelling, you can appreciate the seamless playback that is achieved, particularly when dealing with intricate graphics or captivating effects.

- **Enhanced editing performance**: By removing the processing requirements of a dynamic link, system resources are freed up, resulting in improved efficiency for Premiere Pro. Prepare to be amazed by the lightning-fast responsiveness you'll experience while editing, even when dealing with multiple clips or effects in your project.

- **Ensure workflow flexibility**: Even after generating a new file, the original dynamic link remains accessible for any future requirements. With this feature, you have the flexibility to fine-tune your project in After Effects and effortlessly update the element in Premiere Pro.

Here's how to use the **Render and Replace** option in Premiere Pro:

1. Select a clip in your Premiere Pro timeline and choose the clip or sequence with the dynamic link you want to render.

2. Go to the **Clip** menu at the top of the Premiere Pro interface and select **Render and Replace....**

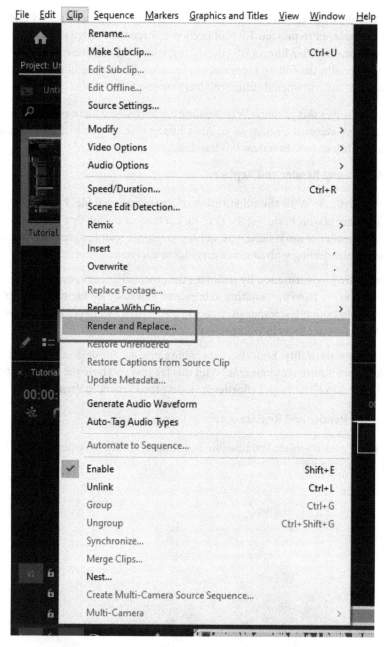

Figure 15.20 – Render and Replace option in sequence menu

3. When the dialog box appears, you can choose to match the format of the original sequence or select a different format and preset for the rendered file. This allows you to optimize the file size and quality based on your needs:

Figure 15.21 – Choosing the sequence settings to match the format of the original sequence

In this window shown in *Figure 15.19*, you can define the location where you want to save the rendered file. Additionally, you can choose whether to replace the dynamic link in the timeline with the rendered file or create a new standalone file.

4. Once everything is set, click **OK** to initiate the process. Premiere Pro will create the pre-rendered file and either replace the dynamic link or create a new clip in your timeline depending on your choice.

5. The key parameter is **Include video effects**. This renders the footage with effects, creating a new video file. The effects won't be editable after rendering, but they'll improve timeline performance.

6. Apply this method to slow timelines, not all footage. Select the clip, click **Clip** at the top of the screen, and choose **Restore unrendered** to restore it if you need to make modifications or export.

Render and Replace is an indispensable tool for every Premiere Pro user who deals with dynamic links, especially when it comes to intricate graphics or effects. By implementing this feature, users can experience seamless playback, enhance editing performance, and have the freedom to make additional adjustments while preserving the integrity of the original dynamic link, if necessary. The next time you encounter slow editing due to dynamic links, try using **Render and Replace** for a smoother and more responsive workflow.

Adjusting playback resolutions

Picture yourself attempting to edit a colossal, high-resolution video on your mobile device. Every single detail is meticulously laid out, yet the process of zooming in and out to make necessary edits can be quite sluggish and exasperating. When it comes to video editing, Premiere Pro operates in a way that showcases the breathtaking quality of high-resolution footage. However, the process of editing such footage seamlessly can put a strain on your computer's capabilities.

Being able to adjust playback resolution in Premiere Pro is quite handy as it allows you to zoom out on your editing view. As a new user, you have the option to select a lower-resolution version of your video for editing purposes.

Here's why this is beneficial for improving Premiere Pro's performance:

- **Enhanced editing**: Premiere Pro effortlessly highlights a lower-resolution rendition of your video during the editing process, reducing the strain on your computer's processing capabilities. With this improvement, you will experience seamless playback without any interruptions or loss of frames. With the ability to make edits and add effects in real time, there's no need to wait for the video to catch up.

- **Faster performance**: Enjoy faster playback at lower resolutions. This can be especially beneficial for newcomers who are using older computers or laptops that may have difficulty handling high-resolution footage. With a more seamless editing experience, the process of mastering Premiere Pro becomes a truly delightful journey.

- **Unleash your creativity**: When editing with lower-resolution playback, feel free to explore different cuts, effects, and transitions without any limitations. With the reduced processing demands, you'll be pleased to find that rendering times for each change are significantly shorter. With this tool, you can delve into the depths of your imagination, effortlessly bringing your creative vision to life.

The good news is that adjusting playback resolution is quite simple in Premiere Pro. Here's how to do it:

1. Find the option in **Program Monitor**. A menu will pop up with various options. Look for the one that says **Playback Resolution**.

2. Now, you must choose a lower resolution. The menu will display a list of different resolutions for your video. Choose a lower resolution option, such as **1/2** or **1/4** of the original size:

Figure 15.22 – Select Playback Resolution in Program Monitor

> **Important note**
> Making this adjustment to the playback resolution only affects how you see the video during editing. The final exported video will always be in the original, high-resolution format you filmed or imported in.

Project decoding speed depends on **playback resolution**. You may easily change playback resolutions to customize your experience. Lowering playback resolution increases decoding speed at your discretion.

Manipulating the playback resolution can be an invaluable tool for novice Premiere Pro users. With these enhancements, you'll be able to seamlessly refine your edits, enjoy improved speed and performance, and have the freedom to explore and experiment with your creative vision. Feel free to customize the resolution to a level that suits your computer, enhancing your editing workflow for maximum efficiency.

Managing project and media files on networked storage for collaboration

Collaborative editing systems rely on easy organization and access to project files. Let's learn how to handle project and media files across networked storage systems.

Choosing the right networked storage:

- **Performance**: To prevent delays or congestion when numerous editors are working with huge media files at the same time, use a high-performance **network-attached storage** (**NAS**) or **storage area network** (**SAN**) that provides rapid data transfer speeds of gigabits per second or more. Imagine a project with many video editors collaborating on intricate scenarios. An advanced NAS system would provide seamless access to these extensive video files, eliminating any potential delays for editors caused by sluggish data transfer.

- **Security**: Make sure that the storage solution has strong access controls. For example, let's say you can establish user groups with precise rights (such as read-only or read/write) to limit illegal entry to project files. As an illustration, a sound designer may just want read-only privileges to see the video footage, whereas editors would need read/write authorization to make modifications.

- **Capacity**: Ensure future preparedness by selecting storage options that possess sufficient capacity to meet both your current project size and prospective expansion in the long run. Imagine a project in which you begin with a small amount of recorded material, but you expect to gather more interviews and supplementary film at a later time. Opting for a high-capacity NAS device will guarantee that you own plenty of storage capacity to accommodate the full project, eliminating the need for a storage update midway.

- **Backup strategy**: Implement a dependable backup system to protect against inadvertent data loss or hardware malfunction. Imagine inadvertently deleting a vital project file. Implementing a resilient backup solution, such as cloud storage or a secondary NAS, will enable you to retrieve the misplaced file and avert significant obstacles.

Project organization:

- **Centralized storage**: Save all project files (including media, project files, and assets) on the centralized network storage to facilitate convenient access for all contributors. This obviates the necessity for editors to maintain copies on their own PCs, hence mitigating version control complications.

- **Clear folder structure**: Establish an organized folder structure that classifies project elements (such as video, audio, graphics, and more) in a manner that facilitates easy browsing and version management. For example, you may organize your files into folders with labels such as `Footage - Raw`, `Footage - Edited`, `Audio`, `Music`, `Graphics`, and `Project Files`. This clear structure makes it easy for editors to find specific assets they need.

- **Naming conventions**: To enhance discoverability and prevent any misunderstandings among collaborators, it is crucial to establish uniform naming conventions for files and folders. This will ensure a seamless workflow and make it easier for everyone to locate the necessary resources. It is advisable to utilize a system that incorporates the project name, clip type (such as `_01_Broll_StreetScene`), and version number (for example, `_v2`). Editors can easily identify specific clips and their versions within the project.

Version control:

- **Version control system (VCS)**: Consider utilizing a VCS such as Git or Subversion. This invaluable tool allows you to track changes effortlessly, revert to previous versions, and safeguard against accidental overwrites, especially when collaborating with multiple editors on a project. Picture two editors collaborating on the same scene at the same time. By utilizing a VCS, individuals can view and track each other's modifications, roll back to previous iterations if needed, and effectively avoid any potential conflicts while preserving a comprehensive record of all edits made.

- **Locking system**: If a VCS isn't feasible, consider implementing a locking system that allows editors to *lock* certain files or projects to prevent conflicts while editing simultaneously. Whether it's a basic spreadsheet or a specialized software program, editors can reserve specific files for their editing needs.

Communication:

- **Clear communication**: Maintain clear communication with collaborators regarding file locations, naming conventions, and version control procedures. Regular team meetings or a communication platform can help ensure everyone is on the same page when it comes to managing project files.

- **Collaboration tools**: Utilize collaboration tools that integrate with your workflow, allowing real-time communication and project updates. Many editing platforms offer built-in collaboration features or integrate with project management software, allowing editors to discuss edits and track progress seamlessly.

- **File permissions**: Set appropriate file permissions to restrict editing or deletion rights based on collaborator roles. For example, an intern might only need read-only access to project files, while senior editors would have full read/write permissions.

- **Offline editing**: Implement a system for handling offline editing scenarios, allowing editors to work on local copies of project files with proper synchronization upon reconnection. This could involve using software that allows editors to check out project files and then sync their edits back to the central storage location once they're back online.

- **Standardization**: Standardize project templates and file structures across projects to streamline collaboration and onboarding of new users. This creates a consistent workflow and reduces the learning curve for new team members joining the project.

By following these guidelines, you can ensure efficient and organized management of project and media files in a networked storage environment, fostering a smooth and productive collaborative editing experience.

Common troubleshooting issues with proxy editing

Let's address the difficulties that occur from proxy processes in Premiere Pro. This section will provide you with guidance to overcome the challenges you are facing, providing a streamlined and effective editing experience. Frequently, if not consistently, problems occur when users do not fully understand the limitations of proxy processes in Premiere Pro and how they operate.

Black bars on proxies

This question is frequently asked. The straightforward explanation is *Because the individual who created the customized proxy preset lacked the necessary expertise.* You must adhere to the instructions provided in this chapter, particularly in the *Understanding proxy workflows in Premiere Pro* section.

A prevalent situation occurs when individuals possess 4K source files and generate proxies specifically designed for UHD, frequently mislabeled as 4K UHD. The resolution is not quite 4K, but it is very similar. UHD has a resolution of 3840×2160 pixels, although cinema 4K typically has a resolution of 4096×2160 pixels. The variation in breadth is responsible for the formation of those black bars.

You can resolve this issue by either configuring your proxy settings using the **Stretch to Fill** option or using the pre-existing built-in defaults:

Figure 15.23 – Selecting the Stretch to fill option in the Export window

Choose the **Stretch to fill** option under the **Scaling** settings, located below the preview window. This will provide compatibility with all aspect ratios, hence preventing the appearance of black bars in your proxies.

The proxies you have do not match the original versions

This issue may arise if the frame rate of your proxy files differs from that of your source files. By employing the techniques outlined in this chapter, this issue should no longer occur. However, if your project was initiated in a previous version, particularly 2022.3 or before, it may still arise.

It is recommended to either generate new proxy files or detach and reattach the existing proxy files. Additionally, you should do the required Interpret Footage workaround, as detailed in the section on resolving the issue with Interpret Footage.

It is possible to connect proxy files to the original video clips in the **Project** window, even if the original files are not currently accessible. To attach proxies to your clips in the **Project** window or bin, simply right-click on them and select **Proxy | Attach Proxies...**:

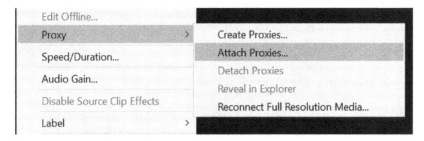

Figure 15.24 – Right-clicking clips in the Project window or bin and selecting Proxy | Attach Proxies...

A dialog box will appear, allowing you to attach proxies. When it comes to attaching your proxy clips, you have the option to choose between the media browser or operating system dialog. If you're looking to reattach proxy files to Offline clips, consider using **Attach Proxies**:

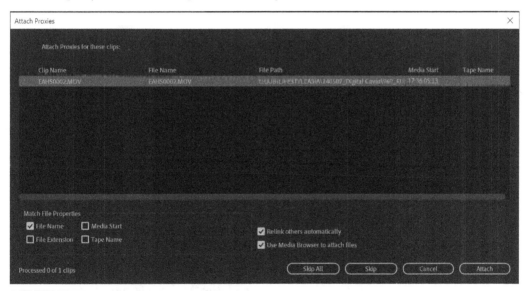

Figure 15.25 – The Attach Proxies window

With Premiere Pro, you can attach proxies using a limited range of frame sizes and pixel aspect ratios. It is crucial for various parameters, including fields, frame rate, duration, and audio channels, to align.

In version 2023.4, a glitch was present that resulted in all transcribed clips starting at frame 1, hence disregarding the in-point specified by the user. However, this issue has been resolved in version 2023.5.

Toggle Proxies not working

One common culprit for this issue is a corrupted preferences file. If you happen to come across any problems with **Toggle Proxies** or **Enable Proxies** not functioning properly, even if you have proxies connected, simply exit Premiere Pro. Then, when you relaunch Premiere Pro, make sure you hold down the *Shift*, *Alt*, or *Opt* key. Then, select the **Reset App Preferences** option. With this solution, the problem should be resolved in the majority of instances.

Match Frame appears odd

Rarely does such an occurrence take place, but when it does, it can cause bewilderment for those who lack comprehension of the situation. It occurs when the editor assigns the proxy files with identical names to the original files, which is often seen in certain offline editing workflows that do not specifically utilize the proxy workflow.

Initially, the setup functions flawlessly. However, when the project is relocated to a different folder, drive, or system, the files necessitate reestablishing the connections. When Premiere Pro prompts you to locate the file, you inadvertently select the proxy file instead of the original, resulting in you losing the link to the original file.

It is highly advisable to consistently include the _Proxy suffix in the filename of the proxy. With Premiere Pro, you can effortlessly link the camera original and the proxy to the same file. However, this is only a temporary solution. Once you save, close, and reopen the project, you will be prompted to relink once more.

You'll find yourself trapped in a never-ending cycle of having to attach proxies every time you open the project. Furthermore, when performing a *Match Frame* to the original, the visual outcome may differ from what was initially observed in the timeline. When editing in an HD timeline with 4K footage, it's important to ensure that the correct file is attached to avoid any scaling issues.

It is important to keep the true identity of your proxy files a secret from Premiere Pro! Aside from the peculiar scaling issues, sending files to color grading outside of Premiere Pro can result in the wrong files being sent, requiring some file acrobatics to rectify the situation.

However, there is a solution to the problem at hand. By taking the necessary steps, such as disconnecting from the internet, renaming or relocating the proxy folder, and then reestablishing the connection with the camera originals using the **Reconnect Full Resolution Media…** feature, the issue can be resolved. You can find this option by right-clicking the proxy clip and choosing **Proxy | Reconnect Full Resolution Media…**:

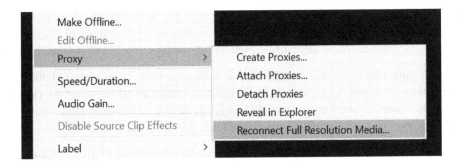

Figure 15.26 – Reconnect Full Resolution Media

When you select **Reconnect Full Resolution Media…** from the right-click menu, you will see the **Reconnect Full Resolution Media** dialog. This dialog is very similar to the **Attach Proxies** dialog:

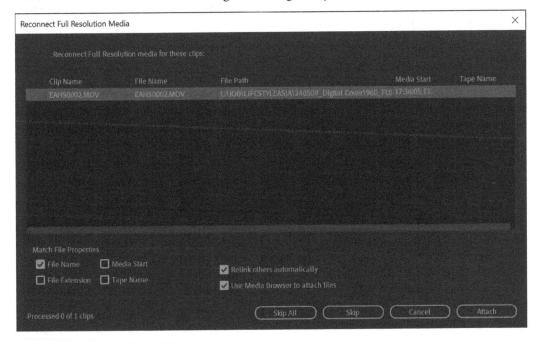

Figure 15.27 – The Reconnect Full Resolution Media dialog

By selecting this option, the chosen clip transitions into the proxy state, while the clip you pick in the **Reconnect Full Resolution Media…** dialog replaces the original clip as the new full-resolution original clip.

If a proxy has previously been linked to your clip, the proxy clip will be retained and just the full-resolution section will be substituted. Reconnecting full resolution is irreversible, but you may rejoin another clip. It is permissible to add more media, even if a full-resolution file has already been uploaded.

If one of the original files becomes inaccessible after saving the project file, a **Link Media** prompt will appear when you reopen the project. To preserve the original files offline, select the **Offline All** option or choose **Cancel** to abort the process. If the original video becomes unavailable while you are working on a project, you will be prompted with the **Link Media** dialog.

After opening the project, you may still utilize the **Link Media** or **Reconnect Full Resolution Media** choices. Make sure you save your work before you begin the process. Then, remember to attach proxies if necessary. Finally, save your work again to ensure that your progress is preserved.

To achieve an almost fully automated proxy workflow, utilize Premiere Pro's capability to generate proxies using the automatic technique. Before importing camera proxies or externally created proxies to reconnect to the source files, it is advisable to test this procedure in advance using a few clips to ensure its intended functionality. It might not.

Summary

By reading this chapter, you should be able to improve the speed and efficiency with which you edit. You've mastered the art of proxy processes, which enable you to edit high-resolution film with silky-smooth playback. You've unlocked a secret layer of processing capability within Premiere Pro by using the capabilities of your graphics card via hardware acceleration. We also covered crucial approaches such as controlling the media cache and altering playback resolution, which provide a responsive editing process even on less capable devices. These deliberate changes have paved the way for a seamless and fast editing experience.

In the next chapter, we'll embark on a new adventure, conquering the world of export settings. Here, you'll gain the knowledge to craft stunning final videos, perfectly tailored to your specific needs and ready to impress any audience. Buckle up and get ready to take your Premiere Pro skills to the next level!

16

Best Export Settings in Premiere Pro

As you approach the finish line of your editing journey in Premiere Pro, the final hurdle awaits: export. This seemingly easy step could be crucial to the success of your video. Selecting the appropriate export parameters guarantees that your work looks and sounds great on every platform, even when it leaves the editing suite. This chapter delves deeply into bitrates, formats, and codecs, giving you the tools you need to confidently handle these technical areas. We'll look at environments designed for high-end productions that demand flawless quality, all the way down to bite-sized social media posts. This chapter provides you with the expertise to export your video with the best quality and efficiency so that your vision is seen by the world exactly as you intended, whether your goal is to win over audiences at a film festival or to capture their attention on Instagram.

In this chapter, we're going to cover the following main topics:

- Quickly exporting videos using the Export button
- In-depth export settings for any screen or device
- Exporting for maximum quality – Premiere Pro best practices
- Exporting in Media Encoder for Premiere Pro

Quickly exporting videos using the Export button

It can be difficult to choose video export settings with so many options. In this chapter, you will learn about the best Adobe Premiere Pro export settings to make your production look and sound amazing on any platform. The **Export** button in Premiere Pro is a lifesaver for situations where you need to get your video out the door quickly without fiddling with extensive settings.

Here's how to use it for a hassle-free export:

1. Open your completed Premiere Pro project with your edited sequence in place. Look toward the top-left corner of the program window. You'll find an **Export** menu tab – that's your **Export** button:

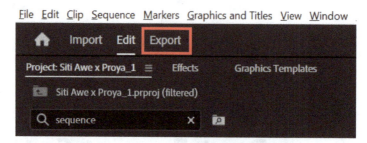

Figure 16.1 – The Export button in the workspace

Finding the optimal Premiere Pro export settings requires balancing quality and playability. On slower internet connections, higher-quality settings may increase the file size, affecting streaming performance.

2. Click the **Export** button. This opens a fullscreen **Export** window. To access browser options for choosing files or settings, you need to click on the blue text within that window:

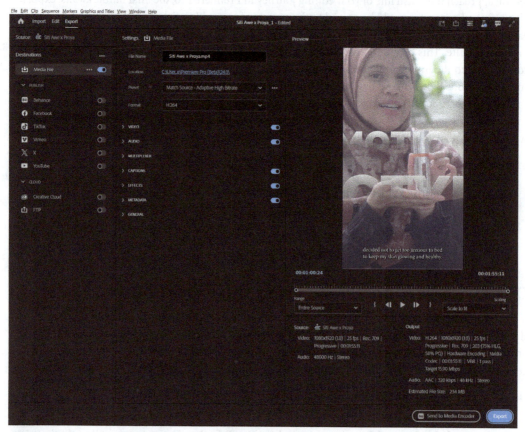

Figure 16.2 – The Export window in Premiere Pro

The menu offers a range of preconfigured export presets tailored for various use cases. These presets eliminate the need to manually configure settings, saving you valuable time.

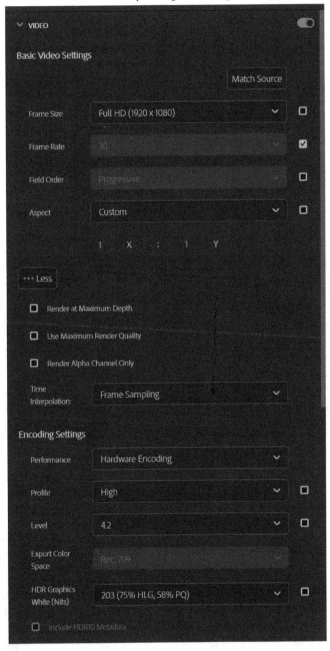

Figure 16.3 – Basic video settings in Export window

These are the optimal video export settings for most apps:

- **Format**: H.264 (`.mp4`)

- **Frame size**: 1920 x 1080 for HD, 1080 x 1920 for vertical video, and 3840 x 2160 for 4K

- **Frame rate**: Typically, you'll see `24`, `29.97`, `30`, `59.97`, `or` `60` **frames per second (FPS)**

- **Field order**: Progressive

- **Aspect**: Custom, Square pixel (1.0)

- **Performance**: Hardware encoding

- **Profile**: High

- **Level**: 4.2 (5.2 for 4K)

- **Export Color Space**: Rec. 709

- **Bitrate encoding: VBR, 1 pass**

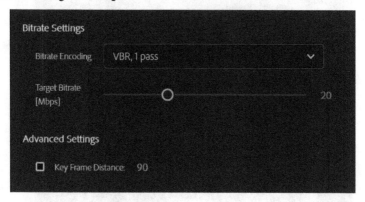

Figure 16.4 – Bitrate settings in Export window

- **Target bitrate**: 20-30 Mbps for HD, 60-80 Mbps for 4K Match Source. This preset maintains the resolution and frame rate that match your original footage, ensuring an accurate representation of your edits.

- **Resolution-Based Presets**: You'll find presets optimized for popular online platforms, such as **HD 1080p**, which is ideal for YouTube uploads or social media content.

- **Bitrate Recommendations**: Many presets come with suggested bitrate settings. Bitrate affects the file size and overall video quality. Higher bitrates result in larger files but sharper visuals, while lower bitrates create smaller files but with some compromise in quality. The presets provide a good starting point, but you can experiment with them based on your specific needs.

For those starting with video encoding, the default **Match Source - Adaptive Bitrate** presets are a great option. They provide a good balance of quality and performance, making them versatile for different projects. These presets adjust the bitrate automatically according to your source material, ensuring smooth playback while maintaining quality. This is especially useful when dealing with various resolutions or frame rates.

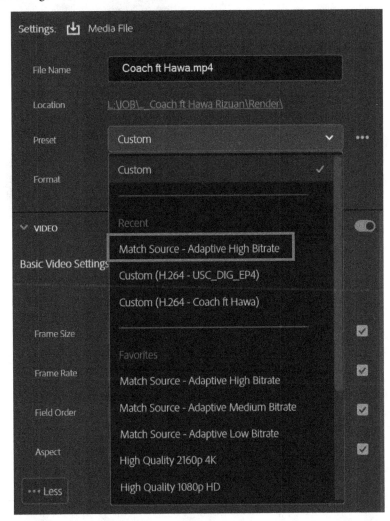

Figure 16.5 – Preset drop-down menu in Export Settings

3. Once you've chosen your destination and a suitable preset, click the prominent blue **Export** button. Premiere Pro will take the reins, automatically initiating the export process using your selected settings:

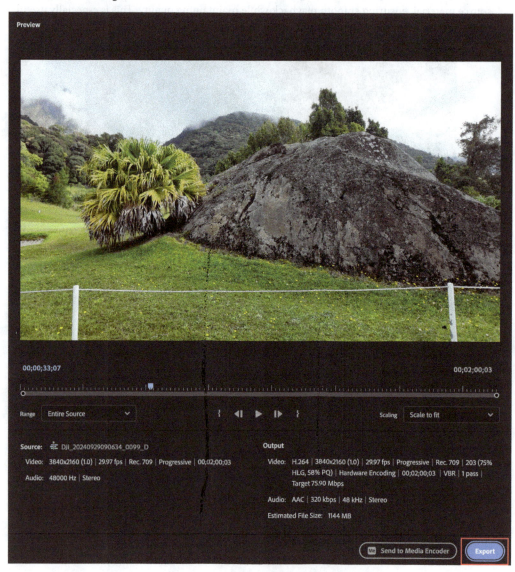

Figure 16.6 – The Export button in Export settings

Since it speeds up export times, hardware encoding is usually better than software. Older computers without GPU cards may not support hardware encoding. Export settings that don't allow hardware encoding will be using software encoding. Choose the proper aspect ratio for your platform before exporting. Instagram prefers a vertical **9:16** aspect ratio for mobile devices; however, higher-resolution videos are **16:9**.

In the following section, we'll explore essential audio export options to enhance your video projects.

Audio export options

Video is the most powerful multimedia format. However, most audio-less videos are incomplete. Users must utilize the appropriate audio settings in addition to video export settings. Doing so ensures that the edited video has great sound and visuals.

Adobe recommends these settings for great video sound:

- **Audio format**: **AAC**
- **Audio codec**: **AAC**
- **Sample rate**: **48,000 Hz**
- **Channel**: **Stereo**
- **Audio quality**: **High**
- **Bitratc**: **320**
- **Precedence**: **Bitrate**

The **Export** button serves as a fantastic tool for swiftly exporting videos with commonly used settings. It's your go-to option for draft exports, social media uploads, or situations where extensive customization isn't required. However, for professional-grade exports with specific requirements or the need for advanced features, the traditional export media settings offer the level of control necessary to achieve those high-quality results.

In the next section, we'll dive into detailed export settings tailored for various screens and devices.

In-depth export settings for any screen or device

Optimizing export parameters for specific platforms is more art than science. It impacts video quality, reach, and engagement. Thus, in addition to knowing how to apply adjustment layers and transitions in Premiere Pro, video creators should know the proper export settings for all main platforms to make their videos stand out online.

We will look at the optimal export options for YouTube, Instagram, TikTok, Facebook, and Vimeo in depth. However, accessing the **Export** window might be intimidating due to its abundance of settings. Don't worry; this guide will give you the skills you need to master video export for a variety of platforms and gadgets.

Understanding the core concept

Knowing how to export is crucial and here are a few things to consider while exporting:

- **Codecs**: Think of codecs as translators. They translate your edited video into a format that is compatible with many gadgets. The standard codec for social media and YouTube-like 'websites is H.264.

- **Resolution**: This is the total amount of pixels that are shown both vertically and horizontally. Higher resolutions offer crisper details; common specifications are 720p (1,280 x 720 pixels) and 1080p (1,920 x 1,080 pixels).

- **Frame rate**: Visualize a flipbook, where every page represents a frame. The speed at which the pages turn gives the impression of motion. For the majority of web material, standard frame rates are 24 FPS for a theatrical effect and 30 FPS for smoother movements.

- **Bitrate**: This controls the trade-off between file size and quality. Larger files with clearer images are produced by higher bitrates, whereas smaller files with some quality loss are produced by lower bitrates.

Understanding fundamental elements such as codec, resolution, frame rate, and bitrate is critical for successful video creation. These components work together to affect the quality, performance, and compatibility of the final product. A thorough mastery of these essentials ensures that your video looks and sounds fantastic while also meeting the needs of diverse platforms and viewers. With this foundation, you can make informed decisions to improve your storytelling and effectively engage your audience.

In the next section, you will learn about the critical role of FPS settings in video production, including common frame rates, their impact on viewer experience, and guidelines for selecting the appropriate FPS for different types of projects.

Understanding FPS settings

FPS is an important video production metric that indicates how many individual frames are presented in a single second of video playback. This rate is critical in determining the overall appearance and feel of a video, impacting not only the smoothness of motion but also the viewer's emotional reaction. A higher FPS often results in smoother motion, which is especially crucial in fast-paced sequences, whereas a lower FPS rate can create a more theatrical atmosphere.

Common FPS rates

Various projects use different FPS settings according to the style and medium they aim to use:

- **24 FPS**: 24 FPS is the typical cinematic standard, offering a rich, filmic quality. It is frequently utilized in narrative films to provide a distinct look that people connect with storytelling.

- **30 FPS**: This rate is common in television broadcasts and internet video material, and it delivers significantly smoother action than 24 FPS. It's commonly utilized in talk shows, documentaries, and online films.

- **60 FPS**: This rate is commonly used in high-motion video settings such as sports broadcasts, video games, and action films. The higher frame rate captures greater detail in rapid motions, making it excellent for dynamic content.

- **Higher frame rates (for example, 120 FPS and 240 FPS)**: These are commonly employed for slow-motion effects, which allow for a dramatic slowdown of quick actions. Such high frame rates are frequently found in action sports footage, nature documentaries, and certain artistic projects that require precise detail capture.

Why is FPS important?

The choice of FPS has a considerable impact on the spectator experience and sense of motion:

- **Viewer experience**: Higher frame rates can provide a more immersive experience by making motion appear smooth and realistic, which is important for action-packed programming. Lower FPS, on the other hand, can inspire nostalgia or drama, which improves storytelling.

- **File size and rendering times**: The number of FPS directly determines the size of the video file. Higher frame rates produce larger files, which may necessitate additional processing power and longer rendering times for export. Understanding this can help you arrange your process more efficiently.

- **Platform considerations**: Each platform may have a recommended or ideal FPS rate. For example, social networking networks may want 30 FPS for ordinary content, whereas cinematic uploads may require 24 FPS. Always review the platform guidelines to ensure compatibility and quality.

Choosing the right FPS for your project

Selecting the appropriate FPS for your project is essential:

- **Narrative films versus documentaries**: Narrative films benefit from the theatrical quality of 24 FPS, whereas documentaries may prefer 30 FPS for a more immediate and interesting presentation.

- **Commercials and corporate videos**: Depending on the intended tone, 30 FPS is standard, although 60 FPS can be used for high-energy advertising with dynamic images.

- **Live events and sports coverage**: 60 FPS is preferable to provide smooth playback of fast-moving subjects and to keep viewers engaged.

- **Consistency in FPS**: It is critical to keep your FPS consistent throughout your project. Combining multiple frame rates can produce visual distortions and a disrupted viewing experience.

Adjusting FPS settings in Premiere Pro

Setting and changing FPS in Adobe Premiere Pro is straightforward:

1. Begin by starting a new project or opening an existing one.

2. Go to the sequence you want to change. Go to **Sequence** in the top menu, then **Sequence Settings...**:

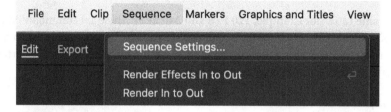

Figure 16.7 – Selecting Sequence Settings... in the Sequence menu

3. In the **Sequence Settings** dialog box, look for the **Timebase:** drop-down menu. Here, you can choose your preferred FPS from the various possibilities:

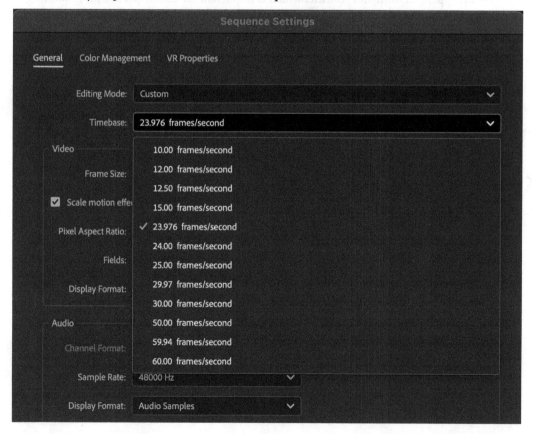

Figure 16.8 – Changing FPS in the Sequence Settings window

4. When altering frame rates, consider the source content. If you're lowering the frame rate of a high FPS project, time remapping can help ensure a smooth transition.

Understanding and selecting the appropriate FPS settings is critical in video production. Your project's quality and emotional impact can be greatly influenced by the frame rate you choose. As you experiment with various FPS settings, you'll learn how to use them most effectively to accomplish your intended aesthetic and viewer experience. Try different frame rates to see how they affect your footage and storytelling!

Exporting in Premiere Pro – essential resources for you

Here are some go-to resources to understand before starting exporting to every screen:

- **Presets**: A wealth of preconfigured presets catering to different platforms are available in Premiere Pro. They serve as an excellent beginning point and do not require delving into complex settings.

- **Match Source**: This preset guarantees an accurate portrayal of your modifications by preserving the source footage's resolution and frame rate.

- **Presets based on resolution**: Locate settings that are suited for widely used web platforms.

The following is a summary of a few popular locations:

- **YouTube HD 1080p (1920x1080)**: An excellent option that offers a decent trade-off between download size and quality for the majority of YouTube material.

- **HD 720p (1280x720)**: Ideal for mobile viewing with constrained data plans or other scenarios requiring a smaller file size.

- **Social Media (1920x1080)**: Perfect for high-resolution Instagram photos or Facebook streams. While these platforms have typically prioritized horizontal content, many now allow vertical video for features such as **Stories** and **Reels**. Consider this when developing content for various platforms.

- **Social Media 720p (1280x720)**: Ideal for news articles or quick social media videos.

- **Square (1080x1080)**: Ideal for Instagram or Facebook posts that work well in square layouts.

Customizing beyond presets

Presets come in quite handy, but if you want more control, go deeper. This is what you can change:

- **Bitrate**: Play around with the bitrate parameters to achieve the ideal balance between file size and quality. 5 Mbps is a reasonable starting point for 1080p YouTube content and 3 Mbps for 720p.

- **Frame Rate**: For most web pages, 23.98 FPS or 30 FPS is sufficient. While platforms such as YouTube may support higher frame rates such as 60 FPS, these are often reserved for specific content types such as gaming or high-speed action. Using 23.98 FPS or 30 FPS can help optimize file size and playback performance on a wider range of devices.

By understanding these concepts and leveraging Premiere Pro's export tools, you'll be well on your way to exporting your video to various devices.

Exporting data to various devices

Even if particular device optimizations aren't always required, take into account these factors:

- **Mobile devices**: A lot of people use tablets and smartphones with different features to view content. Smooth playback on data plans is ensured by lower resolutions (720p or lower) and moderate bitrates (around 3 Mbps).

- **Computers**: Higher resolutions and bitrates can be handled by desktop and laptop computers. For outstanding quality, you can export at 1080p or even higher with bitrates of at least 5 Mbps.

Don't hesitate to experiment and find the settings that best suit your editing style and project requirements. Next, let's see what the best settings are for YouTube.

Best Premiere Pro YouTube export settings

Creators must follow YouTube video and audio criteria to optimize their videos. They should also use the right export settings to ensure video quality, upload times, and, most crucially, platform playback system compatibility.

The easiest way to set up your export settings for YouTube is as follows:

1. In the **Export** window, choose a preset from the **PUBLISH** dropdown. Presets provide preconfigured parameters for a variety of uses (such as YouTube, Vimeo, and H.264).

2. In the **PUBLISH** dropdown, enable the **YouTube** preset. This preset is tailored to YouTube's standards. See the following screenshot:

Figure 16.9 – Enabling the YouTube export option in the Export window

3. The **PUBLISH** option in Premiere Pro is generally used to route exported videos to a specific destination or service. It provides options such as the following:

    - **Media**: This is the default choice, which allows you to save the exported video as a file to your computer

    - **YouTube**: This option uploads the video directly to YouTube and requires you to sign in to your account

    - **Vimeo**: Like YouTube, this option publishes the video directly to Vimeo

    - **Facebook**: You can upload the video directly to your Facebook page or profile

    - **X**: Posts the video directly to X

    - **FTP**: Used to upload files to a remote FTP server

    - **Other**: This option lets you select a specific destination or service

4. After selecting your chosen destination from the **PUBLISH** menu, you will need to define any platform-specific options. This could include entering login information, creating a video title and description, or changing privacy settings. After you've finished these steps, click the **Export** button to begin the process of delivering your video to its designated destination.

5. Next, choose the **YouTube** preset. In the **Export** window, locate the **More presets…** drop-down menu. Here, Premiere Pro offers various presets designed to simplify the export process for specific destinations:

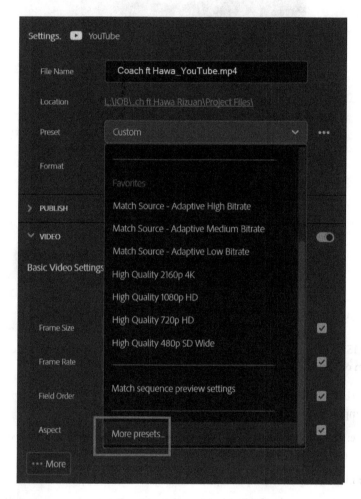

Figure 16.10 – Selecting More presets… in the Custom drop-down menu

6. Look for presets with names such as **YouTube 1080p HD** or **YouTube 720p HD**. These presets are specifically tailored for uploading to YouTube, taking into account factors such as resolution, bitrate, and frame rate, which are crucial for achieving optimal playback quality on the platform.

7. To find the YouTube preset you're looking for, open the **Preset Manager** window (*Figure 16.11*) and enter the preset name in the search bar:

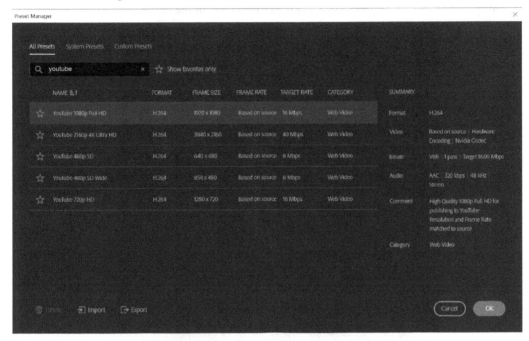

Figure 16.11 – Searching for the YouTube preset name in the Preset Manager window

8. Look up the YouTube options you want depending on the output of your video production, then click **OK** when you're done. Next, select your destination and filename. Locate the **File Name** field. Here, you can give your exported video a descriptive name for easy identification later. It's helpful to include details such as the video title and resolution in the filename to keep your video library organized:

Figure 16.12 – Selecting your destination filename in the Export settings window

9. Click the blue-colored text in the **Location** tab. Navigate to your desired location on your computer where you want to save the exported video. Choosing a well-organized folder structure for your exported videos will help you locate them easily in the future:

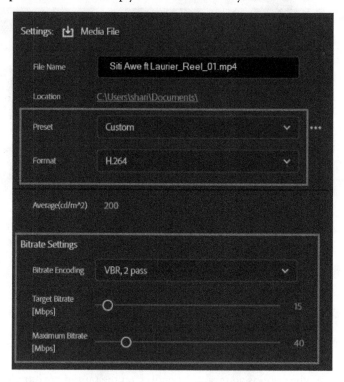

Figure 16.13 – Bitrate settings for YouTube

While the YouTube presets offer a well-balanced foundation, you can make slight adjustments for more control over the final video:

*   **Bitrate**: The bitrate parameter controls the size and quality of the produced video file. While lower bitrates produce smaller files with some quality loss, higher bitrates produce larger files with clearer images. For higher resolutions (such as 1080p), YouTube suggests using higher bitrates to provide a fluid playing experience for viewers. Usually, the presets have a bitrate range appropriate for the selected resolution; nevertheless, you can play around with that range to discover the ideal balance between file size and quality for your particular requirements. 5 Mbps is a decent place to start when uploading 1080p videos to YouTube. When selecting this option, keep in mind that uploading larger file sizes may take longer, so take your internet upload speed into account.

- **Frame rate**: The number of images (or frames) shown in a second is referred to as the frame rate, and it basically determines how smoothly motion flows in your video. Standard frame rates of 24 FPS for a cinematic effect or 30 FPS for a more seamless viewing experience work well for the majority of web material, including YouTube videos. You probably won't need to change this setting unless you're working with footage that has a different frame rate, as the YouTube presets usually have it set correctly at either 30 or 23.98 FPS.

10. Once you've chosen your preset, destination folder, and filename and have made any desired adjustments to bitrate (if applicable), click the blue **Export** button at the bottom of the **Export** window:

Figure 16.14 – Exporting your video and uploading to YouTube

11. Remember to fill out the following form to sign in to your YouTube account where you wish to submit the video:

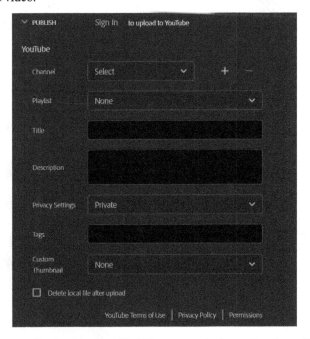

Figure 16.15 – Signing in to your YouTube account before uploading to YouTube

Premiere Pro will initiate the export process, encoding your video using the chosen settings. The progress bar will indicate the remaining time until your video is ready for upload to YouTube.

The best video export settings for YouTube are as follows:

- **Format: H.264**

- **Preset: Custom**

- **Frame Rate: 29.97**

- **Height & Width: 1920 × 1080**

- **Bitrate Encoding**: VBR, **2 Pass** (Increasing passes improves video quality but drastically increases encoding time. **1 Pass** usually suffices for simple jobs.)

- **Target Bitrate: 15**

- **Maximum Bitrate: 40**

12. The appropriate video and audio export parameters are explained here. Make sure to check both the **AUDIO** and **VIDEO** checkboxes in the **Export** settings, as shown in *Figure 16.16*:

Figure 16.16 – Enabling video and audio export options in Export settings

13. The video quality may be enhanced by turning on **Use Maximum Render Quality**; however, the encoding time is greatly increased. It may usually be avoided and is not necessary for most simple tasks. Checking this option is advised, nevertheless, if you're working on a crucial project that needs the best quality possible (see *Figure 16.17*):

Figure 16.17 – Enabling Use Maximum Render Quality

You need to consider two reasons for selecting options in the export settings of Premiere Pro. The checkbox for **Use Maximum Render Quality** is not directly connected to choosing a measurement system, such as imperial. Let's break it down in the following sections.

Keeping efficiency and quality in check

Efficiency and quality are traded off in **Export** settings. Sharper videos are produced with higher-quality settings, such as higher bitrates and resolutions, but the resulting larger files take longer to render (export). Lower-quality options, on the other hand, result in smaller files that render more quickly but might not look as sharp. Because they must find the best balance between quality and efficiency for their particular demands, users are forced to make a decision.

When balancing efficiency and quality in video editing, keep the following key factors in mind:

- **Target platform**:

  - Doing a YouTube upload? For quick upload speeds, you may want to give equal weight to file size and quality.

  - Exporting for a customer's high-resolution project? Maximal quality may need to be prioritized.

- **Project prerequisites**:

  - Does the project require flawless images for an audience of experts? You could select settings of a higher caliber.

  - Is the goal of the video rapid distribution on social media? Perhaps a smaller file size would be better.

- **Hardware restrictions**:

  - For high-quality exports, heavy rendering can be handled by powerful computers.

  - Large files may be difficult for less capable computers to render at optimal quality settings. Setting changes could be necessary for improved performance.

Custom settings versus presets

Presets that are preconfigured with parameters tailored for different platforms, such as social media or YouTube, are available in Premiere Pro. While these defaults are a terrific place to start, full customization is not possible with them.

Depending on their requirements, users must select between presets and custom settings. While custom settings give you greater control over the final movie, presets are useful for speedy exports using typical parameters. You can fine-tune individual characteristics such as bitrate or frame rate.

Regarding Use Maximum Render Quality

You should be aware of the following while deciding whether to check the box or leave it blank:

- Selecting imperial units is irrelevant to this checkbox. It has to do with the rendering engine that Premiere Pro exports data with.

- When enabled, Premiere Pro uses its most sophisticated rendering engine, which may result in output of a better caliber but may also take longer.

- Users must decide whether to turn on this option in order to emphasize speed or possibly acquire some additional quality. Although this parameter may not have as much of an effect on render times in more recent Premiere Pro versions due to the introduction of strong GPUs, it's still important to take into account.

To put it simply, selecting export settings involves striking the ideal balance between output standards, productivity, and project-specific needs. Regarding the rendering engine used during export, there is an additional choice regarding the **Use Maximum Render Quality** checkbox.

Audio export settings for YouTube

Navigate to the **Export Settings** tab and make the following changes to the specifications:

- **Audio Codec**: AAC

- **Audio Format**: AAC

- **Sample Rate**: 48000 Hz

- **Audio Quality**: High

- **Channels**: Stereo

Change these **Bitrate Settings** options:

- **Bitrate**: 320

Premiere Pro offers a YouTube preset specifically designed for audio export. When you choose this preset, it automatically configures the following settings, ensuring compatibility and quality for YouTube:

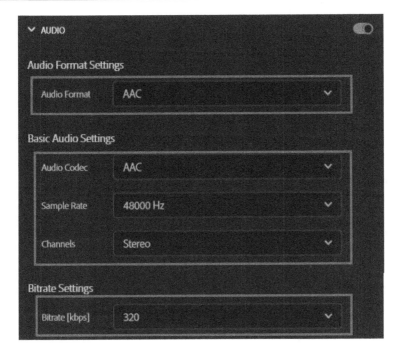

Figure 16.18 – Audio settings for YouTube

Here are some details to help you learn more about the audio options in the **Export** settings:

- **Audio Codec**: **Advanced Audio Coding** (**AAC**) is the industry standard for social media and YouTube, among other online video sites. It provides a decent trade-off between file size and quality.

- **Audio Format**: **AAC** – This format is compatible with the selected codec, making a perfect match.

- **Sample Rate**: **48000 Hertz (Hz)** – This is a typical sample rate that works well for most video footage since it records a broad variety of audio frequencies.

- **Channels**: **Stereo** – This keeps your audio's stereo channels intact, which is perfect for preserving the soundtrack's three-dimensional quality.

- **Bitrate**: A bitrate suitable for high-quality audio on the platform is usually established by the YouTube settings. Something as high as 192 **kilobits per second (kbps)** could be visible to you.

Here's why YouTube works well with these settings:

- **Compatibility**: YouTube's playback technology is guaranteed to work seamlessly while using the AAC codec and format

- **Quality**: The stereo channels provide a genuine sound experience, while the 48 kHz sampling rate records a wide range of sounds

- **Efficiency**: The selected bitrate maintains export manageability without compromising quality by striking a balance between audio fidelity and file size

Even if the YouTube settings work perfectly in most cases, there may be some circumstances in which you'd prefer a little more flexibility:

- **Specific requirements**: You may want to choose a higher sample rate, such as 96 kHz, if your project calls for exceptionally high-fidelity audio. But be aware that doing so will result in larger files.

- **Surround sound**: You'll need to select a new preset or adjust parameters to account for the extra channels for projects containing surround sound audio mixes.

Here are the best practices for exporting audio for YouTube:

- **Matching source quality**: As a general guideline, you should export your audio files with the same bitrate and sampling rate as your original source files. This guarantees that the export process doesn't result in any quality loss.

- **Bitrate experimentation**: If the size of the file is a serious concern, try a slightly lower bitrate (within reason) to see whether you can get a good audio quality without affecting the listening experience too much.

The default YouTube preset in Premiere Pro provides excellent audio export settings for most YouTube content makers. It offers a harmonious blend of effectiveness, compatibility with the platform, and quality. However, you may make well-informed judgments for particular project requirements if you have a solid understanding of the fundamentals of audio codecs, sample rates, and bitrates.

Best Premiere Pro export settings for Instagram

Instagram's move from a photo-centric to a video-centric platform was easy. Creators must meet the top social media platform's quality and compatibility requirements to ensure their reels and IGTV videos perform well in terms of engagement and reach.

Let's define a few key concepts before we get into the settings:

- **Resolution**: This is the total amount of pixels that are shown both vertically and horizontally. Higher resolutions offer crisper details; common specifications are **720p** (1,280 x 720 pixels) and **1080p** (1,920 x 1,080 pixels).

- **Frame rate**: Visualize a flipbook where every page represents a frame. The speed at which the pages turn gives the impression of motion. For the majority of web material, standard frame rates are 24 FPS for a theatrical effect and 30 FPS for smoother movements.

- **Bitrate**: This controls the trade-off between file size and quality. Larger files with clearer images are produced by higher bitrates, whereas smaller files with some quality loss are produced by lower bitrates.

- **Aspect ratio**: This is your video's width-to-height ratio. Typical Instagram aspect ratios are as follows:

  - **1:1 (Square) or 1000 x 1000 pixels**: Perfect for stories and posts on Instagram feeds

  - **9:16 (Portrait) or 1080 x 1920 pixels**: Ideal for Instagram **Stories** and **Reels**

  - **4:5 ratio or 1080 x 1350 pixels**: Ideal for in-feed posts that take advantage of more vertical space

Export options in Premiere Pro for Instagram

Several options are available in Premiere Pro to help you optimize your Instagram export process:

- **Presets**: They are pre-made configurations made for particular websites, such as Instagram. They're an excellent place to start as you don't need to delve into complex settings.

- **Match Source**: This preset guarantees an accurate portrayal of your modifications by preserving the source footage's resolution and frame rate.

- **Resolution-oriented presets**: Premiere Pro has Instagram-specific presets such as **Instagram 1080p** and **Instagram Story**. For the best viewing experience on the platform, these presets take into account variables including aspect ratio, bitrate, and resolution.

Exporting in various formats for Instagram

The suggested settings for the most common Instagram formats are broken down as follows:

- **Square or 4:5 posts on Instagram feeds**:

  Resolution:

  - **Novices**: Commence with a recognizable format such as **720p** (1280 x 720)

  - **Editors with experience**: Try **1080p** (1920 x 1080) for sharper images but be mindful of file size

  - **Frame rate**: For fluid playback, **30** FPS is a good guess

  Bitrate:

  - **Novices**: A bitrate of 3 to 4 Mbps is what you should aim for

  - **Editors with experience**: Try experimenting with between 4 and 6 Mbps to discover the ideal balance between file size and quality for your particular film

- **Aspect ratio**: Depending on the format you want, select either **1:1** (square) or **4:5**

- **Stories on Instagram (9:16)**:

  Resolution:

  - **Novices**: For effective uploads, beginners should start with **720p** (1280 x 720)

  - **Editors with experience**: 1080 x 1920 (portrait orientation) will provide sharper images on modern devices

  - **Frame rate**: **30** FPS guarantees fluid playback

  Bitrate:

  - **Novices**: Aim for a bitrate of 2 to 3 Mbps

  - **Editors with experience**: Try different speeds between 3 and 5 Mbps, but pay attention to file sizes

  - **Aspect ratio**: Select the **Portrait 9:16** aspect ratio for a smooth narrative flow

Above and beyond – advanced tips (optional)

To take your video editing to the next level, consider these additional tips and tricks:

- **H.264 codec:** The industry standard for websites such as Instagram is the **H.264** codec. For most export options in Premiere Pro, it is used by default.

- **Bitrate experimentation:** The previously suggested bitrates are just a place to start. To determine the ideal ratio of file size to quality for your particular material and upload speed over the internet, you can do a little trial and error.

- **File size limitations:** Uploads to Instagram are subject to file size restrictions. Depending on how long the video is, these restrictions change. For instance, in-feed video posts have a maximum file size of 25 GB and a maximum duration of 60 minutes. Conversely, stories have a file size limit of 250 MB per clip and a lesser time limit of 15 seconds per clip, with a maximum of 10 clips combined.

- **Examining the Instagram rules:** Instagram refreshes its suggested videos on a periodic basis. For the most recent information, it's a good idea to consult its official rules at `https://help.instagram.com/1038071743007909`.

By following these guidelines and leveraging Premiere Pro's export tools, you'll be well on your way to exporting Instagram-ready videos that capture attention and ignite engagement on your profile. Use the following video and audio export parameters to achieve this:

1. Navigate to the **Export Settings** tab and make the given changes:

   - **Frame Rate: 30**

   - **Frame Size: 1080 × 1920**

- **Format**: H.264

- **Match Source**: **High Bitrate**

- **Render**: **Maximum Depth and Maximum Render Quality**

- **Bitrate Encoding**: **VBR, 2Pass**

- **Target Bitrate**: **2 Mbps**

- **Maximum Bitrate**: **3 Mbps**

While Premiere Pro provides a number of encoding options, **H.264** is the recommended option for Instagram uploads. This profile strikes a compromise between quality and Instagram's playback system compatibility. Here's where you can adjust your export settings for Instagram:

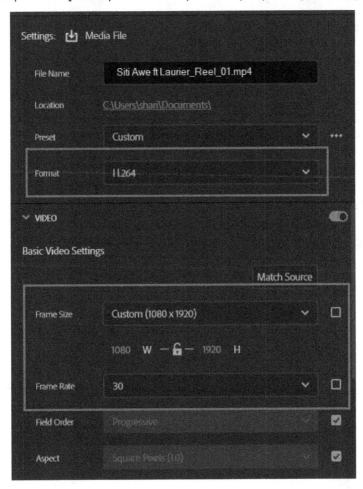

Figure 16.19 – Video settings for Instagram

> **Tip**
>
> Save all settings as a preset after adjusting them. Doing so will save you from manually adjusting parameters when exporting to Instagram.

2. To acquire the best audio export settings for Instagram, make the following changes as per the following screenshot:

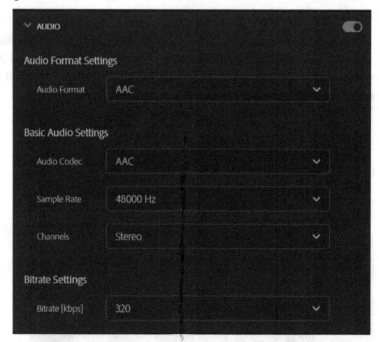

Figure 16.20 – Audio settings for Instagram

From the preceding screenshot, we can see the following settings:

*   **Audio Format: AAC**

*   **Audio Codec: AAC**

*   **Sample Rate: 48000 Hz**

*   **Bitrate: 320 Kbps**

*   **Channels: Stereo**

While the default settings are excellent for most situations, there might be a few scenarios where you want a bit more control:

- **Extremely high-fidelity audio**: For projects with exceptionally high-quality audio, such as professional music videos, consider using a higher sample rate such as *96 kHz*. However, keep in mind that this will increase file size and may not be noticeable to most Instagram users, who are typically less sensitive to subtle audio differences. For most Instagram content, a sample rate of *44.1 kHz* is sufficient, and *48 kHz* can offer slightly improved quality.

The Premiere Pro default audio settings work incredibly well for the vast majority of Instagram video outputs. They provide a harmonious blend of effectiveness, compatibility with the platform, and quality. On the other hand, if you are familiar with the fundamentals of audio codecs, sample rates, and bitrates, you will be able to make well-informed judgments for project requirements that call for extraordinarily high-fidelity audio.

Best Premiere Pro export settings for TikTok

Due to its short-form structure, TikTok is the most popular social media platform. Exporting content after selecting the proper export parameters is crucial for producers using the platform to submit and exhibit their work.

For TikTok creators, these video and audio export options will help your videos succeed:

- **Aspect ratio**: Verify that the aspect ratio and resolution of your video are set to 9:16 vertically, with 1080 x 1920 pixels.

- **Frame rate**: To ensure fluid playback on TikTok, stick to a conventional frame rate of either 30 or 24 FPS.

- **Bitrate**: This controls the trade-off between file size and quality. For TikTok content, 5 to 8 Mbps is a reasonable starting point. Try to find the ideal balance between file size and quality that will allow you to upload videos at the desired quality and upload speed over the internet.

- **File size restrictions**: Videos that last up to 10 minutes on TikTok are limited to a maximum file size of 500 MB. For the majority of short-form content, this shouldn't be a problem, but for longer videos, bear that in mind.

- **Efficiency in encoding**: Premiere Pro has a number of encoding settings. For TikTok uploads, **H.264 (Main Profile)** is the suggested format. This profile strikes a compromise between playback system compatibility and quality on TikTok.

Change the following options (as seen in *Figure 16.21*) after visiting the **Export** options:

- **Preset**: Match Source - Adaptive High Bitrate
- **Format**: H.264

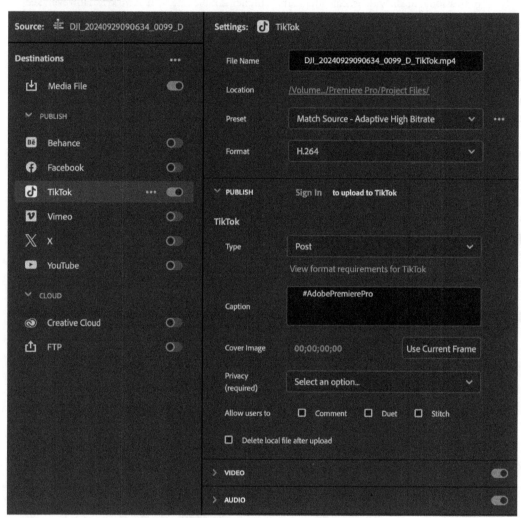

Figure 16.21 – Export settings for TikTok

To ensure optimal video quality, check the **Render at Maximum Depth** and **Use Maximum Render Quality** boxes in the render options before exporting your project; see *Figure 16.22*:

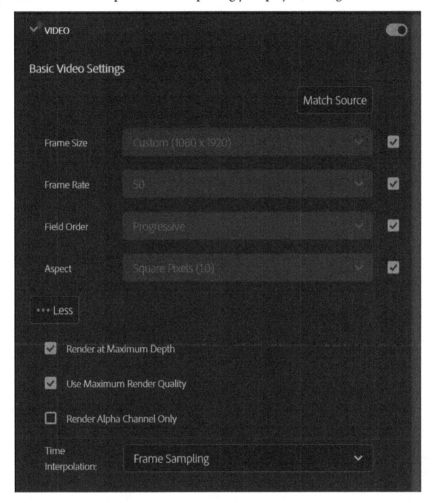

Figure 16.22 – Render at Maximum Depth and Use Maximum Render Quality checkboxes

Several concepts need to be clarified together in the remark about checking these boxes during export settings. Let's dissect it in the following subsections.

Render at Maximum Depth

Understanding the relationship between preview quality and export settings is essential for achieving the best results in your Premiere Pro projects. Here is why:

- This parameter relates to Premiere Pro's preview quality and has nothing to do with export settings.

- Premiere Pro can use more intricate effects and compositing with more accuracy when the **Render at Maximum Depth** option is enabled during playback. To make sure your edits appear as intended when working on your project, this can be useful.

- It is crucial to remember that a higher quality final output video does not always equate to maximum render depth.

Use Maximum Render Quality

To refine the details and clarity of your exported video, check this render setting:

- This export settings option tells Premiere Pro to use the Mercury Playback Engine, which is its most sophisticated rendering engine, for possibly better output quality.

- Turning this option on may improve the output video's clarity and playback, but it may also lengthen rendering times. This is a result of the engine running more complex computations to maybe attain higher quality.

When working on your project, choose Premiere Pro's Render at Maximum Depth option to see a more accurate preview of your adjustments. For potentially sharper visuals, think about exporting with maximum render quality enabled, but be aware that this could lengthen the rendering time. When adjusting export settings for maximum quality and efficiency depending on your intended platform, pay attention to bitrate, frame rate, and resolution.

To make sure your exports live up to your standards for quality, preview them.

Audio export settings for TikTok

Premiere Pro uses audio export defaults that work exceptionally well for TikTok. These defaults are typically used by both the built-in social media presets and custom export settings:

- **Audio Codec: AAC** – This is the industry standard for online video platforms such as TikTok. It offers a good balance between quality and file size.

- **Audio Format: AAC** – This format aligns with the chosen codec for a seamless pairing.

- **Sample Rate: 48 kHz** – This is a common sample rate that captures a wide range of audio frequencies, suitable for most video content.

- **Channels: Stereo** – This preserves the stereo channels of your audio, ideal for maintaining the spatial dimension of your soundtrack, especially for videos with dialogue or music.

As a general guideline, you should export your audio files with the same bitrate and sampling rate as your original source files. This guarantees that the export process doesn't result in any quality loss.

> **Tip**
> Save the preceding parameters as your default export settings to avoid having to alter them every time you upload a video.

The Premiere Pro default audio settings work incredibly well for the great majority of TikTok video exports. They provide a harmonious blend of effectiveness, compatibility with the platform, and quality. On the other hand, if you are familiar with the fundamentals of audio codecs, sample rates, and bitrates, you will be able to make well-informed judgments for project requirements that call for extraordinarily high-fidelity audio.

Best Premiere Pro export settings for Facebook

Facebook has over 2.9 billion members and a variety of material, but videos perform best. Thus, many artists upload videos as their main content. Most viewers watch videos on smartphones, so artists must optimize their videos for small screens.

Recognizing Facebook's prerequisites

Before exporting your video, here's what you should understand about Facebook's requirements:

- **Supported format**:

  - Facebook mostly allows videos that are encoded in **H.264** (MP4) format. It matches perfectly because Premiere Pro exports files in this format by default.

- **Aspect ratio and resolution**:

- Facebook offers versatility with aspect ratios for posts and stories. You can select a vertical rectangle (**9:16**) for mobile-friendly viewing, a horizontal rectangle (**16:9**) for a cinematic effect, or a square format (**1:1**) for a more static image-like experience. When selecting the aspect ratio, take your target audience and content into account:

  - Facebook suggests that live or pre-recorded in-stream movies have a minimum resolution of 1280 x 720 pixels (**720p**).

  - Make use of Premiere Pro's integrated presets for a dependable and quick export experience. Search for presets such as **H.264 for Social Media** or **Facebook 1080p**. A strong starting point for exporting Facebook videos is provided by these settings.

Facebook requires video makers to optimize their films, just as other social media networks. Simply utilize the following Premiere Pro video export settings:

- **Resolution: 1080 x 1920**
- **Video Codec: H.264**

- **Format**: MP4

- **Target Bitrate**: 15 MB/s

- **Bitrate Encoding**: VBR, 1 pass

> **Tip**
>
> Keep the compression rate below 4 MB. Facebook has file size restrictions that change based on the duration of the video. For instance, the maximum file size for in-feed videos is 10 GB, but they can last up to 240 minutes. For the most recent information, always refer to Facebook's guidelines as of right now.

Use the following audio settings:

- **Audio Format**: AAC

- **Audio Quality**: High

- **Channel**: Stereo

- **Sample Rate**: 48000 Hz

Always check your exported videos to be sure the format on Facebook is exactly how you meant it to appear and sound.

Try new things and discover your balance. Experiment with bitrate settings to get the ideal ratio of file size to quality for your particular need and upload speed over the internet. Facebook places accessibility as a top priority when it comes to closed captions. Think about using third-party tools or Premiere Pro's features to add closed captions to your videos. Engagement and viewership may rise as a result.

Best Premiere Pro export settings for Vimeo

Vimeo is another great venue for sharing HD videos with the world. Creators must use Vimeo-compatible export options to ensure their videos work well on Vimeo. The recommended export settings for Premiere Pro editors can be seen in the next section.

Recognizing Vimeo's prerequisites

Before exporting your video, here's what you should understand about Vimeo's requirements:

- **Supported formats**: When it comes to codecs, Vimeo supports more than some other services. The most often used and advised codec is **H.264** (MP4), but Vimeo also supports DNxHR, Apple ProRes, and HEVC (**H.265**).

- Aspect ratio and resolution are two areas where Vimeo offers a lot of versatility. You have the ability to upload videos in a range of aspect ratios and resolutions, from common choices such as 720p (16:9) and 1080p (16:9) to more cinematic formats such as **4K (UHD)** and even 8K.

Use the presets that Premiere Pro comes with to ensure a dependable and speedy export procedure. Go through social media presets or search for presets such as **Match Source - High Bitrate**. These presets provide a strong starting point for Vimeo video exporting. Select these options after accessing the **Export** settings:

- **Match Source**: Unchecked

- **Format: H.264**

- **Frame Size: HD – 1280 x 720 pixels (720p), Full HD – 1920 x 1080 pixels (1080)**, and **4K – 3840 x 2160 pixels (UHD)**

- **Aspect Ratio**: Vimeo allows various aspect ratios, including **16:9** (widescreen), **1:1** (square), and **9:16** (vertical). Choose the one that best suits your content.

- **Output Name**: Video output name and destination

- **Bitrate Encoding: VBR, 2 Pass**

> Tip
> Render at maximum depth.

Remember that there are additional factors to consider while exporting, such as the following:

- **Vimeo's compression guidelines**: H.264-compressed movies are recommended for best playback performance, even if the platform supports a larger variety of codecs. For advanced reference, you can check their comprehensive compression instructions at `https://vimeo.com/help/compression`.

- **File size restrictions**: Vimeo has limits on individual video uploads, even though it gives a lot of storage based on your plan. The weekly allotment for free accounts is 500 MB; larger capacities are available with paid subscriptions. When selecting bitrate levels, keep these limitations in mind.

- **Efficiency in encoding**: Premiere Pro has a number of encoding settings. Vimeo uploads should use **H.264** (**Main Profile** or **High Profile** for HD and higher). This profile strikes a compromise between Vimeo's playback system compatibility and quality.

Make use of Premiere Pro's integrated presets for a dependable and quick export experience. Go through social media presets or search for presets such as **Match Source - High Bitrate**. These presets provide a strong starting point for Vimeo video exporting.

Audio export settings for Vimeo

The audio export settings for Vimeo in Premiere Pro are similar to other platforms.

Use the following audio settings:

- **Audio Format**: AAC
- **Audio Quality**: High
- **Channel**: Stereo
- **Sample Rate**: 48000 Hz

Complete the following actions for checkboxes:

- **Use Maximum Render Quality**: Checked
- **Use Frame Blending**: Unchecked
- **Use Previews**: Unchecked
- **Import into Projects**: Unchecked

> **Tip**
>
> You may need to utilize a separate audio encoder to export the audio in a format that is compatible with Vimeo if you select a video format other than H.264, such as ProRes or DNxHR (usually AAC).

Vimeo is a great place to find excellent video material, so make sure your exports look great. For both novice and expert users, here is a setting for exporting videos for Vimeo in Premiere Pro: You can make sure your Vimeo uploads are of the highest caliber and wow your viewers by adhering to these rules.

- **Format**: H.264
- **Preset**: Vimeo 1080p HD
- **Resolution**: 1920 x 1080 (or the resolution of your source video)
- **Frame Rate**: Match the frame rate of your source video
- **Bitrate Settings**:

    - **Bitrate Encoding**: VBR, 2 pass
    - **Target Bitrate**: 10 Mbps
    - **Maximum Bitrate**: 20 Mbps

- **Audio Settings**:

  - **Audio Codec**: AAC

  - **Sample Rate**: 48000 Hz

  - **Channels**: Stereo

  - **Audio Quality**: High

  - **Bitrate**: 320 kbps

These settings should help you achieve high-quality uploads that look great on Vimeo

4K export settings for Adobe Premiere Pro

4K (Ultra High Definition) is one of the highest resolutions available for video. It is widely popular among video editors due to its superior clarity, sharpness, color reproduction, and compatibility with various screens and devices. Adobe Premiere Pro requires particular settings to export 4K files.

Adobe's advanced editing software's 4K export settings are as follows:

- **Format**: **H.264** (MP4) is the industry standard for online platforms and playback devices. Premiere Pro defaults to this format, making it a perfect choice.

- **Resolution**: Choose **3840 x 2160** pixels for true 4K resolution.

Select these options in the **Export** settings:

- **Format: H.264**

- **Preset: Custom**

- Check **Match Sequence**

- Check **Use Maximum Render Quality**

- **Frame Rate: 60**

- **Bitrate: 66-85 MB/s**

- **Audio Bitrate: 512 KB/s**

Utilize Premiere Pro's built-in presets for a swift and reliable export:

- **Match Source - High Bitrate**: This preset automatically adjusts settings based on your project's resolution and frame rate, offering a good starting point

- **Social media presets**: Some platforms such as YouTube have specific 4K presets that ensure compatibility

While presets are convenient, experienced users can fine-tune settings for more control:

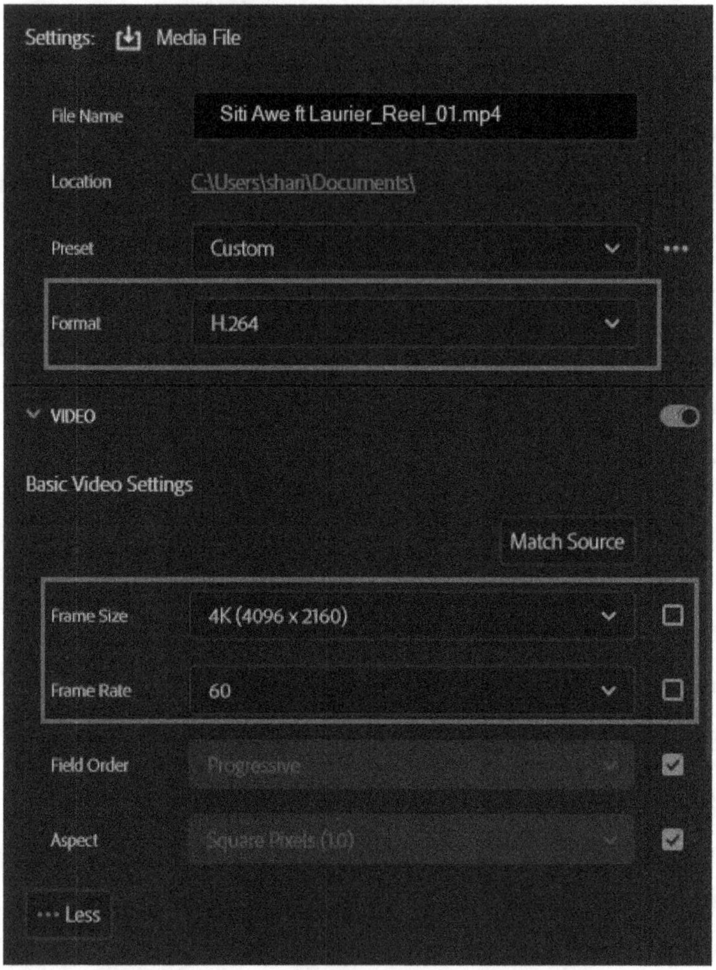

Figure 16.23 – 4K export settings in Premiere Pro

The settings in the **VIDEO** tab are as follows:

- **Resolution**: Ensure it's set to **4096 x 2160** pixels.

- **Frame Rate**: Maintain a standard frame rate such as **24** FPS, **25** FPS, or **30** FPS and above for smooth playback.

- **Bitrate**: This determines the file size and quality. Here's a breakdown of different scenarios:

- **High quality (large files)**: Start with 50 Mbps to 100 Mbps for exceptional quality, ideal for offline viewing or archival purposes.

- **Online platforms (balance)**: Aim for 20 Mbps to 40 Mbps for a good balance between quality and manageable file size for upload to platforms such as YouTube or Vimeo. Consider their specific recommendations for 4K uploads.

  - **Profile**: **Main Profile** is a common choice, but **High Profile** can offer more control over video quality, especially at higher bitrates.

After making the configuration adjustments, simply click **Export**. Doing so starts 4K rendering.

Here's what you should consider while exporting 4K videos in Premiere Pro:

- **Encoding for efficiency**: Hardware encoding speeds up export times by making use of your graphics card, particularly when working with 4K videos. Software encoding, however, might occasionally provide somewhat higher quality. To discover the ideal balance for your project, try different things.

- **Depth of color and sampling**: For the majority of web systems, 8-bit depth and 4:2:0 chroma sampling are usually adequate. Higher settings should only be taken into account for color grading or professional broadcast operations.

- **Platform of interest**: Make sure to always review the platform's guidelines or special criteria before uploading a 4K video. There may be restrictions on the maximum bitrate or file size on some platforms.

By adhering to these rules and making use of Premiere Pro's export capabilities, you should have no trouble producing gorgeous 4K videos that effectively convey your artistic vision. Recall that the ideal configuration may change based on the objectives of your particular project and the intended platform. To get the best outcomes for your 4K masterpieces, try different things and improve your strategy. In the following section, we'll cover best practices for exporting in Premiere Pro to achieve the highest quality results.

Exporting for maximum quality – Premiere Pro best practices

Quality, file size, and compatibility must be balanced to get the *best* export options. High-quality settings produce spectacular images but larger files, whereas low-quality settings prioritize compactness over visual fidelity. Remember that your needs and audience determine the best settings. In the upcoming subsections, you'll learn how to select the best format for your project and the importance of choosing the right codec. Understanding these elements is crucial for optimizing your video quality and compatibility across different platforms.

Choosing your format

The format you choose affects video playback and sharing. Some popular choices are as follows:

- **MP4** (`.mp4`): The king of online video, suitable with most devices and platforms

- **H.264** (`.h264`): MP4 compression codec that balances quality and file size

- **H.265** (`.h265`): A newer codec with better compression but slower encoding and less compatibility

- `.mov`: A flexible format used for professional editing but incompatible with many websites

The ideal export parameters are determined by your project's objectives, the intended platform, and the desired ratio of file size to quality. Try different things and improve your strategy to get the greatest output for your Premiere Pro video exports.

Picking the right codec

Choosing the right codec for video editing in Premiere Pro is crucial for several reasons:

- **Editing performance and efficiency**:

  - The degree of complexity varies amongst codecs. High-end, lossless codecs such as ProRes and DNxHR are built for professional editing. Even though they provide better image quality, they may cause poorer playing and editing performance on less powerful computers since they demand more processing power from your system.

  - Editor-friendly codecs are Avid DNxHD and Apple ProRes. When editing, they enable faster frame access and manipulation than compressed codecs such as H.264 (which are typically used for final delivery). This more seamless editing process can greatly enhance your productivity.

- **Compression and quality**:

  - There are two types of codecs: lossless and lossy. ProRes and DNxHR are examples of lossless codecs that maintain all of the original data from your video, giving it the best quality possible. For professional editing operations where preserving the original quality is crucial, this is perfect.

  - To minimize file size, lossy codecs (such as H.264) compress the video data. They are, therefore, appropriate for online distribution and final delivery, but some image quality is lost in the process. The selected bitrate determines the extent of quality degradation (greater bitrate = better quality and larger file size).

- **Playback and compatibility**:

  - Not every device can play every codec. Professional editing environments are the primary use case for codecs such as ProRes or DNxHR, which may require additional software to play back on consumer devices.

  - One popular and well-supported codec is H.264. This makes it a viable option for final delivery because it guarantees fluid playback on most devices and web platforms.

When editing, for best results and quality preservation, use editing codecs such as ProRes or DNxHR on compatible devices, and to balance quality and file size, choose H.264 for online platforms and final export, taking into account the bitrate and resolution recommendations of the destination platform.

Each format has a codec that compresses video data. Some popular options are as follows:

- **H.264**: MP4's default mode, with good quality and wide compatibility

- **Variable Bitrate (VBR)**: Dynamic bitrate adjustment based on video complexity produces higher-quality but larger files

- **Constant Bitrate (CBR)**: For predictable playback and streaming, maintain a constant bitrate

When working with video in Premiere Pro, knowing how codecs affect editing quality, performance, and compatibility gives you the power to make wise choices. You can make sure that the editing process runs smoothly, retain excellent quality throughout, and produce videos that are tailored to your target audience by selecting the appropriate codec for each step (editing versus delivery).

After selecting your format, codec, and preset, examine the settings:

- **Bitrate**: File size and quality are balanced by bitrate. Higher bitrates produce clearer images but larger files.

- **Frame Rate**: Smoothly plays source footage at its frame rate.

- **Resolution**: Select the right resolution for your audience and platform.

- **Field Order**: Choose the source footage field order for proper playing.

- **Audio Settings**: Select the format and bitrate for best sound.

You may have more power and flexibility than just the basic defaults by looking through the options. The setting lets you customize the export procedure to get the best results for your movie, be it optimizing quality, limiting file size for upload, or adhering to platform guidelines.

Excellent tips for exporting

To ensure your exported videos meet the highest standards of quality and efficiency, follow these expert tips:

- **Hardware encoding**: H.264 and VBR encoding are faster with the GPU

- **Multi-pass encoding**: Two-pass encoding improves quality but takes longer

- **Test quality and size**: Before exporting, export brief test clips with different parameters to test quality and file size

- **Consider your audience**: Use YouTube-/Vimeo-optimized export settings

- **Automation**: Save time and effort with automated export tools and procedures

To achieve the best Premiere Pro exports, follow the advice provided by your target platform and play around with the bitrate parameters to find the ideal balance between file size and quality. Although presets are a fantastic place to start, you can adjust the parameters to suit your needs. Recall that while H.264 with an optimized bitrate is perfect for final distribution and web platforms, editing codecs such as ProRes guarantee fluid editing. In the following section, you'll learn the process of exporting your projects using **Media Encoder** alongside Premiere Pro.

Exporting in Media Encoder for Premiere Pro

Exporting via **Media Encoder** allows you to render your video in the background while continuing to work in Premiere Pro. **Media Encoder** processes the most recently saved version of each sequence in the queue. It offers a dedicated workspace for handling video exports, freeing up Premiere Pro for continued editing while your video renders. Here's how to leverage it:

1. To send a sequence video to **Media Encoder** in the **Export** window, click the **Send to Media Encoder** button; see *Figure 16.24*:

Figure 16.24 – Sending a sequence to Media Encoder in the Export window

2. To send a video to **Media Encoder** for background rendering from the timeline, select **File |
    Export | Send to Adobe Media Encoder** or use the *Option + Shift + M* (macOS) or *Alt + Shift
    + M* (Windows) keyboard shortcut. By default, the currently open sequence in the timeline is
    sent, but you can also choose specific sequences or clips in the **Project** panel using the
    same method; see *Figure 16.25*:

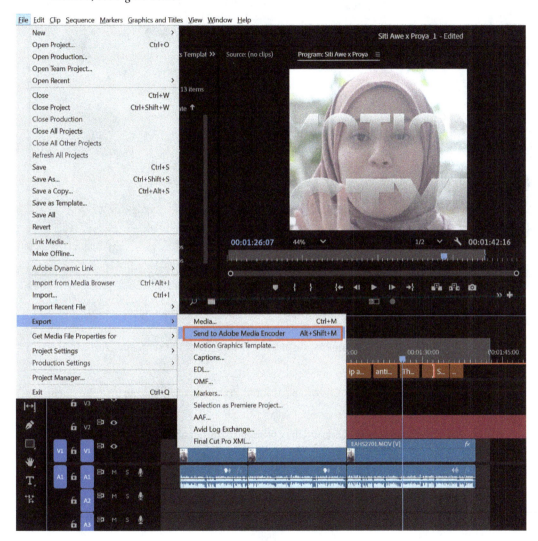

Figure 16.25 – Send to Adobe Media Encoder in Premiere Pro from the File menu

3. Adobe **Media Encoder** will automatically launch, and the selected sequences will be added to the queue, ready for you to start the rendering process:

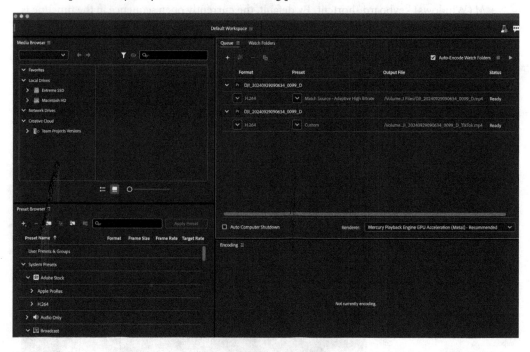

Figure 16.26 – Adobe Media Encoder window for rendering

4. The **Media Encoder** interface opens, displaying your project in the queue. You can then do the following:

- **Add more projects**: Drag and drop additional Premiere Pro projects into the queue for batch exporting.

- **Rearrange the queue order**: Click and drag projects in the queue to change the processing order.

- **Adjust presets and settings (for multiple projects)**: If you export multiple projects, you can adjust presets or settings directly within the **Media Encoder** queue for each project.

- **Drag and drop**: Select and hold the *timeline* thumbnail, then drag it to the **Media Encoder** window. Once you've got the timeline in Media Encoder where you want it, release the mouse button.

5. Click the green **Play** button in the **Media Encoder** queue to begin the export process:

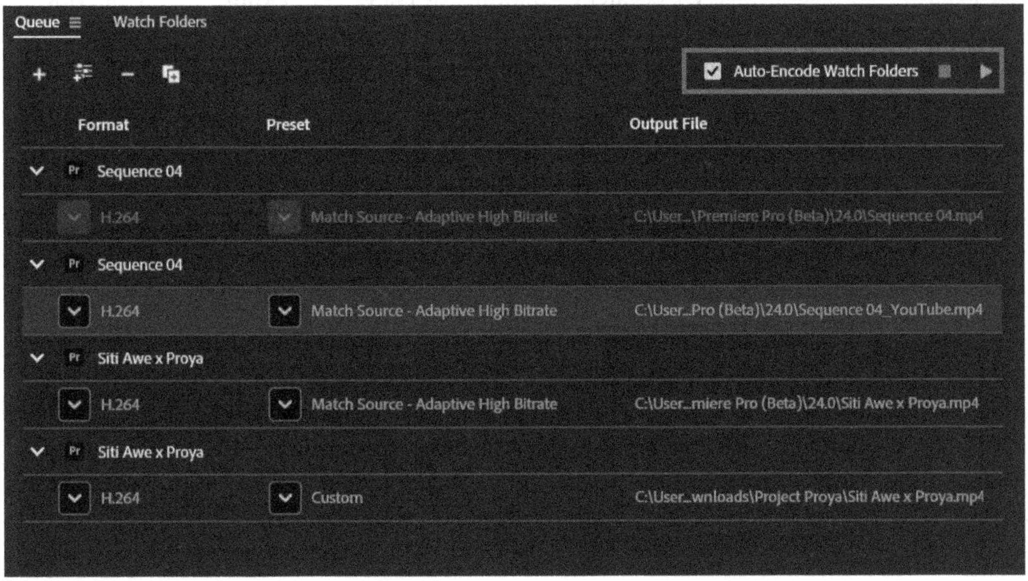

Figure 16.27– Exporting media in Adobe Media Encoder

6. **Media Encoder** will leverage your system's resources to render the video according to the specified settings. This is useful for exporting numerous Premiere Pro sequences simultaneously.

Every project in the queue has a progress bar showing how much encoding is left to do. This enables you to schedule your workflow and predict the completion time of the export. You can also work in Premiere Pro while **Media Encoder** exports. Since Premiere Pro struggles to handle everything, I export using this method most often.

The sequence is exported from that window by clicking **Export**. You won't be able to utilize Premiere Pro while rendering occurs if you export straight from the program. The ability of **Media Encoder** to render in the background comes in handy in this situation as it lets you finish working on other chores or projects while your video exports.

Summary

Creators who seek quality on any device benefit from Adobe Premiere Pro's export settings. The nicest aspect is that Premiere Pro exports videos easily. However, the software's exporting speed depends on the user's hardware. The perfect export settings are a tool to be used with knowledge and intention, not a holy grail. Adapt your settings to your project and audience, experiment, and keep learning. With this chapter's advice, you'll confidently export your video masterpiece to the world.

This chapter explored the intricacies of exporting videos in Premiere Pro, providing a comprehensive guide to ensure optimal results. We began by exploring the convenient **Export** button, offering a streamlined approach for basic exports. For those seeking more granular control, we explored the in-depth export settings, allowing you to customize your videos for various screens, devices, and specific requirements.

To achieve the highest quality exports, we provided expert tips and best practices. These included optimizing settings such as frame rate, resolution, and bitrate, as well as leveraging advanced features such as **Render at Maximum Depth** and **Use Maximum Render Quality**. Additionally, we explored the option of exporting directly to **Media Encoder**, enabling efficient background rendering and allowing you to continue working in Premiere Pro while your videos are processed.

The export settings in Premiere Pro allow you to customize your video for various platforms and quality objectives. You can continue editing in Premiere Pro and expedite the export process by utilizing **Media Encoder**. We looked at important parameters such as frame rate (keep it at 24 FPS, 25 FPS, or 30 FPS), resolution (choose based on your project and target platform: SD, HD, Full HD, or 4K), and bitrate (the higher the bitrate, the better the quality but larger file size). While presets (such as **YouTube 1080p**) are an excellent place to start, checking the parameters enables customization such as bitrate adjustment for best quality and file size balance.

By following the guidelines we outlined in this chapter, you'll be equipped to export your Premiere Pro projects with confidence, ensuring that your videos meet the highest standards of quality and are optimized for their intended platforms.

In the next chapter, we will explore the collaborative aspects of Premiere Pro by discussing team projects. You'll learn how to work seamlessly with other editors via the cloud, enabling efficient teamwork and real-time collaboration on shared projects.

17

Team Projects in Premiere Pro — Collaborating with Other Editors via the Cloud

No more editing alone in dimly lit rooms. Teams across continents can now collaborate to realize creative ambitions in the current video industry. This chapter introduces Adobe Premiere Pro's strong team project feature, giving you the skills to handle collaborative editing efficiently. You'll learn how to set up your team, work on edits simultaneously, navigate conflicts smoothly, and keep track of changes. We'll even explore advanced features for larger teams and show you how Premiere Pro integrates with other creative tools. By the end, you'll be equipped to collaborate like a pro and take your video editing to the next level. This chapter aims to equip you with the knowledge and skills to confidently utilize Premiere Pro's Team Projects feature for seamless cloud-based collaboration on video editing projects.

In this chapter, we're going to cover the following main topics:

- Team Projects in Premiere Pro
- Using Frame.io with Premiere Pro for review and collaboration
- Productions in Premiere Pro

Team Projects in Premiere Pro

Adobe launched Creative Cloud almost a decade ago to go to the cloud. It's one of the most popular content creation platforms since it adapts to user needs.

Remote work has created one of these needs. Now that content creation is a worldwide endeavor, team members – especially post-production workers – don't need to live together. Smooth, cloud-based, collaboration-first remote content creation is needed. Adobe Team Projects enables this.

Advantages of collaborative projects

Premiere Pro has collaborative editing capabilities that enable smooth collaboration with other editors on the same project. In this section, we'll examine the process of establishing Team Projects, allocating roles, overseeing timeframes, and ensuring an efficient collaborative workflow.

Here are the key benefits of using Team Projects:

- Simultaneous editing allows multiple editors to collaborate on different areas of a project at the same time, speeding up the editing process
- All project assets, such as media files and sequences, are stored in a central cloud location that can be accessed by all collaborators
- Version control enables modifications that have been made by individual editors to be tracked, allowing prior versions to be reverted or edits to be combined if necessary
- Team Projects facilitates efficient communication among editors, promoting a cooperative atmosphere

Collaborative projects in Premiere Pro enable users of varying levels of expertise to increase their productivity by enhancing their speed and efficiency. It helps to produce projects of superior quality and greater creativity. Editors and teams can acquire knowledge and develop by exchanging ideas and experiences with one another to ensure a very efficient and optimized process. Let's understand what Team Projects is and how we can work with it.

What is Team Projects?

Adobe's Team Projects tools simplify collaboration. This enables seamless Premiere Pro and After Effects project collaboration.

Team Projects has allowed collaborative editing for years, but only on Adobe's **Team** and **Enterprise** plans. Adobe gave all Creative Cloud users free access to Team Projects throughout the COVID-19 pandemic.

Team Projects lets the lead editor construct a cloud-hosted project. This project file allows several editors and post-production collaborators to edit the timeline, which can be beneficial in most instances.

Let's check out some Premiere Pro features that Team Projects enables.

Before using Team Projects

All Team Projects collaborators need source footage. Due to this, using a cloud-based file-sharing system with Team Projects is recommended. Editors can set scratch discs in a cloud-based file to share Premiere Pro project metadata and media with colleagues. Avoiding film transfers is beneficial when using cloud-based file storage as it ensures the media will never go offline.

Google Drive and Dropbox are good choices for this. All editors must download and install the desktop client, then set the cloud drive as a Premiere Pro location. Upon doing this, your team will have real-time access to the media, and any modifications (such as uploads) will be reflected to all users.

The following subsections will show you what users should do and prepare before diving into Team Projects and collaboration features in Premiere Pro.

Effective planning and clear communication are crucial for success

Effective planning and clear communication are the cornerstones of successful team projects in Premiere Pro for a few key reasons:

- **Project goals and scope**: It's essential to have a clear understanding of the project's objectives, the intended audience, and the overarching vision. This ensures that all individuals are aligned creatively.

- **Exploring the roles and responsibilities of a team**: Ensure that every team member has a well-defined role and clear set of responsibilities. One approach could be to break the project down into different scenes, types of edits (such as motion graphics or sound design), or specific tasks.

- **Methods of communication**: Create a comprehensive communication plan for the team. Consider the best way to communicate your updates, inquire about any concerns, and offer constructive feedback. You have a variety of options to choose from, such as video calls, messaging platforms, or project management software.

Preparation from a technical standpoint

From a technical standpoint, minimal preparation is required for team projects and collaboration in Premiere Pro itself. However, there are a few key things to consider to ensure a smooth workflow:

- **Software updates**: It's crucial to make sure that all team members have the most up-to-date version of Premiere Pro installed. This will help prevent any potential compatibility problems that may arise when working on Team Projects.

- **Cloud storage**: Establish a dependable cloud storage solution such as Dropbox or Google Drive to conveniently store project files and media assets in one central location. By ensuring everyone can easily access the most up-to-date versions, any worries or difficulties with file management are eliminated.

- **Internet connection**: Having a stable and robust internet connection is essential when ensuring seamless collaboration. This is crucial when it comes to uploading and downloading project files as it can be quite resource-intensive.

- **File naming**: Establishing clear file naming conventions for project files and media assets is crucial to avoid any confusion that may arise. By implementing a systematic approach to naming files, you can ensure that everyone involved in the project can easily locate and identify the necessary files. This will not only save time but also enhance overall efficiency. So, take the time to establish a well-thought-out file naming convention that suits your project's needs. With this feature, anyone can find and access the files they require effortlessly.

- **Color coding**: Utilize the color coding feature in Premiere Pro to visually differentiate the work of different editors on the timeline. This fosters a sense of openness and minimizes the chance of unintentional alterations.

- **Backup strategy**: It's crucial to always keep a backup of your project files in a separate location from the cloud storage location. This extra precaution ensures enhanced security for your valuable work.

By implementing these considerations, users can guarantee a seamless and productive collaborative editing experience in Premiere Pro. It's crucial to emphasize the importance of effective communication, thorough planning, and having a solid grasp of the project's features to fully leverage the advantages of collaborative endeavors.

Setting up shared projects

To create a shared project, you must open Premiere Pro. Follow these steps:

1.   On the home screen, click **New Team Project** at the bottom left, as shown in *Figure 17.1*:

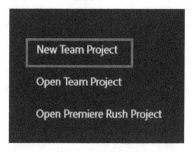

Figure 17.1 – New Team Project

2. Name the project and add collaborators. All collaborators need Adobe email addresses. An example of this is shown in *Figure 17.2*:

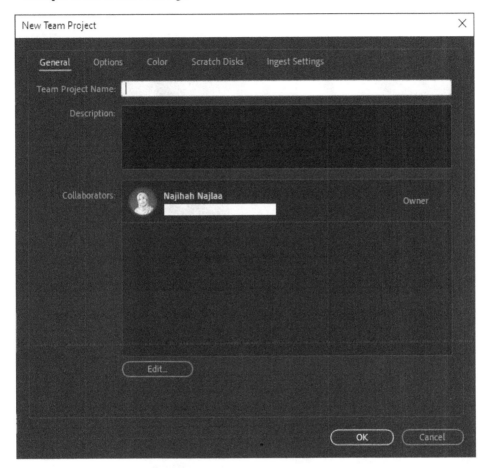

Figure 17.2 – Naming the project and adding collaborators

3. Users can also change their **Options**, **Scratch Disks**, and **Ingest Settings** values in this pop-up box. After finishing, click **OK** to see the Team Projects timeline.

4. Premiere Pro can also convert a local project file into a shared team project file with one click. Go to the **Edit** drop-down menu and select **Team Project** to see the available commands. Select **Convert Project to Team Project…**, as shown in *Figure 17.3*:

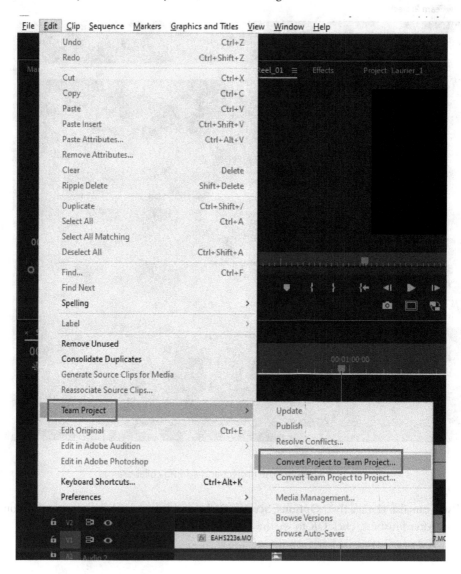

Figure 17.3 – Convert Project to Team Project…

5. Please provide a name for your Team Projects, along with a brief description, and begin adding collaborators.

6. Click **OK** to finalize the process. Upon doing so, your collaborators will receive a notification in their Creative Cloud Desktop application. You'll also find that the invitation is displayed in the **Manage Team Projects** dialog, in the **Invites** tab.

Next, we'll cover the best features that are available in Team Projects.

Team Projects features

No repetitive file transmission is needed between participants since the project file is saved to the cloud. Editors always view the same file. This speeds up upload and download time, making editors more productive.

Premiere Pro's Team Projects offer a robust set of features that are designed to streamline collaborative editing workflows. The following subsections provide a breakdown of the key features.

Essential features

Here are the essential features in Team Projects for Premiere Pro that enable seamless cloud-based collaboration:

- **Cloud-based project hosting**: Team projects are effortlessly stored in the cloud, enabling numerous editors to access and collaborate on the same project simultaneously, no matter where they're located.

- **Centralized asset management**: By storing all project assets in a central location, the hassle of file transfers and version control issues is eliminated.

- **Locking and unlocking timelines**: To avoid any potential clashes, editors can *lock* certain sequences before they start working on them. Those who come across the sequence will be informed that it's been locked to prevent any unintended alterations.

Exploring the various collaboration features

Here's a breakdown of how you can explore the various collaboration features in Team Projects for Premiere Pro:

- **Invite and manage collaborators**: The project administrator can invite collaborators via email, giving them different levels of access (Editor or Viewer), depending on their role in the project.

- **Check version history**: In the version history, Team Projects keeps a record of all the changes that are made to sequences. This feature allows you to easily revert to previous versions or merge edits as necessary. This provides a safety net and encourages new ideas to be explored.

- **Perform real-time collaboration**: Although edits may not appear immediately on everyone's screen, collaborators can track who's working on specific sections of the timeline and stay informed about the progress that's being made.

Effective communication and strong organizational skills are essential

Effective communication and strong organizational skills are the cornerstones of successful team projects in Premiere Pro for several reasons:

- **Color coding**: In Premiere Pro, you can assign vibrant colors to different editors, adding visual organization to your workflow. The timeline beautifully captures the essence of each individual's contribution through its vibrant colors.

- **Project locking**: The administrator has the power to secure the entire project, ensuring that no edits can be made until it's unlocked. This serves as a valuable tool for ensuring final approvals or deliveries.

- **The Project panel**: This panel provides valuable information, such as the status of the project and the person responsible for editing a locked sequence. This fosters transparency and keeps the team well-informed.

- **Offline editing**: Editors can work on the project seamlessly, regardless of any internet connection hiccups. With Premiere Pro, you have the convenience of being able to download media files so that you can work on them offline. And the best part? Your changes will sync up seamlessly once you're back online.

- **Frame.io integration**: Premiere Pro integrates with Frame.io effortlessly, a widely used online platform for review and collaboration. With the smooth integration of feedback and annotations, the Team Projects workflow becomes even more efficient and streamlined.

By utilizing these Team Projects features, editors can collaborate effectively, establish a structured project framework, and guarantee a seamless editing experience.

Premiere Pro's publishing feature allows numerous editors to work on the same timeline and eases this process. Videos can be imported, edited, and rendered separately. Editors can **Publish** their version when they're ready, updating the project timetable for other participants. The **Publish** button can be seen in *Figure 17.4*:

Figure 17.4 – Publishing edits in Team Projects

Editors can write comments or notes in a text field when publishing edits to the team. This lets editors inform the team about completed modifications and upcoming tasks. The **Comment** text field is shown in *Figure 17.5*:

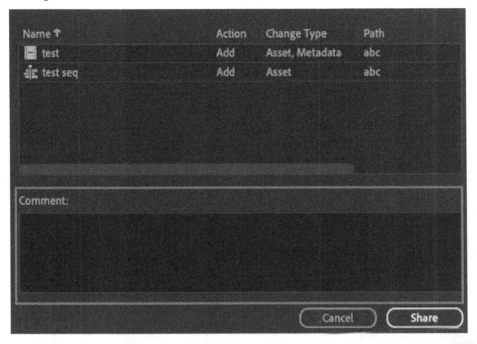

Figure 17.5 – Adding comments

Premiere Pro's automatic *sequence locking* prevents timeline duplication. Collaborators can view the project file in **View-Only Mode** when the timeline is locked as seen in *Figure 17.6*:

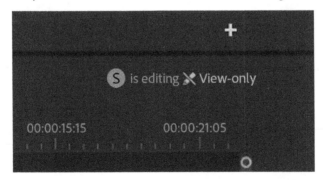

Figure 17.6 – View-only mode in the Timeline panel

Editors working on a project file in Premiere Pro use the visual signals we've learned about to stay on track. Users receive these cues when they may publish modifications, are in read-only mode, or have an updated timetable.

Editing Team Projects in post-production might be stressful as various edits must be done simultaneously. Users can relax knowing that all edits are stored in the cloud and can never be lost. The project owner can also resolve version discrepancies that are reported since changes that have been made by collaborators are automatically logged in a **Version History** tab. As shown in *Figure 17.7*, users can utilize the right-hand scroller in the **Media Browser** tab to view older timelines. Here, they can cycle through all released timeline variations:

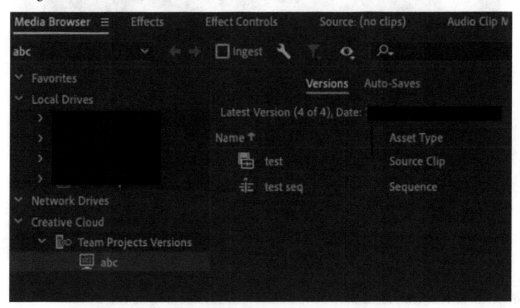

Figure 17.7 – Team Projects edits are stored in the cloud

Right-click the Team Project file in the **Media Browser** tab and select **Team Project Versions** to view earlier versions. A window will open that contains all cloud-published project versions. See *Figure 17.8*:

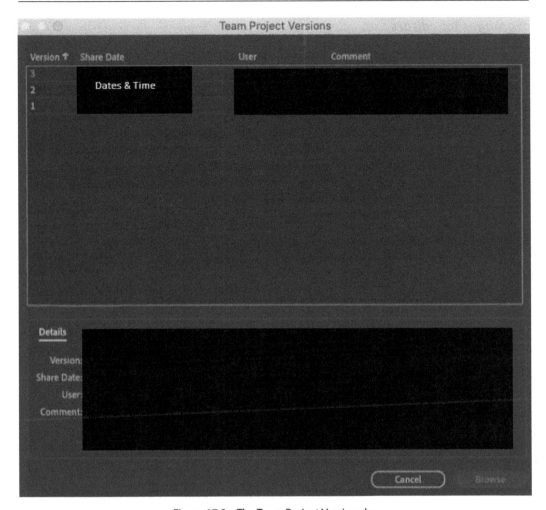

Figure 17.8 – The Team Project Versions log

Users can reset the timeline if needed. A previously recorded version can be used to produce a local or Team Project file.

Understanding the benefits of Team Project version logs for editors and collaborators

In Premiere Pro, version logs for team projects serve as a valuable tool for meticulously tracking changes and maintaining a comprehensive history of the project's progression. The upcoming subsections provide a comprehensive analysis of the advantages they offer to editors and collaborators.

Advantages for editors

Here are the advantages of Team Project version logs for editors in Premiere Pro:

- **Version tracking**: The logs that are provided of each alteration that's made to a sequence offer a comprehensive account of all modifications. Let's take a closer look:

  - Editors have the option to revert to a previous version from the log if an edit isn't achieving the desired outcome. This tool is an absolute godsend for those moments when you accidentally delete something or when you want to experiment with various creative approaches. It's like having a safety net for your work, ensuring that you never lose anything valuable and allowing you to explore different ideas freely.

  - Version logs meticulously document the precise modifications that have been made, including the user responsible, the date, and the time. Editors can easily identify the person responsible for a particular change and gain insight into the project's past.

- **Comparing versions**: Editors can analyze various versions of a sequence, then view them side-by-side to observe the progression of the edit and make well-informed choices.

With the help of version logs, we can easily track the latest changes that have been made to a sequence and identify the editor responsible for them. This collaboration awareness feature enhances transparency and facilitates efficient teamwork. By implementing this system, editors can prevent any inadvertent conflicts in their work and ensure a more streamlined workflow.

Advantages for collaborators

There are several advantages of Team Project version logs for collaborators in Premiere Pro, even if they aren't directly editing the project themselves:

- **Transparency and communication**: Version logs serve as a clear and open record of the project's progress. The log is accessible to all collaborators, allowing them to review the details of any changes that have been made, including the person responsible, the timing, and the nature of the modifications. This promotes enhanced communication and comprehension among team members.

- **Version logs**: Version logs are an invaluable resource when it comes to troubleshooting problems. They provide valuable insights and help in finding solutions. If a problem occurs during the final edit, collaborators can utilize version logs to track down the issue to a particular edit and determine who's responsible.

- **Remote collaboration**: Version logs prove to be invaluable for teams spread across different locations. Even when collaborators aren't working together at the same time, they can easily stay informed about any changes that have been made to the project by referring to the version log.

Version logs for team projects play a crucial role in facilitating collaborative editing within Premiere Pro. Editors are given the power to track changes, maintain complete creative control, and effortlessly manage the workflow. In addition, they cultivate an environment of openness, effective communication, and problem-solving among team members, resulting in a streamlined and prosperous collaborative editing process.

Team Projects supports Premiere Pro and After Effects

While Team Projects offers a robust collaboration solution within Premiere Pro, it's important to understand that it doesn't directly integrate with After Effects functionalities. This section provides a breakdown of the current limitations and some alternative workflows.

Limitations of Team Projects with After Effects

While Team Projects offers a powerful solution for collaborative video editing, there are limitations when it comes to integrating After Effects directly within the collaborative workflow:

- **Direct integration limitations**: Unfortunately, Team Projects can't support After Effects compositions directly. Collaborative editing of After Effects projects isn't supported in a Team Projects environment.

- **Issues with Dynamic Link**: Unfortunately, Team Projects (as of March 2024) doesn't fully support Dynamic Link, which means that live linking of After Effects compositions within Premiere Pro timelines isn't possible. Changes that have been made to the After Effects composition within the Team Project won't automatically update in the linked Premiere Pro timeline.

Here are some alternative workflows you can implement to achieve a collaborative environment between Premiere Pro and After Effects:

- **Shared folder and version control**: Take advantage of a cloud storage solution such as Dropbox or Google Drive so that you can store your Premiere Pro project files and After Effects compositions securely. To manage changes and prevent conflicts effectively, it's crucial to incorporate a version control system such as Git. By doing this, editors can focus on their tasks, such as fine-tuning edits in Premiere Pro or creating captivating compositions in After Effects. By effectively communicating updates, they can ensure their work is integrated smoothly.

- **Export and import while providing clear communication**: With clear communication, editors can export their finished After Effects compositions as video files and import them into the Premiere Pro timeline seamlessly. Ensuring compatibility and maintaining a smooth workflow requires clear communication and well-defined export settings, such as resolution and codecs.

- **Third-party collaboration tools**: When it comes to collaboration, exploring options beyond the traditional methods can be a game-changer. Platforms such as Frame.io and Wipster offer a fresh perspective and enhanced functionality for working together seamlessly. These platforms provide the convenience of uploading After Effects compositions and Premiere Pro sequences for review and feedback in a centralized location.

With Adobe's unwavering commitment to enhancing its software, we can expect that upcoming updates to Team Projects will bring about even more seamless integration with After Effects. At the time of writing, alternative workflows serve as dependable methods for facilitating collaborative editing between these two robust applications.

Using Frame.io with Premiere Pro for review and collaboration

The Team Project format makes it easy for several users to open, edit, and save the same project and resolve problems. This makes it a natural communication layer for Frame.io, even in Beta. These technologies complement each other.

The Frame.io screen displays real-time shot and edit annotations. Syncing Frame.io and Team Projects maintains their connectivity. You should sync Frame.io edits anywhere the Team Project is open. Updates will appear in a `.aep` or `.prproj` file.

Let's take a closer look at how to use Frame.io within Premiere Pro.

Frame.io provides users with a convenient Frame.io panel located within Premiere Pro and After Effects. This can be accessed by navigating to **Window** | **Workspaces** | **Review or Window** | **Review with Frame.io**. In addition to this panel, Frame.io offers a web application and a range of collaborative features that you can use to enhance your workflow:

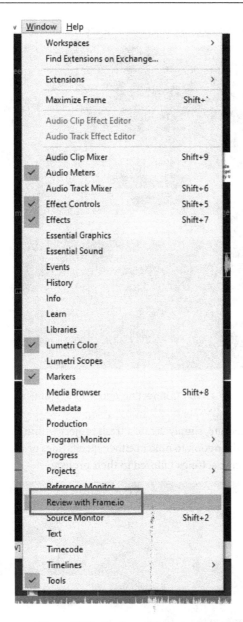

Figure 17.9 – Review with Frame.io

Within Premiere Pro and After Effects, the **Frame.io** panel allows seamless access to media, collaboration features, review sharing, timeline uploads, and presentation mode sharing. It also allows you to import comments and annotations directly into your project. To fully harness the power of Frame.io, begin your journey within the application and then seamlessly transition to the web interface to unlock a plethora of advanced features.

Connect your Adobe ID with your Frame.io account in the window that appears:

Figure 17.10 – Connecting Adobe ID to Frame.io

Once you're prepared to collaborate, simply create a fresh project within Frame.io. Within the Frame.io panel menu bar, users have the option to upload either specific files or the currently active sequence, all while customizing the specific settings tailored to their project:

Figure 17.11 – Managing projects in Frame.io

Frame.io seamlessly integrates with Premiere Pro by offering a central hub for project assets, streamlining collaboration. Upload all your footage, graphics, and audio. Invite editors and reviewers to leave frame-accurate comments and approvals directly in the cloud. Frame.io even tracks versions and facilitates communication, keeping your project on track and everyone in the loop.

Uploading to Frame.io directly from Premiere Pro

As mentioned previously, Frame.io integrates seamlessly with Premiere Pro, allowing you to upload your project for review and feedback without the need to leave the editing software. Here's how to do it:

1. Choose the sequence you wish to upload for review within your project panel.

2. Find the **Upload** button in the Frame.io panel and click it:

Figure 17.12 – The upload sequence in Frame.io

Once the upload is finished, Frame.io swiftly generates hover scrubs for your videos and thumbnails for your still images. File icons are used to identify non-media file types. Collaborators can access the sequence, leave frame-specific comments and feedback directly on the timeline, and provide approvals efficiently.

Available upload options

Frame.io offers several ways for you to get your edited sequence into the platform for collaboration:

*   Uploading the active sequence allows you to share the entire sequence you currently have open in the timeline effortlessly.

*   With the **Upload from Bin** feature, you can handpick and upload chosen clips or media files from your project bin. It's a convenient way to selectively share your content.

Uploading your project file can be a valuable option for collaborating with editors who work on different workstations. It allows you to share your entire Premiere Pro project effortlessly. The following screenshot shows the options that are available when you're uploading:

Figure 17.13 – Upload options in Frame.io

Feel free to give the uploaded file a new name if necessary:

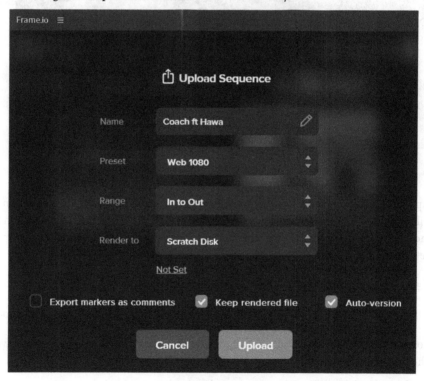

Figure 17.14 – Upload sequence settings in Frame.io

Let's take a closer look at the options shown in the preceding screenshot:

- **Name**: Choose a name for the file in Frame.io.

- **Preset**: You can choose the preferred upload format according to the requirements of your reviewer. You may consider utilizing optimized presets or personalized settings.

- **Range**: You have the option to upload the entire sequence or handpick specific **In** and **Out** points to create a more targeted review.

- **Render to**: Specify the location of the exported file on your disk.

- **Export markers at comments**: Transform your timeline markers into insightful Frame.io comments upon upload.

- **Keep rendered file**: Preserve the exported file on disk at the specified location. When you turn off the device, the files are automatically deleted after the upload finishes.

- **Auto-version**: A powerful tool that seamlessly incorporates new versions of a sequence into your Frame.io version stack.

By utilizing the **Active Sequence** feature in Premiere Pro, you can effortlessly render and upload your timeline directly to Frame.io for seamless sharing, all within the confines of the application.

Sharing and collaboration

The following screenshot shows how you can share projects for team collaboration purposes:

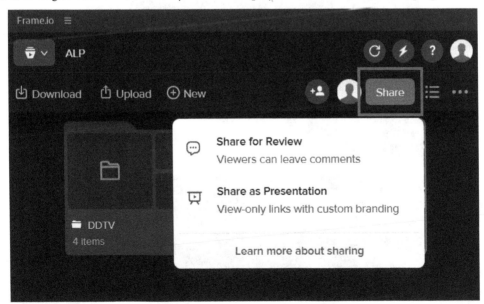

Figure 17.15 – Sharing and collaboration in Frame.io

Once you've selected the project you wish to share, click **Share for Review**. A shareable link will be automatically generated:

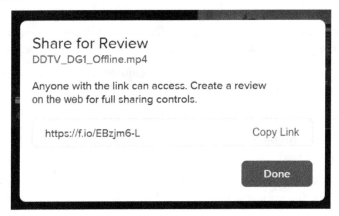

Figure 17.16 – Share for Review in Frame.io

Make sure you copy the link to the dashboard and share it offline by using the chain link icon. If you're looking to take your sharing capabilities to the next level, make your way over to Frame.io on the web.

To present your project as a presentation, select **Share as Presentation** and view the available options:

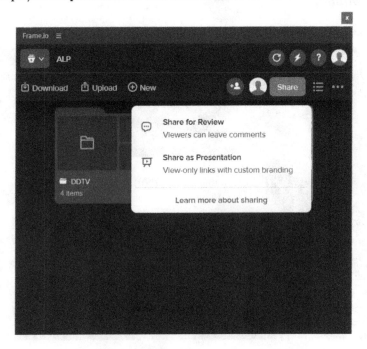

Figure 17.17 – Share as Presentation in Frame.io

The following screenshot shows what options are available:

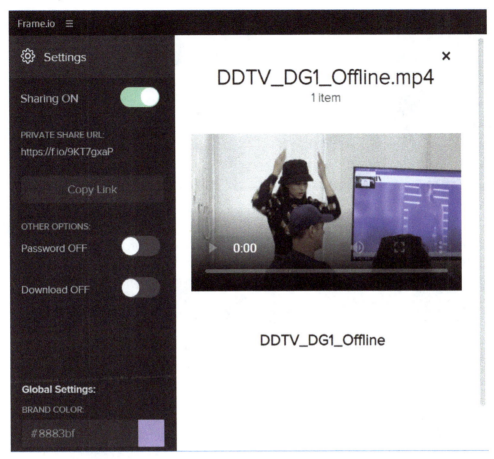

Figure 17.18 – Options available in Share as Presentation in Frame.io

Optionally, you can personalize your preferences before sharing them, making sure to fine-tune settings such as due dates, password protection, and download permissions. After configuring these settings, you can choose to generate a shareable link for reviewers by clicking **Copy Link** or directly upload the sequence to your Frame.io account by clicking **Share ON**.

Adding collaborators

You can extend an invitation to potential reviewers by providing the email addresses of the collaborators you wish to invite for review.

Here's where you can find the **Add collaborator** button:

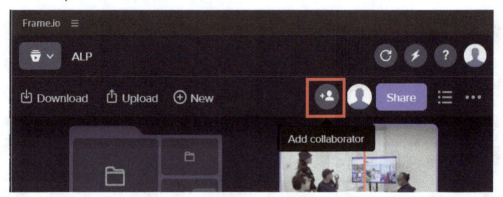

Figure 17.19 – The Add collaborator button in Frame.io

In the Frame.io panel, simply follow the steps provided to search for collaborators and then click **Add**. New contributors can be welcomed or invited to join your project:

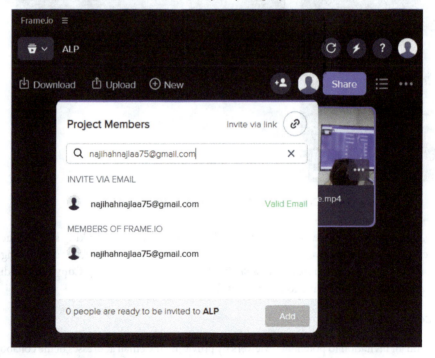

Figure 17.20 – Searching for collaborators in the Frame.io panel

By seamlessly integrating Frame.io into Premiere Pro, your collaborative editing workflow will be taken to new heights. Say goodbye to inefficiencies and hello to a more productive feedback loop for all your projects.

Traditional video editing workflows often meant juggling multiple project files, version control headaches, and limited collaboration options. To address these challenges, Premiere Pro introduced Productions, a powerful tool that streamlines organization and collaboration for complex video projects. But what exactly is a Production in Premiere Pro? Let's break it down.

Enhanced organization and efficiency

Here's how Productions elevate your editing experience:

- **Divide and conquer large projects**: Productions allow you to carefully break down a feature film into reels or scenes, giving each segment its own dedicated project. This approach ensures that project files are kept organized and speeds up the process of opening and saving them.

- **Efficiency gains**: You can achieve this by focusing on specific sections of the project, rather than loading the entire thing. This allows for streamlined workflows and eliminates unnecessary burdens.

- **Eliminate repetition**: Bid farewell to the tedious task of constantly duplicating clips or sequences. Productions allow for effortless element reuse across different projects within the Production.

A seamless collaboration experience

Here's how Productions elevate teamwork:

- By unlocking the power of shared local storage synergy, a multitude of editors can seamlessly collaborate on separate projects within a single Production, all thanks to their access to a shared storage drive.

- You can secure projects for peace of mind by safeguarding against unintended modifications while a colleague is actively engaged in a project. Nevertheless, editors can access clips for reference purposes.

- In the world of centralized asset management, certain elements play a crucial role. These elements, such as title sequences and sound effects, are stored in a central location within the Production. This centralized location allows easy access for all editors, ensuring that consistency is maintained and workflows are streamlined.

Unveiling the depths

With offline editing, you have the freedom to make changes to your work even when you're not connected to the internet. Productions are stored locally, allowing for seamless editing without any disruptions.

Perfectly complementing traditional projects, Productions are a match made in heaven for those seeking to tackle large-scale endeavors or engage in fruitful collaborations. Feel free to stick with regular projects for those smaller, individual tasks.

Productions in Premiere Pro

Productions offers a versatile and adaptable framework for efficiently managing workflows across multiple projects. Productions allows you to organize and coordinate large and intricate workflows, ensuring optimal efficiency and fostering collaboration through the utilization of shared local storage. Assets can be easily shared between projects within a Production, eliminating the need for creating duplicate files.

Editors can group related projects, which can greatly enhance organization and efficiency. When it comes to tackling large projects such as documentaries, films, or TV shows, one effective approach is to divide them into reels or episodes. This allows multiple editors to come together and work collaboratively, each following their own preferred workflow. The key to seamless collaboration is a shared storage network, which ensures that everyone has access to the necessary files and resources.

The foundational structure of Productions is built upon the well-established Premiere Pro project format. Productions bring an extra dimension, connecting the various projects and assets they contain. Within a Production, a project retains all the attributes of a `.pproj` file. Existing Premiere Pro projects can be seamlessly incorporated into a Production. If necessary, you have the option to remove them and utilize them as independent Premiere Pro projects.

Now that you understand the foundation of Productions, let's delve into the specific advantages they offer for both individual editors and teams.

What advantages can Productions offer?

So far, we've explored how Productions can transform Premiere Pro into a collaborative hub. But what specific advantages do they offer for both individual editors and teams working on video projects? Here's a breakdown of the key benefits:

- **You can manage multi-project workflows**: For those with extensive or intricate workflows, Productions can be broken down into more manageable segments by utilizing the familiar Premiere Pro project format. Productions seamlessly connect projects, transforming them into integral components of a larger workflow, ensuring impeccable organization and optimal efficiency for your projects and assets.

- **You can keep everything organized and synchronized**: By employing media referencing across projects, you can reuse assets within your production efficiently, eliminating the need for unnecessary duplicates. This allows you to maintain a sense of agility and efficiency in handling each project.

- **You can utilize the Production panel**: With the introduction of the new **Production** panel in Premiere Pro, users now have a centralized hub to oversee and control their multi-project workflows. It's like having a command center at your fingertips, allowing you to seamlessly manage all your projects with ease. Once any projects are added to the `Productions` folder, they become an integral part of the production. Regardless of whether you're using macOS or

Windows, any modifications you make to your computer's storage will be immediately reflected in Premiere Pro. Similarly, any alterations that are made within Premiere Pro will be applied to the files on your disk. Productions ensures that everything remains perfectly synchronized.

- **You can design for collaboration**: With the help of shared local storage, a group of editors can collaborate on various projects simultaneously, enhancing the efficiency of the production process. With Project Locking, your valuable work remains safe and secure. Your colleagues can still access and reference your project, but they won't be able to alter anything until you've finished your edit. This feature provides you with peace of mind and ensures the integrity of your work. Every project within a Production is equipped with identical settings, including scratch disks. Having preview files accessible to all editors working on a project guarantees seamless playback and saves valuable time for the entire team.

- **You can control your media**: With Productions, you're given complete autonomy over your content. Your projects and assets have the freedom to reside solely in your local storage. Everything remains off the cloud until you upload it. With the absence of an internet connection, you can complete all tasks at hand with ease.

Setting up a Production

Before starting a Production or joining one that's been set up by a colleague, ensure Premiere is ready. Follow these steps:

1. Uncheck the following settings in **Preferences** | **Media**;

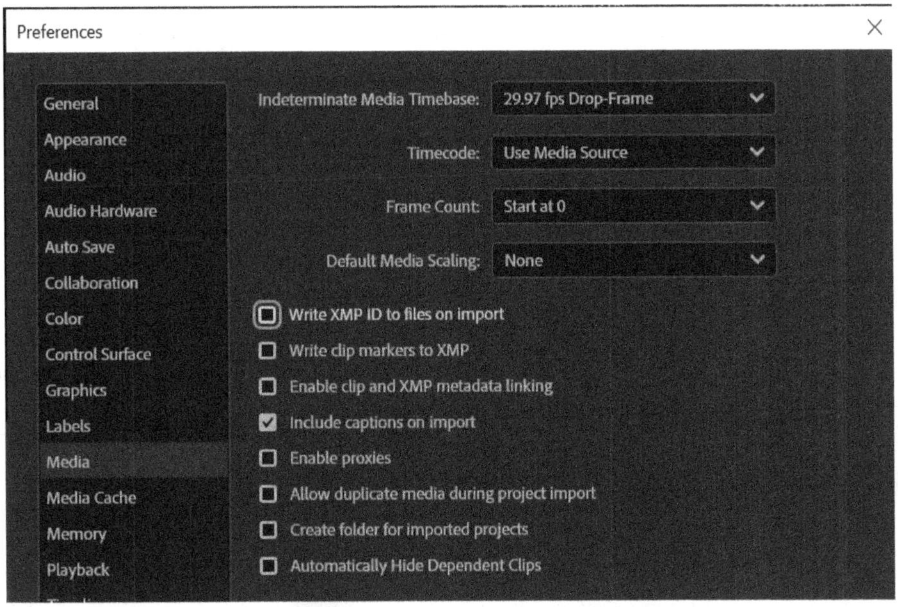

Figure 17.21 – Setting up Production in Preferences

2. Configure your desired preferences by accessing the **Edit | Preferences (Windows) or Premiere Pro | Preferences (macOS)** dialog box.

3. In **Preferences | Media**, deselect the following options:

    *   **Write XMP ID to files on import**

    *   **Write clip markers to XMP**

    *   **Enable clip and XMP metadata linking**

    *   Select **Collaboration** and **Project Locking** from the **Options** window sidebar. Your username will help people identify closed projects for editing. Save your changes by clicking **OK**.

    Keep in mind that adjusting preferences in Premiere Pro for collaboration and project locking purposes will primarily impact how multiple users can work on the same project.

    Next, you'll learn how to configure your preference for collaboration.

4. In **Preferences | Collaboration**, do the following:

    *   Ensure that the option for project locking is selected

    *   Choose a captivating username that will leave a lasting impression on others as they delve into your project

5. To modify your settings, navigate to the **Window** menu and select **Workspaces**. From there, uncheck the **Import Workspaces from Projects** option.

By ensuring that your workspace remains consistent, you can avoid any disruptions that are caused by opening projects that have been worked on by different editors.

Using Productions

Premiere Pro's Productions takes project organization and collaboration to a new level. Instead of a single, monolithic project file, Productions acts as a central hub that contains multiple, focused sub-projects. This allows you to break down a large film into edits, sound design, and motion graphics projects, each with its own editor working simultaneously. Productions also streamlines teamwork by allowing assets such as clips and sequences to be shared across these sub-projects. This eliminates the need for cumbersome hand-offs and ensures everyone has access to the latest version of each element.

Unlike individual project files, you can only open one production at a time. Here's how:

1. Select **Open Production** from Premiere's file menu to start a production.

2. Click **Explore**, then choose **Production Folder**.

3. Every project and folder in your production will appear in the **Production** panel. Open any project file to see Premiere's standard interface.

4. Reopen the **Production** panel for cross-project navigation. It can be found in the **Window** menu (primary toolbar).

Figure 17.22 shows the **Production** panel in Premiere Pro:

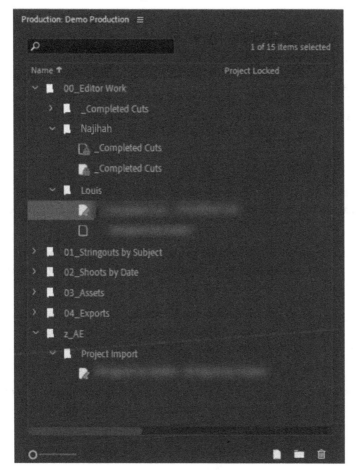

Figure 17.22 – The Production panel

5. Project icon variations indicate project status in the **Production** panel:

    *   White icons denote open projects

    *   A gray outline signifies a closed project

    *   A green pen icon means project write access

    *   A red lock means someone else edited a project

6. Double-click an unlocked project to edit it. Holding *Option/Alt* while launching a project opens it in read-only mode. On the other hand, double-clicking a locked project opens it in read-only mode. In read-only mode, you can do the following:

    -   Insert clips and sequences into the source monitor

    -   Watch the program monitor/timeline sequences

    -   Copy elements to editable projects

    -   Export read-only projects

Remember, project locking is used for managing access during editing while exporting is the final output process after edits are complete. We'll look at this next.

Work recovery and importing projects

Sometimes, you need to incorporate external projects such as auto-save into your production. If you copy a project into a production folder with File Explorer, it will cause issues until you remove it and import it properly.

Thankfully, the process is simple! Right-click anywhere in the **Production** panel and choose **Add to Production**. Premiere will scan and copy an external project into production. Project addition ensures media management and smooth operations.

If you're looking for an in-depth guide on Productions, I highly recommend checking out the *Premiere Pro Best Practices & Workflow Guide*. It provides a comprehensive overview of the best practices and workflows for long-form episodic projects. You can find it here: `https://helpx.adobe.com/premiere-pro/using/long-form-episodic-best-practices.html`.

From this, we can see that Productions provides a robust project management framework within Premiere Pro that promotes efficiency, enhances organization, and enables seamless collaboration for extensive projects or teams.

Summary

This chapter unpacked the collaborative features that are available in Premiere Pro, equipping you to streamline your video editing workflow across geographical distances. We started with project locking, a crucial tool that prevents multiple editors from making conflicting changes simultaneously. By temporarily locking a project, you can ensure everyone is working on the same version and prevent editors from accidentally overwriting each other's edits. Once edits reach the collaboration stage, unlocking the project allows other team members to jump in and contribute.

Then, we looked at Frame.io, which Premiere Pro integrates with to enhance collaboration further. This eliminates the cumbersome process of exporting video files for review. Team members can directly provide feedback and annotations within Premiere Pro itself, saving time and ensuring everyone is on the same page. Annotations are automatically reflected as markers in the timeline, making it easy for editors to address feedback efficiently.

After, we considered Productions. For projects with a massive volume of assets and multiple versions, Productions offers a centralized management solution. Imagine a project with numerous video clips, graphics, and audio files. Productions keeps everything organized in a single location, accessible to all collaborators. Version control allows you to track changes and revert to previous versions if needed, fostering a sense of security and flexibility.

By combining project locking, Frame.io integration, and Productions, Premiere Pro empowers you and your team to collaborate effectively on video projects, regardless of location. These features transform Premiere Pro from a powerful editing tool into a collaborative hub that fosters seamless communication and efficient project management for geographically dispersed teams.

At this stage, you have the tools you need to optimize your editing process and work seamlessly with others on extensive projects in Premiere Pro. With a deep understanding of these features, you're now ready to take on ambitious projects such as feature films, episodic series, or any other lengthy endeavor in Premiere Pro. Your newfound efficiency and collaborative skills will be invaluable in bringing your vision to life!

In the next and final chapter, you'll learn how to integrate AI video features into Premiere Pro. We'll cover how AI tools enhance editing efficiency, how to use AI models to generate more clips, and how to improve content quality. We'll also discuss the potential future impact of AI on video production workflows, helping creators leverage these advancements to elevate their projects.

18
AI-Powered Video Editing

The combination of **artificial intelligence** (**AI**) with digital media has ushered in a transformational era, changing the landscape of content creation. Premiere Pro seamlessly integrates AI capabilities to improve productivity, creativity, and overall production quality.

AI, with its learning, reasoning, and problem-solving abilities, has the potential to transform many elements of video editing. Premiere Pro leverages **machine learning** (**ML**) algorithms to provide a set of AI-powered features that expedite processes, expand creative possibilities, and produce remarkable results. AI has the potential to alter the function of the video editor by intelligently automating monotonous activities and creating totally new creative components.

This chapter digs into the complex link between AI and Premiere Pro, focusing on the various AI-powered capabilities that have been built into the program. Special emphasis will be placed on AI-powered audio augmentation capabilities, which have the potential to transform sound design and post-production. Furthermore, the integration of the Adobe Firefly generative AI model will be explored, shedding light on its potential to generate creative assets, such as images, videos, and graphics, directly within the editing environment. This chapter also examines the complexities of AI in Premiere Pro, exploring its skills, uses, and the potential consequences of this potent technology. The goal of this chapter is to present an overview of several AI capabilities, such as audio augmentation and generative AI, and to examine their potential influence on video editing workflows and creative opportunities.

In this chapter, we're going to cover the following main topics:

- Harnessing AI in Adobe Premiere Pro
- Understanding AI in Premiere Pro
- AI-powered features in Premiere Pro
- Third-party generative AI models with Adobe Firefly
- Future exploration with third-party models
- AI-powered audio enhancement in Premiere Pro

Harnessing AI in Adobe Premiere Pro

Premiere Pro is equipped with AI capabilities that streamline intricate operations and enhance the efficiency of video editing. Furthermore, with the imminent arrival of generative AI tools this year, the future appears more promising than ever.

In April 2024, Adobe showcased cutting-edge generative AI advancements in Adobe Premiere Pro. These improvements will revolutionize video creation and production processes, offering professional editors additional creative opportunities to match the fast-paced nature of video production. Premiere Pro introduced advanced generative AI features this year, allowing users to optimize video editing processes by effortlessly manipulating scenes, such as adding or deleting objects and expanding clips. The implementation of these new editing workflows will be facilitated by a novel video model, which will be added to the existing lineup of Adobe Firefly models, including image, vector, design, and text effects. Adobe is actively advancing the development of Firefly AI models in areas where it possesses extensive knowledge and skill, such as photography, video, audio, and 3D. These models will be seamlessly integrated into Creative Cloud and Adobe Express.

In the future, professional video editors may be able to use Premiere Pro's integrated video-generating models from **OpenAI**, **Runway**, and **Pika Labs** to create B-roll that can be edited into their projects. It also demonstrates how a shot may be extended by a few seconds by using Pika Labs in conjunction with the **Generative Extend** tool.

In the next section, we'll look at how ML algorithms evaluate video material and automate time-consuming chores to give you a better understanding of the potential of AI in Premiere Pro.

Understanding AI in Premiere Pro

AI in video editing refers to the utilization of ML algorithms to analyze and comprehend video footage. These algorithms analyze large quantities of data, detecting patterns and trends that allow software to carry out activities that often need human involvement. For example, the AI in Premiere Pro can evaluate a video sequence and identify scene changes, transitions, and potential audio problems without human intervention.

It is important to note that Adobe has already attempted to provide AI improvements to its consumers before venturing into generative AI. For several years, Adobe has been engaged in research and development of AI solutions through its **Adobe Sensei** platform. Even if you are unfamiliar with Sensei, it is quite probable that you have seen its integrations throughout several Creative Cloud apps. Within Premiere Pro, we have observed the integration of AI capabilities that have significantly enhanced the efficiency of my editing processes over a considerable period.

Core AI technologies

ML is the foundational technology that supports many AI capabilities in Premiere Pro. Through the process of training algorithms on extensive datasets, the software acquires the ability to identify recurring trends and generate forecasts. For instance, the auto-cropping tool in Premiere Pro uses ML to ascertain the most suitable crop for various aspect ratios.

Deep learning is a specific branch of ML that uses artificial neural networks to analyze intricate data, such as photos and movies. Premiere Pro utilizes AI-driven effects, such as Morph Cut, that employ deep learning techniques to meticulously examine and perfectly merge video frames.

The AI-powered capabilities that Premiere Pro provides, such as object manipulation, scene identification, and generative tools that help speed up the editing process, will be covered in more detail in the section that follows.

AI-powered features in Premiere Pro

The new generative AI workflows will be powered by a new video model for Adobe Firefly. Several cutting-edge AI-powered capabilities are being added to Adobe Premiere Pro to improve the editing experience. Here are some of the main features that have been revealed:

- **Scene Edit Detection**: Editors can use this to find cuts in previously altered video
- **Object Selection**: With the help of this function, editors may quickly include or exclude items from their video
- **Generative Extend**: This effortlessly append frames to increase the duration of clips, facilitating precise timing of changes and seamless integration of transitions
- **Speech to Text with transcription**: AI-driven technologies are improving transcription by giving text output for voiceovers or conversations that are more accurate and automatically creating captions
- **Enhanced Speech**: Designed to dramatically improve the clarity and quality of dialogue audio, this is a boon for video editors dealing with noisy or subpar audio recordings
- **Content Credentials**: With the help of this feature, content creators may accurately credit their work and cultivate audience faith in the legitimacy of their material

These AI-powered tools are intended to streamline the editing process, reduce workload, and free up editors time to concentrate on ideas while maintaining the quality of content. The Scene Edit Detection tool in Premiere Pro will be discussed in the following section. You will discover how AI is used to automatically detect cuts and speed up the editing process.

Scene Edit Detection

Scene Edit Detection in Premiere Pro uses ML and AI to instantly locate original edit locations in video files, considerably speeding up the editing process. This convenient feature, readily available on a timeline, will automatically divide lengthy movies, such as B-roll stringouts, into their own pieces. The software can generate modifications, include separate subclips to a storage container, and insert markers during transitions between scenes.

Understanding Scene Edit Detection in Premiere Pro

This function provides three primary capabilities: applying cuts, building a bin of subclips, and placing clip markers at each cut point. This adaptability accommodates various editing requirements.

To apply Scene Edit Detection in Adobe Premiere Pro, follow these detailed steps:

1. Choose the video clip that you wish to analyze for scene edits in the timeline. You may choose to divide this clip into parts according to identified scene changes.

2. In the timeline, right-click on the clip you've chosen.

3. Click the context menu and choose **Scene Edit Detection…**. This option is available in the latest versions of Adobe Premiere Pro.

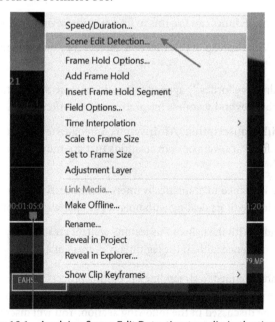

Figure 18.1 – Applying Scene Edit Detection to a clip in the timeline

4. Next, a **Scene Edit Detection** pop-up box will appear with configurations for detection options, as shown in the following screenshot:

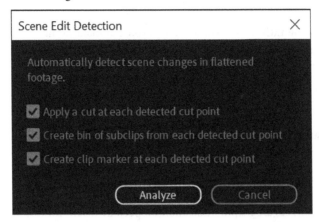

Figure 18.2 – The Scene Edit Detection pop-up window

There will be a dialog window with three options:

- **Apply a cut at every detected cut point**: Selecting this option will insert cuts into the timeline at each detected scene change.

- **Create bin of subclips from each detected cut point**: Select this option if you wish to arrange the detected cuts into a different bin. Every cut will be stored in the bin as a distinct clip.

- **Create clip marker at each detected cut point**: Select this option if you would rather mark the cut spots that have been detected than cut the clip. Instead of cutting with each scene change, this will insert markers.

1. After you've made your selections, click **Analyze**. The program will start evaluating the footage for scene alterations. This process may take some time, particularly with lengthy clips. You may notice a progress indication throughout this analysis.

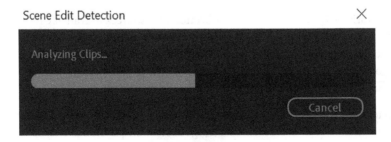

Figure 18.3 – Analyzing the clip for scene changes

2. Once the analysis is finished, Premiere Pro will apply the cuts, produce the subclips, or place the markers, depending on what you choose to do. You may now go through the timeline to examine how the footage has been separated or tagged.

3. Following the **Scene Edit Detection** workflow, you can make additional edits to the clips or markers. You may remove undesired cuts, prolong clips, or utilize the markers as reference points while editing.

4. If you created a bin of subclips, you can find it on the **Project** panel. This structure will make it easier to handle your film, especially when working with B-roll or other resources.

By following these instructions, you can effectively use Scene Edit Detection in Adobe Premiere Pro, saving time and improving your editing productivity.

Advantages of editing with Adobe Premiere Pro

When editing videos, markers are helpful indications, especially when working with B-roll material. They facilitate the editing process by effectively classifying and highlighting key footage.

Markers can help you traverse your project timeline more easily while editing by highlighting specific portions or places of interest in your video. This tool is very useful for intricate modifications. B-roll film may be managed more effectively and accessed more easily when it is arranged into bins. Time is saved, and the editing process is improved overall, with this structure.

It is anticipated that the use of AI technology in editing software will increase its effectiveness and usefulness. Future iterations of these upgrades should provide more beneficial features for consumers.

As you will see in the next section, Adobe has released new generative AI capabilities that allow users to access a multitude of new features without having to give up on the workflows they are used to using in Premiere Pro. These capabilities are powered by a range of third-party models and Adobe Firefly. Now that we have explored the capabilities of Adobe Firefly, let's delve into the wider world of third-party generative AI models.

Third-party generative AI models with Adobe Firefly

In the age of generative AI, a completely new collection of resources is available for discovery and integration into your work process. For this reason, Adobe has integrated Firefly, a collection of generative AI models, directly into its products. The Firefly models were specifically constructed to cater to the categories and use cases that clients prioritize. Furthermore, these models were meticulously designed to ensure your safety and suitability for commercial applications.

Though your preferences and the available resources still have an impact on the final product, generative AI has already shown itself to be a novel and amazing source of inspiration. Firefly refines the output that the AI model generates, incorporates it into your larger project, and continues working until you realize your vision. Whether utilizing Generative Fill in Photoshop, text effects in Express, Firefly variation generation in GenStudio, or other tools and capabilities, the great bulk of content creation with Adobe Firefly has happened inside Adobe's flagship apps.

The next section will provide a detailed explanation of the **smart masking** feature in Adobe Firefly, demonstrating how it can be used to remove objects from videos with ease.

Adobe Firefly video model – Object Selection with smart masking

The Object Selection Tool is something you've presumably used in Photoshop. This application makes it simple to select items in a picture with a single click by automatically highlighting them.

Figure 18.4 – Example of the Object Selection Tool in Photoshop

The functionality of smart masking in Premiere Pro appears to be similar; however, it may be more comparable to Roto Brush 3.0 in After Effects. The eventual outcome within Premiere Pro is expected to fall halfway between the capabilities of Photoshop and After Effects. However, the essential point is that it should enable convenient concealment and monitoring of items without the need to exit Premiere Pro. Not only does it save time, but it also integrates compositing tools directly into your timeline.

This is quite significant. Things getting accidentally left in the frame when filming, such as boom mics, is a typical occurrence. While Premiere Pro has always provided basic compositing tools and methods for removing undesired items, none of them are as sophisticated, user-friendly, or quick as what is shown in the following screenshot:

Figure 18.5 – The object masking feature in Premiere Pro

Premiere Pro's AI-powered smart masking makes it easier to quickly and precisely remove objects between frames, which improves editing accuracy and productivity. Selecting objects in motion is now faster and easier than ever thanks to new AI-based smart masking and tracking technologies. You may now easily add set dressings, such as a painting or a lifelike flower arrangement on a desk, change moving objects in a shot, and remove undesired elements, such as boom mics or stray coffee cups, when combined with the **object selection** and **object removal** tools. While it has greatly improved in recent revisions, it is crucial to note that it may not always work flawlessly in every situation. Experiment with different settings and strategies to get the required level of accuracy and precision.

One of the most interesting new features of the Adobe Firefly video model is the ability to add objects to films, which opens up new creative possibilities for improving and editing footage. Let's look at the following section.

Adobe Firefly video model – object selection

Filmmakers usually prefer to delete elements in a photo rather than add them. However, there is a lot of merit to the idea that generative AI may be used to alter a watch's dial or an actor's attire, for instance—especially if Adobe manages to figure out how to control the created content's unique design components. Here's where you can find the **Add object** feature in Premiere Pro:

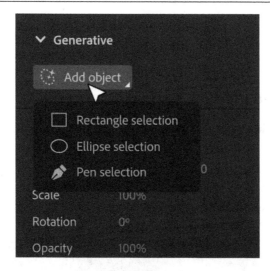

Figure 18.6 – Object selection new feature in Premiere Pro

Using the **Pen selection** tool, make a selection, then create a prompt and include whatever you can think of. The Adobe Firefly video model is used to build the extra item. As shown in the following screenshot, a pop-up box will appear and allow you to add a prompt to add an object based on your object selection:

Figure 18.7 – The Add object feature in Premiere Pro

The **Add object** feature in Adobe Firefly represents a major advancement in video editing, as it allows users to insert new elements into existing footage. Unlike other cleanup tools, this tool might be able to change things in a scene, such as watch dials or clothes. This technology is still being worked on, but it has the potential to make film creation much more creative and efficient.

The Adobe Firefly video model's creative versatility for storytelling and visual effects is further enhanced by its capacity to stretch video sequences beyond their original parameters. Let's look at the following section.

Adobe Firefly video model – Generative Extend

In many cases, a subject's face may need to remain on screen for longer than the original footage permits. Perhaps the individual blinks, continues to speak, sneezes, or does something else entirely.

The go-to method, which has produced a mixed bag of results over the years, is to slow down the final 60% of the interview and switch the clip's interpolation to optical flow. While it usually goes unnoticed, it does need several stages to complete and may produce odd outcomes. The following screenshot shows footage being generated using the Generative Extend feature:

Figure 18.8 – The Generative Extend feature in Premiere Pro

The new Generative Extend AI technology has the potential to completely remove the workaround procedure and may be used for a variety of shots, not only interviews. The final product would enable editors to maintain control over the pacing of an edit by utilizing perfect shots that could have otherwise been rendered useless by being cut too short. You will always have the precise media you want for flawless editing without sacrificing quality thanks to the Generative Extend tool, which dynamically adds frames to film.

Premiere Pro 2025 includes Generative Extend, an AI-powered tool for extending clips, filling gaps, and smoothing transitions. It produces new frames based on current video, which helps to preserve narrative flow and saves editing time.

The following screenshot shows how to extend footage using the Generative Extend tool:

1. In the timeline, click on the video clip you want to extend. This could be a clip that needs lengthening to cover a gap or one that requires smoother transitions.

2. Right-click the chosen clip. Look for and pick the option labeled **Generative Extend Tool** from the toolbar.

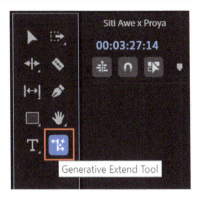

Figure 18.9 – Generative Extend Tool in Premiere Pro

3.   Simply stretch the clip farther in time, and Adobe Firefly will artificially extend it. The greatest thing is that the change is practically invisible; if you use it unexpectedly, you won't even notice. The following screenshot shows the Adobe Firefly generating to extend the original clip:

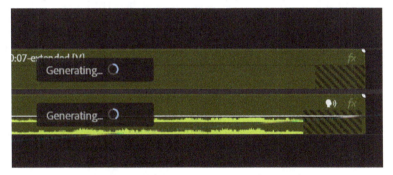

Figure 18.10 – Generative Extend Tool in Premiere Pro

4.   After applying, you may wish to make other tweaks, such as cutting or changing the time of the extended clip to better match your project's flow. The extended frames of the clip will be labeled as **AI-generated**, as shown in *Figure 18.11*:

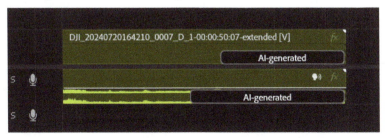

Figure 18.11 – Generative Extend in Premiere Pro

Run through your revised timeline to confirm that everything runs well. Once you're finished, export your project as normal.

Important considerations

When using Generative Extend, it's essential to keep a few key points in mind. Video clips that perform best typically have minimal contextual shifts, such as those featuring fast camera sweeps. Additionally, audio samples with consistent noise or ambient sounds lend themselves well to this feature.

Generative Extend allows you to add up to 2 seconds of video footage and extend audio elements for up to 10 seconds. This means you can effectively lengthen your video segments by 2 seconds and stretch audio components, such as room tone or background sounds, by an impressive 10 seconds.

Currently, Generative Extend supports only landscape videos in the *16:9* aspect ratio, specifically the *1920 x 1080* and *1280 x 720* resolutions. Unfortunately, vertical videos and other aspect ratios commonly used on social media platforms are not supported at this time. We recognize the growing importance of vertical formats and are actively evaluating them for potential enhancements in future updates. For further details, please refer to the official Adobe documentation here (`https://helpx.adobe.com/premiere-pro/using/generative-extend-faq.html/`).

Object Selection may be used to extend the limits of a video frame in a manner akin to that of Generative Fill in Photoshop. Everybody has seen circumstances where a source material, such as an interview, is edited too closely to our preference. Consider how pleasant it would be to give your video's sides, top, and bottom a bit more breathing room—Premiere Pro may struggle to fill longer spaces with content. The current models may start to behave strangely after a while. So, for now, it's best to use them for shorter applications, such as a few seconds.

We'll look at how Adobe's Content Credentials may help resolve issues with AI-generated content and enhance process transparency in the creative process in the following section.

Improving credibility via Content Credentials

In terms of reality versus fiction and intellectual property, AI has unlocked a lot of doors. Adobe is once again setting the standard for the industry by proposing a solution to allay worries about created content.

Adobe has committed to adding **Content Credentials**, a kind of open source nutrition label, to AI assets generated in its Creative Cloud services under the Content Authenticity Initiative. You will be able to observe the creation process of content, including which particular AI models were employed. As generative AI spreads throughout the creative industries, this is a significant step in the right direction.

The purpose of Premiere Pro's Content Credentials function is to improve the veracity and integrity of edited material. It enables creators to include metadata with their films, which includes details on the work's author, place of origin, and any editing-related changes. As soon as you apply Content Credentials to a Premiere Pro project, you'll get the following message:

Figure 18.12 – Applying Content Credentials in Premiere Pro

They promote transparency in material sharing, reliability, and the prevention of disinformation. Creators can provide their identity and contact information to facilitate relationships with viewers.

When exporting from Premiere Pro or Media Encoder using Adobe AI-generated assets, you are informed that Content Credentials will be included in supported formats, such as **MP4**, **MOV**, **AVI**, **WAV**, **MP3**, **JPEG**, **PNG**, and **TIFF**. However, Adobe cannot guarantee that all publishing platforms will accept these credentials.

To add Content Credentials, choose a sequence including AI-generated assets, then navigate to **File | Export | Media**. The **Content Credentials:** stamp will appear under **Output** of the **Export** window in Premiere Pro.

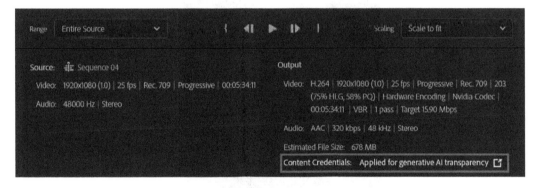

Figure 18.13 – Content Credentials applied in Premiere Pro

When you export media using Adobe Media Encoder, the **Content Credentials:** stamp appears in **Output Preview**.

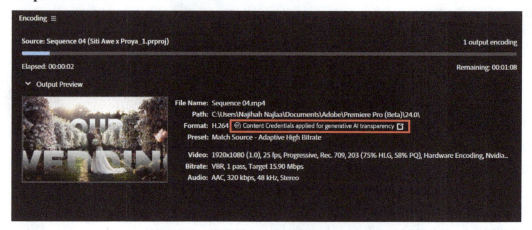

Figure 18.14 – Content Credentials applied in Media Encoder

As you can see in the project's details, you should be clear about whether AI was employed, and which model was used in the construction of the media.

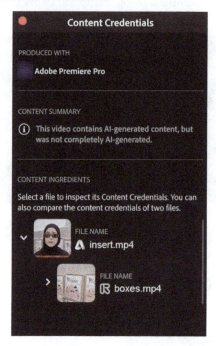

Figure 18.15 – Content Credentials is now available in Premiere Pro

By assisting viewers in understanding how the material they are seeing was created, this feature seeks to promote confidence in digital media. In an era of false information, it can be especially useful since it enables creators to provide crucial information about the process of making a movie, such as the use of AI technologies and any major changes made to the original material.

Content Credentials attach additional information during export or download, which is kept in tamper-evident metadata. This appears alongside the content, allowing users to see both content and context. Multiple Content Credentials can accumulate a version history over time, which helps with trust choices.

A thorough explanation of the **Properties** panel's features and how to effectively manage a project's settings will be given in the next section.

The Properties panel

The **Properties** panel resembles the **After Effects** feature that many motion designers have come to adore. The **Properties** panel lets you see settings and controls in the context of the work you're doing at the moment. The buttons on this panel are easy to get to when you need them because it was made with ease of use in mind. The following screenshot shows the new **Properties** panel in Premiere Pro:

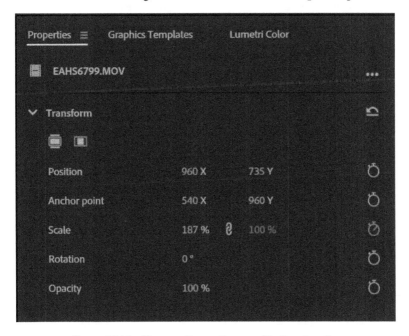

Figure 18.16 – The new Properties panel in Premiere Pro

What we're witnessing today is only the tip of the iceberg when it comes to AI filmmaking, which will elevate the position of an editor to unprecedented heights. Assignments will change and the number of hats editors can don will only get larger.

To be honest, this is nothing new when you consider the history of editing. With these new AI capabilities, it will be even simpler to get over the tiresome duties that used to get in the way of creative endeavors.

The potential of enhancing Premiere Pro's AI capabilities through third-party plugins and integrations, including style transfer functions, will be discussed in the following section.

Future exploration with third-party models

Although most AI elements in Premiere Pro prioritize user-friendliness, the software still provides sophisticated functionalities tailored for proficient editors. Although not an essential component of Premiere Pro, third-party plugins and integrations can facilitate style transfer functionalities.

Generative AI, an emerging technology, has the capability to generate novel video content by utilizing provided cues. Premiere Pro's new AI-powered tools, such as object selection/removal and generative extension, will change video editing using Adobe Firefly and third-party models. This feature is driven by generative AI, making it easier to add, remove, and extend frames for precise editing.

With text prompts, you may now easily add or change objects in footage with the new Adobe Firefly video model, increasing creative possibilities. Editors can now choose the ideal model for their work from the upcoming sub-sections.

Next, let's explore how Adobe's integration with OpenAI's Sora can enhance Premiere Pro's capabilities, particularly in areas such as scene object creation and distraction reduction.

Future exploration – OpenAI

Adobe incorporates third-party AI solutions, such as **Sora** from **OpenAI**, into Premiere Pro. This integration utilizes the Firefly AI paradigm to enhance capabilities, such as scene object creation and distraction reduction. By using a simple text prompt to make B-roll for any scene, you can get a variety of new scenes created by AI. The Adobe Firefly Video Model will be used to turn text into video. A lot of businesses have become very popular with their products in the past year. Every single one seems to do things a little differently, and they all have their own pros and cons.

You can see how to use OpenAI for prompting in the following screenshot:

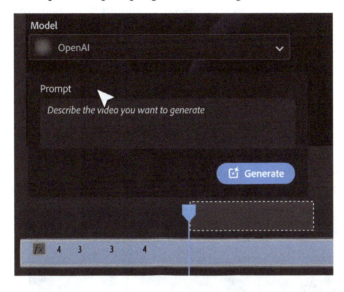

Figure 18.17 – OpenAI model in Premiere Pro

OpenAI has showcased its Sora model's ability to produce realistic videos in response to text prompts. Sora is being utilized to generate video in Premiere Pro, as shown in the following screenshot:

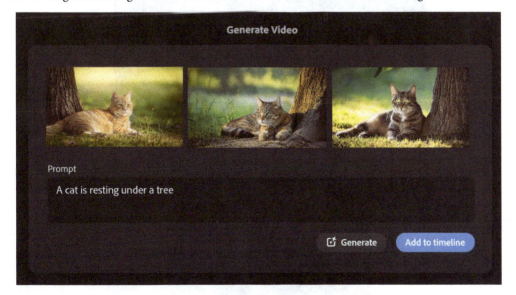

Figure 18.18 – Using a text prompt to generate video in Premiere Pro

Enhance the program by including AI-driven functionality, such as the capability to automatically insert AI-generated items into certain areas of a movie or eliminate distractions from a scene without requiring laborious manual intervention by a video editor.

Next, let's explore how Premiere Pro can be used in conjunction with third-party AI tools, such as Runway, to create and edit AI-generated footage.

Future exploration – Runway

Premiere Pro users will now be able to edit and work with live-action video taken on regular cameras, as well as AI footage. The goal is to give Premiere Pro users new options, such as extending shots with models such as Pika or producing B-roll for their projects using Sora or Runway AI. Sora generates options based on straightforward text prompts, as you can see in the following screenshot:

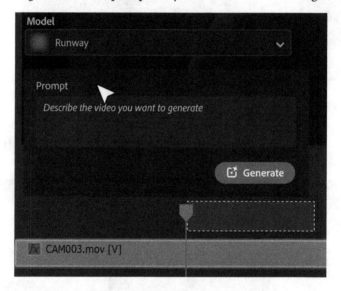

Figure 18.19 – Prompting text using the Runway model in Premiere Pro

You can use video generation models from OpenAI and Runway in Premiere Pro to create B-roll that you can easily edit into your project and quickly add to your timeline, as illustrated in the following screenshot:

Figure 18.20 – Adding a prompted clip to the timeline

Consider capturing a video of an actor fleeing from a monster and then producing the monster with AI – no props or costumes are required, but both pieces of footage are available and are integrated into the same video file in the same editor. The same is true for animation made using more established technologies, or hand-drawn frames, which might be blended with AI footage that matches it in the same Premiere Pro file.

Next, let's see how the Generative Extend tool in Pika Labs can be used to make a shot last a little longer by generating a new video clip.

Future exploration – Pika

Pika Labs is well known for its picture-generating abilities. It can be used to create stunning and realistic graphics from written descriptions. The addition of a native connection with Premiere Pro bridges the gap to endless discovery and invention. You can now use Generative Extend with Pika Labs, as shown in the following screenshot:

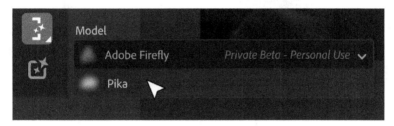

Figure 18.21 – Pika powering Generative Extend to make a scene flow better

The Generative Extend tool may be used to extend shots by creating whole new frames at the beginning and end of a clip. Use the extra material to fine-tune edits, pause a shot for an extra beat, or add a few frames to cover a transition. Simply click and drag for the perfect edit:

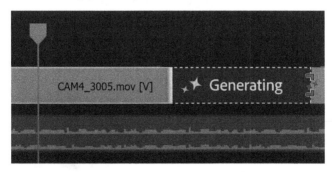

Figure 18.22 – Use of the Generative Extend tool to create new frames in the timeline

The Pika Labs model quickly generates a new video clip and adds it to the timeline. Here's the extended clip:

Figure 18.23 –The new extended frames of the clip in the timeline

AI is undergoing rapid development, and its influence on the field of video editing will continue to expand. Anticipate progress in the areas of instantaneous editing, automated narrative creation, and AI-powered optimization for many platforms. With the increasing sophistication of AI, it is probable that it will assume further creative responsibilities, allowing editors to concentrate on more advanced storytelling and visual expression.

Nevertheless, it is crucial to contemplate the ethical ramifications of AI. The emergence of deepfakes and other forms of AI-generated material has sparked worries over the spread of disinformation and the preservation of authenticity. It is imperative to employ AI in a responsible and transparent manner.

In the next section, you will get an overview of the AI-powered audio enhancement tools in Premiere Pro, highlighting their capabilities and how they can be used to improve your audio quality.

AI-powered audio enhancement in Premiere Pro

Adobe's latest generative AI video capabilities, along with new audio workflows in Premiere Pro, have been available to clients since May 2024. These workflows will provide editors with comprehensive tools to effectively manage and enhance the sound quality of their projects.

Premiere Pro's revised audio process increases productivity by enabling users to create final sound mixes with fewer clicks. Improved effects management, AI-driven audio type detection, and visual fade handles are among the new features. For both novices and experts, audio editing is made easier with features such as the remix function and improved voice processing.

Furthermore, the AI-powered **Enhance Speech** feature, which promptly eliminates undesirable noise and enhances inadequately recorded speech, has been widely accessible since February 2024. Let's dive deeper into the new AI-powered audio workflow.

To understand how AI can enhance the clarity and production value of your audio, we'll delve into the Enhance Speech feature and its capabilities.

Enhance Speech – studio-quality sound with a single click

Enhance Speech, a new addition to Premiere's extensive toolset, incorporates the remarkable technology from Adobe Podcast into Premiere's Essential Sound panel. Denoising and EQ-ing (equalization) dialog with a single click may easily increase its production value. It significantly reduces background noise and improves audio clarity. You can use the Essential Sound panel to classify clips as conversation, change the mix intensity, and analyze audio while editing. The following example significantly improves voice distinctness, making it simpler to understand.

How can improved speech boost audio quality?

Premiere Pro includes an enhanced speech capability that successfully reduces background noise, resulting in much better audio quality. This is very handy for editing voice recordings in loud areas.

The Essential Sound panel in Premiere Pro includes options for classifying clips as conversation, which is critical for improving audio quality. The tagging procedure is simple and user-friendly.

To access the necessary sound panel in Adobe Premiere Pro, perform these steps:

1. Select the audio clip. Click on the audio clip in your timeline that you wish to alter. Make sure it's highlighted.

2. Switch to the **Audio** workspace. Alternatively, use the toolbar at the top of the screen to navigate to **Window**, then **Essential Sound**.

Figure 18.24 – Enabling the Audio workspace in Premiere Pro

3. This will bring up the **Essential Sound** panel, where you can tag your clips and alter audio parameters. Tag the audio type. You may tag the selected audio clip as **Dialogue**, **Music**, **Sound Effects**, or **Ambience** in the **Essential Sound** panel by selecting the respective button. This will allow options related to that audio type.

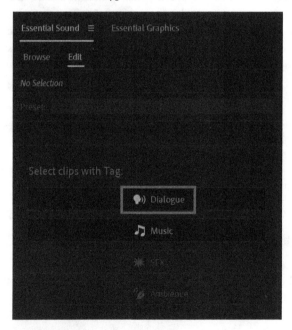

Figure 18.25 – Tagging an audio clip as Dialogue in the Essential Sound panel

4. Once tagged, you may utilize the panel's buttons and sliders to fine-tune your audio, including volume, clarity, and improved voice. Depending on the scenario and the footage, you may require more or less improvement. The **Mix Amount** control allows you to change the amount of enhancement you wish to utilize by sliding the slider to the left or right, as shown in the following screenshot:

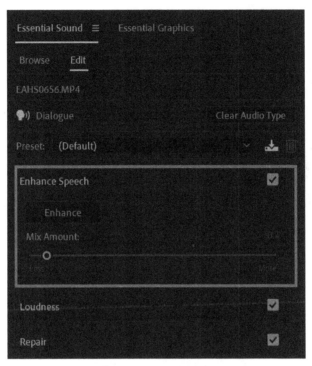

Figure 18.26 – Tagging an audio clip as Dialogue in the Essential Sound panel

You can continue to edit while the audio is being improved. The audio analysis activity runs in the background, enabling you to focus on other areas of your project uninterrupted.

With its integration with Adobe Podcast, Enhance Speech has amassed around a million monthly active users across all Adobe products. People are using it to speed up their editing for lectures, presentations, and interviews. It has been reported that editors have used Enhance Speech to restore the sounds of loved ones from low-quality cassette recordings taken 20 years ago, when the devices were far less advanced. It is just priceless!

Premiere Pro has interactive fade handles that let you effortlessly build and change fades between clips for precise control over transitions. Let's have a look.

Interactive fade handles

The new Premiere Pro audio workflow greatly improves user experience by streamlining and speeding up the process of creating a quality sound mix. The procedure is streamlined by new AI-powered capabilities, making audio editing simple.

By enabling users to generate a variety of fades with ease by only dragging, the new visual fade handles improve the editing experience. This element encourages efficiency and inventiveness in audio mixing. The following screenshot illustrates the fade handles in the timeline:

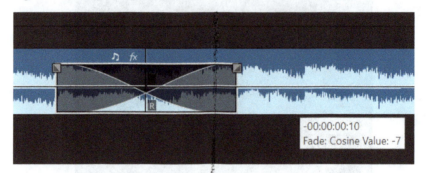

Figure 18.27 – New fade handles in Premiere Pro

It's now easier for users to construct seamless transitions by adjusting audio fades directly in the timeline with visible handles. In order to optimize your audio workflow and optimize the editing process, learn how to efficiently manage and organize your audio assets with Premiere Pro's interactive audio badges and Audio Category Tagging. Let's examine this next.

Audio Category Tagging and interactive audio badges

The new **Audio Category Tagging** feature in Premiere Pro automatically classifies audio clips as ambiance, sound effects, music, or chat, automatically presenting the most pertinent tools in the Essential Sound panel, which saves editors time. The **Auto Tag** feature can be seen in the **Essential Sound** panel as shown in the following screenshot:

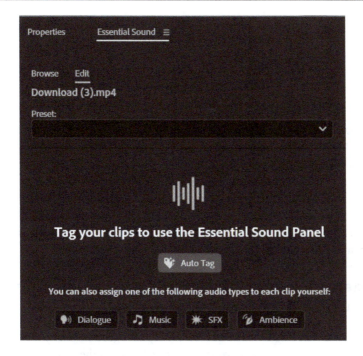

Figure 18.28 – The Auto Tag tool in the Essential Sound panel

The power of AI detects if clips are **Dialogue**, **Music**, **SFX**, or **Ambience** and adds a new interactive badge. Simply click to have fast access to the most important tools for that audio type in the **Essential Sound** panel.

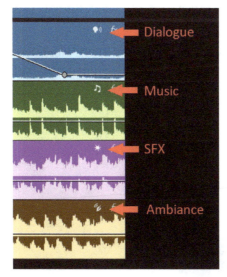

Figure 18.29 – New audio tagging in Premiere Pro

Simply click to have fast access to the most applicable tool for that audio type inside the **Essential Sound** panel.

Adobe has conducted years of internal research to develop auto-category tagging technology. Adobe has been developing models that utilize AI to truly comprehend what is happening in audio and incorporate the technology into the product. It aids novice users in their creative process.

AI-driven technologies, such as the **Remix** tool, automatically modify music timing to flawlessly suit video footage, resulting in time savings and enhanced audio production quality. Within five seconds of the intended duration, a remix can typically locate a corresponding section of the song. Occasionally, the length of the song may vary depending on how much you've stretched it. It is possible that some manual modifications will still need to be made. Users with and without expertise can both profit from this innovation. Use Premiere Pro's filler word detection feature to enhance the clarity and quality of your text-based changes. It will automatically remove frequent filler words, such as "um" and "uh." Let's examine it in more detail next.

Filler word detection in text-based editing – automatically eliminating "um" and "uh"

The text-based editing tool in Premiere Pro has completely changed how many users edit audio and video. This function allows you to modify your discussion like any other text document once it has been automatically transcribed. Your modifications will appear in the video right away. A frequently requested feature in Premiere Pro is the ability to automatically identify and eliminate filler words, such as "uh" and "um."

Video editors sometimes have to cut out words such as "um" and "uh" while editing interviews. In the past, this was a laborious procedure that required carefully listening to the full audio file and deleting every filler word by hand.

The Adobe Research team developed an AI model called **Filler Word Detection** to simplify this process. With the help of this program, users can easily find and eliminate every filler word in a transcription. Just choose **Filler words** from the **Transcript** panel when the transcript opens.

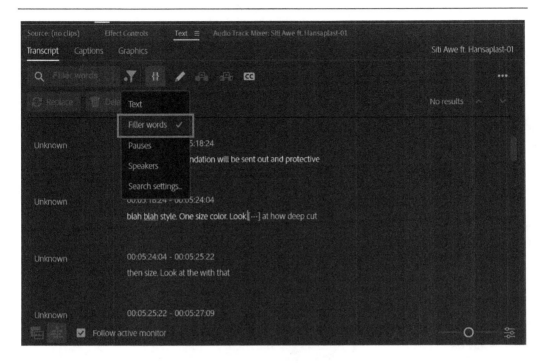

Figure 18.30 – Filtering filler words in the Text panel in Premiere Pro

Previously, it might have taken many minutes or hours. But now, you can easily eliminate all of the filler words with a single click.

Next, let's use Premiere Pro's Speech to Text feature to quickly and accurately transcribe audio or video information. This feature translates spoken words into written text.

Speech to Text with transcription

With the use of Premiere Pro's automated transcription features, users can edit more effectively by making changes to the visuals directly through the transcript. By enabling text-based editing and speech-to-text capabilities, these technologies improve your workflow.

Premiere Pro's automatic transcription tools make editing easier by letting you alter clips from the transcribed text. Time is saved, and accuracy is increased. Take a look at the following example:

Figure 18.31 – Creating a rough cut by duplicating and inserting text with transcription

Using AI-powered text-based editing, you can create a rough cut from your transcript, move clips around by cutting and pasting blocks of text, search for certain terms, locate and eliminate pauses and gaps as indicated by the [...] symbol, and place your footage in order faster than before.

Summary

Premiere Pro's video editing has been revolutionized by AI. It now provides features that greatly increase creativity and productivity. Editors can enhance their storytelling and discover new opportunities by becoming proficient with these AI functionalities.

This chapter explored how AI is revolutionizing the video editing industry. It began by presenting the idea of using AI in the context of Adobe Premiere Pro, a popular video editing program. A more thorough examination that explains how AI is incorporated into Premiere Pro's features came next.

After that, we turned to the emerging field of AI-powered features and discussed how these developments are completely changing the way that videos are edited. It covered the possibility of future partnerships with AI models, such as Runway, OpenAI, and Pika Labs, and presented Adobe Firefly, a platform that makes use of third-party generative AI models. Finally, we examined the use of AI in audio augmentation, revealing AI's broad effect across different facets of video creation.

As AI technology advances at a rapid rate, industry experts and fans alike anxiously await further integration and development of AI features in Adobe Premiere Pro. The potential for innovative advances in video editing is enormous, and future enhancements are primed to reshape the creative environment for filmmakers, editors, and content producers worldwide.

Congratulations on completing this comprehensive guide to Adobe Premiere Pro! You have developed a thorough grasp of the software's features and a knowledge of how to use its tools to produce visually appealing films by going through the various chapters. From learning the fundamentals to exploring more complex methods, you've gained the information and abilities required to create material of a high caliber. I'm pleased with your commitment and perseverance in achieving this goal. Thank you for choosing this book as your guide, and I hope your video editing pursuits continue to be fruitful.

Index